Server Controls → html!

Code behind -20.

Includes

Components

ASP.NET for Web Designers

Contents At a Glance

ASP.NET for Web Designers

Peter Ladka

New
Riders

201 West 103rd Street, Indianapolis, Indiana 46290
An Imprint of Pearson Education
Boston • Indianapolis • London • Munich • New York • San Francisco

ASP.NET for Web Designers

International Standard Book Number: 0-7357-1262-X

Library of Congress Catalog Card Number: 2001099564

Printed in the United States of America

First edition: September 2002

06 05 04 03 02   7 6 5 4 3 2 1

Interpretation of the printing code: The rightmost double-digit number is the year of the book's printing; the rightmost single-digit number is the number of the book's printing. For example, the printing code 02-1 shows that the first printing of the book occurred in 2002.

Trademarks

Warning and Disclaimer

PUBLISHER
David Dwyer

ASSOCIATE PUBLISHER
Stephanie Wall

PRODUCTION MANAGER
Gina Kanouse

MANAGING EDITOR
Kristy Knoop

ACQUISITIONS EDITOR
Deborah Hittel-Shoaf

PRODUCT MARKETING MANAGER
Tammy Detrich

PUBLICITY MANAGER
Susan Nixon

DEVELOPMENT EDITOR
John Rahm

SENIOR PROJECT EDITOR
Lori A. Lyons

COPY EDITOR
Margo Catts

INDEXER
Christopher Morris

PROOFREADER
Ben Lawson

COMPOSITION
Wil Cruz

MANUFACTURING COORDINATOR
Jim Conway

BOOK DESIGNER
Barb Kordesh

COVER DESIGNER
Aren Howell

First, I would like to dedicate this book to my wife, Janet, who has shown a simple man that Faith, Hope, Loyalty, and Love are the pillars upon which life is balanced and that the greatest of these is…Love.

Second, I must dedicate this book to Brooke Lindsay. A small wonder who showed the colors of life to a man who before could only see in black and white. Thank you, my little love muffin.

Whatever greatness anyone sees in me is merely a dim reflection of these two amazing women who have revealed the wonders of life and love to me.

And lastly, to the son I've yet to meet but am very eagerly anticipating. It's hard to believe that I can bear any more joy and happiness than I am currently enduring; but I am already experiencing you and know that you won't just add pride, joy, and happiness to my life but are causing it to multiply.

Dear God,

Should a man be so happy? I don't know, but for these three things, I am forever indebted.

Thank You

Love, Peter

Table of Contents

About the Author

Peter Ladka is the Chairman and President of Nexus Media Inc. Nexus Media is a web development firm located in New York with a focus on providing business with advanced database-driven web applications.

Peter founded Nexus Media in 1997 after years of servicing clients as a freelance graphic designer. As the Internet became more prominent, he began to see more interest from clients in the area of web development and began to explore the possibilities of providing these services to his customers. Out of this, Nexus Media was born (www.nexusmediagroupcom).

With the emergence of the .NET Framework, Peter has guided Nexus Media into the forefront as a development firm focused on providing applications based on this technology. This focus has brought Nexus Media into the national spotlight as a leader in ASP.NET technologies, developing a wide range of applications that can be found across the Internet and within businesses around the world.

About the Technical Reviewers

These reviewers contributed their considerable hands-on expertise to the entire development process for *ASP.NET for Web Designers*. As the book was being written, these dedicated professionals reviewed all the material for technical content, organization, and flow. Their feedback was critical to ensuring that *ASP.NET for Web Designers* fits our reader's need for the highest-quality technical information.

Mike Ahern is the President of a web development and network consulting firm in New Jersey. He has been involved with the Internet and web development since 1995 and has been developing with .NET since its early Beta 1 days. His experience includes ASP, COM, C++, everything .NET (almost...), SQL, Visual Basic, and Windows NT/2000. Mike also holds MCSE and MCDBA certifications. When he's not working on various projects into the early hours of the morning, he can usually be found either fishing or mountain biking.

Steve Heckler is President of Accelebrate, an IT training and technical writing firm in Atlanta. An avid ASP.NET, Java, and XML developer and trainer, Steve served more than six years as a senior manager and trainer at a leading east-coast IT training firm prior to founding Accelebrate. He holds a Bachelor and Masters degrees from Stanford University.

Acknowledgments

I would like to acknowledge a few people here in the order that they participated—from before this title was even a dream until I penned my last sentence. First, the New Riders gang, starting with Theresa Gheen, whose moment of temporary insanity or sheer brilliance (still to be determined) thought that a goofball like me could write a book. Deb Hittel-Shoaf, whose belief that I shouldn't write a good book, but that I must find the great book inside of me led us through a three-month journey of refinement for which I am grateful. John Rahm, who, without him even knowing it, was my conscience, defining where the line between fun and idiocy lie. More than once I found myself consulting with him in my mind ("Will John think that's stupid…Nah!). I would look at his picture on the New Riders website, and then nothing seemed too far-out. To all of you at New Riders who I know by name and those who I've never met but made this possible. Thanks.

To Mark Ahern and Steve Heckler for keeping me on the straight and narrow road and making me look smarter than I am by letting me borrow from their intelligence. For all the mistakes you will never see, I must thank them. Thanks, guys!

I must acknowledge my right-hand man, Jay Oliver, here at Nexus Media. Jason is an extraordinary man who continually keeps me thinking one step ahead—otherwise, he'd leave me in the dust. He is someone who I can always go to whenever I need an honest and sound opinion. If anyone can sniff out a flaw in your coding or your thinking, it's him; and he is hardly embarrassed about letting you know. A co-worker who I most definitely consider a treasured friend.

Then, not to sound like a broken record, I must thank my wife and family for putting up with the absurd, ridiculous, unending, limitless, and all-consuming nature of writing a book. They are an unending flow of inspiration and support. Without them I never could have done it.

Tell Us What You Think

As the reader of this book, you are the most important critic and commentator. We value your opinion and want to know what we're doing right, what we could do better, what areas you'd like to see us publish in, and any other words of wisdom you're willing to pass our way.

As the Associate Publisher for New Riders Publishing, I welcome your comments. You can fax, email, or write me directly to let me know what you did or didn't like about this book—as well as what we can do to make our books stronger. When you write, please be sure to include this book's title, ISBN, and author, as well as your name and phone or fax number. I will carefully review your comments and share them with the author and editors who worked on the book.

Please note that I cannot help you with technical problems related to the topic of this book, and that due to the high volume of email I receive, I might not be able to reply to every message.

Fax: 317-581-4663

Email: stephanie.wall@newriders.com

Mail: Stephanie Wall
         Associate Publisher
         New Riders Publishing
         201 West 103rd Street
         Indianapolis, IN 46290 USA

Introduction

Are you sick and tired of long technical manuals that act more like a sleep aid than give you a digestible way of understanding something? Well…ME TOO! I have spent a gazillion hours explaining ASP.NET in an understandable way to web designers and programmers alike.

I've jam-packed a gazillion hours into this easy-to-read book so that someone who can't quote the value of Pi out to the 412th decimal place from memory can easily use Microsoft's new exciting web technology called ASP.NET.

Seriously, though, I've tried really hard to explain ASP.NET and its complexities in a way that everyday people like you and I can understand. I make every effort to take the complexities and give everyday (sometimes silly) examples and parallels to how ASP.NET operates. I've found that if you give people metaphors that are easy to understand, and then tie them to features or aspects of ASP.NET, it's much easier to grasp.

So, pour yourself a glass/cup of your favorite beverage, fluff up the old reading chair, and dig on into this page turner. You won't be sorry.

Who Should Read This Book

Are you are a web designer, experienced or just starting? How about a programmer moving from Traditional ASP or any other programming language to ASP.NET? Do you HATE big fat books about technology that demand you shut your brain off from all other activities so that all your processing power can be devoted to attempting to understand what you are reading?

In other words, if you want a book that teaches ASP.NET in plain English, then this book is for you. (Buy two—it's twice the fun.)

Who This Book Is Not For

This book isn't for someone who is currently reclining in a big chair, clutching a café latte in one of the giant bookstore chains with the intention of reading it from cover to cover without paying for it. Oh, it also isn't for someone who already has an advanced understanding of ASP.NET.

Overview

I've tried desperately to organize this book in a simple and progressive fashion so that as you make your way through the book, you are being fed tidbits that will help you to understand what is about to follow.

In Part I, I lay some of the required groundwork that will help you understand ASP.NET's personality and how to talk to it. I cover paradigms, languages, and concepts so that you have a good understanding of some of the base things you need to move forward with ASP.NET.

In Part II, I investigate the members—the participants, if you will—of ASP.NET and how to interact with them. I go through Server Controls, List Controls, Data Controls, and so on to build your vocabulary so that you can speak (and write) the language. Between the first section's foundational information and this section, you are now ready to move into more advanced concepts.

By the time you get to Part III, you will be well-versed in ASP.NET's concepts to the point where you can get into advanced data manipulation, site personalization and identity, security, and XML integration. After finishing this section, you will have all the tools you need to conceptualize and build some very complex web applications.

Conventions

This book is hardly conventional, but there are a few things to note before you move on. A lot of the book is in plain English where I banter on, explaining things about ASP.NET, but because this is a programming language, there are TONS of code examples. I use a few different techniques to make reading and comprehending code easier.

- The code blocks have been separated from the text for easier reading and appear in a monospace font.

- A code continuation character, ➡, appears at the beginning of code lines that have wrapped down from the line above it.

- All code examples are in two languages: VB.NET and C# (pronounced C Sharp). This is clearly delineated before each code block for easy reference.

- The code that I want to focus on is highlighted in bold.

- In more complex code examples, I have written comments right within the code examples to explain key factors about the code.

Relax, and I hope you enjoy. I can say I've certainly enjoyed writing *ASP.NET for Web Designers*, and I hope you find it helpful as you venture into the depths of ASP.NET.

<Part> I

ASP.NET Overview

chapter 1

ASP.NET Basics

On the move with ASP.NET

It was a dark and stormy night in Chicago. The kind you expect to see in a black-and-white 1940's movie. Frank Garrison stood with his back tight against the wall, expecting the worst.... WAIT A MINUTE!!! This is the wrong book for that type of opening. Sorry.

Seriously now. I'm guessing that you are reading this book because you're interested in learning about Microsoft's newest web technology: ASP.NET. If you spent any time perusing newsgroups on web design, or any of the zillions of web sites dedicated to the topic of web applications, you probably have heard at the very least a murmur about this mysterious creature.

For the most part, the people talking about .NET are programmers. They speak in a language all their own, discussing things such as objects, namespaces, scope and the like as if everyone should know what these terms mean and how they apply to .NET. Even books on the subject of .NET are being written by programmers with this same outlook. "Well, it's obvious that the page class is used to create an instance of the page object which falls under the system.web.UI namespace." Sheesh. Who wants to read and attempt to decipher that? I'm assuming you don't, and that's why I'm writing this book. To explain to web designers what ASP.NET is in plain English.

I want to avoid—just like you, I'm assuming—the techno-babble associated with typical programming books and help you understand how powerful ASP.NET is without boring you with every technical nook and cranny in the language.

I am going to explain ASP.NET and its concepts through simple examples, metaphors, and everyday language that you and I can understand. Through this I hope you will see that grasping ASP.NET isn't like scaling a towering skyscraper of information, but like bringing together a series of small building blocks of logical systems to lay a foundation on which you can create powerful web function without being a master architect.

ASP.WHAT?

A question that may be looming in your mind and may be part of the reason you bought this book is "What is ASP.NET?" This is a good question considering it is important to understand what you are learning about before you learn it.

Some people may believe that it is a new programming language. Others may think it is another attempt of Microsoft's to dominate and rule the world. (Insert sinister music and image of evil-looking man wringing his hands together.)

In reality, ASP.NET is truly a new paradigm, or in other words, a new way of thinking when it comes to creating web applications.

To give you a better grasp of what I'm saying, we need to take a look back into the mysterious world of the web, where souls are gained and lost and the hearts of men and children…oh, sorry. I'm getting carried away again.

What we must do is look over the progression of the web and how we got to where we are today and examine the problems this created.

Back in the olden days, the Internet was used as a means of trading text-based documents within different medical, scientific, and collegiate circles. There was a need for a language to control this, and hence HTML was born.

Now, let's shoot forward to the early 1990s when the World Wide Web began to demand that this language take on traits that it didn't possess. These functions were things like interactivity, moving and flashing images, and from that languages such as JavaScript became a popular addition to web site design. JavaScript in this form ran on the client's machine enabled by the browser's capability to execute JavaScript function.

Next was the demand for dynamic data integration or database-driven web sites, and from that languages such as CGI, Active Server Pages, ColdFusion, Java Server Pages, and PHP were born. These technologies ran on the server, which enabled dynamic and personalized data to be delivered to the client's browser.

All these languages solved problems presented by the demands and needs that shaped web design and web applications. But with these solutions came new problems—problems that were associated with the intermingling of languages and the nature of how a web server had to deliver this data.

My firm used to program applications in Active Server Page technology, the predecessor of ASP.NET. In using this technology we found ourselves programming in seven different languages when we created applications for our clients. The code from these languages was all intertwined. In other words, one line of code would contain HTML, with the next containing a combination of HTML and JavaScript, and the next containing Active Server Page code.

And on and on the intermingling of code went. As an application grew, so did the confusion within our development teams and its different members about which code was doing what, in who knows what language. Are you beginning to see the problem?

This is just the way it was for a web development company. We learned to deal with it and put into place some systems to help us deal with these types of complications when designing web sites.

Microsoft had some different ideas, as they always do. In early 1998 a few people within Microsoft began to examine the pros and cons of its Active Server Page technology. They noted the powerful applications that could be built with the technology, but also saw many of the problems that I have previously stated and many more that I haven't.

They began to open up a debate about how to resolve these issues and build on the power of ASP's core strengths, and ASP.NET was born. What emerged was a completely new way of addressing web development when it comes to dynamic function and data integration. ASP.NET is only part of a much bigger initiative called the .NET Framework.

N o t e

Don't be intimidated by terms like "Framework" that are used when describing .NET. These are just fancy programmer words for very practical things. Throughout the book I will help you to decipher this "programmer speak" with easy-to-understand examples. For instance, the word "Framework" can be represented with a word like "skeleton." It's the supporting structure on which .NET applications and services are built.

Understanding ASP.NET

The .NET Framework is a programming model for building, deploying, and running XML web services and applications, including Windows and web applications. ASP.NET includes the XML web services and web forms portions of the .NET Framework as seen Figure 1.1.

FIGURE 1.1

The .NET Framework with the portion that makes up ASP.NET highlighted.

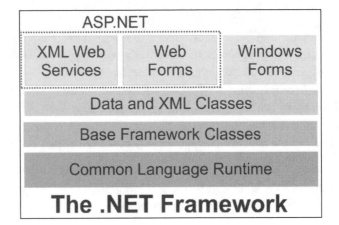

If you look at Figure 1.1, you can see that XML web services and web forms have been encapsulated by a dashed line denoting that they are the portions that are exclusive to ASP.NET. We will be exploring the web forms portion of ASP.NET within this book very heavily and will briefly touch on web services. Truly, web services is a book title unto itself and demands more than I could cover within the scope of this book.

As you can see, there is much more involved with the .NET Framework than just ASP.NET, and I will be investigating the data classes, the base classes, and the common language runtime portions of the Framework throughout this book. Although this may look very confusing and a bit overwhelming, you will see as you progress that these layers or bones of the .NET skeleton make perfect sense. They fit together and give you flexibility, strength, and stability to create, deploy, run, and maintain powerful web applications while avoiding the pitfalls of runtime languages like traditional ASP.

You will see how much easier it is to build applications from the concept of structure instead of relying on the traditional method of runtime-interpreted scripting languages such as traditional ASP.

It's a Whole Different Animal

ASP.NET turns web development from a runtime environment to an object- and event-centric environment. It actually uses full-fledged traditional and new programming languages to produce its results. In actuality, ASP.NET isn't really a language as much as it is a technology.

It is a technology that is driven by a programming language to produce the results you are looking for when you develop applications. It allows you to use languages such as Visual Basic .NET, C# (pronounced C Sharp), and C++ to drive ASP.NET. Don't let this frighten you. You don't need to learn a zillion programming languages to create ASP.NET applications. Just one will do.

"But wait," you're thinking, "I have to learn ASP.NET and Visual Basic .NET or C#. That's got to be a ton of stuff to learn." Fear not. Remember, ASP.NET isn't a language. It's a technology, and you use a language to tell it what to do.

Think of it this way. ASP.NET is like a car. It is potentially very powerful, but by itself it is powerless. It needs fuel to run and direction to guide it. That fuel is the programming language of your choice and the direction is the things you tell it to do through the programming language.

The Differences Between Traditional ASP and ASP.NET

Like I said, ASP.NET is a whole different animal, and the differences between traditional ASP and ASP.NET are many. One of the core differences, as I've mentioned, is that ASP is a runtime language or can also be called an interpreted scripting environment. I've also said that ASP.NET is an object- and event-oriented environment. Let's take a look at this with an example.

Oh No! Not Another "Hello World"!!!

I can hear you now. "Okay, Peter. I thought you said this wasn't going to be a typical programmer's book. But your first example is 'Hello World.' Every programming book starts out with this example."

Please bear with me. I'll try to deviate a bit from the traditional "Hello World" example; but if you can humor me, the simplicity of a "Hello World"-type example will help you to easily understand the differences between the two types of environments.

Below is an example coded in traditional ASP:

```
<html>
<head>
<title>No!! Not Hello World!!</title>
</head>
<body bgcolor="#FFFFFF" text="#000000">
<% Response.Write "It was a dark and stormy night with traditional ASP. "%>
</body>
</html>
```

The way this code executes is from top to bottom, starting with the opening `<html>` tag and ending with the closing `</html>`. The result is shown in Figure 1.2.

FIGURE 1.2

Traditional ASP intertwines HTML and ASP code and progresses from the first line of code through the last.

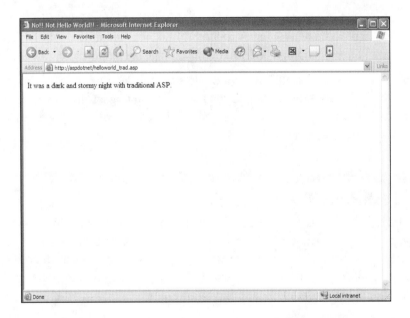

As you can see, the results are exactly as expected. And when the page was requested, it ran, and when server reached the line that read

```
<% Response.Write "It was a dark and stormy night with traditional ASP. "%>
```

it processed the code, and through ASP the line of text was written to the HTML page. Classic ASP is like a snowball that rolls downhill: The code starts at the top and rolls to the bottom and builds as it rolls, executing functions as the code runs. This is what makes it a runtime language.

ASP.NET is more like a car. For you to operate your car, you have interactions with parts of the car. Those parts could be thought of as objects in ASP.NET.

So if you want to get into the car, you grab the door handle and open the door. The door handle is an object and opening the door is an event. Then you may sit down on the seat. Sitting is an event and the seat is an object.

Then you take the key (object), insert (event) it in the ignition (object), turn (event) the key (object), and start (event) the engine (object). Are you beginning to see how the interaction with a car is a series of events and objects and how these are associated with one another?

In the following code you can see a similar example to the traditional ASP page, but written in ASP.NET code using Visual Basic .NET as the scripting language. When you look at this code, try to figure out what the objects and events are (note that throughout this book, code I want to focus on appears in bold):

```
<script language="vb" runat=server>
Sub Page_Load(Source As Object,E As EventArgs)
    labelText.text = "It was a dark and stormy night in ASP.NET World!"

End Sub
</script>
<html>
<head>
<title>No!! Not Hello World!!</title>
</head>
<body>
<asp:label id="labelText" runat="server" />
</body>
</html>
```

As you can see, the code looks a bit different, and in fact it is quite different from the traditional ASP example. Were you able to pick out the event and the object in this example? If not, don't sweat it—before long you will be able to look at even more complex code blocks and figure out what's happening like it's second nature.

> **N O T E**
>
> *You may even be thinking that it appears more complex than traditional ASP. In this particular example there are more lines of code to achieve a similar result than there are in the traditional ASP example, but ASP.NET code reduces the amount of code you write dramatically when you are creating full applications. I have found consistently at least a 30% reduction in code, sometimes reaching as high as 60% reduction in a side-by-side comparison between traditional ASP and ASP.NET*

Let's take a look at the code and identify the event and object. The object in this code is an ASP.NET server control called a Label, and its code looks like this:

```
<asp:label id="labelText" runat="server" />
```

You'll learn about ASP.NET server controls in depth in later chapters, so for now let's just say that server controls are objects within the ASP.NET Framework that result in HTML output to the user's browser.

All ASP.NET objects must contain an ID attribute, and this label's ID is "labelText" and is set using `id="labeltext"`. The ID is used to identify an object within ASP.NET, so you may address it within your ASP.NET code.

The `runat="server"` attribute tells the server that it is a control to be processed at the server to generate HTML and isn't just text to be passed to the browser.

So now I have an object, just like the car, but it can do little without interaction from an event of some sort. When a page is requested, a multitude of events take place, but the one that we are dealing with here is the Page Load event.

```
Sub Page_Load(Source As Object,E As EventArgs)
    labelText.text = "It was a dark and stormy night in ASP.NET World!"
End Sub
```

During the Page Load event, I set the text of the labelText object to the sentence I want displayed when the page is rendered. This can be seen in the line `labelText.text = "It was a dark and stormy night in ASP.NET World!"` So during the Page Load event the text attribute is set, and during rendering that object is displayed. Look at the result in Figure 1.3.

FIGURE 1.3

ASP.NET uses the paradigm of events and objects to process its code.

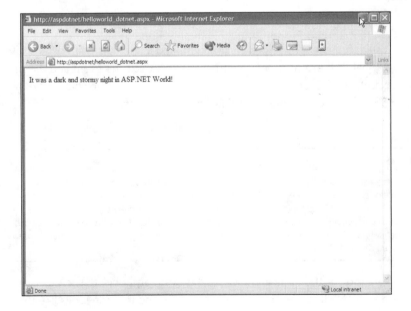

Looks pretty similar to the traditional ASP example, but the way it is achieved—through the use of events and objects—is completely different.

Just to reinforce the concepts of event- and object-driven programming and to further illustrate how ASP.NET is different from traditional ASP, I thought it would be fun to take the last example, change the text, and move the Page_Load event to the bottom of the page.

```
<html>
<head>
<title>Show Event Example</title>
</head>
<body>
<asp:label id="labelText" runat="server" />
</body>
</html>
<script language="vb" runat=server>
Sub Page_Load(Source As Object,E As EventArgs)
    labelText.text = "Notice the event still sets the label's text"
End Sub
</script>
```

Now that I've moved the block of code that sets the text of the label to the bottom of the page, look at the results in Figure 1.4.

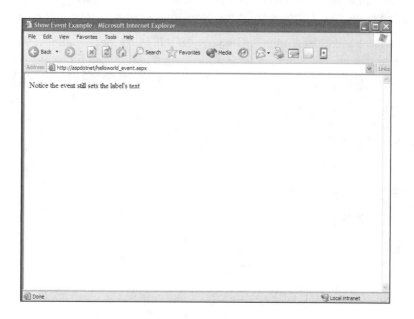

FIGURE 1.4

Even when I place the Page_Load event at the end of the code, it still executes when expected because it is an event.

As you can see, the results are exactly the same because the Page_Load event happens before the page is rendered to the user's browser and the label's text is properly set regardless of where the Page_Load block is placed in the page.

Again, ASP.NET code doesn't execute from top to bottom anymore; it is completely driven by events and how you use those events to affect what is delivered in HTML form when the page is rendered.

You will see as we progress that this paradigm of event- and object-oriented application development is a powerful departure from traditional ASP. It is more logical, concise, and productive than its predecessor. If you come to the table with some experience in traditional ASP, I would encourage you to open your mind to the different and more efficient methods that ASP.NET uses. It may take you some time to let go of old thinking and wrap your brain around this programming model, but after you do you'll never go back.

Let Me Show You the Shiny New Model: The ASP.NET Advantage

There are many new advantages to ASP.NET, but I will try to highlight the main points and how they solve some of the problems discussed earlier in this chapter.

The following points best encapsulate how ASP.NET provides a platform for power application development while addressing these nagging problems:

- Multiple Language Support
- Code Separation Support
- Server Controls
- User Controls
- Smart Code Output
- Deployment

Multiple Language Support

Multiple language support is made possible by an ingenious layer of the .NET Framework called the *common language runtime*. I could spend pages and pages trying to explain all that the common language runtime does with regard to the .NET Framework, but this isn't really the point of this book.

What I will explain is that the common language runtime enables people to write ASP.NET applications in a boatload of languages, both old and new. The most common languages are:

- Visual Basic .NET
- C# (Pronounced C Sharp)
- C++
- JScript.NET

.NET allows third parties to implement other languages for the common language runtime, and there are languages numbering in the dozens, including Cobol, Pascal, and a version of Java for .NET.

This opens up a world of options for people coming from different backgrounds of design and programming to take advantage of the power of ASP.NET. This is possible because the .NET Framework takes all the languages that are supported and breaks them down into what is called "Intermediate Code."

Basically, .NET has a universal language that it uses no matter what code language you program in. As long as it is a .NET-supported language, you can program your .NET application in it and common language runtime will interpret it down to intermediate code. On top of that, you can program different languages in the same application and .NET is prepared to handle that as well. Your objects are available to each of the different languages no matter what language you are using.

For example, if you are programming just one bit of code in Visual Basic .NET and you create an object while using that language, and you then have someone else in your crew of designers who loves to code in C#, they can access that object as well. Previous to .NET, this was an impossible task. If you needed access to an object, you needed to program in the language that the object was created in. *There is power in ASP.NET.*

Let's take a look at how we can use different languages, and how .NET can produce the same results. I'll use a similar example to the dreaded "Hello World" example from before, create it in both Visual Basic .NET and C#, and see what results we get.

The following is the example in Visual Basic .NET:

```
<script language="vb" runat=server>
Sub Page_Load(Source As Object,E As EventArgs)
    labelText.text = "Our VB.NET Example"
End Sub
</script>
<html>
<head>
<title>Multi Language Support - VB.NET</title>
</head>
<body>
<asp:label id="labelText" runat="server" />
</body>
</html>
```

The results are shown in Figure 1.5.

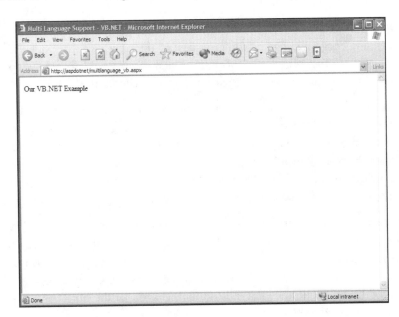

FIGURE 1.5

The simple example in Visual Basic .NET.

Now here's a similar example in C#:

```
<script language="C#" runat="server">
void Page_Load(Object src, EventArgs E){
    labelText.Text = "Our C# Example";
    }
</script>
<html>
<head>
<title>Multi Language Support - C#</title>
</head>
<body>
<asp:label id="labelText" runat="server" />
</body>
</html>
```

The results are shown in Figure 1.6.

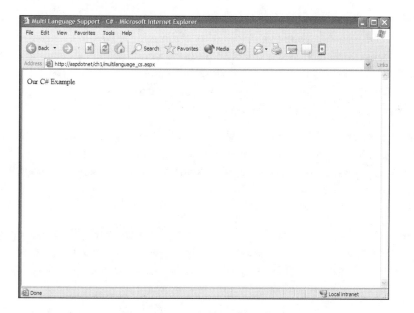

FIGURE 1.6

The simple example in C#.

As you can see, for the common language runtime it doesn't matter what language you program in. If it is a .NET-supported language, the common language runtime interprets it and converts it to Intermediate Language and processes it exactly the same.

C A U T I O N

I specifically wrote the `label.Text` *in the Visual Basic .NET version with the "t" in "text" in lowercase to illustrate that Visual Basic .NET is a bit more forgiving than C#. If "Text" had a lowercase "T" in the C# example, this would have thrown an error that read:* `'System.Web.UI.WebControls.Label' does not contain a definition for 'text'`. *Be careful when referencing object attributes when writing in C# because it's quite picky.*

Multiple language support creates a powerful environment in which people from all different backgrounds, with different likes and dislikes, can build .NET applications without prejudice. Gone are the days of arguing over what language is better.

Code Separation Support

As a web designer, if you have done any programming in dynamic languages such as Active Server Pages, you probably have been faced with being confused over code that jumped back and forth between programming logic and physical display code. This has no doubt led to confusion—even in circumstances where you were the only person working on a project.

I remember back a few years ago, while I was developing a commerce application, I was faced with loads of conditional code while trying to display the contents of a shopping cart. This page jumped back and forth with all kinds of branches to accommodate if this, that, or the other thing was true. Then we needed to display—well, this, that, or the other thing.

Several times I found myself in a trance, staring like a drooling idiot at my monitor, only to be brought back to the present time and place by the burning sensation in my eyeballs from a lack of blinking. The only thing that seemed to help was a break for coffee or an ice cream cone.

Although these things gave me small moments of clarity, they really did little else but give me heartburn or increase my belt size. Out of this a new tag was developed in our firm. We call it the `<insanity>` tag. Feel free to use it any time you are close to losing your mind. It looks like this:

```
<INSANITY>
Insert any totally insane, uninterruptible code here
</INSANITY>
```

We have been petitioning the W3C committee to include this in the next standardized version of HTML. I'm sure many web designers would use this on every project. We can only hope.

Another problem with programming web applications is that code reuse was a nightmare at best. It was parallel to untangling a wet, dirty garden hose. Pleasant thought? Neither was the concept of code reuse in traditional ASP. Frankly, I can't think of a single situation where we could easily reuse code from one ASP application to another without picking out the dirt. Bleck!!

But Microsoft has an answer for the <insanity> tag and code reuse problems. It's called *code separation*. Because ASP.NET is an event-and object-oriented program-ming model, the concept of code separation is possible. Business logic and display code can be placed in different places within the page.

Let's revert back to traditional ASP and see how you might build a drop-down box from an array of values. If some of this confuses you, don't worry; I'll cover these concepts in greater detail in later chapters.

```
<html>
<head>
<title>Code Separation - Traditional ASP</title>
</head>
<body>
<% Dim arrNames(4)
arrNames(0)="Tom"
arrNames(1)="Frank"
arrNames(2)="Bill"
arrNames(3)="Larry"
arrNames(4)="Mike"
%>
<select name="select">
<%for i=0 to Ubound(arrNames)%>
<option value="<%=arrNames(i)%>"><%=arrNames(i)%></option>
<%
Next
%>
</select>
</body>
</html>
```

I've highlighted in bold the ASP code to make it easier to spot.

The resulting HTML is exactly as you'd expect:

```
<html>
<head>
<title>Code Separation - Traditional ASP</title>
</head>
<body>
<select name="select">
<option value="Tom">Tom</option>
<option value="Frank">Frank</option>
<option value="Bill">Bill</option>
<option value="Larry">Larry</option>
<option value="Mike">Mike</option>
</select>
</body>
</html>
```

As you can see with this code, you are moving in and out of HTML and ASP code. This is the reason that ASP has been tagged as a "Spaghetti"-type language. This is just a simple example of code mingling when you're programming in traditional ASP. Even in this small scale, understanding where the programming begins and ends and where the HTML begins and ends is a bit confusing. Imagine more complex situations where you are dealing with data being delivered from multiple tables in a database, with all the other blocks of ASP code blended in. It can become quite a mess.

Now let's look at a small example of how code separation can simplify your development and make your code more readable, as well. The following are ASP.NET examples of the previous ASP code.

Visual Basic .NET

```
<script language="vb" runat=server>
Sub Page_Load(Source As Object,E As EventArgs)
    Dim arrNames(4) as string
    Dim counter as Integer
    arrNames(0)="Tom"
    arrNames(1)="Frank"
    arrNames(2)="Bill"
    arrNames(3)="Larry"
    arrNames(4)="Mike"

    For counter = 0 to Ubound(arrNames)
        NameList.Items.Add(arrNames(counter))
    Next
```

```
End Sub
</script>
<html>
<head>
<title>Code Separation - VB.NET</title>
</head>
<body>
<form runat="server">
<asp:dropdownlist id="NameList" runat="server"/>
</form>
</body>
</html>
```

C#

```
<script language="cs" runat=server>
void Page_Load(Object src, EventArgs E){
    string[] arrNames = new string[5];
    int counter;
    arrNames[0]="Tom";
    arrNames[1]="Frank";
    arrNames[2]="Bill";
    arrNames[3]="Larry";
    arrNames[4]="Mike";

    for(counter=0;counter < arrNames.Length;++counter){
        NameList.Items.Add(arrNames[counter]);
    }
}
</script>
<html>
<head>
<title>Code Separation - C#</title>
</head>
<body>
<form runat="server">
<asp:dropdownlist id="NameList" runat="server"/>
</form>
</body>
</html>
```

Once again, I've highlighted the ASP.NET code. Can you see how the programming or logical code has been separated out from the display code? This provides a logical way to create and control the development of programming and interface design separate from each other.

The resulting HTML for both these examples is exactly the same with the exception of the `<title>`. Look familiar?

Visual Basic .NET

```
<html>
<head>
<title>Code Separation - VB.NET</title>
</head>
<body>
<select name="NameList" id="NameList">
<option value="Tom">Tom</option>
<option value="Frank">Frank</option>
<option value="Bill">Bill</option>
<option value="Larry">Larry</option>
<option value="Mike">Mike</option>
</select>
</body>
</html>
```

C#

```
<html>
<head>
<title>Code Separation - C#</title>
</head>
<body>
<select name="NameList" id="NameList">
<option value="Tom">Tom</option>
<option value="Frank">Frank</option>
<option value="Bill">Bill</option>
<option value="Larry">Larry</option>
<option value="Mike">Mike</option>
</select>
</body>
</html>
```

These are the same basic results as traditional ASP produced. The `dropdownlist` object is smart, as are all the other ASP.NET objects. It knows what HTML to produce without you even telling it.

Microsoft has also provided a way to even further separate out code with a technique called *code-behind*. Code-behind, simply put, is a technique of placing your programming code in a totally separate file from your display page. I'll take the previous examples and program them with the "code-behind" technique.

First I can create the content page that contains the HTML content code:

Visual Basic .NET

```
<%@Page Inherits="NameArrayClass" Src="codebehind_vb.vb"%>
<html>
<head>
<title>Code Behind - VB.NET</title>
</head>
<body>
<form runat="server">
<asp:dropdownlist id="NameList" runat="server"/>
</form>
</body>
</html>
```

C#

```
<%@Page Inherits="NameArrayClass" Src="codebehind_cs.cs"%>
<html>
<head>
<title>Code Behind - C#</title>
</head>
<body>
<form runat="server">
<asp:dropdownlist id="NameList" runat="server"/>
</form>
</body>
</html>
```

These pages contain the content, including the standard HTML tags and the ASP.NET DropDownList server control. Also notice the first line of code, which is called the Page Directive. Think of the Page Directive as what the name seems to imply: directions or instructions for the page. Again, this is covered later in Chapter 4.

Now let's look at the code-behind pages. Again, don't fret at the sight of stuff like "inherits" and "import." This example is just to demonstrate how you can use the code-behind technique to further separate code out.

Visual Basic .NET

```
Imports Microsoft.VisualBasic
Imports System
Imports System.Web.UI
Imports System.Web.UI.WebControls

Public Class NameArrayClass
    Inherits Page
    Public NameList as DropDownList

    Sub Page_Load(Source As Object,E As EventArgs)
        Dim arrNames(4) as string
        Dim counter as Integer
        arrNames(0)="Tom"
        arrNames(1)="Frank"
        arrNames(2)="Bill"
        arrNames(3)="Larry"
        arrNames(4)="Mike"


        For counter = 0 to Ubound(arrNames)
            NameList.Items.Add(arrNames(counter))
        Next
    End Sub
End Class
```

C#

```
using System;
using System.Web.UI;
using System.Web.UI.WebControls;

public class NameArrayClass : Page {
    public DropDownList NameList;

    void Page_Load(Object src, EventArgs E){
        string[] arrNames = new string[5];
        int counter;
        arrNames[0]="Tom";
        arrNames[1]="Frank";
        arrNames[2]="Bill";
        arrNames[3]="Larry";
        arrNames[4]="Mike";

        for(counter=0;counter < arrNames.Length;++counter){
            NameList.Items.Add(arrNames[counter]);
        }
    }
}
```

And the resulting HTML:

Visual Basic .NET

```
<html>
<head>
<title>Code Behind - VB.NET</title>
</head>
<body>
<select name="NameList" id="NameList">
    <option value="Tom">Tom</option>
    <option value="Frank">Frank</option>
    <option value="Bill">Bill</option>
    <option value="Larry">Larry</option>
    <option value="Mike">Mike</option>

</select>
</body>
</html>
```

C#

```
<html>
<head>
<title>Code Behind - C#</title>
</head>
<body>
<select name="NameList" id="NameList">
    <option value="Tom">Tom</option>
    <option value="Frank">Frank</option>
    <option value="Bill">Bill</option>
    <option value="Larry">Larry</option>
    <option value="Mike">Mike</option>

</select>
</body>
</html>
```

I'm sure you can begin to see the options and advantages of using code separation and code-behind techniques. This also makes the reuse of the programming code a cinch. You can include this file in a zillion other files without having to strip out anything. Just like that—instant reusable code.

Throughout this book I will go through some very cool examples of how this frees up designers to be creative with designs without having the programming code getting in the way. I feel, as I'm sure you do, that anything that will free me up to focus on "look and feel" aspects and compartmentalizes programming is a welcome friend.

Server Controls

We have touched (actually just scratched the surface) on server controls in some of the past examples, such as the Label control or the DropDownList control.

Imagine what it would be like if you could design web sites and include advanced stuff by just saying to the browser "Put one of those whatcha callits right here, and a thingy there, and give me a big, blue whosit here." Well, this is a bit of a silly way of saying that ASP.NET gives you that capability.

If you look, you can see that in my silly babble all I was really doing was talking about…what? You guessed it: objects!

I have often thought and discussed with other people in our firm what programming would have been like if someone who was right-brained had named some of the elements used in the programming world. We joke that an object would have been a "thingy."

Server controls are just things used in ASP.NET to return predictable blocks of HTML code to the end user's browser. As you saw with the DropDownList, I simply added values to the list in the `Page_Load` event from the array, and the DropDownList server control knew what to output.

It created the `<Select>` tags, as well as the `<Option>` tags with value attributes, without me ever writing a single `<Select>` or `<Option>` tag.

"Great Peter," you say. "But that looks like a plain vanilla drop-down box. This seems like a solution written by a programmer for a programmer who doesn't want to be bothered by coding visual aspects of web design. He just wants to output the data and that's it."

And I say "Patience." There are plenty of sparkly, fun, and exciting aspects for designers, as well, in ASP.NET, and you'd better believe we will be digging deep into that stuff all throughout the book. I can't wait to get to those parts, either, but you must be patient and understand some basic concepts of ASP.NET first.

What ASP.NET provides is a thingy (object) for all the base chunks of HTML code that you need to build ASP.NET applications. From tables, to forms, to images, ASP.NET has an object that is ready to do what you tell it.

There are even a bunch of advanced functioning objects, such as the Calendar
server control, that with a single line of code (highlighted in bold)

```
<html>
<head>
<title>Calendar</title>
</head>
<body>
<form runat="server">
<asp:Calendar id="Calendar" runat="server" />
</form>
</body>
</html>
```

you can produce something as advanced as a fully functioning Calendar with
navigation, as shown in Figure 1.7.

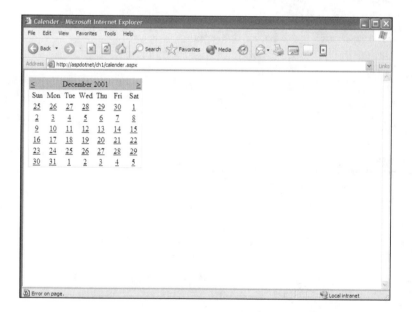

FIGURE 1.7

*With a simple single
line of code, ASP.NET
can produce a
very powerful,
rich function.*

NOW THAT'S TOTALLY AWESOME!!! With a small bit of additional code, you
can capture the user's selection and navigate to a different page or whatever your
heart desires. All that, and it took me about 30 seconds to code.

The following is the generated HTML from the unmodified Calendar server control. How long do you think it would take you to write this? "A long time" is the answer. Longer than 30 seconds, for sure!

Calendar.aspx

```
<html>
<head>
<title>Calendar</title>
</head>
<body>
<table id="Calendar" cellspacing="0" cellpadding="2" border="0"
➥style="border-width:1px;border-style:solid;border-collapse:collapse;">
<tr><td colspan="7" style="background-color:Silver;">
<table cellspacing="0" border="0" style="width:100%;border-collapse:collapse;">
<tr><td style="width:15%;"><a href="javascript:
➥__doPostBack('Calendar','prevMonth')" style="color:Black">&lt;</a></td>
<td align="Center" style="width:70%;">December 2001</td>
<td align="Right" style="width:15%;">
<a href="javascript:__doPostBack('Calendar','nextMonth')"
➥style="color:Black">&gt;</a></td></tr></table></td></tr>
<tr><td align="Center">Sun</td>
<td align="Center">Mon</td>
<td align="Center">Tue</td>
<td align="Center">Wed</td>
<td align="Center">Thu</td>
<td align="Center">Fri</td>
<td align="Center">Sat</td></tr>
<tr><td align="Center" style="width:14%;">
<a href="javascript:__doPostBack('Calendar','selectDay0')"
➥style="color:Black">25</a>
</td>
<td align="Center" style="width:14%;">
<a href="javascript:__doPostBack('Calendar','selectDay1')"
➥style="color:Black">26</a>
</td>
<td align="Center" style="width:14%;">
<a href="javascript:__doPostBack('Calendar','selectDay2')"
➥style="color:Black">27</a>
</td>
<td align="Center" style="width:14%;">
<a href="javascript:__doPostBack('Calendar','selectDay3')"
➥style="color:Black">28</a>
</td>
<td align="Center" style="width:14%;">
<a href="javascript:__doPostBack('Calendar','selectDay4')"
➥style="color:Black">29</a>
</td>
<td align="Center" style="width:14%;">
<a href="javascript:__doPostBack('Calendar','selectDay5')"
➥style="color:Black">30</a>
```

```
</td>
<td align="Center" style="width:14%;">
<a href="javascript:__doPostBack('Calendar','selectDay6')"
➡style="color:Black">1</a>
</td></tr
><tr><td align="Center" style="width:14%;">
<a href="javascript:__doPostBack('Calendar','selectDay7')"
➡style="color:Black">2</a>
</td>
<td align="Center" style="width:14%;">
<a href="javascript:__doPostBack('Calendar','selectDay8')"
➡style="color:Black">3</a>
</td>
<td align="Center" style="width:14%;">
<a href="javascript:__doPostBack('Calendar','selectDay9')"
➡style="color:Black">4</a>
</td>
<td align="Center" style="width:14%;">
<a href="javascript:__doPostBack('Calendar','selectDay10')"
➡style="color:Black">5</a>
</td>
<td align="Center" style="width:14%;">
<a href="javascript:__doPostBack('Calendar','selectDay11')"
➡style="color:Black">6</a>
</td>
<td align="Center" style="width:14%;">
<a href="javascript:__doPostBack('Calendar','selectDay12')"
➡style="color:Black">7</a>
</td>
<td align="Center" style="width:14%;">
<a href="javascript:__doPostBack('Calendar','selectDay13')"
➡style="color:Black">8</a>
</td></tr>
<tr><td align="Center" style="width:14%;">
<a href="javascript:__doPostBack('Calendar','selectDay14')"
➡style="color:Black">9</a>
</td>
<td align="Center" style="width:14%;">
<a href="javascript:__doPostBack('Calendar','selectDay15')"
➡style="color:Black">10</a>
</td>
<td align="Center" style="width:14%;">
<a href="javascript:__doPostBack('Calendar','selectDay16')"
➡style="color:Black">11</a>
</td>
<td align="Center" style="width:14%;">
<a href="javascript:__doPostBack('Calendar','selectDay17')"
➡style="color:Black">12</a>
</td>
<td align="Center" style="width:14%;">
<a href="javascript:__doPostBack('Calendar','selectDay18')"
➡style="color:Black">13</a>
```

continues

Calendar.aspx (continued)

```
</td>
<td align="Center" style="width:14%;">
<a href="javascript:__doPostBack('Calendar','selectDay19')"
➡style="color:Black">14</a>
</td>
<td align="Center" style="width:14%;">
<a href="javascript:__doPostBack('Calendar','selectDay20')"
➡style="color:Black">15</a>
</td></tr>
<tr><td align="Center" style="width:14%;">
<a href="javascript:__doPostBack('Calendar','selectDay21')"
➡style="color:Black">16</a>
</td>
<td align="Center" style="width:14%;">
<a href="javascript:__doPostBack('Calendar','selectDay22')"
➡style="color:Black">17</a>
</td>
<td align="Center" style="width:14%;">
<a href="javascript:__doPostBack('Calendar','selectDay23')"
➡style="color:Black">18</a>
</td>
<td align="Center" style="width:14%;">
<a href="javascript:__doPostBack('Calendar','selectDay24')"
➡style="color:Black">19</a>
</td>
<td align="Center" style="width:14%;">
<a href="javascript:__doPostBack('Calendar','selectDay25')"
➡style="color:Black">20</a>
</td><td align="Center" style="width:14%;">
<a href="javascript:__doPostBack('Calendar','selectDay26')"
➡style="color:Black">21</a>
</td>
<td align="Center" style="width:14%;">
<a href="javascript:__doPostBack('Calendar','selectDay27')"
➡style="color:Black">22</a>
</td></tr>
<tr><td align="Center" style="width:14%;">
<a href="javascript:__doPostBack('Calendar','selectDay28')"
➡style="color:Black">23</a>
</td>
<td align="Center" style="width:14%;">
<a href="javascript:__doPostBack('Calendar','selectDay29')"
➡style="color:Black">24</a>
</td>
<td align="Center" style="width:14%;">
<a href="javascript:__doPostBack('Calendar','selectDay30')"
➡style="color:Black">25</a>
```

```
</td>
<td align="Center" style="width:14%;">
<a href="javascript:__doPostBack('Calendar','selectDay31')"
➥style="color:Black">26</a>
</td><td align="Center" style="width:14%;">
<a href="javascript:__doPostBack('Calendar','selectDay32')"
➥style="color:Black">27</a>
</td>
<td align="Center" style="width:14%;">
<a href="javascript:__doPostBack('Calendar','selectDay33')"
➥style="color:Black">28</a>
</td>
<td align="Center" style="width:14%;">
<a href="javascript:__doPostBack('Calendar','selectDay34')"
➥style="color:Black">29</a>
</td></tr>
<tr><td align="Center" style="width:14%;">
<a href="javascript:__doPostBack('Calendar','selectDay35')"
➥style="color:Black">30</a>
</td>
<td align="Center" style="width:14%;">
<a href="javascript:__doPostBack('Calendar','selectDay36')"
➥style="color:Black">31</a>
</td>
<td align="Center" style="width:14%;">
<a href="javascript:__doPostBack('Calendar','selectDay37')"
➥style="color:Black">1</a>
</td>
<td align="Center" style="width:14%;">
<a href="javascript:__doPostBack('Calendar','selectDay38')"
➥style="color:Black">2</a>
</td>
<td align="Center" style="width:14%;">
<a href="javascript:__doPostBack('Calendar','selectDay39')"
➥style="color:Black">3</a>
</td>
<td align="Center" style="width:14%;">
<a href="javascript:__doPostBack('Calendar','selectDay40')"
➥style="color:Black">4</a>
</td>
<td align="Center" style="width:14%;">
<a href="javascript:__doPostBack('Calendar','selectDay41')"
➥style="color:Black">5</a>
</td></tr>
</table>
</body>
</html>
```

Are you beginning to see how ASP.NET will help you to concentrate on design, speed up your productivity, and cut down the lines of code you have to write? I thought so.

User Controls

This subject is as juicy as server controls and also is another big part of the equation when it comes to code reuse.

In the past, one of the ways that both designers and programmers tried to reuse code was through Server Side Include files. Server Side Includes were files that contained code "snips" that could be reused in many pages simply by including these file in your ASP or HTML pages. They were a step in the correct direction, but unfortunately they brought some problems with them as well.

One problem with traditional Server Side Includes is that if the file contained images, the images' paths were relative to the include file. You could make image paths absolute by including the full path, but this created problems because the paths in the development environment were very often different from the path of the deployed application.

Another issue in a traditional ASP environment is that Server Side Includes are processed prior to any ASP code. Now that doesn't sound like that big of an issue, but what if you wanted to dynamically decide between loading different include files within your dynamic code? For instance

```
<% If variable = 1 then %>
<!--#include file="include1.asp" -->
<%Else%>
<!--#include file="include2.asp" -->
<%End If%>
```

In this code block, both `include1.asp` and `include2.asp` would fully load. Then the dynamic code would take over after and determine which block to execute. "What's the big deal?" you say. Imagine having ten include files with 100 lines of code each in a statement like this. Your file would contain 900 more lines of code from the 9 unnecessarily loaded pages than needed for what you want to achieve.

As you can see, Server Side Includes are hardly the perfect solution for code reuse, but they were all we had. So we made do.

Now ASP.NET has provided a solution with all the advantages (and more) of the Server Side Include, while resolving the problems associated with it.

User controls can contain images, and the file path issues are resolved properly by the .NET server. This opens up huge doors for design issues and reusing code blocks across multiple pages.

For instance, in my firm we are in the process of developing a content management system for a client that will allow them to build templates by specifying the use of modularized User controls. In other words, the client can specify where a "News" highlight control or a "Hot Point" dialog box appears and create a completely new template in their content management system this way.

In addition, User controls can also be dynamically loaded, allowing many more usable possibilities without sacrificing the application's performance.

One other small issue is that User controls actually are executed in a different process than the file in which they are included. This alleviates some potential problems that conventional include files created with regard to variable name conflicts. With conventional includes, variable names needed to be unique across all included files and the host file as well.

Think of the dynamically selected include file example earlier, and the complications this could create. Most times the differences between the include files in these instances are minimal, with just some small semantic changes. The fact that variables of the same name could and usually were contained in many of the files only added to the problems. ASP.NET User controls make this a moot point.

Smart Code Output

I must mention briefly a super-powerful feature in ASP.NET. It has the capability to produce device-specific code without any intervention by the designer. Did you catch that? Maybe you were so overwhelmed by the statement, you fainted. I'll repeat it again. ASP.NET HAS THE CAPABILITY TO PRODUCE DEVICE-SPECIFIC CODE WITHOUT ANY INTERVENTION BY THE DESIGNER!!!

Being a web designer myself, I don't have to ask if you've been cursed with browser compatibility problems. I know you have! Every web designer has faced this issue with every project.

Suffice it to say that this is an area powerfully addressed by ASP.NET. It can produce code specifically for a boatload of different browsers and devices, including all standard web browsers, many mobile devices, hand-held devices, and more. It also enables you to add definitions for additional devices to accommodate new or existing technologies that are not included in the base .NET Framework.

For instance, ASP.NET has some very powerful form validation server controls. ASP.NET can determine the browser's capabilities and produce browser-specific client-side validation or, if a browser doesn't support this, it can force Server Side validation with you as a designer doing anything but setting some parameters in the server control. All I can say is WOW!

Deployment

Again in the vein of solving problems that are common to web designers, ASP.NET has provided a way for many applications to run on the same server with complete independence from one another, and it has also overcome some of the biggest deployment problems known to people developing ASP applications when using installed components.

The problems are addressed through at least two things that are unique to every possible application on a .NET server. These are an application's Configuration file and the application's bin directory.

N o t e

The term application *is another fancy programmer term used to describe a group of ASP.NET pages that are contained within the confines of a directory or folder. It is the same thing as a web site's root directory. All things contained in that directory are considered part of the web site. The same is true for ASP.NET applications. Everything contained within that root directory is considered part of the application.*

The Configuration file, named web.config, is contained in your application's root directory. It is basically an XML file that tells the application how to behave under certain circumstances and situations.

N o t e

XML (Extensible Markup Language) is an open source language that allows the creation of self-describing, structured information in a standard text document. This is a very powerful concept that is covered in later chapters.

The web.config file isn't necessary for your ASP.NET application to run, but it is available for you to use to further control your application and achieve the results and actions you want. For example, if you want to be able the view detailed errors when you are creating your ASP.NET pages, a simple web.config file might look like the following:

```
<configuration>
    <system.web>
        <compilation debug="true"/>
    </system.web>
</configuration>
```

Web.config files can contain much more information than this, but this gives you an idea of what a web.config file looks like.

When looking at how ASP.NET has simplified application deployment, you also must consider the use of components. Components are blocks of code that are compiled into a closed file type called a DLL (dynamic link library). The code contained in the DLL is not accessible directly, but you can interact with these components through predetermined methods. I will go into this in more depth as you proceed through the book.

In traditional ASP, components were used for everything from email functionality to file upload functions. The components required some annoying—if not disruptive—treatment to make them available for use in ASP pages.

First a system's web service would need to be stopped, making the pages on that system unavailable to web browsers. Then the component would need to be copied to the web server. It would need to be registered through a command line execution with Window's RegServ32.exe file. Only then could the web service be restarted. In a shared web hosting environment, many hosting companies won't install custom components at all.

If you created the component yourself and made changes to it, you would need to repeat the process of stopping web service, copying and registering the component, and restarting web service for the changes to be available.

Do you want to hear how you make components available for ASP.NET applications? You copy the component to the bin directory. That's it! Do you want to know how you update a component on the server with a new version? You guessed it! Copy it to the bin directory. What could be simpler than that?

Summary

In this opening chapter, I have just wanted to tickle your fancy or wet your whistle with regard to the possibilities of ASP.NET. I'm sure you are beginning to feel the same excitement at the possibilities ASP.NET provides for web designers that I did when I first discovered it. Many of the annoying issues of dynamic web development have been addressed with simple Server Controls. As you progress through the book, you'll dig deeper into these subjects and discover the rich and powerful functions of ASP.NET in more detail.

Understanding Object-Oriented Programming

Get your object outta my
namespace or I'm calling the cops!

We spent quite a bit of the first chapter discussing the differences between
traditional ASP and ASP.NET. One of the main recurring topics that arose was the
different paradigm under which ASP.NET operates: the paradigm of event- and
object-driven programming. That sounds all well and good, but to understand the
impact that this will have on you as a web designer, we must explore more deeply
what this really means.

You need to have a pretty good understanding of what object-oriented programming (OOP) is and how objects are used in ASP.NET. You need to know what
makes up an object, how to use it, and how to manipulate it to truly understand
the power of programming in this fashion. Then you will see how using this type
of programming environment opens up whole new worlds to you and will enable
you to program very complex functionality.

What Is Object-Oriented Design?

To truly understand object-oriented design, you must look at what is at the center of this way of designing. You guessed it—the object.

What is an object, you ask? Are they similar to objects we use, see, and touch every day? Yes! They are just like that. Objects can be exactly paralleled to physical objects we deal with every day.

Imagine you and I were on the phone and you bought a new ball recently at the store. I ask you to tell me about this new ball. Now you are in a position to explain conceptually something that is physical and apparent to you. You begin to tell me about its shape, color, texture, and so on. You are using attributes of the ball to give me a conceptual description of that ball.

Then imagine I have no idea what a ball is and need you to explain we can do with the ball. You would tell me that you can roll, bounce, throw, and kick the ball.

Through this description of the ball's attributes and what it can do, I can formulate a conceptual picture of this object and what it can do. I can picture in my mind what it looks like and how it will react to my interaction with it.

I think web designers and right-brained individuals have a distinct advantage over a typical programmer when it comes to understanding these concepts. It requires a bit of imagination and even creative thinking to understand it. You see, an object is a concept when relating to programming. It's a conceptual representation of something, or a "thingy" as I've said before. The concept of object-oriented programming enables us to create and build more complex "thingies."

So looking at our ball we can agree that as an object it is made up of things that describe it and what we can do with it.

Things that describe it:

> Shape
>
> Color
>
> Texture

What we can do with it:

> Roll
>
> Bounce
>
> Throw
>
> Kick

From a programming standpoint there are proper names for these descriptions. The things that describe an object's attributes are the object's *properties*. What we can do with an object are the object's *methods*.

Instances and Classes

When people talk about objects within the realm of programming it is important to understand that the word "object" could potentially have two meanings. There is a distinct difference between an object class and an object instance.

"Oh no, here we go again. We are being sucked into the tornado of programmer's terms with no way out and headed for the 'Land of Snooze.' Classes, Instances, Properties, and Methods, OH MY!! Auntie Em, I'm not in Kansas anymore. There's no place like home…There's no place like home… There's know pla…"

Let's try to alleviate any anxiety you may have about this and help you to understand that what we are talking about is common sense. You don't need to fear these terms or feel that this is too complex for you to understand. It is actually quite simple.

The other day I was playing with my daughter and I asked her if she wanted me to go into her room and get a ball. Now there is a toy chest full of balls but I wasn't specific with her about what one I would get for her.

Her toy chest is filled with *instances* of balls. There are all different colors, shapes, and textures of balls. There are blue, red, brown, green and all the other colors of the rainbow. There are foam, rubber, vinyl, and plastic balls—tons of instances of balls.

Notice that although there are lots of different balls, they all seem to have certain things in common. They all have a common set of properties and if you think about it, they all have a common set of methods, as well. They all have a color, shape, and texture, and they can all be rolled, bounced, thrown, and kicked.

Let's use the word "template" to describe what a class is. A class is a template of common properties and methods across a group of objects. It is a conceptual representation of the properties and methods of an object. So if I said to my daughter "Do you want me to get a ball from your toy chest?" I am referring to the concept or "class" of a ball. Objects in the toy box that are based on the Ball class all have color, shape, and texture, and can be rolled, bounced, thrown, and kicked.

After I retrieve a ball, I am bringing her a specific "instance" of a ball. It has a defined value for these different properties.

Methods are common among all instances of objects, so there aren't really differing methods among object instances. These are constant across the whole group, as shown in Figure 2.1.

FIGURE 2.1

Classes describe the properties and methods of an object. An instance is a named version with specific property values describing the instance's individuality.

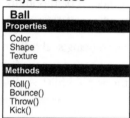

As shown in Figure 2.1, the `Ball` class is made up of the color, shape, and texture property and includes several methods of using a ball object. The `Roll()`, `Bounce()`, `Throw()`, and `Kick()` methods are available to all ball objects.

> **NOTE**
>
> *The parentheses are containers for variables that are passed to the method. So, for instance, if the `Kick()` method had variable strengths of how hard we kick the ball, we could pass this information through this variable, as in `Kick("hard")` or `Kick("soft")`.*

`objMyBall` has values that describe the properties as a color of white, a shape of round, and a texture of smooth. `objYourBall` has its own property values that describe it, as well. But this doesn't make our objects uniquely identifiable. It is our objects' names that make them unique, and in programming it is important—actually required—that instances of objects have unique names. How else is ASP.NET going to know which object we are talking about?

The diagram has two unique balls, objMyBall and objYourBall. The way to create new instances of objects is to assign names to the objects through variable creation. Variables are simply containers. They can hold objects and values, as well. You can name a variable anything you want, with the exception of reserved words such as "integer," "object," and "new," but it is good practice to use a uniform system when naming variables. In the diagram and for the ball, I used "obj" as a prefix to help you identify these as objects. The reason behind this is if I create a bunch of objects with such names in my ASP.NET pages, they will be easy to locate because they will all contain this prefix.

Creating Instances of Objects

How do you create a new ball object? First you have to assume that the Ball class is a part of the .NET Framework, which it isn't. If you can allow this stretching of reality, then you can declare a ball in this fashion in ASP.NET.

W A R N I N G

In the next few sections, I will display code examples that will throw errors if you try to plug them into a page and run them. This is because I am using an object that isn't native to ASP.NET, but one that you will discover how to create later, and if you refer to Appendix B, "Compiling Custom Objects," you will see how to turn this class into a full-fledged object that can be used in your applications. After you learn how to build your own class later in this chapter, you can use these examples as references.

Visual Basic .NET

```
dim objMyBall as Ball
dim objYourBall as Ball

objMyBall = new Ball()
objYourBall = new Ball()
```

C#

```
Ball objMyBall;
Ball objYourBall;

objMyBall = new Ball();
objYourBall = new Ball();
```

> **N O T E**
>
> *Please feel free to get excited. You now understand something that a programmer has a big fancy word for again and you didn't even know it. The operation of creating an instance of an object is called a "Constructor." Now I wonder whether you can guess the big programmer word for the operation of destroying an object. You guessed it. A "Destructor." We will discuss this a bit later.*

We now have two ball objects with the name `objMyBall` and `objYourBall` available to use, define, and interact with in your ASP.NET application.

You may be asking "Why do I have to create a variable as a ball and then create a `New Ball()` after that?" In the initial line I'm just creating a variable that will contain an object and telling the variable what shape it is—or in other words, what the variable will hold. ASP.NET doesn't actually make the ball until we stick it in the container. The variable name is the label on the container. You use the `New()` constructor to fill the container with the `Ball`.

To consolidate the function of creating like variables (containers), ASP.NET allows you to perform declarations of like object types on one line like this:

Visual Basic .NET

```
Dim objMyBall,objYourBall as Ball
```

C#

```
Ball objMyBall,objYourBall;
```

You still need to fill those variables with a `Ball` object by using the `New()` constructor.

Visual Basic .NET

```
Dim objMyBall,objYourBall as Ball

objMyball = new Ball()
objYourBall = new Ball()
```

C#

```
Ball objMyBall,objYourBall;

objMyball = new Ball()
objYourBall = new Ball()
```

ASP.NET has also provided a shortcut for this by enabling you to do both functions on a single line for each individual object.

Visual Basic .NET

```
Dim objMyBall as New Ball()
Dim objYourBall as New Ball()
```

C#

```
Ball objMyball = new Ball();
Ball objYourBall = new Ball();
```

This shortcut makes it possible to create the variable and construct the object all in one shot for each object. No method is really better than the other. This is pretty much a personal preference issue, so feel free to use the method that you are most comfortable with.

Objects are pretty cool, huh? You bet they are! ASP.NET has hundreds of pre-built object classes to create and interact with in your applications. You can also create objects of your own like the ball. ASP.NET basically treats everything as an object, and you will see as the examples develop function and form that we are also creating objects to interact with. Kinda like building a log cabin with Play-Doh: If you need another log you just grab some more Play-Doh and roll it between your palms. If you need another object in ASP.NET, you massage your code to build another object in the application. We will do this later, but first you must understand some other stuff, so you get the whole thing under control.

Properties

Now that the `Ball` objects are alive and ready to use, you can begin to tell ASP.NET what they look like. Looking at an object class and object instances from the previous example, there is something you should understand.

When you create an instance from a class, the class builds the object with default properties. These properties may simply have a default value that is empty. A ball has a color attribute because the class defines it. However, it may not have a value yet. Or maybe the `Ball` class creates a ball with a default color property of white. This is determined within the class; you'll learn more later when we investigate the `Ball` class in detail.

Setting Properties

As we've discussed before, the `Ball` has properties—things that describe what the object is like. It has a color, shape, and texture property. When you create an instance of an object, you can now set and retrieve the value of a property for a specific instance.

Visual Basic .NET

```
objMyBall.Color = "White"
objYourBall.Color = "Blue"
```

C#

```
objMyBall.Color = "White";
objYourBall.Color = "Blue";
```

Notice that the statements are virtually the same with the exception of the semicolon at the end of each line in the C# version. This is how you set the value of property in ASP.NET.

C A U T I O N

If you choose C# as your language for programming in ASP.NET, you must remember that it is very picky (as I stated in Chapter 1 when showing that C# would misbehave because it is case sensitive). Another thing to be aware of is that C# loves semicolons. It needs semicolons to terminate a line of code. This has advantages and disadvantages. In Visual Basic .NET there is an assumption that every line in the document is equal to a line of code and if you want to continue your code on the next line you must indicate this with an underscore. So Visual Basic .NET terminates a line of code by default unless otherwise told. C#, on the other hand, continues a line of code unless it is terminated with a semicolon.

Properties can be set in other ways, too, as you'll see in the next section on methods. Properties can have values assigned to them in three ways:

- When an instance of an object is created, the class (template) has a default value, even if it's nothing.

- You can set it by writing `objectname.propertyname = value`.

- They can be set by an object's methods.

There isn't any limitation on how many times you can set these properties within a page or application. It's there for you to manipulate and you can feel free to go hog wild and change these values as much or as little as is necessary to suit what you are trying to do in your application.

Retrieve Properties

Now that we've set these properties , you need to know how to retrieve them. Just as writing `Objectname.PropertyName` sets the `Ball`'s `Color` property, you also retrieve its value this way. Following are two different examples of situations that involve getting the value of the `Color` properties.

Visual Basic .NET

```
dim strMyBallColor,strYourBallColor as String
strMyBallColor = objMyBall.Color
strYourBallColor = objYourBall.Color

OurLabel.Text = objMyBall.Color
OurLabel.Text = objYourBall.Color
```

C#

```
String strMyBallColor,strYourBallColor;
strMyBallColor = objMyBall.Color;
strYourBallColor = objYourBall.Color;

OurLabel.Text = objMyBall.Color;
OurLabel.Text = objYourBall.Color;
```

In this example, you first create two variables and then set their values to the value of the objects' color properties. Next, you set the text of an ASP.NET Label server control to the value of the property.

So we can say that properties are the attributes that describe the condition of an object. This can be what an object looks like, but as you'll see as we start to explore the balls methods, it also can include a new property that can't be paralleled to its "appearance" but deals with its condition.

Imagine being in Hawaii (I wish!!!!). The sun is beating down on you and the things around you. You decide that it's time to go to the beach and enjoy some of the beautiful Hawaiian surf. You step off the boardwalk onto the sand and begin to hop around like a kangaroo. Why, you ask? Because of this:

```
Sand.Temperature = "Hot"
```

The `Sand.Temperature` property is `"Hot"`, as you can feel. It doesn't describe an attribute of what sand looks like, but what type of state it is in. Properties describe objects and have the potential of describing any type of attribute. They outline what something is like.

Methods

Methods are simply ways for us to tell an object what to do. They can be simple things such as rolling the ball, which actually could be considered complex, but for this example we will keep it simple. Methods can also be very complex, as well. For instance, imagine you have a car object and want to call its `StartEngine()` method. This method must put many things into motion before you can alter the state of the car object from not having a running motor to having a running motor.

Executing a method or calling a method is not a whole lot more difficult than referring to a property. You simply refer to the `ObjectName.MethodName()`. The parentheses are required when calling a method, so be sure to include them.

Let's take a look at the `Roll()` method of the ball object and see how it affects the state of the ball. The `Roll()` method does just that: It rolls the ball. But you need a way to see that the ball is rolling. I am going to introduce you to an additional property of the ball now. It is the Motion property. This property identifies whether the ball is in motion or not. It has a default value of 'still' set by the `Ball` class. This code is run in the `Page_Load()` event and the text attribute of the label is set to the values of the ball at different times. So, now let's roll the ball.

Visual Basic .NET—`ball_roll_method_vb.aspx`

```
dim objMyBall as New Ball()

OurLabel.Text = "<u>Before Roll Method</u><br>"
OurLabel.Text += "MyBall: " & objMyBall.Motion & "<br><br>"


objMyBall.Roll()

OurLabel.Text += "<u>After Roll Method</u><br>"
OurLabel.Text += "MyBall: " & objMyBall.Motion
```

C#—`ball_roll_method_cs.aspx`

```
Ball objMyBall = new Ball();

OurLabel.Text += "<u>Before Roll Method</u><br>";
OurLabel.Text += "MyBall: " + objMyBall.Motion + "<br><br>";

objMyBall.Roll();

OurLabel.Text += "<u>After Roll Method</u><br>";
OurLabel.Text += "MyBall: " + objMyBall.Motion;
```

Now you see how to call a method. Tough? I don't think so! Figure 2.2 shows how this code will appear in a browser.

FIGURE 2.2

Notice that the ball is still before the roll() *method is called and rolling after it is called.*

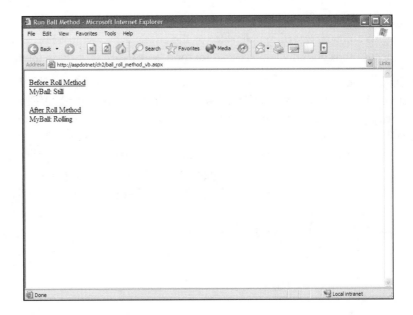

You can see that the ball initially is still, which is its default property set by the class (Remember Template) when objMyBall was created. After you call the Roll() method, you can see that the ball is rolling. Keep in mind that this is over-simplified. Under this situation the ball would roll infinitely without some other intervention, but ignore this problem for this example so we can move on.

You can even pass directives to your methods if they allow for it. Imagine that the Roll() method allowed you to adjust how hard you roll the ball. Maybe you can determine whether you want to roll the ball softly, moderately, or hard. You can pass these values in the parentheses and affect how hard the ball rolls. You can even pass directives to your methods if they allow for it. You'll learn more about this later after you learn how to create methods.

Creating a Class

Now we're gonna take some time to put together all this stuff you've learned on the last few pages about objects, properties, and methods. We are going to build a real living object in ASP.NET, and you will see how easy it is to come up with a concept and turn it into an object.

Remember, you don't have to build your own objects to use ASP.NET; there are hundreds of pre-built ones that cover tons of typical web application situations. We are going to build this object as a demonstration of how to build one if you want to. The greatest part is YOU CAN!!! This is part of the freedom that ASP.NET gives to you when you program web applications in this language.

Inside the Class

Let's take a look at the full-fledged Ball class—with properties of Color and Motion and a method of Roll()—and dissect it into its different parts so you can easily understand it. Don't be overwhelmed by the big block of code that follows. Think of it as a sizzling, juicy steak that is being placed in front of you. It would be difficult to enjoy if you tried to swallow it whole (and I'd be hard pressed to save you from choking considering you're only reading a book and I'm not there with you). But if you cut it up into bite-sized pieces you can chew it, savor it, and finally swallow the whole steak.

Visual Basic .NET

```
Public Class Ball
    Private _Color as String
    Private _Motion as String

    Public Sub New()
        _Motion = "Still"
    End Sub

    Public Property Color as String
        Get
            Return _Color
        End Get
        Set
            _Color = value
        End Set
    End Property

    Public ReadOnly Property Motion as String
        Get
            Return _Motion
        End Get
    End Property

    Public Sub Roll()
        _Motion="Rolling"
    End Sub
End Class
```

C#

```
public class Ball {
    private string _Color;
    private string _Motion;

    public Ball(){
        _Motion = "Still";
    }

    public string Color{
        get {
            return _Color;
        }
        set {
            _Color = value;
        }
    }


    public string  Motion {
        get {
            return _Motion;
        }
    }

    public void Roll() {
            _Motion="Rolling";
    }
}
```

The first thing I think you'll notice is that the C# language is definitely more compact or concise—maybe less wordy is a way to say it. Visual Basic .NET does tend to be wordier to accomplish the same thing in a side-by-side comparison with C#, but there are tradeoffs to writing less characters of code in C#. Keep in mind that C# is *very* picky. Did I mention C# is picky? As you can see, Visual Basic .NET, in references to keywords such as return, is indifferent to case sensitivity. Not so in C#. So the tradeoff is that to program in C# you might have to type fewer characters, but you must pay special attention to what those characters are.

Class Delimiter

Now let's get out our steak sauce, a knife, and a fork, and carve up some of that delicious steak. The first thing you need to do when building a class is to define it.

Visual Basic .NET

```
Public Class Ball
```

C#

```
public class Ball {
```

This line lets the .NET Framework know that you're going to build an object. It works in this manner in its simplest form: accessibility level, class keyword, and class name.

Let's look at accessibility levels first. We are going to touch on only the two contained in this example—Public and Private—but there are many possible accessibility levels that help you to control how a class or its members (Properties and Methods) are available for use within your applications. The Public and Private accessibility levels can be described as follows:

- **Public.** A class or a class member that is available anywhere the class is present.

- **Private.** A class or a class member that is available only within that class that it is part of.

So if you look at the code above, you can see that this class is available for creating ball objects.

The only noticeable difference between the Visual Basic .NET code and the C# code is that the C# code has a curly bracket ({) at the end of the line. This is C#'s opening delimiter for a block of code. If you are familiar with JavaScript, this will look familiar because it uses the same character. Both Visual Basic .NET and C# require that you delimit the beginning and end of encapsulated code blocks such as classes, properties, and methods, to mention a few. This is similar to all the two-part tags in HTML, such as the <html></html> tags or <table></table> tags. You must provide a start delimiter and an end delimiter to the block of code.

In Visual Basic .NET, all keywords that need delimiting inherently are the opening delimiter for itself but must be closed with the keyword's proper matching end delimiter:

```
Public Class Ball
    //Class Code Here
End Class
```

C# must have an opening curly bracket and must also have a partner closing curly bracket as well.

```
Public Class Ball{
    //Class Code Here
}
```

So now we've covered the first and last lines of the class and we've also talked about how many members of ASP.NET—including classes, properties, and members—need to be delimited to work properly. Now it's time to move on to our next juicy morsel.

Class Private Variables

Next it's time to create the variables for the properties. These aren't the properties that you access, but the variables that contain them inside the class. Notice the private access level on these variables. As mentioned earlier, this means they are available to only the class that they are part of. This means you can't directly get the value of _Color or _Motion. This just holds the current value of the objects _Color and _Motion. You get these values through calling the properties.

Visual Basic .NET

```
Private _Color as String
Private _Motion as String
```

C#

```
private string _Color;
private string _Motion;
```

> **T I P**
>
> The underscore that begins the property name in _Color and _Motion is a pretty standard way of naming variables that are private inside a class and are used to store property values with matching names. So _Color is holding the value of the color property and _Motion is holding the value of the motion property in this class. This makes it easy to identify these variables in your code as property value containers.

Let's move on.

Class Constructor

The following is the class constructor code. It is the block of code that is executed during a call to the New() method when you're creating a new instance of the Ball object. It is not a required part of code when you write a class. You need it only if you need to do something when you create each instance of your object.

Visual Basic .NET

```
Public Sub New()
    _Motion = "Still"
End Sub
```

C#

```
public Ball(){
    _Motion = "Still";
}
```

Follow this...an "object" has a class in the eyes of the .NET Framework and it has a template as well. It is called the Object class. All objects in the .NET Framework get their base structure from the Object class and thus have all of its properties and methods. In that Object class there is a New() constructor by default, so even if you don't insert it into your class code, you can still use the New() constructor because your object will have gotten the constructor from the base Object class.

You need to set a default value of "Still" for the motion property of the ball, so you need the constructor code. You can basically do anything within the constructor code. For instance, you could have called a Roll() method from the constructor if you wanted to be able to create a rolling ball right off the bat.

Class Properties

The next thing to study is the properties.

Visual Basic .NET

```
Public Property Color as String
    Get
        Return _Color
    End Get
    Set
        _Color = value
    End Set
End Property

Public ReadOnly Property Motion as String
    Get
        Return _Motion
    End Get
End Property
```

C#

```
public string Color{
    get {
        return _Color;
    }
    set {
        _Color = value;
    }
}

public string  Motion {
    get {
        return _Motion;
    }
}
```

These are our two properties, Color and Motion, being created in the class. These are two different types of properties. The Color property is something you want to retrieve and be able to set a value for, as well. So this property has a Get function, for retrieving the value of the parameter, and a Set function, for setting the value of the parameter. Pretty self-explanatory! If you want a parameter value, you Get it; if you want to assign it, you Set it.

In the Get function, all you're doing is returning the value of the private variable that matches the parameter in the case of both the Color property and the Motion property. Ask for the value as follows:

Visual Basic .NET

```
dim strMyBallColor as String
strMyBallColor = objMyBall.Color
```

C#

```
String strMyBallColor;
strMyBallColor = objMyBall.Color;
```

You are calling the Get portion of the property and receiving the value of the private variable in return.

If you look at the Color property, you can see an additional function called Set. The Set function is also pretty simple to understand. When you want to change the value of a property, you use code like this, as mentioned before:

Visual Basic .NET

```
objMyBall.Color = "White"
```

C#

```
objMyBall.Color = "White";
```

With this type of code, you're calling the Set function. Notice that the Motion property doesn't have a Set function. This is because you don't want to give people the ability to set the value of a ball's motion: We're trying to programmatically mirror reality here, and a ball doesn't just start moving. You need to restrict the ability to set a property's value by making it a read-only property. Again the differences in Visual Basic .NET and C# are apparent here. We must tell Visual Basic .NET that a property is read-only by placing "ReadOnly" in the line where you create the property.

C#, on the other hand, figures that if there's no Set property, it must be read only. This makes sense, and again leads to having to type less code than in Visual Basic .NET to accomplish the same thing.

Class Methods

Now on to the method. You want to be able to roll the ball, but the Motion property is read-only so we can't get our ball to move. This example of a method is over-simplified to help give you some basic understanding of how a method is created and what it can do. If we took time to really investigate what happens to a ball when you roll it, how gravity, friction, wind, and other things affect it, we could be here forever writing a gazillion lines of code to accommodate what the ball's Motion property would look like when the ball is rolled. I say all this to point out that it's possible to do so. You could programmatically create these scenarios and affect the ball with these things, but we are only investigating what methods are, not how complex they can get. This is kinda like the whole "fishing/feeding" metaphor, which goes, "Give a man a fish and you feed him for a day; teach him how to fish and you feed him for a lifetime," or something like that. I'm trying to teach you how to fish so that tomorrow you can create your own methods and understand how to do it successfully.

Visual Basic .NET

```
Public Sub Roll()
    _Motion="Rolling"
End Sub
```

C#

```
public void Roll() {
        _Motion="Rolling";
}
```

When you call the Roll method, you can see it simply sets the private variable _Motion to Rolling. Next time you check the ball's Motion property, it will return a value of "Rolling".

As I mentioned, you can do very complex things in methods—and with properties, too, for that matter. In the following, the Roll() method has been adapted to allow you to dictate how hard the ball rolls.

Visual Basic .NET

```
Public Sub Roll(Strength as String)
    If _Motion = "Still" then
        If Strength = "Soft" then _Motion = "Rolling Softly"
        If Strength = "Medium" then _Motion = "Rolling Medium"
        If Strength = "Hard" then _Motion = "Rolling Hard"
    End if
End Sub
```

C#

```
public void Roll(string strength) {
    if ( _Motion == "Still"){
        if (strength == "Soft") _Motion = "Rolling Softly";
        if (strength == "Medium") _Motion = "Rolling Medium";
        if (strength == "Hard") _Motion = "Rolling Hard";
    }
}
```

Now let's say you've edited your page to look like the following. Remember that this code block is running in the page's Page_Load() event and is setting the text attribute of a Label object:

Visual Basic .NET—**ball_roll_method_strength_vb.aspx**

```
dim objMyBall as New Ball()
dim objYourBall as New Ball()
dim objNewRidersBall as New Ball()

OurLabel.Text += "<u>Before Roll Method</u><br>"
OurLabel.Text += "MyBall: " & objMyBall.Motion & "<br>"
OurLabel.Text += "YourBall: " & objYourBall.Motion & "<br>"
OurLabel.Text += "NewRidersBall: " & objNewRidersBall.Motion & "<br><br>"

objMyBall.Roll("Soft")
objYourBall.Roll("Medium")
objNewRidersBall.Roll("Hard")

OurLabel.Text += "<u>After Roll Method</u><br>"
OurLabel.Text += "MyBall: " & objMyBall.Motion & "<br>"
OurLabel.Text += "YourBall: " & objYourBall.Motion & "<br>"
OurLabel.Text += "NewRidersBall: " & objNewRidersBall.Motion & "<br><br>"
```

C#—`ball_roll_method_strength_cs.aspx`

```
Ball objMyBall = new Ball();
Ball objYourBall = new Ball();
Ball objNewRidersBall = new Ball();

OurLabel.Text += "<u>Before Roll Method</u><br>";
OurLabel.Text += "MyBall: " + objMyBall.Motion + "<br>";
OurLabel.Text += "YourBall: " + objYourBall.Motion + "<br>";
OurLabel.Text += "NewRidersBall: " + objNewRidersBall.Motion + "<br><br>";

objMyBall.Roll("Soft");
objYourBall.Roll("Medium");
objNewRidersBall.Roll("Hard");

OurLabel.Text += "<u>After Roll Method</u><br>";
OurLabel.Text += "MyBall: " + objMyBall.Motion + "<br>";
OurLabel.Text += "YourBall: " + objYourBall.Motion + "<br>";
OurLabel.Text += "NewRidersBall: " + objNewRidersBall.Motion + "<br><br>";
```

This can be seen in Figure 2.3.

FIGURE 2.3

You can have your method perform multiple tasks, including changing the strength at which roll the ball rolls.

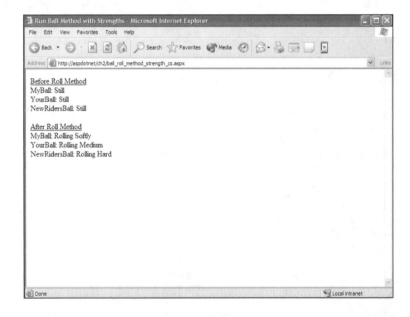

As you can see in Figure 2.3, passing a parameter to the method affects how hard the ball rolls. The method is structured to check how hard you want to roll the ball and then change the Motion property.

One more thing that I would like to touch on is what programmers call "overloading methods," and what Boy scouts call "being prepared." Overloading a method is nothing more than providing a bunch of different potential ways to use a method.

Let's take the Roll() method, for instance. You may want to give people two ways to describe how hard to roll the ball. You might want to leave the ability to pass in "Soft, Medium, or Hard" to the method, but also want to be able to pass in 1, 2, or 3 to affect this method the same way "Soft, Medium, and Hard" do. You would create another Roll() method to accommodate this different situation.

Visual Basic .NET

```
Public Sub Roll(Strength as String)
    If _Motion = "Still" then
        If Strength = "Soft" then _Motion = "Rolling Softly"
        If Strength = "Medium" then _Motion = "Rolling Medium"
        If Strength = "Hard" then _Motion = "Rolling Hard"
    End if
End Sub

Public Sub Roll(Strength as Integer)
    If _Motion = "Still" then
        If Strength = 1 then _Motion = "Rolling Softly"
        If Strength = 2 then _Motion = "Rolling Medium"
        If Strength = 3 then _Motion = "Rolling Hard"
    End if
End Sub
```

C#

```
public void Roll(string strength) {
    if ( _Motion == "Still"){
        if (strength == "Soft") _Motion = "Rolling Softly";
        if (strength == "Medium")  _Motion = "Rolling Medium";
        if (strength == "Hard") _Motion = "Rolling Hard";
    }
}
public void Roll(int strength) {
    if ( _Motion == "Still"){
        if (strength == 1) _Motion = "Rolling Softly";
        if (strength == 2)  _Motion = "Rolling Medium";
        if (strength == 3) _Motion = "Rolling Hard";
    }
}
```

Again, this is an oversimplified example and methods can contain more than one variable, but it demonstrates what it means to overload a method and "be prepared!"

> **WARNING**
>
> *Each overloaded method must have a unique footprint or "signature." A method's signature is a combination of the method's name and its parameter types. In the previous example, the first overloaded method has a signature of* `Roll(string)`*, and the second has a signature of* `Roll(int)`*. These create two unique signatures so that .NET can know which version of the method you are trying to address. You can't overload a method with two matching signatures no matter how many parameters it has.*

With the class dissected, you now have a clearer understanding of what objects are made of and how they work. It's not as complicated as you may have thought, and I'm sure you are feeling a bit more comfortable with objects now.

As I've said before, the .NET Framework provides a boatload of pre-made objects so you won't have to go through this process of creating classes and their properties and methods. A vast majority of typical web function is already covered in classes that come standard with .NET.

"Okay Peter, so a 'boatload' of objects is available. What are they and what they do?" Not as big a deal as you think, and later we'll go through many of them in more detail. The bigger question that needs to be answered is *where* they are. The answer to this question really provides a platform to answer *what* they are.

(Fade to black and white)…We will now unveil another one of the .NET mysteries as we enter the "Namespace" zone!!

Namespaces

Let's just say that the concept of namespaces is like an addressing system, similar to the Dewey decimal system used by libraries for categorizing, grouping, and locating books. It's really that simple.

As I've said before, .NET has tons of object classes ready for you to use to build applications. If I just provided a list of these, it would be longer than a football field—and finding an object would be a pain in the posterior!

Imagine that you and I are standing outside your house in your backyard. We are enjoying a barbeque of succulent ribs and a few ice-cold beverages. You are slaving over the hot open barbeque and realize that you forgot to bring the tray of bacon-topped baked beans outside. You ask me to go inside and get them for you. Well, I've never been in your house before, because I came straight from the car to the backyard. (I know, I know!! Come on Peter, get to the point and stop talking about food again.)

"Where are the beans?" I ask.

"Go through the back door into the house, turn left into the kitchen. They are in the oven on the top rack," you say. These directions are easy enough to follow, and I successfully find the beans and return outside to our lovely barbeque.

"What does this have to do with namespaces?" you ask. I'll tell you in a way that's easy to understand. Your house could be looked at from the viewpoint of namespaces, and it would provide thorough directions to find baked beans in your house. The beans are in a namespace:

```
House.FirstFloor.Kitchen.Oven.TopRack
```

Your socks in a namespace:

```
House.SecondFloor.Bedroom.Dresser.TopDrawer
```

Aspirin, lawnmower, fine china, laundry detergent:

```
House.SecondFloor.Bathroom.MedicineCabinet
House.FirstFloor.Garage
House.FirstFloor.DiningRoom.ChinaCabinet
House.FirstFloor.LaundryRoom.Shelf
```

Are you getting it? Namespaces are just like this in .NET. It is a system to describe where objects are stored. And let me tell you that it is a *very* logical system. We will be looking deeper into this in the next section of this chapter and investigating some of the namespaces we will commonly use when making ASP.NET applications.

Creating a Namespace

When we created the `Ball` class earlier in the chapter, we included the `Ball` class code right in the top of the web page. Every time this page is called, that class is available for use by that page. This is the way we did it for the example, but it may not be the optimal way to achieve what you want.

You may want to create a component out of the `Ball` object. This is a fancy way of saying you will create the `Ball` as an object that will be available just as all the .NET objects are.

Describing how to create components is a bit out of the scope of this chapter, but I provide a teaser and some more detailed information on component creation in Appendix B. Right now, you're just investigating how to create a namespace. It isn't very different from creating an object. You must just call the correct keyword and follow the correct syntax.

Visual Basic .NET

```
Namespace Peter.Toybox
    Public Class Ball
        //Our Class Code
    End Class
End Namespace
```

C#

```
Namespace Peter.Toybox{
    public class Ball {
        //Our Class Code
    }
}
```

In the appendix you can see more about how the ball component is created, but for the next example let's imagine you've created your component and it's available for use in your application.

Using a Namespace

To use the `Ball` object in your application, you simply need to just let .NET know where the `Ball` object is, using its namespace, just like I could have found the baked beans in the oven by following its namespace directing.

Visual Basic .NET

```
Import Peter.Toybox
```

C#

```
using Peter.Toybox
```

Notice that the keyword used by Visual Basic .NET and C# is different. `Import` is used to address a namespace in Visual Basic .NET and the word `using` is used in C#.

ASP.NET and Objects

We've been talking a lot about objects in this chapter, and I've mentioned several times that the .NET Framework provides a huge number of ready-to-use objects for you to use when you build web applications. These objects are organized in namespaces.

If you are familiar with traditional ASP, things such as the `Request` and `Response` objects will be familiar to you. They are used in a very similar way in ASP.NET. There are also object versions of just about every significant HTML element you've ever used for creating web pages, from simple anchor tags to very complex objects like the calendar object I demonstrated in chapter one.

In the scope of the .NET Framework, objects cascade from general objects down to very specialized objects the deeper you get into the namespace hierarchy. Just like in the barbeque example, the house is a very general thing, but the first or second floor is more specific. And as you go, the directions become more and more specific, down to the top drawer of the dresser where are socks are kept. That drawer has a very specific function in comparison to all the other things in the house. The second floor holds all the rooms within it, as well as the things each room contains.

So out in the root of the .NET Framework, where the `System` namespace is located, some very basic object classes are contained there, such as the data type objects like `System.String` or `System.DateTime`, which aren't linked to any specific task but are used in just about everything.

Then deeper in the Framework you can see objects that are function-specific, such as the `HTMLAnchor` object that resides in `System.Web.UI.HTMLControls`. As you can see, the deeper you look into the Framework, the more specific the function an object performs.

So out at the root is the `System` namespace. This is like the house in the barbeque example. Every other namespace is contained in this namespace, just like every floor of the house—every room, every element, and every thing—is contained in your house.

For you as a web designer, and for the rest of this book, we will primarily, with a few exceptions, be paying attention to just a few namespaces in the .NET Framework. They are

- `System.Web`. This namespace •contains the vast majority of objects that you would use to build your web applications. It contains the objects we will focus on in the later chapters in this book, plus many others.

- `System.Web.UI`. This namespace contains nearly all the objects and namespaces, including `System.Web.UI.HTMLControls` and `System.Web.UI.WebControls`, that you use to build your ASPX pages.

- `System.Data`. This namespace contains all the objects needed for manipulating data and interfacing with databases.

- `System.XML`. This namespace is explored later in the book and provides objects for reading, manipulating, and writing XML data.

T I P

You can find a very powerful web application called "The .NET Framework Class Browser" located at the following URL. It allows you to browse the entire list of .NET namespaces, the namespace hierarchy, and the objects contained within in a logical navigable format. When you locate any particular object, it shows you all its constructors, properties, and methods.

```
http://samples.gotdotnet.com/quickstart/aspplus/samples/
classbrowser/vb/classbrowser.aspx
```

As you continue to explore ASP.NET, you'll dig deeper into objects and discover how the object-oriented design paradigm is really liberating after you can sink your teeth into it. If you are curious and want to learn more about object-oriented design, there are many good books available on the subject, including

The Art of Objects by Yun-Tung Lau. Addison Wesley, 2000.

Design Patterns—Elements of Reusable Object Oriented Software. Erich Gamma, Richard Helm, Ralph Johnson, and John Vlissides. Addison Wesley, 1995.

Please be forewarned that these books are *very* programmer-oriented, go *very* deep into the concepts of object-oriented design, and required a bit of patience on my part to follow. They are books that focus on teaching the concept of this programming method and don't have web-specific examples. I simply provide these titles as additional resources if you want to learn more about the concepts of object-oriented programming.

Summary

As you've seen, objects are very powerful things. But they are power unrealized if they don't get some fuel and direction from us. We are going to move forward into understanding how to use your chosen scripting languages to get the results you want out of your web applications. With what you've learned in this chapter, plus the knowledge of scripting that you'll get in the next, you will have a more thorough understanding of the power of objects and how to manipulate them.

chapter 3

Scripting Basics

This has nothing to do with penmanship, but your writing style is still being graded!

I spent quite a bit of the first chapter discussing the common language runtime, and I'll touch on it a bit here too. Dozens of languages are supported in .NET, either natively or through third parties.

I am very often asked the question, "If there are so many languages, which one should I use?" You may as well ask me "What shampoo should I use?" because the answer is the same. It's your own personal choice.

If you come with some understanding of a particular supported .NET language, then I might recommend you use your experience in that language to help you move forward faster into building .NET applications. You can easily understand many of the concepts in this book and they'll be a cinch for you to port over to your chosen language.

Common Language Runtime—Which Language Should I Use?

If you haven't decided on a language yet, I suggest that you consider either Visual Basic .NET or C#. These two languages seem to have emerged as the most popular languages in .NET circles and will provide you with the richest amount of support material in both reading and web resources.

I chose to include examples in the book in both Visual Basic .NET and C# because I think that these two languages cater to two different types of people. I've made several points about some general characteristics and attributes of both Visual Basic .NET and C# so far to try to help you decide. I guess I can sum it up this way:

> **Visual Basic .NET** is a bit wordier but closer to regular English in its performance of form and function. (By the way, this is the language I generally use, but I'm also fond of C#).

> **C#** is more compact, picky, and specific. It is a bit harder for the untrained eye to read, but as you become more accustomed to it you will habitually pay more attention to capitalization, line termination, and a few other of the common faux pas associated with the language.

I found myself rubbing my forehead and gouging my eyes while learning C# because I had become VERY, VERY!, VERY!! lazy about being careful during coding of ASP/VBscript applications when we built traditional ASP applications. VBScript is quite a forgiving language, but unfortunately I allow this liberty to reinforce bad coding practices that became painfully apparent when I learned C#. C# is not only unforgiving, it's brutal. But I've come to love it in its simplicity.

I know it sounds like I harp on C# more often than Visual Basic .NET, and if we went back and counted complaints or "Warnings" so far, this may be true. But this isn't because I think Visual Basic .NET is better than C#. It is just me communicating to another designer about the bumps I've hit in the road. I know that as a designer and conversely as an ASP/VBScript programmer, I was never very concerned about something like capitalization. C# is very concerned about capitalization, and if you choose to program in it you're going to need to be, too.

What I suggest is that if you haven't already decided which language you will use, read this chapter and see some of the different ways that common functions and controls are written in both Visual Basic .NET and C#. Then decide which one will best suit you.

I spend the rest of this chapter exploring the guts behind these two languages. You'll investigate variables and something called control structure and how these are handled in both languages.

Many of the code samples in this chapter require writing information to pages. In an effort to reinforce the Object/Event thing discussed in Chapter 1, I have made the following template page for you to use as a base for many of the examples in this chapter. Simply drop the blocks of code in the examples into the `Page_Load()` event (which has been highlighted in bold) and you should be good to go!!

Visual Basic .NET—`template_vb.aspx`

```
<%@ page language="vb" runat="server"%>
<script  runat=server>

Sub Page_Load()
    'Replace this with your code
End Sub

</script>
<html>
<title>VB.NET Template</title>
<body>
<asp:label id="OurLabel" runat="server"/>
</body>
</html>
```

C#—`template_cs.aspx`

```
<%@ page language="c#" runat="server"%>
<script  runat=server>
public void page_load(){
    //Replace with your code
}
</script>
<html>
<title>C# Template</title>
<body>
<asp:label id="OurLabel" runat="server"/>
</body>
</html>
```

Variables

I've been using variables throughout the first two chapters, and you may have a loose idea of what a variable is and does. Remember—a variable is nothing more than a container.

If you come from a traditional ASP background, variables created sloppy coding behavior because variables weren't really variables in the truest sense of the word. They were variants and could basically hold anything without ever indicating what type of data the variable was holding. Now variables must be told what they are holding, otherwise…BOOM!!! It won't work.

We are going to explore variables and their data types in both languages. There are some differences in names, the way you address variables, and how you manipulate them. First I must show you what data types are available and what their names are.

Data Types

The language-specific data type names in the following table aren't really the data types themselves. They are pointers. Do you know what they point to? You guessed it—objects! These objects handle the data types and their properties and methods. These can also be explored in the .NET Framework Class Library explorer mentioned at the end of Chapter 2.

Table 3.1 shows the pointer names for both languages, their corresponding .NET object, and an explanation of what that data type can hold.

TABLE 3.1 Data Types

Visual Basic .NET Type	C# Type	.NET Framework Type	Range
Boolean	bool	System.Boolean	True or False
Byte	byte	System.Byte	0-255
Char	char	System.Char	0-65535 Unicode Character
Date	DateTime	System.Datetime	January 1, 0001 to December 31, 9999
Decimal	decimal	System.Decimal	Approx. 1.0_10^{-28} to 7.9_10^{28}

Visual Basic .NET Type	C# Type	.NET Framework Type	Range
Double	double	System.Double	Approx. $\pm5.0\_10^{-324}$ to $\pm1.7\_10^{308}$
Integer	int	System.Int32	$-2,147,483,648$ to $2,147,483,647$
Long	long	System.Int64	$-9,223,372,036,854,775,808$ to $9,223,372,036,854,775,807$
N/S	sbyte	System.SByte	-128 to 127
Short	short	System.Int16	$-32,768$ to $32,767$
Single	float	System.Single	Approx. $\pm1.5\_10^{-45}$ to $\pm3.4\_10^{38}$
String	string	System.String	0 to approximately 2 billion Unicode characters
N/S	ushort	System.UInt16	0 to 65,535
N/S	uint	System.UInt32	0 to 4,294,967,295
N/S	ulong	System.UInt64	0 to 18,446,744,073,709,551,615

N/S = Not Supported

Don't be intimidated by all the different data types and numbers. I really only put this in the book to impress you with my knowledge of the vast and seemingly infinite range of data one can manipulate with these data types and their corresponding objects.

YEAH...RIGHT!!!

Seriously, this is best way I can explain data types to you: The raisin between my ears has boiled it down to the descriptions in the sections that follow.

Boolean

Boolean, which is shown in Table 3.2, is about as simple a data type as there can be. True or false. That's it.

TABLE 3.2 Boolean

Visual Basic .NET Type	C# Type	.NET Framework Type	Range
Boolean	bool	System.Boolean	True or False

Numbers

There are numbers with decimals, numbers without decimals that can have negative numbers, and numbers without decimals that start at 0 and go up. (The latter are available only in C#.) Big, Bigger, and Super Size, for all three as seen in Table 3.3 and Table 3.4.

Table 3.3 Numbers without Decimals

Visual Basic .NET Type	C# Type	.NET Framework Type	Range
Byte	byte	System.Byte	0-255
N/S	sbyte	System.SByte	-128 to 127
Short	short	System.Int16	Big number, no decimal, can start below 0
Integer	int	System.Int32	Bigger number, no decimal, can start below 0
Long	long	System.Int64	Super Size number, no decimal, can start below 0
N/S	ushort	System.UInt16	Big number, no decimal, that starts at 0
N/S	uint	System.UInt32	Bigger number, no decimal, that starts at 0
N/S	ulong	System.UInt64	Super Size number, no decimal, that starts at 0

TABLE 3.4   Numbers with Decimals

Visual Basic .NET Type	C# Type	.NET Framework Type	Range
Single	float	System.Single	Big number with decimal
Double	double	System.Double	Bigger number with decimal
Decimal	decimal	System.Decimal	Super Size number with decimal

To give you an idea how big a Super Size number is, its largest possible value is

```
+/-79,228,162,514,264,337,593,543,950,335
```

That's like 9 trillion or zillion or something like that. Like I said…SUPER SIZED!!!

> **N O T E**
>
> The size differences of the variables in the Table 3.3 and 3.4 bring up an issue that I'd like to address. The larger the variable you use, the more server memory you use, so it is good practice to use variables that are sufficient enough in capability to contain what you will be placing in them but to not use anything larger. Using larger variables puts undue requirements on the server and allocates memory that you will never use. That said, I can tell you that in all my years of programming I've NEVER needed to use a Long or Super Size integer before.

Characters

This data type includes any type of character such as letters, numbers, and special characters. There are only two kinds of character data types. One is very small and the other is very large, as shown in Table 3.5.

TABLE 3.5   Characters

Visual Basic .NET Type	C# Type	.NET Framework Type	Range
Char	char	System.Char	Any single one of the 65535 Unicode characters
String	string	System.String	0 to approximately 2 billion Unicode characters

If you need to use more than one character, you've go no choice but to use a string—not a difficult choice to make.

Dates and Times

This data type is pretty self-explanatory. It's used to store dates and times, as shown in Table 3.6.

TABLE 3.6   Date & Time

Visual Basic .NET Type	C# Type	.NET Framework Type	Range
Date	DateTime	System.Datetime	January 1, 0001 to December 31, 9999

Declaring and Initializing Variables

In the previous chapters, you've seen a bit of variable declaration and initialization, but let's make it official and discuss some different techniques and shortcuts.

Remember, we declare variables like this:

Visual Basic .NET

```
dim var1 as integer
```

C#

```
int var1;
```

And variables are initialized like this:

Visual Basic .NET

```
var1 = 1
```

C#

```
var1 = 1;
```

It's also possible to declare multiple variables of the same type at the same time. They simply need to be separated by commas:

Visual Basic .NET

```
dim var1,var2,var3 as integer
```

C#

```
int var1,var2,var3;
```

You can declare and initialize variables on the same line, as well, for a shortcut of sorts.

Visual Basic .NET

```
dim var1 as integer = 1
```

C#

```
int var1 = 1;
```

Now here's a place where C# has some advantage over Visual Basic .NET. C# allows you to declare and initialize multiple variables of the same type on the same line.

C#

```
int var1 = 1, var2 = 2, var3 = 3;
```

You cannot use this type of technique in Visual Basic .NET.

Manipulating Data

Now that you can make all kinds of variables with different data types, it will be helpful for you to understand how to manipulate your data as well.

What happens when you need to add two number type variables together? Or what if you need to find out whether a specific word appears in a string? The following sections look at a bunch of these types of functions.

Number Manipulation

Manipulating numbers is nothing more than doing math. It's either addition, subtraction, multiplication, or division. Let's look at the operations and their operators.

Let's declare some variables and perform some mathematical operations and see what we get. We'll use some of our cool short cuts for declaring and initializing variables.

Visual Basic .NET—**basic_math_vb.aspx**

```
'Cool variable declaration
Dim var1,var2,var3,var4,vartotal As Integer
var1 = 3
var2 = 4
var3 = 5
var4 = 6
varTotal = 0

'Addition
varTotal = var1 + var2
OurLabel.Text+= "Addition: " & varTotal & "<br>"

'Subtraction
varTotal = var3 - var2
OurLabel.Text+= "Subtraction: " & varTotal & "<br>"

'Multiplication
varTotal = var1 * var2
OurLabel.Text+= "Multiplication: " & varTotal & "<br>"

'Division
varTotal = var4 / var1
OurLabel.Text+= "Division: " & varTotal & "<br>"
```

C#—**basic_math_cs.aspx**

```
/* Very cool C# declaration and initialization
code that lets us perform this on one line */
int var1=3,var2=4,var3=5,var4=6,varTotal=0;
//Addition
varTotal = var1 + var2;
OurLabel.Text += "Addition: " + varTotal + "<br>";

//Subtraction
varTotal = var3 - var2;
OurLabel.Text += "Subtraction: " + varTotal + "<br>";

//Multiplication
varTotal = var1 * var2;
OurLabel.Text += "Multiplication: " + varTotal + "<br>";

//Division
varTotal = var4 / var1;
OurLabel.Text += "Division: " + varTotal + "<br>";
```

The results are delivered as expected in Figure 3.1.

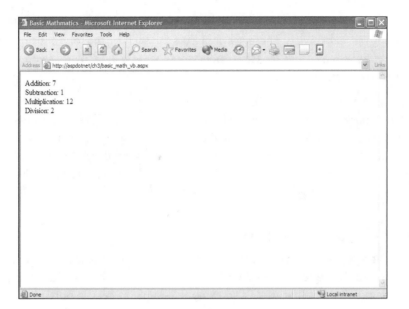

FIGURE 3.1

Computers excel at doing math and have no problem handling very complex mathematical operations.

T I P

I have added comments to these two previous code blocks to demonstrate how you can add comments to both Visual Basic .NET and C#. The single quote (') is the character in Visual Basic .NET that signifies a line is a comment, and anything on that single line is ignored. The comment indicator for a single line in C# is two forward slashes(//). C# also has a way for you to insert a multi-line comment, which is displayed above the variable declaration in the C# example. Anything between a forward slash–star combination for the opening of the comment and a star-forward slash combination (/* put your comment in here */) for the close of the comment will be ignored. Note that comments can be on a line with executed code. Anything after the comment delimiter will be ignored.

As you can see, math operates just as you would expect it to. Addition, subtraction, multiplication, and division are basic functions of the numeric operators. Both Visual Basic .NET and C# offer some shortcuts for some common situations in math operation. For instance, you might want the value of a variable to be set to the value of adding another variable to itself. This typically would look as follows in both languages (with the exception of a semicolon at the end of the line in C#):

```
var1 = var1 + var2
```

We now have a shortcut option that produces the same results:

```
var1 += var2
```

The += operator sets var1 to the sum of var1 + var2, but saves the trouble of writing out var1 twice. There are shortcuts for each of the four basic math functions, as well as other timesaver operators that you'll discover as you progress through the book.

"Thanks for the math lesson, Peter, but I learned all that in 3rd grade." Sorry, but I think it's important to cover some of the most basic concepts on which we will build more complex functions later in the book. Otherwise, I fear that there will be weak spots in your understanding that will make everything else more difficult to pick up. Understanding these basic functions and how they are properly executed will prove to be an invaluable asset as we dig into the deeper stuff later.

String Manipulation

Manipulating strings of characters is a bit more challenging than some of the math concepts. You'll see some basic functions in the following sections—such as joining two strings together—but you'll also explore lopping off certain portions of a string, or checking to see whether a certain word appears in a string.

There are a ton of different functions available to mess around with strings, and you'll see that they come in very handy in many situations.

Concatenation

Concatenation? No, it isn't a country full of criminal felines! It's another one of those REALLY BIG programmer words. The definition of concatenate is "to link things together." So concatenating is simply sticking strings together. Take a look:

Visual Basic .NET—**string_concate_vb.aspx**

```
dim var1,var2,var3 as string
var1 = "ASP.NET is "
var2 = "very cool!"
var3 = var1 + var2 '<<< Yippee!! Concatenation
OurLabel.Text = var3
```

C#—**string_concate_cs.aspx**

```
string var1,var2,var3;
var1 = "ASP.NET is ";
var2 = "very cool!";
var3 = var1 + var2; // <<< WAHOO!! Concatenation
OurLabel.Text = var3;
```

And you get a concatenated string as shown in Figure 3.2.

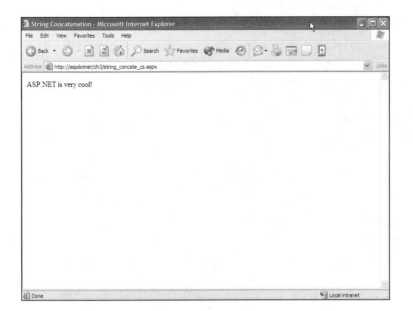

FIGURE 3.2

Concatenating strings is the process of linking strings together.

> **N O T E**
>
> *As you saw when we manipulated numbers, the same operators are used in both languages to perform a mathematical function. There is a difference in the operator when it comes to string concatenation. In Visual Basic .NET, the ampersand (&) or the plus (+) sign can be used as the operator to concatenate strings, but only the plus (+) sign is used to perform this function in C#. The ampersand is basically a holdover from VBScript, but for the sake of consistency I recommend you use the plus sign. Using the ampersand allows you to concatenate a string and a number without creating an error, but this is the beginning of a slippery slope of bad coding habits that is easy to fall into. It's better to use the plus sign and use the number's* ToString() *method if you need to concatenate a string and a number.*

As you continue to investigate all the fabulous things you can do with strings, I would again encourage you to go to the .NET Framework class browser I mentioned in Chapter 2 and look at all the built-in properties and methods for the System.String class, which is what we are dealing with here. We are going to go over a bunch of them, but there are like a wheelbarrow full—Too many to cover thoroughly here.

Just a note if you come from a traditional ASP programming background: This is gonna be a bit of a change for you from what you are accustomed to when manipulating strings with ASP functions. Most of the function is still there, with a few exceptions and consolidations, but they aren't functions anymore—they are methods.

Length

Let's start by looking at the Length property. It's the only property we are going to cover here. The rest are System.String methods. The Length property returns (without any surprise) the length or number of characters in the string.

Visual Basic .NET—string_length_vb.aspx

```
dim var1 as string
var1 = "ASP.NET is very cool!"
OurLabel.Text = var1.length + " characters long"
```

C#—string_length_cs.aspx

```
string var1;
var1 = "ASP.NET is very cool!";
OurLabel.Text = var1.Length + " characters long";
```

And you can see the results in Figure 3.3.

FIGURE 3.3

If you need to find out how many characters (including spaces) are in a string, you ask for the length property.

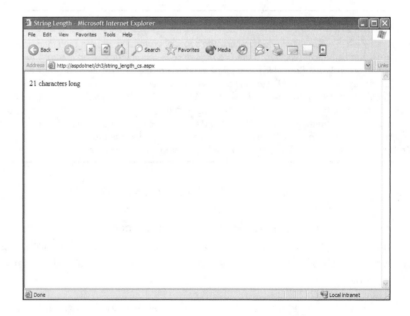

W A R N I N G
Remember when calling properties and methods in C# that you must match the case of the Frameworks' property. For instance in the System.String *class the* Length *property has a capital* L. *If you use a lowercase* l, *you will throw an error that says that a string doesn't have a length property. In C#'s eyes it doesn't have* length *property, it has* Length *property.*

Substring( )

A very useful System.String method is called Substring(). You may be familiar with a similar method in JavaScript with the same name. When we were still programming in ASP using VBScript as our script language, there were three different functions that this single Substring() function replaces: Left, Right and Mid. These functions no longer exist, and just about anything that you could perform with them can be achieved with this single method of the System.String class.

To demonstrate the Substring() method, I'll use the opening line from the book, "It was a dark and stormy night in Chicago." We are going to use Substring() to hack, pick, and prod this string apart.

Visual Basic .NET—**string_substring_vb.aspx**

```
dim OurString,MySubStr as String
OurString = "It was a dark and stormy night in Chicago"

'Show first 11 characters
MySubStr = OurString.Substring(0,11)
OurLabel.Text += "First 11 Characters: " + MySubStr + "<br>"

'Show last 4 characters
MySubStr = OurString.Substring(37)
OurLabel.Text += "Last 4 Characters: " + MySubStr + "<br>"

'Show 3 character from the middle
MySubStr = OurString.Substring(10,3)
OurLabel.Text += "3 Middle Characters: " + MySubStr
```

C#——`string_substring_cs.aspx`

```
String OurString,MySubStr;
OurString = "It was a dark and stormy night in Chicago";

//Show first 11 characters;
MySubStr = OurString.Substring(0,11);
OurLabel.Text += "First 11 Characters: " + MySubStr + "<br>";

//Show last 4 characters;
MySubStr = OurString.Substring(37);
OurLabel.Text += "Last 4 Characters: " + MySubStr + "<br>";

//Show 3 character from the middle;
MySubStr = OurString.Substring(10,3);
OurLabel.Text += "3 Middle Characters: " + MySubStr;
```

Now look at the results in Figure 3.4.

FIGURE 3.4

You can cut out portions of a string by using the `Substring()` *method.*

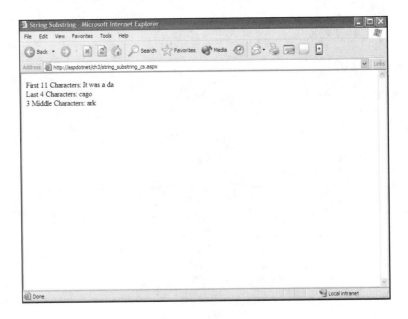

Now let's investigate. Let's start with the first call to the method, where we extract the first 11 characters of the string.

```
OurString.Substring(0,11)
```

The first parameter of 0 tells the Substring() method where to start the chopping. The second parameter of 11 tells the method how many character to chop. So, basically, we can say that the Substring() method was told: "Start chopping at character 0 and give me 11 characters from there.

The third example that pulls the characters out of the middle of the string is not really different. It simply starts at character 10 and proceeds to return 3 characters.

```
OurString.Substring(10,3)
```

Now you can look at a real-world version of an overloaded method in the second example of the Substring() method:

```
OurString.Substring(37)
```

You can see that only one parameter of 37 is being passed into the Substring() method . This Substring() method knows that if you provide only one parameter, you want everything from the starting provided parameter to the end of the string. Basically, the previous example told the Substring(): "Give me everything from character 37 to the end of the string."

N O T E

Just an aside here. If you remember back in Chapter 2, overloaded methods enable you to send multiple "variable signatures" to a method, and then the .NET Framework figures out which version of the method you are referencing. The Substring() *method is a perfect example of an overloaded method, and the previous examples illustrate passing different "variable signatures" to the overloaded method.*

Now I am even going to touch on some other methods briefly to show how you can use multiple methods and properties to achieve the results you want.

Let's imagine we are trying to locate and extract a certain word from a string. For instance, maybe you're trying to see whether the word "stormy" appears in the string. You don't know where it is exactly, but you need to find and extract it. Here's a tricky way to pull it out using some combinations of methods and properties.

Visual Basic .NET—**string_substring_findword_vb.aspx**

```
dim OurString,OurWord,OurFoundWord as String
OurString = "It was a dark and stormy night in Chicago"
OurWord = "stormy"

OurFoundWord = OurString.Substring(OurString.IndexOf(OurWord),OurWord.Length)
OurLabel.Text = OurFoundWord
```

C#—**string_substring_findword_cs.aspx**

```
String OurString,OurWord,OurFoundWord;
OurString = "It was a dark and stormy night in Chicago";
OurWord = "stormy";

OurFoundWord = OurString.Substring(OurString.IndexOf(OurWord),OurWord.Length);
OurLabel.Text = OurFoundWord;
```

This block of code writes the word "stormy" to the page. Let's see how. If you investigate the Substring() method call, you can see that two parameters are being passed.

```
1: OurString.IndexOf(OurWord)
2: OurWord.Length
```

The first parameter uses another method of the System.String class called IndexOf(). You pass this method a parameter of OurWord that contains the word "stormy." Basically, the IndexOf() method returns a number value of the start position of the first occurrence of the parameter passed to it. In this case it passed the value of 18, which is the first character of the word "stormy" in OurString.

The second parameter is next. It contains the length of OurWord, "stormy", which is 6, using the Length parameter of the String object. Basically we are passing

```
OurString.Substring(18,6)
```

You can begin to see how you might use this to pass parameters that depend on a user's input or a dynamically determined variable to manipulate strings using the Substring() method.

ToUpper( ), ToLower( )

There may be times when you are messing around with strings and you need to adjust the case of a string's characters. System.String has provided two ways: the ToUpper() and ToLower() methods. The names are pretty self-explanatory, so look at some examples of this action:

Visual Basic .NET—**string_casechange_vb.aspx**

```
dim OurString as String
OurString = "It WAs a DaRk aND sToRMy Night in ChicAgo"

OurLabel.Text += "Original String:" + OurString + "<br><br>"
OurLabel.Text += "ToUpper Example:" + OurString.ToUpper + "<br><br>"
OurLabel.Text += "ToUpper Example:" + OurString.ToLower
```

C#—string_casechange_cs.aspx

```
String OurString;
OurString = "It WAs a DaRk aND sToRMy Night in ChicAgo";

OurLabel.Text += "Original String:" + OurString + "<br><br>";
OurLabel.Text += "ToUpper Example:" + OurString.ToUpper() + "<br><br>";
OurLabel.Text += "ToUpper Example:" + OurString.ToLower();
```

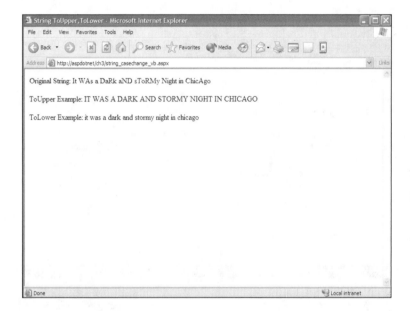

FIGURE 3.5

Use the ToUpper() *and* ToLower() *methods to manipulate a string to uppercase or lowercase.*

As you can see by the results in Figure 3.5, the ToUpper() method capitalizes all the characters of the string and the ToLower() method makes all the characters lowercase.

I purposely left out the parentheses of the ToUpper() and ToLower() method calls of the Visual Basic .NET example to illustrate another situation where Visual Basic .NET will allow you to "get away" with something. Again, I recommend you avoid these types of habits because they will create issues for you if you need to move across languages and program in C#.

Replace( )

Replace() is a handy-dandy method for string manipulation if you need to locate occurrences of a particular word or phrase and replace it with something else.

Visual Basic .NET—`string_replace_vb.aspx`

```
dim OurString as String
OurString = "It was a dark and stormy night in Chicago"

OurLabel.Text += "Original String: " + OurString + "<br><br>"
OurLabel.Text += "Replaced String: " + OurString.Replace("dark and stormy
➥night","bright and shiny day")
```

C#—`string_replace_cs.aspx`

```
String OurString;
OurString = OurString = "It was a dark and stormy night in Chicago";

OurLabel.Text += "Original String: " + OurString + "<br><br>";
OurLabel.Text += "Replaced String: " + OurString.Replace("dark and stormy
➥night","bright and shiny day");
```

You can see the results in Figure 3.6.

FIGURE 3.6

The Replace() *method provides a way to find and replace occurrences of a string inside another string.*

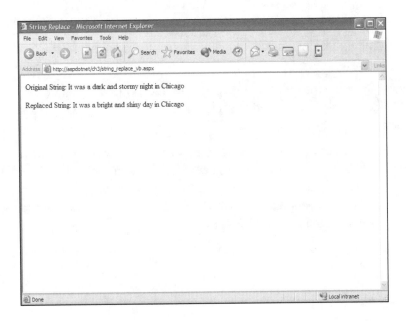

You will find many uses for the `Replace()` method, as it provides you with ways to achieve desired results very easily. For instance, I had a client who didn't like that the results of a Boolean variable were displaying `True` and `False`. I simply used the `Replace()` method to change this to `Yes` and `No` as the client wanted.

The `Replace()` method is case sensitive. If you are attempting to replace a word such a "Dark" and it appears in lowercase in the string as "dark," the `Replace()` method will not see this as a match. This is not language-specific; it is a characteristic of the method and not any language.

Date Manipulation

Dates are pretty standard and are used quite often when building web applications. There are many times when you will need dates and times formatted in a certain way, or you may need to display only a certain portion of a date or time.

The .NET Framework provides many functions and properties to deal with dates and times. The following code block demonstrates a whole bunch of the available properties and methods, but remember this isn't an exhaustive list, just a sampler.

Visual Basic .NET—**datetime_vb.aspx**

```
dim MyDate as DateTime = DateTime.Now
OurLabel.Text = "MyDate: " + MyDate + "<BR><BR>"


OurLabel.Text += "<B><U>Date Properties:</U></B><BR>"
OurLabel.Text += "MyDate.Hour: " + MyDate.Hour.tostring + "<BR>"
OurLabel.Text += "MyDate.Day: " + MyDate.Day.tostring + "<BR>"
OurLabel.Text += "MyDate.DayOfWeek: " + MyDate.DayOfWeek.tostring + "<BR>"
OurLabel.Text += "MyDate.DayOfYear: " + MyDate.DayOfYear.tostring + "<BR>"
OurLabel.Text += "MyDate.Month: " + MyDate.Month.tostring + "<BR>"
OurLabel.Text += "MyDate.Year: " + MyDate.Year.tostring + "<BR><BR>"


OurLabel.Text += "<B><U>Date Methods:</U></B><BR>"
OurLabel.Text += "MyDate.ToShortTimeString: " + MyDate.ToShortTimeString + "<BR>"
OurLabel.Text += "MyDate.ToLongTimeString: " + MyDate.ToLongTimeString + "<BR>"
OurLabel.Text += "MyDate.ToShortDateString: " + MyDate.ToShortDateString + "<BR>"
OurLabel.Text += "MyDate.ToLongDateString: " + MyDate.ToLongDateString + "<BR>"
OurLabel.Text += "MyDate.AddDays(2): " + MyDate.AddDays(2) + "<BR>"
OurLabel.Text += "MyDate.AddMonth(4): " + MyDate.AddMonths(4) + "<BR>"
OurLabel.Text += "MyDate.AddYear(1): " + MyDate.AddYears(1) + "<BR>"
```

C#—**datetime_cs.aspx**

```
DateTime MyDate = DateTime.Now;
OurLabel.Text = "MyDate: " + MyDate + "<BR><BR>";

OurLabel.Text += "<B><U>Date Properties:</U></B><BR>";
OurLabel.Text += "MyDate.Hour: " + MyDate.Hour + "<BR>";
OurLabel.Text += "MyDate.Day: " + MyDate.Day + "<BR>";
OurLabel.Text += "MyDate.DayOfWeek: " + MyDate.DayOfWeek + "<BR>";
OurLabel.Text += "MyDate.DayOfYear: " + MyDate.DayOfYear + "<BR>";
OurLabel.Text += "MyDate.Month: " + MyDate.Month + "<BR>";
OurLabel.Text += "MyDate.Year: " + MyDate.Year + "<BR><BR>";
OurLabel.Text += "<B><U>Date Methods:</U></B><BR>";

OurLabel.Text += "MyDate.ToShortTimeString: " + MyDate.ToShortTimeString() +
➡"<BR>";
OurLabel.Text += "MyDate.ToLongTimeString: " + MyDate.ToLongTimeString() + "<BR>";
OurLabel.Text += "MyDate.ToShortDateString: " + MyDate.ToShortDateString() +
➡"<BR>";
OurLabel.Text += "MyDate.ToLongDateString: " + MyDate.ToLongDateString() + "<BR>";
OurLabel.Text += "MyDate.AddDays(2): " + MyDate.AddDays(2) + "<BR>";
OurLabel.Text += "MyDate.AddMonth(4): " + MyDate.AddMonths(4) + "<BR>";
OurLabel.Text += "MyDate.AddYear(1): " + MyDate.AddYears(1) + "<BR>";
```

As you can see in Figure 3.7, there is a lot of built-in functionality for formatting and manipulating dates and times. Figure 3.7 displays the original date we are working with, and then displays some of the available properties and methods. In this example, in the browser window you can see the time on top, then a label for MyDate.PropertyOrMethod to tell you what we are displaying, and then that property or method displayed as described. In the code examples a ToString() method is applied to all of these, so they can be concatenated into one string and displayed in the label. If you are going to use any of these properties and methods to manipulate your dates or times, and want to append them to a string, you must use the ToString() method as well.

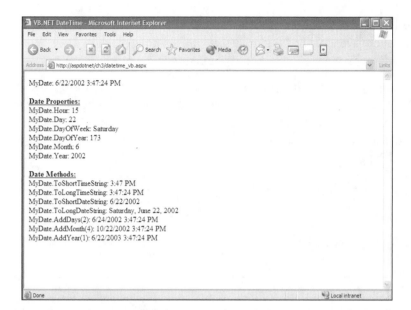

FIGURE 3.7

The DateTime *object provides many of the necessary properties and methods to extract and manipulate dates and times in just about any way you would need.*

Control Structure

Control structure—like all the other words and phrases that you've encountered so far that have made you think, "What the heck is that?"—is just as simple to understand when explained in plain English.

When creating dynamic web applications, there are two types of code you program: code that always executes and code that conditionally executes. Control structure deals with the latter. It deals with controlling the flow of code that executes based on conditions.

At its heart, control structure is checking to see whether something is true or false and running code based on the answer.

In real life, we do this type of thing all the time as we go about our day. We may have never have identified the processes or even considered that our brains use what in programming is called control structure, but we do.

Think back to the last time you had lunch at a restaurant. You were presented with a menu, and you read down it looking for an item that tickled your fancy. Something that would fulfill your desire for some good eatin'. Maybe the menu looked like this:

1. Garden Salad w/Soup

2. Grilled Chicken Sandwich

3. Bacon Double Cheeseburger

4. Turkey Sandwich Wrap

N o t e

I must make a disclaimer that although most of the examples in this book to this point have been about food, I am not preoccupied with food.

(Note from Publisher: Peter is lying about his love for food. We're betting he will pick the Bacon Double Cheeseburger. Let's watch!)

Now you are faced with a few choices here. As you proceed down the menu, you will find yourself asking some questions. To simplify this example, I'll use just one question: "Do I want it?" Pretty simple. Let's go through the menu.

1. Garden Salad

   • Do I want it? Nah!

2. Grilled Chicken Sandwich

   • Do I want it? Nah!

3. Bacon Double Cheeseburger

   • Do I want it? YES!

4. Turkey Sandwich Wrap

   • No need to look at this; I've made my decision

(Note from Publisher: We told you he'd pick the cheeseburger.)

With this process, I am basically going through the list of items in the menu and asking the same question for each item. The following isn't a working code example but a plain English model of a thought process that will give you an example of a looping and branching process.

```
1.Garden Salad
2.Grilled Chicken Salad
3.Bacon Double Cheeseburger
4.Turkey Sandwich Wrap

menuitem = "Garden Salad"
do this until I have said "yes!" to something on the menu
    if I want (menuitem)then
        Say "Yes!"
    Otherwise
        Say "Nah!"
    And move on
Go to the next menu item and do it again
```

This is a crude example of the process, but you can see both a loop statement as I go through the menu items and a branching statement as I decide whether I want the particular item I happen to be considering.

So the first time through the loop the question was "Do I want a garden salad?" Because I didn't, I said "Nah!" and moved on, went to the next menu item, and started over. I went through this process until I got to the cheeseburger, where my answer was "Yes!" When I went to the next item, there was no reason to proceed because I found something on the menu I liked.

As you can see, all day long we're branching and looping and looping and branching in our decision-making processes. Let's begin to take a look into each of these processes in more depth. You will see that dynamic programming as a whole and ASP.NET specifically depends heavily on different types of control structures.

Branching

To solidify what branching is, it's a test that helps us to control what blocks of code are executed based on the results of the text. There are two basic kinds of branching statements:

- **If > Then > Else**. This provides a way to select a block of code to execute based on whether a specific condition is met. This is generally used when there are two or maybe a few possible conditions that need to be evaluated, but it is generally not used when there are many possibilities.

- **Select/Switch**. This type of branch has a different name in each language, but they all perform the same action. In Visual Basic .NET, it is called a `Select Case` statement; and in C#, it is called a `switch`. This statement is used when there are many possible conditions that need to be checked.

If > Then > Else

When you are trying to assess the condition of something and execute a certain block of code based on that condition, the `if` statement in all its forms provides a powerful and versatile way to go about it. Look at the simple form of the `if` statement:

Visual Basic .NET

```
if Test then
    Code that gets executed if test returns true
end if
```

C#

```
if (test){
    Code that gets executed if test returns true
}
```

The way it works is pretty simple. If the test returns true, everything between the opening delimiter and closing delimiter executes. If it returns false, it ignores this code. Take a look at a working example now:

Visual Basic .NET—branch_if_simple_vb.aspx

```
dim i as Integer
i=10

if i = 10 then
    OurLabel.Text = "It matched"
end if
```

C#—branch_if_simple_cs.aspx

```
int i;
i = 10;
if (i == 10){
    OurLabel.Text = "It matched";
}
```

This block of code would return true, and "It matched" would be written to the page. Now let's go a step farther and give the statement an option if the test fails to match.

Visual Basic .NET—**branch_if_else_vb.aspx**

```
dim i as Integer
i=10

if i = 11 then
    OurLabel.Text = "It matched"
else
    OurLabel.Text = "It didn't match"
end if
```

C#—**branch_if_else_cs.aspx**

```
int i;
i = 11;

if (i == 10){
    OurLabel.Text = "It matched";
}else{
    OurLabel.Text = "It didn't match";
}
```

Because the value of the i variable is now 11, the test returns a value of false and the if > else statement now hits the else portion. This is where the word *branching* comes from. These different sections of code are known as code branches and, depending on the condition of the test results, determine which branch is run, just like the menu item that returned a positive response from my stomach/brain to determine what I would have for lunch.

If statements can be more complex as well. They can contain multiple branches using the elseif statement in Visual Basic .NET and else if statement in C#.

W A R N I N G

Be mindful that in Visual Basic .NET elseif is a single word and in C# it is two separate words—else if. I have more than a few times had ASP.NET yell at me about mixing and matching these two across languages.

Visual Basic .NET—**branch_if_elseif_vb.aspx**

```
dim i as integer
i=12

if i = 11 then
    OurLabel.Text = "It matched the 11 branch"
elseif i = 12 then
    OurLabel.Text = "It matched the 12 branch"
else
    OurLabel.Text = "It didn't match"
end if
```

C#—**branch_if_elseif_cs.aspx**

```
int i;
i = 12;

if (i == 11){
    OurLabel.Text = "It matched the 11 branch";
}else if(i == 12){
    OurLabel.Text = "It matched the 12 branch";
}else{
    OurLabel.Text = "It didn't match";
}
```

This branching structure would execute the middle elseif/else if branch because i = 12.

If statements can contain any code inside a branch that is operable in the programming language you are using. You can conditionally run code, write, or a host of other things with the branches of if statements. You can even have nested if statements in your if statements. Believe it or not, you can have nested if statements in your nested if statements that are in your if statements. I know it may be hard to believe but you can have nested if statements…and on and on. You get the point. I'll demonstrate a bunch of nested statements at the end of this section.

Now for clarity, if statements don't just check for equality, and they can also contain multiple questions in each test. Let's look at our operators for a minute so we can look out over the wild blue yonder and see that the world is our oyster when it comes to if statements and control structure as a whole.

Operators

Let's simplify this right from the start. Operators are something you started to learn about in the second grade.

Remember when…*Enter dream sequence*:

> **Miss Applebee**: "Susie, I've got two blocks and you have three. Do you have more blocks than me?"
>
> **Peter**: "Ooo, Ooo, Ooo!!! Miss Applebee, I know, I know!" says Peter with much excitement.
>
> **Miss Applebee**: "Hush child!!! You're speaking out of turn for the third time today."
>
> (Peter slumps in his seat. Feeling dejected, he swears he'll never open his mouth again to utter even a single peep. He will forever deprive the world of his great wisdom.)
>
> **Susie**: "I have more blocks than you, Miss Applebee, because 3 is greater than 2."
>
> **Miss Applebee**: "Good! That's correct."
>
> **Peter** (muttering): "I knew that!!"
>
> **Miss Applebee**: "Now. If I have 7 blocks and you have 4, do you have more blocks than me?"
>
> **Peter**: "Ooo, Ooo, Ooo!!! Miss Applebee, I know, I know!"
>
> **Miss Applebee**: "Okay Peter, what do you think?"
>
> **Peter**: "4 is less than 7, so…"

Exit dream sequence.

As you can see, operators are nothing more than simple comparison tools you can use in your code. You'll see that branching and control structure is full of comparison operators. Table 3.7 lists the most common and basic operators.

TABLE 3.7 Operators

Visual Basic .NET	C#	Explanation
=	==	Boolean Equality (True or False)
=	=	Equality
< >	! =	Inequality
<	<	var1 less than var2
>	>	var1 greater than var2
<=	<=	var1 less than or equal to var2
>=	>=	var1 greater than or equal to var2
OR	OR	Provides for multiple comparisons such as (var1 = var2 OR var3 = var4); this returns true if either statement is true
AND	AND	Provides for multiple comparisons such as (var1 = var2 AND var3 = var4); this returns true only if both statements are true

These operators provide a full palette of colors you can use to paint your code and get what you want out of your web applications. We will be exploring the use of these throughout the rest of this chapter (and the rest of the book, for that matter).

Select/switch

Select and switch statements are the same animal, with the Select Case statement being used in Visual Basic .NET and switch being used in C#.

This branching statement is used in a similar way to the if statements, except it requires a whole lot less code. You will see the power of Select/switch statements immediately in their capability to test multiple values.

Let's try comparing a variable to days of the week using the if/elseif statements first so you have something to compare your select statement against.

Visual Basic .NET

```
dim WeekDay,OurString as String
WeekDay = "Tuesday"
OurString = "This day of the week is "

If Weekday = "Monday" then
OurString += "the first day of the work week"

elseif Weekday = "Tuesday" then
OurString += "the second day of the work week"

elseif Weekday = "Wednesday" then
OurString += "the third day of the work week"

elseif Weekday = "Thursday" then
OurString += "the fourth day of the work week"

elseif Weekday = "Friday" then
OurString += "the last day of the work week"

else
OurString += "on the weekend"

End If

OurLabel.Text = Ourstring
```

C#

```
String WeekDay,OurString;
WeekDay = "Tuesday";
OurString = "This day of the week is ";

if (Weekday == "Monday"){
    OurString += "the first day of the work week";
}else if(WeekDay == "Tuesday"){
    OurString += "the second day of the work week";
}else if(WeekDay == "Wednesday"){
    OurString += "the third day of the work week";
}else if(WeekDay == "Thursday"){
    OurString += "the fourth day of the work week";
}else if(WeekDay == "Friday"){
    OurString += "the last day of the work week";
}else{
    OurString += "on the weekend";
}

OurLabel.Text = OurString;
```

Pretty wordy for a simple statement to check what day of the week a `Weekday` variable matches. Now look at an example of how the `Select` or `switch` statement code for this similar function looks.

Visual Basic .NET—`select_days_vb.aspx`

```
dim WeekDay,OurString as String
WeekDay = "Tuesday"
OurString = "This day of the week is"

Select Case Weekday

    Case "Monday"
    OurString += "the first day of the work week"

    Case "Tuesday"
    OurString += "the second day of the work week"

    Case "Wednesday"
    OurString += "the third day of the work week"

    Case "Thursday"
    OurString += "the fourth day of the work week"

    Case "Friday"
    OurString += "the last day of the work week"

    Case Else
    OurString += "on the weekend"

End Select

OurLabel.Text = Ourstring
```

C#—`switch_days_cs.aspx`

```
String WeekDay,OurString;
WeekDay = "Tuesday";
OurString = "This day of the week is ";

switch(WeekDay){
    case "Monday":
    OurString += "the first day of the work week";
    break;

    case "Tuesday":
    OurString += "the second day of the work week";
    break;

    case "Wednesday":
```

```
    OurString += "the third day of the work week";
    break;

    case "Thursday":
    OurString += "the fourth day of the work week";
    break;

    case "Friday":
    OurString += "the last day of the work week";
    break;

    default:
    OurString += "on the weekend";
    break;
}

OurLabel.Text = OurString;
```

Look at Figure 3.8 to see the results.

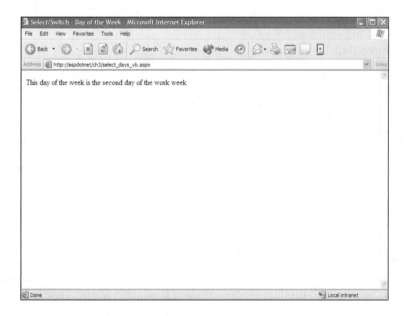

FIGURE 3.8

The Select *statement in Visual Basic .NET and the* switch *statement in C# are a clean way of making multiple comparisons.*

When you look at this code, you can see that it is a lot cleaner than the redundant `elseif` and `else if` statements. And as my old pappy use to say, "Cleaner is better." My mom used to say this about my room when I was young. I didn't think it really applied, but it definitely applies to code.

This branching statement is an area where there is a degree of separation between Visual Basic .NET and C#, and the pickiness of C# become a bit more evident (to me, at least).

The Visual Basic .NET `Select` statement flows from top to bottom, checking to see whether each case in the statement is true or not and executing each branch that returns true. Pretty simple.

C# is a bit less forgiving. C# does not "fall through" to the next `switch` section by default. You must explicitly tell C# what behavior you want the `switch` to do if that particular branch returns true. You will find that you generally will use the `break` statement, which causes the `switch` to jump to the next block of code after the full `case` statement. For instance:

C#

```
String WeekDay,OurString;
WeekDay = "Monday";
OurString = "This day of the week is ";

switch(WeekDay){

    //This branch would return true
    case "Monday":
    OurString += "the first day of the work week";
    //This break would execute the end of the switch
    break;

    case "Tuesday":
    OurString += "the second day of the work week";
    break;

}
//The break would move us to this point to follow executing code after the switch
```

The break provides a way to exit the `switch` and proceed processing code. There are two other ways to end a `switch` section or each case of a `switch` statement. They are the `goto` statement and the `return` statement. I would recommend that you consult the .NET Framework SDK (Software Development Kit) Documentation to learn more about the `goto` and `return` statements. These topics are a bit too broad to cover here and apply to things other than the `switch` statement.

> **N O T E**
>
> *The .NET Framework SDK Documentation is the full master cookbook for the .NET Framework. It will be available on your machine if you've done a full installation of the .NET Framework. This doesn't come with the redistributable version of the .NET Framework. The .NET Framework SDK Documentation is a very powerful and extremely thorough help center for the entire .NET Framework. I would suggest you go there first when you are stumbling or struggling with any issue surrounding .NET. It usually can be found on the Start Menu in Programs > Microsoft .NET Framework SDK > Documentation on the machine on which the .NET Framework is installed. It has a full Contents, Index, and Search of the SDK documentation and is quite an impressive collection of information, examples, code samples, language references and tutorials.*
>
> *There will be times throughout the book that I will also provide direct links to documents in the SDK. Just pop them in a browser address bar on the machine that has the SDK installed and it will take you directly to the page I have referenced.*

Both Visual Basic .NET and C# provide ways for you to check for multiple conditions in a single `Select Case` branch or `switch` section. Again be careful to notice the differences in the way that these are performed in the different languages.

Visual Basic .NET—`select_days_multivarialbes_vb.aspx`

```
dim WeekDay,OurString as String
WeekDay = "Tuesday"
OurString = "This day of the week is "

Select Case Weekday

    Case "Monday","Tuesday","Wednesday","Thursday","Friday"
    OurString += "during the work week"

    Case "Saturday","Sunday"
    OurString += "on the weekend"

End Select

OurLabel.Text = OurString
```

C#—switch_days_multivarialbes_cs.aspx

```
String WeekDay,OurString;
WeekDay = "Tuesday";
OurString = "This day of the week is ";

switch(WeekDay){
    case "Monday":
    case "Tuesday":
    case "Wednesday":
    case "Thursday":
    case "Friday":
    OurString += "during the work week";
    break;

    case "Saturday":
    case "Sunday":
    OurString += "on the weekend";
    break;
}

OurLabel.Text = OurString;
```

You can see the results in Figure 3.9:

FIGURE 3.9

Checking across multiple conditions is a useful way to create clean code from what would be a complicated If statement.

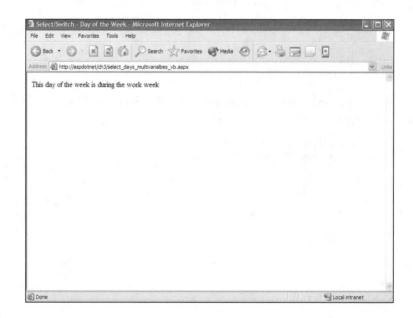

Can you see how this has expanded the function of the `Select Case` statement? The first case is the equivalent of either 10 separate `case` statements (`case 1`, `case 2`, and so on) or `case 1,2,3,4,5,6,7,8,9,10`. You can see again how this creates possibilities to clean up your statements to another level. These can also can have multiple expressions per `case` statement as well.

These keywords can also be used in `string` expressions as well. Again I would refer you to the SDK where you can find out more information about this. Place the following link in a web browser's address line:

```
ms-help://MS.NETFrameworkSDK/vblr7net/html/vastmSelectCase.htm
```

We must deal with one more quick issue regarding `Select` and `switch` statements. They are case sensitive and this could create some problems when comparing strings. If your case branch contains the word "Flower," but you try to compare "flower," your branch doesn't execute. You might think a solution would be to put a branch for "Flower" and "flower," but what if this value comes from a text box on a web page and the person has Caps Lock on? Then you'd also need to test for "fLOWER" and "FLOWER". The combinations are virtually endless.

"Bah, Humbug!" you may be thinking. `Select` and `switch` statements are going to be a pain. Not so fast, (Insert your Name)!!! Have you forgotten already? The `String` class has the `ToLower()` method, and it will work perfectly here. Watch!

Visual Basic .NET—`select_tolower_vb.aspx`

```
dim messString,OurString as String
messString ="FloWeR"
OurString = ""

Select Case messString.ToLower()

    Case "flower"
    OurString += "It matched the lower case flower"

    Case "FloWeR"
    OurString += "It matched our wacky case FloWeR"

End Select

OurLabel.Text = OurString
```

C#—`switch_tolower_cs.aspx`

```
String messString,OurString;
messString = "FloWeR";
OurString = "";

switch(messString.ToLower()){
    case "flower":
    OurString += "It matched the lower case flower";
    break;

    case "FloWeR":
    OurString += "It matched our wacky case FloWeR";
    break;
}

OurLabel.Text = OurString;
```

We can see in Figure 3.11 how using the `ToLower()` method allows us to force uniform comparisons.

FIGURE 3.11

Using the `ToLower()` *method to force strings to lowercase makes matching expressions in* `Select` *and* `switch` *statements a breeze.*

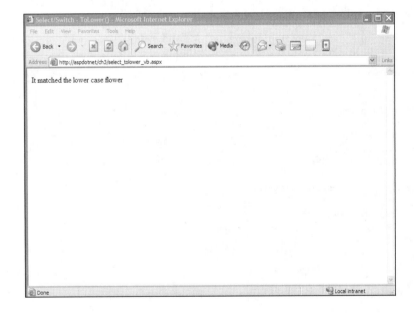

We've covered a lot of basic information with regard to branching, and I'm sure you can see how this is going to be a key for you in creating applications that perform the way you want.

Think back to the example where I said that ASP.NET is like a car, but that you need fuel to drive and steer the car, and scripting is that fuel and steering device. You might be beginning to see how you use scripting to fuel and steer your applications where we want them to go.

Looping

Just like branching statements, looping statements have parallels to our everyday lives. We loop whenever we need to do repetitive tasks a certain number of times.

Take sending holiday cards. Picture the stack of 100 envelopes, containing holiday greetings for your friends and family. To make sure that each of your friends and family members gets a card (and doesn't have an excuse to be mad at you), you must look up the address in your handy-dandy phone book, write that on the envelope, place a stamp on the envelope, lick and seal the envelope, and then place it on the "done" pile. Now go back to the stack and do it all over again and again and again till your stack is gone and your "done" pile is 100 envelopes tall.

You just looped through your holiday cards. Looping in programming is no different. Repetitive processes are performed over and over until all the items have been processed according to the loop's conditions.

The loops that are available in Visual Basic .NET and C# can be grouped into two different types. The first group is the `for` loop. `for` loops run through a certain number of times.

The second group is made up of two different types of loops that have different names in the two languages. The first type is called `Do Until` in Visual Basic .NET and `do` in C#. The second is called `Do While` in Visual Basic .NET and `while` in C#. Both types of loops continue until a condition is met, just like when the pile of holiday cards is finished. The only difference between the two types is when the test for the condition is performed.

- **`Do Until`/`do`**. The code inside the loop is executed, and then the test is performed. If the condition returns false, the loop is executed again.

- **`Do While`/`while`**. The condition is checked before the code is ever executed. If it returns true, the loop is executed, and then returned to be tested again.

These concepts may be a bit difficult to wrap your brain around right now while they're just being explained in words, but after you see them in action they will make perfect sense.

for Loops

Like I said earlier, for loops run a certain number of times. This number can be determined in just about any way that you can create a numbered expression. For instance:

Visual Basic .NET—**loop_for_simple_vb.aspx**

```
dim i as Integer

for i=1 to 5
    OurLabel.Text += "This is line number " + i.ToString() + " in our loop.<br>"
next
```

C#—**loop_for_simple_cs.aspx**

```
int i;

for(i = 1;i <= 5;++i){
    OurLabel.Text += "This is line number " + i.ToString() + " in our loop.<br>";
}
```

You can see the results in Figure 3.12.

FIGURE 3.12

for loops help you go through repetitive blocks of code in a controlled fashion.

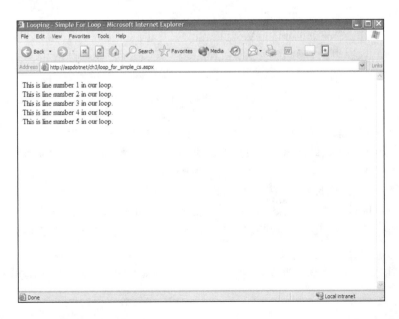

What you'll notice right away about the two different languages' interpretation of the condition statement is that Visual Basic .NET seems to make one sweeping statement, i=1 to 5, and C#'s statement is broken into three sections separated by semicolons (i=1;i >= 5; ++i).

Actually, all three elements present in C# are also present in Visual Basic .NET; they are just not as apparent. It's easier if you understand the C# example first and work back to Visual Basic .NET after that.

The first statement, i = 1, is the initialization of the i variable. This is a nice thing about for loops—they save an extra line of code for initialization. Not a big deal, but it's nice. The second statement, i <= 5, is pretty familiar in its use of the "less than or equal to" operator. This second segment controls the condition of the for loop. Last is a strange-looking fellow, ++i, which is simply a shortcut that adds 1 to the value of i. Its longhand equivalent would be i=i+1. It is called an *increment operator*. Of course it has a counterpart that is called…Anyone? Right!! A *decrement operator*. BIG WORDS, look out!!

Although you've gone over a bunch of operators in this chapter, you can dig a whole lot deeper in the SDK. The following are URLs for the operator section for both Visual Basic .NET and C#.

- Visual Basic .NET:

  ```
  ms-help://MS.NETFrameworkSDK/vblr7net/html/vagrpOperatorSummary.htm
  ```

- C#:

  ```
  ms-help://MS.NETFrameworkSDK/csref/html/vclrfcsharpoperators.htm
  ```

The Visual Basic .NET version of the for loop also has all these as well. Two are bunched together and one is assumed by default. The declaration of the variable is highlighted in bold in the following line of code.

```
for i=1 to 5
```

The condition statement is in there, too, and is basically made up of the whole statement highlighted in bold as follows:

```
for i = 1 to 5
```

After the variable is set, we are looping from the variable's value, or 1 in this case, to 5. Notice the use of the word to in the statement. Remember to from the Select statements earlier in this chapter? The keyword to in Visual Basic .NET can be likened to the word "span." From *here* 'To' *there*. Or, in other words, carry on this function across this span of numbers. The question then becomes, how do you get across these numbers, or move from 1 to 5? C# had the blessed Increment operator to do this for you. How does Visual Basic .NET magically do this?

Well, Visual Basic .NET doesn't do magic. This loop has a default counter built into it that automatically increments the value of the counter by 1 each time through the loop. Great for knuckleheads like me that have more than once forgotten to increment loops and have sent a page into an infinite loop until the web server came crashing down. Whoops!

But are you stuck with single digit increments? Hardly! You can do whatever you want in your loops with regard to incrementing numbers. The mysteriously hidden default incrementor is a keyword called Step. Let's look at a for loop with different incrementing values to see how this is done.

Visual Basic .NET—**loop_for_increment_vb.aspx**

```
dim i as Integer

for i=1 to 10 Step 2
OurLabel.Text += "Odd Numbers: " + i.ToString() + "<br>"
next


OurLabel.Text += "<br><br>"

for i=2 to 10 Step 2
OurLabel.Text += "Even Numbers: " + i.ToString() + "<br>"
next


OurLabel.Text += "<br><br>"

for i=3 to 10 Step 3
OurLabel.Text += "Multiples of 3: " + i.ToString() + "<br>"
next
```

C#—loop_for_increment_cs.aspx

```
int i;

for(i = 1;i <= 10;i += 2){
    OurLabel.Text += "Odd Numbers: " + i.ToString() + "<br>";
}

OurLabel.Text += "<br><br>";

for(i = 2;i <= 10;i += 2){
    OurLabel.Text += "Even Numbers: " + i.ToString() + "<br>";
}

OurLabel.Text += "<br><br>";

for(i = 3;i <= 10;i += 3){
    OurLabel.Text += "Multiples of 3: " + i.ToString() + "<br>";
}
```

You can see the results of this code in a browser in Figure 3.13.

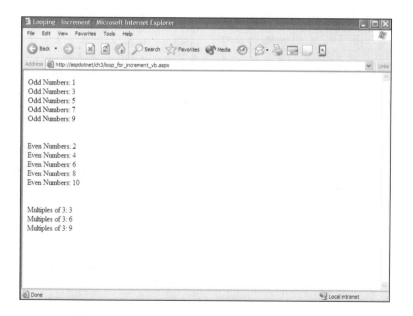

FIGURE 3.13

for *loops can increment in just about any way you can imagine.*

As you can see, the first two examples are incremented by 2 each time through the loop until the condition of <= 10 is met. The third example increments by 3 until the condition of <= 10 is met.

You use the Step keyword to add value to your variable each time through the loop in Visual Basic .NET, and in C# you simply use the shortcut operator that adds the value following the += sign to the current value of i.

The Step keyword or the operation of the for loop isn't limited to addition. You can count down, as well, by setting the step value to a negative number in Visual Basic .NET or by using the -- operator in C#.

Visual Basic .NET—loop_for_decrement_vb.aspx

```
dim i as Integer

for i=5 to 1     Step -1
    OurLabel.Text += "Countdown: " + i.ToString() + "<br>"
next
```

C#—loop_for_decrement_cs.aspx

```
int i;

for(i = 5;i >= 1;--i){
    OurLabel.Text += "Countdown: " + i.ToString() + "<br>";
}
```

As you can see in Figure 3.14, you aren't limited to just addition; you can do subtraction as well. Now let's move on to a smart for loop that knows how many times to loop without ever being told.

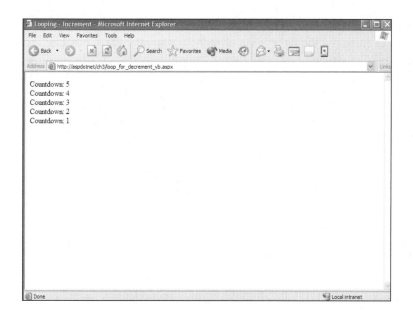

FIGURE 3.14

*And now for something completely different...
Backward looping!*

for each/foreach **Loops**

for each type loops are just like for loops in the previous section in that they go through the loop a specific number of times, but you don't predetermine that number and enter it yourself. It is determined by the number of elements in an array of information.

You'll learn more about arrays later in the book, but for the sake of these examples I'll just say that an array is a variable that can hold multiple values that are identified by an index number. Huh? Not bad for a brief explanation.

So the for each loop is pretty easy to understand if you just think of it in plain English. Execute the loop for each element in the multi-value variable (array). Take a look:

Visual Basic .NET—loop_for_each_vb.aspx

```
dim Beatles(3) as String
dim eachBeatle as String

Beatles(0) = "John Lennon"
Beatles(1) = "Paul McCartney"
Beatles(2) = "George Harrison"
Beatles(3) = "Ringo Starr"

OurLabel.Text = "<u><b>The Beatles</b></u><br>"

for each eachBeatle In Beatles
    OurLabel.Text += eachBeatle + "<br>"
next
```

C#—loop_for_each_cs.aspx

```
string[] Beatles = new string[4];

Beatles[0] = "John Lennon";
Beatles[1] = "Paul McCartney";
Beatles[2] = "George Harrison";
Beatles[3] = "Ringo Starr";

OurLabel.Text = "<u><b>The Beatles</b></u><br>";

foreach (string eachBeatle in Beatles){
    OurLabel.Text += eachBeatle + "<br>";
}
```

Look at all the Beatles gathered together in Figure 3.15.

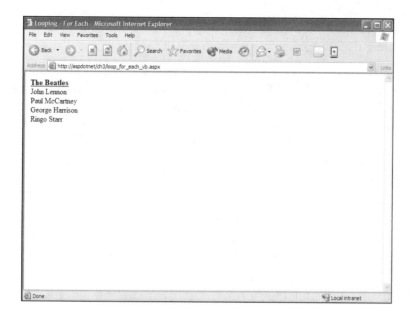

FIGURE 3.15

for each/foreach
*loops enable you to
just feed an array of
data into a loop and,
wiz-bing-bang, it
knows how many
times to go through
the loop like magic.*

"Pay no attention to that array behind the curtain!!!" I mean, try not to get hung
up wanting to understand arrays now. You're trying to understand the for each
loop here, not the array. The first time through the loop, it sets the value of
eachBeatle, which is a string variable, to the first value in the array, which is
Beatles(0) or John Lennon. Then you write the eachBeatle to the page using
the Response.Write() method and proceed to the end of the loop, which shoots
you to the top again and moves you forward to the next element in the Beatles()
array. Then the process starts all over again and proceeds to do this for each
element in our array. Get it? Got it? Good!!

Do Until/do Loops

You use this type of loop when you want something to happen until something
else happens, and you know the first something needs to happen at least
once before the second something can even possibly happen. Whew! Now
I'm confused.

In other (and more understandable) words, you want the loop to execute at least once before the condition that causes you to exit the loop is met.

For a hypothetical example, imagine you have a piggy bank with $10 dollars in it, and you know you can put $45 a week into the piggy bank. You are shooting for $500 dollars in the piggy. You want to know how many weeks it will take and what your piggy bank will contain each week. You know if you cracked her open now she'd have $10 in her, and this is less than your goal, so you must run through your code at least once to exceed your value. This is what this do until/do loop would look like:

Visual Basic .NET—`loop_do_until_vb.aspx`

```
dim Piggy,Deposit,Goal,Week as integer
Piggy = 10
Deposit = 45
Goal = 500
Week = 0

OurLabel.Text = "<u><b>Our Piggy Bank</b></u><br>"
OurLabel.Text += "Opening Balance: " + Piggy.ToString() + "<br>"

Do Until Piggy > Goal
    Piggy += Deposit
    Week +=1
    OurLabel.Text += "Week# " + Week.ToString() + " Piggy's Balance: $" +
    ➥Piggy.ToString() + "<br>"

Loop

OurLabel.Text += "<br>It will take " + Week.ToString() + " weeks to reach
➥our goal."
```

C#—`loop_do_until_cs.aspx`

```
int Piggy,Deposit,Goal,Week;
Piggy = 10;
Deposit = 45;
Goal = 500;
Week = 0;

OurLabel.Text = "<u><b>Our Piggy Bank</b></u><br>";
OurLabel.Text += "Opening Balance: " + Piggy.ToString() + "<br>";

do{
    Piggy += Deposit;
    ++Week;
```

```
        OurLabel.Text += "Week# " + Week.ToString() + " Piggy's Balance: $" +
        ➥Piggy.ToString() + "<br>";
}
while (Piggy < Goal);


OurLabel.Text += "<br>It will take " + Week.ToString() + " weeks to reach
➥our goal.";
```

Again, you need to concentrate. Now look into my eyes. You are getting loopy…loopy…loopy.

Now that you are as loopy as I am, you can dissect the loops shown in Figure 3.16. Remember that this type of loop always executes once before the condition is checked. This is much more apparent when you look at the code in the C# example, because the condition is actually after the code that you want to execute. Visual Basic .NET's way of doing this is a bit deceiving, because the conditions of the loop aren't really executed where they are. They are actually executed by the keyword loop. When you look at it this way, the conditions don't execute until the loop statement, even though they are at the top of the statement.

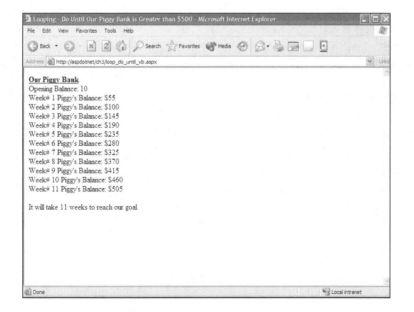

FIGURE 3.16

The Do Until/do loop executes the code inside the loop at least once, then checks the condition to see whether it's true.

Also take notice that C# uses the keyword `while` at the end of the loop, which changes how the statement is evaluated. In Visual Basic .NET, you ask it to "Do this until piggy is greater than $500," and then stop. You're checking to see whether piggy is greater than $500. The `while` statement requires you to evaluate this differently. C# says, "Continue do this while piggy is less than $500," and then stop. You are checking to see whether piggy is still less than $500.

As you examine this code, you can see things inside the loop happen like this:

1. Piggy gets her deposit.

2. You increment the week so that you can keep track of what week you're on and how many weeks it takes.

3. Write to the page the week you're on and what that week's balance is.

Now this do-type loop that always executes once is just fabulous if you know that you want to execute your loop at least once. You might use it, for instance, to see how many times through a loop it would take to pick a specific name out of a random list of names. You know that the answer can't be 0 because no name can be randomly picked if the loop never executes.

But what if you take your loop from the piggy bank example and already have $505 in piggy? If you use this do-type loop that always executes at least once, you'll be depositing money unnecessarily into piggy during the first loop. What do you do? You don't want to overstuff piggy!! Enter the `Do While/while` loop.

Do While/while Loops

This type of loop makes it possible to protect piggy's gorgeous figure and prevents her from getting overstuffed because it checks her condition before a deposit is made, or more seriously, before the loop ever executes.

We are also going to add an `if` statement to the bottom of this code to check whether a deposit was made and to display what happened depending on these conditions.

Take a look:

Visual Basic .NET—`loop_do_while_vb.aspx`

```
dim Piggy,Deposit,Goal,Week as integer
Piggy = 505
Deposit = 45
Goal = 500
```

```
Week = 0

OurLabel.Text += "<u><b>Our Piggy Bank</b></u><br>"
OurLabel.Text += "Opening Balance: " + Piggy.ToString() + "<br>"

Do While Piggy < Goal
    Piggy += Deposit
    Week +=1
    OurLabel.Text += "Week# " + Week.ToString() + " Piggy's Balance: $" +
    ➥Piggy.ToString() + "<br>"

Loop

if Week <> 0 then
    OurLabel.Text += "<br>It will take " + Week.ToString() + " weeks to reach
    ➥our goal."
else
    OurLabel.Text += "Piggy's balance already exceeds our goal. Whahooey!!"
end if
```

C#—loop_do_while_cs.aspx

```
int Piggy,Deposit,Goal,Week;
Piggy = 505;
Deposit = 45;
Goal = 500;
Week = 0;

OurLabel.Text += "<u><b>Our Piggy Bank</b></u><br>";
OurLabel.Text += "Opening Balance: " + Piggy.ToString() + "<br>";

while (Piggy < Goal){
    Piggy += Deposit;
    ++Week;
    OurLabel.Text += "Week# " + Week.ToString() + " Piggy's Balance: $" +
    ➥Piggy.ToString() + "<br>";
}

if (Week != 0){
    OurLabel.Text += "<br>It will take " + Week.ToString() + " weeks to reach
    ➥our goal.";
}else{
    OurLabel.Text += "Piggy's balance already exceeds our goal. Whahooey!!";
}
```

Survey says…For the number one answer, see Figure 3.17.

FIGURE 3.17

The `Do While`/ `while` loop checks whether the condition is true before it executes the code inside the loop.

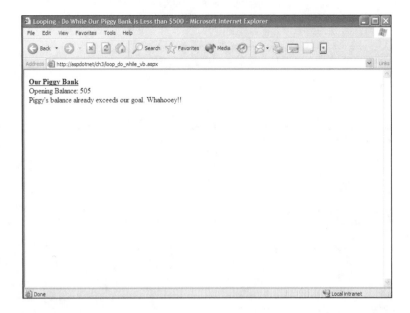

Thank goodness we have these types of loops. Piggy will live to see another day because a deposit was averted. The `Do While`/`while` statement checked the condition to see whether piggy's balance was less than $500. Her balance was $500, and so the loop jumped to the next block of code, which was the `if` statement.

What would happen if piggy's beginning balance was $390 and you ran this code? You can see the results in Figure 3.18, where you are informed of what your weekly balances will be and how long it will take to fill up piggy, just as in the `do until`/`do` loop examples earlier.

You have been through many types of branches, including a plethora of `if` and `looping` statements. These create a bunch of tools and concepts from which you can choose to manipulate your data and code flow. What you've learned about control structure will enable you to control what your code will do under just about any condition or situation. The more you work with branches and loops, the more you can see how wide the possibilities are. Just keep playing and have fun.

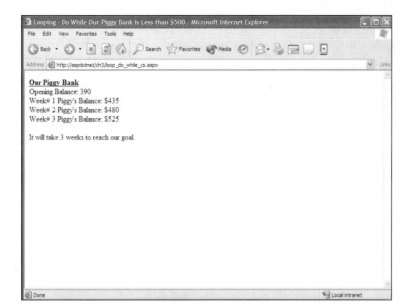

FIGURE 3.18

When the condition calls for the code, it executes and provides the proper information.

Functions and Subs and *void*, OH MY!

So far in this chapter and in this book you've been dealing with code blocks that are self-contained, or in other words, that do all the work within themselves. What if I told you there was another way in certain instances to write less code, reuse code, save loads of time when you're debugging, and separate out your code into compartmentalized blocks that are easier to use and to read? Would that be exciting? Okay, you're not gonna jump out of your chair and do cartwheels, but it is a *little* exciting, isn't it?

Functions and subs, enter stage right. Functions provide a great way to achieve all the above-mentioned benefits and probably many more I can't think of. They give us a way to use blocks of code over and over from anywhere in pages or even whole applications.

I think before we even get into it, I should address what functions and subs are and how both languages handle them. Now how to unscramble this mess? Ok, gotta start somewhere.

In Visual Basic .NET there are both functions and subs. C# has only functions, but C#'s functions can accomplish what both the Visual Basic .NET function and sub can do.

Whew! I can't believe I explained that in one sentence.

Think of it this way: Imagine you're at a Little League baseball game and your son comes running up to you asking for money for ice cream. You have four choices:

- Tell him to forget it, because he didn't clean his room and is not getting any ice cream.

- Give him a few dollars and let him get ice cream.

- Say, "Hey, you've already got money. Buy it yourself. And in fact, while you're at it, bring me back a toasted almond bar."

- Give him a few dollars to get ice cream and tell him to bring back a toasted almond bar for you.

That pretty much sums it up.

Now I will interpret for Visual Basic .NET. The first two options represent subs. Subs do stuff and don't return any data to you directly. They can effect change on something with your application, but they don't directly return anything to you. In both instances, you spoke to your child and the child performed an action, in the latter instance with some input from you. They can accept input from you to perform their actions or, in other words, you can require parameters to be passed to them.

The second two options represent functions. They return something to you, namely a delicious toasted almond bar. In one instance you gave a directive without input from your wallet, and in the second instance you passed your kid a few bucks.

Functions operate in exactly the same way as subs do, but they return values to you, like your toasted almond bar. They too can accept input from you to in the form of parameters.

As I've said before, C# uses its form of a function for what both subs and functions perform in Visual Basic .NET. Take a look at how these are structured to understand this better:

Visual Basic .NET

```
'This is a Sub that doesn't take parameters
Sub SubName()
    Code to be performed
End Sub

'This is a Sub that takes parameters
Sub SubName(ParameterName as ParameterType)
    Code to be performed
End Sub

'This is a Function doesn't that take parameters
Function FunctionName()
    Code to be performed
    return WhatYouWantReturned
End Function

'This is a Function that takes parameters
Function FunctionName(ParameterName as ParameterType)
    Code to be performed
    return WhatYouWantReturned
End Function
```

C#

```
//This is a C# Function that doesn't return anything that doesn't take parameters
void FunctionName(){
    Code to be performed;
}

//This is a C# Function that doesn't return anything that takes parameters
void FunctionName(ParameterType ParameterName){
    Code to be performed;
}

//This is a Function that returns data but doesn't that take parameters
ReturnDataType FunctionName(){
    Code to be performed;
    return WhatYouWantReturned
}

//This is a Function that takes parameters
ReturnDataType FunctionName(ParameterType ParameterName) {
    Code to be performed;
    return WhatYouWantReturned
}
```

As you can see, Visual Basic .NET uses the words Sub and Function to differentiate between whether or not you need something returned. C# differentiates these by using the word void in place of declaring a return data type. Now let's look at a Sub/void function to understand it in practical application.

Sub/void

In one of the previous loops, you added a <br> directly in the string as you went through the loop. This created line breaks in the browser so the loop code doesn't just show up on one line. This example uses a Sub/void function to add <br> tags as it runs through the loop, instead of adding them to the string inside the loop. To make the generated code more readable, you are also going to insert a carriage return in code so you can view the rendered code. In the previous examples, if you viewed the source of the generated HTML it would have been a giant string like: <span id="OurLabel">This is line number 1 in our loop.
This is line number 2 in our loop.
This is line number 3 in our loop.
This is line number 4 in our loop.
This is line number 5 in our loop.
</span>.

N O T E

For all the examples that follow, you need a new template for testing code. Use the following templates for all these examples.

```
functiontemplate_vb.aspx
    <%@ page language="vb" runat="server"%>
    <script runat=server>
        'Replace this with your code
    </script>
    <html>
    <title>VB.NET Template</title>
    <body>
    <asp:label id="OurLabel" runat="server"/>
    </body>
    </html>

functiontemplate_cs.aspx
    <%@ page language="c#" runat="server"%>
    <script runat=server>
        //Replace with your code
    </script>
    <html>
    <title>C# Template</title>
    <body>
    <asp:label id="OurLabel" runat="server"/>
    </body>
    </html>
```

Now for the example:

Visual Basic .NET—`sub_simple_vb.aspx`

```
Sub InsertLineFeed()
    OurLabel.Text += "<br>" + ControlChars.CrLf
End Sub

Sub Page_Load()
    dim i as Integer
    for i=1 to 5
        OurLabel.Text += "This is line number " + i.ToString()
        InsertLineFeed()
    next

End Sub
```

C#—`function_void_cs.aspx`

```
void InsertLineFeed(){
    OurLabel.Text += "<br> \n";
}

void page_load(){
    int i;
    for(i = 1;i <= 5;++i){
        OurLabel.Text += "This is line number " + i.ToString();
        InsertLineFeed();
    }
}
```

And now the generated HTML, which is identical for both languages:

```
<html>
<title>Function - Void</title>
<body>
<span id="OurLabel">
This is line number 1<br>
This is line number 2<br>
This is line number 3<br>
This is line number 4<br>
This is line number 5<br>
</span>
</body>
</html>
```

As you can see, the sub or function (depending on your language) has performed its duty as it was called each time through the loop. It didn't return any data to use, but it did the work it was asked to by adding the <br> and a carriage return to OurLabel.Text each time through the loop.

N O T E

The way to insert a carriage return in Visual Basic .NET and C# is quite different. Visual Basic .NET has an object called ControlChars *that contains a property called* CrLf. *In C# you simply insert* \n *as a string and the interpreter recognizes this as a desired carriage return.*

Now look at a similar example where you pass in a parameter to the Sub/void and use this parameter to determine what action you want taken.

Visual Basic .NET—sub_param_vb.aspx

```
Sub AppendText(OurString as String)
    OurLabel.Text += OurString + ControlChars.CrLf
End Sub

Sub Page_Load()
    dim i as Integer
    OurLabel.Text = ControlChars.CrLf

    AppendText("This is a line we insert before the loop<br>")

    for i=1 to 5
        OurLabel.Text += "This is line number " + i.ToString()
        AppendText("<br>")
    next

    AppendText("This is a line we insert after the loop")

End Sub
```

C#—function_void_param_cs.aspx

```
void AppendText(String OurString){
    OurLabel.Text += OurString + "\n";
}

void page_load(){
int i;
OurLabel.Text = "\n";

AppendText("This is a line we insert before the loop<br>");
```

```
for(i = 1;i <= 5;++i){
        OurLabel.Text += "This is line number " + i.ToString();
        AppendText("<br>");
}

AppendText("This is a line we insert after the loop");

}
```

You can see the results of the Sub/function in Figure 3.19.

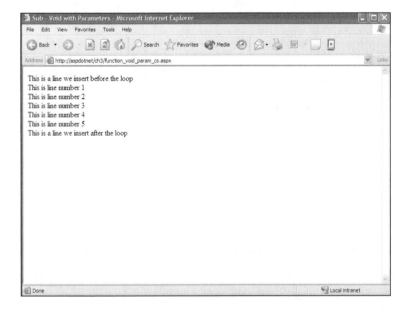

FIGURE 3.19

Passing parameters to subs or functions allows you to better control what they actually do and multiply their power.

As you can see, a parameter called OurString has been set up in the function and you can define what you want added to the string by passing in the text you want appended when you call the Sub/void function. This really just scratches the surface of what you can do, but it demonstrates the basic concept of passing parameters to functions.

Let's move on to functions that can return data that can be used in function calls. We aren't going to demonstrate functions that don't receive any parameters. Reason? You will VERY RARELY run into a situation where you won't be passing a parameter to a function. Besides—it isn't too difficult to project how a function of this type will work after you understand a function with parameters. It works exactly the same way, but without parameters. Got it?

Visual Basic .NET—`function_single_param_vb.aspx`

```
Function AddToTen(OurNum as Integer)
    dim FuncNum as Integer = 10
    return FuncNum + OurNum
End Function

Sub Page_Load()

    OurLabel.Text = AddToTen(89).ToString()
    OurLabel.Text += " Bottles of Beer on the Wall<br>"
    OurLabel.Text += AddToTen(88).ToString()
    OurLabel.Text += " Bottles of Beer on the Wall<br>"
    OurLabel.Text += AddToTen(87).ToString()
    OurLabel.Text += " Bottles of Beer on the Wall<br>"

End Sub
```

C#—`function_single_param_cs.aspx`

```
int AddToTen(int OurNum){
    int FuncNum = 10;
    return FuncNum + OurNum;
}

void page_load(){

    OurLabel.Text = AddToTen(89).ToString();
    OurLabel.Text += " Bottles of Beer on the Wall<br>";
    OurLabel.Text += AddToTen(88).ToString();
    OurLabel.Text += " Bottles of Beer on the Wall<br>";
    OurLabel.Text += AddToTen(87).ToString();
    OurLabel.Text += " Bottles of Beer on the Wall<br>";


}
```

And you can see the results in Figure 3.20

N O T E

Notice that to call to the function, the `ToString()` *method needed to be appended to the calls. After the* `Text` *property of* `OurLabel` *is appended to, it becomes impossible to append an integer to a string. You cannot add* 98 *to* `" Bottles of Beer on the Wall."` *It is mathematically impossible. So you must tell ASP.NET that you want to concatenate and not add these values by turning the* `Int` *into a* `String`.

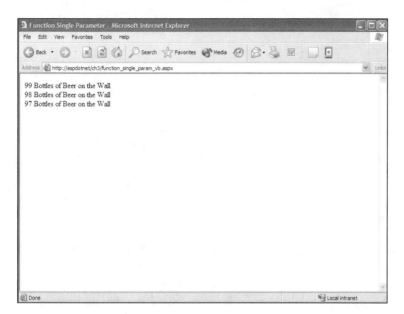

FIGURE 3.20

Functions can return data that can be used in function calls.

You can also pass multiple parameters to a function. In the next example you are going to pass two parameters to the function, do some math, and return the results.

Visual Basic .NET—**function_mutli_param_vb.aspx**

```
Function Add(Num1 as Integer, Num2 as Integer)
    return Num1 + Num2
End Function

Sub Page_Load()

    OurLabel.Text = "10 + 5 = " + Add(10,5).ToString() + "<br>"
    OurLabel.Text += "32 + 11 = " + Add(32,11).ToString()+ "<br>"
    OurLabel.Text += "77 + 44 = " + Add(77,44).ToString()+ "<br>"
    OurLabel.Text += "212 + 458 = " + Add(212,458).ToString()+ "<br>"
    OurLabel.Text += "1493 + 716 = " + Add(1493,716).ToString()+ "<br>"

End Sub
```

C#—**function_mutli_param_cs.aspx**

```
int Add(int Num1,int Num2){
    return Num1 + Num2;
}

void page_load(){

    OurLabel.Text = "10 + 5 = " + Add(10,5).ToString() + "<br>";
    OurLabel.Text += "32 + 11 = " + Add(32,11).ToString()+ "<br>";
    OurLabel.Text += "77 + 44 = " + Add(77,44).ToString()+ "<br>";
    OurLabel.Text += "212 + 458 = " + Add(212,458).ToString()+ "<br>";
    OurLabel.Text += "1493 + 716 = " + Add(1493,716).ToString()+ "<br>";

}
```

You can see in Figure 3.21 that more parameters can provide you with a door
for more functions.

FIGURE 3.21

*Passing multiple
parameters to
functions opens up
a whole world of
possibilities for
reusing code
to create and
manipulate data.*

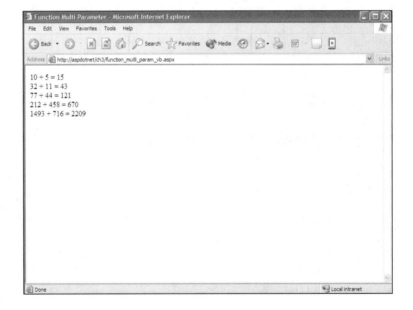

Now just to demonstrate something simple you can do inside a function, I threw together a quick and dirty calculator for simple addition, subtraction, multiplication, and division. I've only included this to illustrate that there are virtually no limits to what can be performed in a function, and that you can now reuse this code numerous times on a page without having to write specific blocks of code all over to calculate your numbers. Notice how there is a `Select`/`switch` statement inside the function to evaluate the third parameter passed in, named `Type`, to control what type of mathematical operation is performed. Pretty cool!

Visual Basic .NET—**function_calc_vb.aspx**

```
Function OurCalc(Num1 as Integer, Num2 as Integer,CalcType as String)
     dim MathType as String
     MathType = CalcType

     Select Case MathType
         Case "+"
             Return Num1 + Num2
         Case "-"
             Return Num1 - Num2
         Case "*"
             return Num1 * Num2
         Case "/"
             return Num1 / Num2
     End Select
End Function


Sub Page_Load()

     OurLabel.Text = "10 + 5 = " + OurCalc(10,5,"+").ToString() + "<br>"
     OurLabel.Text += "32 - 11 = " + OurCalc(32,11,"-").ToString()+ "<br>"
     OurLabel.Text += "77 * 44 = " + OurCalc(77,44,"*").ToString()+ "<br>"
     OurLabel.Text += "736 / 16 = " + OurCalc(736,16,"/").ToString()+ "<br>"


End Sub
```

C#—function_calc_cs.aspx

```
int OurCalc(int Num1,int Num2,String CalcType){
    String MathType;
    int MyReturn;
    MathType = CalcType;
    MyReturn = 0;

    switch(MathType){
        case "+":
            MyReturn = Num1 + Num2;
            break;
        case "-":
            MyReturn = Num1 - Num2;
            break;
        case "*":
            MyReturn = Num1 * Num2;
            break;
        case "/":
            MyReturn = Num1 / Num2;
            break;
    }
    return MyReturn;
}


void Page_Load(){

    OurLabel.Text = "10 + 5 = " + OurCalc(10,5,"+").ToString() + "<br>";
    OurLabel.Text += "32 - 11 = " + OurCalc(32,11,"-").ToString()+ "<br>";
    OurLabel.Text += "77 * 44 = " + OurCalc(77,44,"*").ToString()+ "<br>";
    OurLabel.Text += "736 / 16 = " + OurCalc(736,16,"/").ToString()+ "<br>";

}
```

Take a look at Figure 3.22 to see the results.

We had to jump through a few hoops to get the C# example to work, whereas Visual Basic .NET is much more liberal. Visual Basic .NET enables you to return straight out of the Select statement, whereas C# forces you to populate a variable and return it at the end of the function.

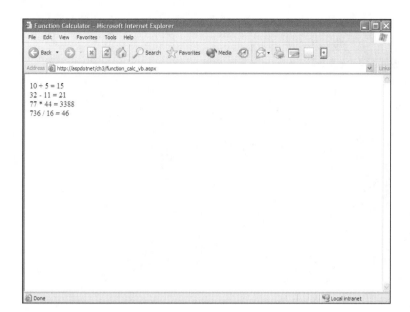

FIGURE 3.22

Functions can be used for a multitude of things such as performing different types of mathematical calculations.

Summary

This chapter has covered a lot of ground, from variables to branch statements, loops, and functions. These become part of a good tool box for you to have when trying to build your ASP.NET applications.

What has been presented is by no means exhaustive. If it were, it would have to contain the full SDK—which is around 110 megabytes of data. I have given you a base understanding of many of the common skills you'll need. As you move on and venture out to build your own application, you will build on these techniques and probably throw a zillion compiler errors in the process. Pushing through this and forcing yourself to learn ASP.NET is the process that will make you a better code writer, and it is all part of the fun of creating ASP.NET applications.

Now that you've been through this chapter, I think you have seen enough code examples to shake a stick at. You've seen the looser but more wordy nature of Visual Basic .NET and the more concise but more critical side of C#. You will have plenty of opportunity to see more examples through the book.

Next, we're going to be looking deep into the nooks and crevasses of ASP.NET pages. We'll see how they differ from typical HTML pages and explore the fact that in ASP.NET, even the page is…you guessed it—an object!

4

ASP.NET Pages

Alive!!! It's alive!!…
The page is ALIVE!!!!!

I don't want to sound like a nag or like I'm harping on the same issue over and over, but ASP.NET is really about events and objects. The ASP.NET page is no exception. It is an object in the eyes of ASP.NET just like anything else. It has properties and methods and can be interacted with, similar to the other objects you've seen so far, and the plethora of things to come as you move through the remainder of this book.

Because events are a big part of ASP.NET and also a huge part of the power of the ASP.NET page object, it's important to look closely at these event and the order in which they occur so that you can utilize them to their fullest potential.

Understanding Page Events

Maybe this isn't the best way to explain this. Maybe my mother wouldn't be so proud of my openness. Maybe these examples will be too graphic for you, but it's the best way I can describe it, so please bear with me.

Every morning of every workday I start my day the same way. I get up, drag my carcass into the living room, and turn on the television. I stare at overpaid morning show hosts like a dribbling fool, with about as much cerebral activity as an earthworm trying to figure out what to eat. After the first flicker of lights goes off in my cranium, I drag my carcass to the shower to defrost my brain.

In the shower I have a set routine so as not to miss any vital, proper hygienic functions and to ensure that the other people in my office and our clients don't give me those strange looks anymore when I enter the room. I think if you took the time to analyze this portion of your life, you'd see that without conscious thought, you pick up the bar of soap and proceed to cleanse without ever putting a thought into what you are doing. You may be singing or thinking about the day you are about to face and before you know it…Boom! You're finished.

It's a routine that I go through every morning almost without thought. And that's a good thing; if I needed to be able to think before I could shower, I wouldn't arrive at work until 10:00 a.m., or until I've had several cups of joe. This practice is part of a subconscious, programmed routine that has been burned into my mind from years of habit.

When I then go to work, I respond to the world around me. I make decisions based on what stimulus comes my way. Maybe someone comes to the office for a meeting. They ask questions and I answer them. The phone rings and I pick it up. I get e-mail and I occasionally read it and less often answer it. I am affected by the world around me and what kind of input it gives me. I then go home and enjoy the solace (this isn't a joke and I'm not kidding) of my family.

At the end of the day I get into my pajamas and go to sleep.

ASP.NET pages are a lot like this. They go through a routine every time they are called. These routines are the ASP.NET pages' *events*. They are like the steps I go through every morning to prepare for my day, or like showering by the same routine everyday.

ASP.NET pages have a routine of events that happen, and they happen in the same way, in the same order, every time. You've seen one of these events, Page_Load, in some of the previous examples. Let's look into these events and the others that a page goes through when it is executed.

The three main events, although there are others, are as follows:

- Page_Init
- Page_Load
- Page_Unload

Page_Init

The Page_Init event is the first to occur when an ASP.NET page is executed. This is where you should perform any initialization steps that you need to set up or create instances of server controls. Server controls are discussed in later chapters, so just keep this event in mind.

You don't want to try to access controls in this event because there is no guarantee that they have been created yet. It is during this event that they are created, and you can control whether your attempt to use these objects will be thwarted by the server processing your request before the object has been created.

The following is an example of the structure of how to use the Page_Init event

Visual Basic .NET

```
Sub Page_Init()
    'Place your Page_Init code here
End Sub
```

C#

```
void Page_Init(){
    //Place your Page_Init code here
}
```

Note that the Page_Init event fires only the first time the page is loaded. When you use a web form and post back to this page again, the Page_Init event doesn't fire. But the Page_Load event fires each time the page loads.

Page_Load

This is the page event where you will be doing most of your work. This event occurs only when all the objects on the page have been created and are available for use. You will see—within this book and in other examples available in the .NET Framework SDK and ASP.NET-related web sites—that the lion's share of work on ASP.NET pages is done during this event. We've been using this event since the beginning of the book and will continue to use it in just about every example.

Although you've seen it a zillion times already in the book, for consistency's sake I'll show you the form here. It doesn't look a whole lot different from the Page_Init example, and for all intents and purposes the only thing that's different is that the word Init is substituted with the word Load.

Visual Basic .NET

```
Sub Page_Load()
    'Place your Page_Load code here
End Sub
```

C#

```
void Page_Load(){
    //Place your Page_Load code here
}
```

Page_Unload

Page_Unload is the counterpart to Page_Init. Just as Page_Init is an event that happens *before* anything else happens, Page_Unload happens *after* everything else happens. It is available for you to perform any operation you need to after you are completely finished with the page.

For instance, imagine that you temporarily needed to create a file on the server during the page's processing. You wouldn't want to leave it there for eternity, especially if the file was unique to each visitor of the web site. You could have loads and loads of files building on your server without any way to get rid of them. But if you were a good boy or girl, you could destroy the file during the page's Page_Unload event and make the server administrator a happy camper.

Just to be fair and impartial, I don't want to leave out showing you the structure of the Page_Unload event. Look familiar?

Visual Basic .NET

```
Sub Page_Unload()
     'Place your Page_Unload code here
End Sub
```

C#

```
void Page_Unload(){
    //Place your Page_Unload code here
}
```

Getting back to my morning routine, it looks like this:

1. `Peter_Init`. Roll carcass from bed to in front of the television.

2. `Peter_Load`. Take shower brainlessly, get dressed (make sure socks match and colors coordinate—check with wife for confirmation). Get into car and drive to the office.

3. Handle the day in all its glory and all the blessings that come with it.

4. `Peter_Unload`. Get into jammies and go to sleep.

It's that routine, and I behave just like the `Page` object does. When I run through these events, I am investigating and affecting all kinds of things. I'm finding out the condition of the world that morning by listening to news, changing the state of my brain to somewhat functional, changing the direction that my hair points from an erratic bird's nest to some semblance of a hairdo, and more.

I'm doing this through checking and setting properties and executing methods, so to speak. During `Peter_Init`, I execute the `RollCarcass()` method to change the `Peter.Sleeping` property from true to false.

During `Peter_Load` I'm checking the value of the `eye.bags` property and seeing what the value of the `hair.color` property is, which is generally grayer than the day before. I'm assuring that the `body.odor` property is set to zero by executing the `Shower()` method.

I then have the ability to respond to events and stimulus from the world around me throughout the day. Then during the `Peter_Unload` event, I execute the `CollapseFromExaustion()` method to set the `Peter.Sleeping` property to true.

Can you see how these different events at different times have a direct affect on my condition? ASP.NET pages can be affected just like this with their different events. Now are you beginning to see more clearly how events and objects interact in ASP.NET and how this is a totally different paradigm from any traditional way of web programming in HTML or Active Server Pages.

As I said in the beginning of the chapter, ASP.NET is all about events and objects, and the ASP.NET page is no exception. You know that objects are made up of their properties and methods, and now you know that objects can also have events, as well.

The page object has the three mentioned events, as well as others that execute without intervention from the designer, but other events also affect ASP.NET pages.

User-Initiated Events

Just as I am faced with input from the world around me after the Peter_Onload event has finished, a page can also deal with events initiated by the web page's visitor.

Let's look at an example of some events, both self executing and user initiated. Below is a page that shows the date and asks you to pick what mood you're in. In the code samples, you'll also be shown another neat server control called a RadioButtonList and a cool feature of the .NET Framework called Databinding. You will also see a property of the Page object called IsPostBack. We will discuss this later in this chapter, but again, don't get hung up on these things—just concentrate on the events in the page.

Visual Basic .NET

```
<%@ page language="vb" runat="server"%>
<script runat=server>

Sub Page_Load()
    dim TodaysDate as Date
    TodaysDate = DateTime.Now.ToShortDateString
    OurTitle.Text = "<u><b>Today's Date is " + TodaysDate    + "</b></u>"

    If Not IsPostBack then
        dim MoodArray(3) as String
        MoodArray(0) = "Good Mood"
        MoodArray(1) = "Okay Mood"
        MoodArray(2) = "Bad Mood"
```

```
            MoodArray(3) = "Totally Melancholy "

            YourMood.DataSource = MoodArray
            YourMood.DataBind()
        End If

End Sub

Sub CheckMood(sender As Object, e As System.EventArgs)
    If YourMood.SelectedIndex > -1 then
        SelectedMood.Text = "The Mood that you selected is " +
        ➥YourMood.SelectedItem.Text
    Else
        SelectedMood.Text = "What? You don't feel anything?"
    End If
End Sub

</script>
<html>
<title>What's Your Mood?</title>
<body>
<form id="MoodForm" runat="server">
<asp:label id="OurTitle" runat="server"/><br>
<asp:RadioButtonList id="YourMood" runat="server"/>
<asp:Button id="MoodButton" text="What's Your Mood?" onClick="CheckMood"
➥runat="server"/>
<br><br>
<asp:label id="SelectedMood" runat="server"/><br>
</form>
</body>
</html>
```

C#

```
<%@ page language="c#" runat="server"%>
<script  runat=server>

void Page_Load(){
    String TodaysDate;
    string[] MoodArray = new string[4];

    TodaysDate = DateTime.Now.ToShortDateString();
    OurTitle.Text = "<u><b>Today's Date is " + TodaysDate    + "</b></u>";

    if (!IsPostBack){
        MoodArray[0] = "Good Mood";
        MoodArray[1] = "Okay Mood";
        MoodArray[2] = "Bad Mood";
        MoodArray[3] = "Totally Melancholy ";

    YourMood.DataSource = MoodArray;
```

continues

C# (continued)

```
    YourMood.DataBind();
    }

}

void CheckMood(object Source, System.EventArgs s){
    if (YourMood.SelectedIndex > -1) {
        SelectedMood.Text = "The Mood that you selected is " +
        ➥YourMood.SelectedItem.Text;
    }else{
        SelectedMood.Text = "What? You don't feel anything?";
    }
}

</script>
<html>
<title>What's Your Mood?</title>
<body>
<form runat="server">
<asp:label id="OurTitle" runat="server"/><br>
<asp:RadioButtonList id="YourMood" runat="server"/>
<asp:Button id="MoodButton" text="What's Your Mood?" onClick="CheckMood"
➥runat="server"/>
<br><br>
<asp:label id="SelectedMood" runat="server"/><br>
</form>
</body>
</html>
```

If you look at Figure 4.1, you can see the results of the initial load of the page. The Page_Load event fires, at which time the date is created. I then set the Text property of OurTitle and I build an array that will make up the radio buttons.

If you look back at the code samples again, you can see that attached to the button is an onClick event that calls a function called "CheckMood". I know that this looks pretty similar to a client-side JavaScript function call, but remember that ASP.NET is a server-side technology. If you look at the code delivered to the browser, you see that there is no onClick event to be seen.

```
<input type="submit" name="MoodButton" value="What's Your Mood?" id="MoodButton" />
```

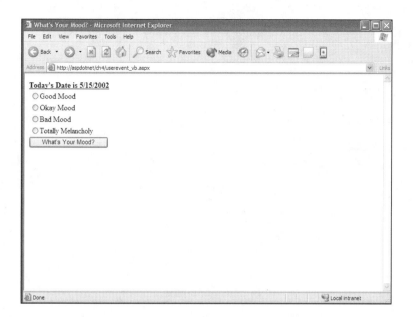

FIGURE 4.1

The Page_Load *event has built the page, but the* onClick *event hasn't had any effect because the button hasn't been pressed yet.*

ASP.NET knows whether you pressed this button—not by a typical client-side onClick event, but by inspecting the form that is posted and seeing whether this button was pressed. The terminology is similar to client-side JavaScript, but the function and method is totally different.

Now it's time to pick a mood and click the button. You can see in Figure 4.2 that the mood is now displayed because the onClick event that took place server-side executed the function called CheckMood, which sets the text of the label.

FIGURE 4.2

The onClick event
is fired by clicking
the button.

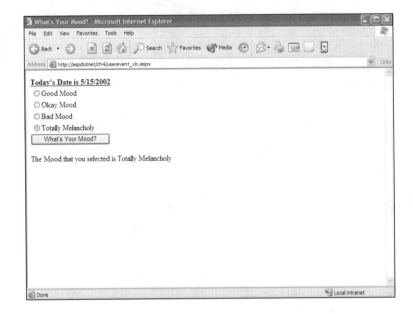

FIGURE 4.2

The onClick event
is fired by clicking
the button.

To reinforce the point that ASP.NET is smart about calling functions and that what
is executed is determined by the onClick event of the button, I have put together
a sample with two different buttons that call two different functions. Each button
uses its own onClick event.

Visual Basic .NET

```vb
<%@ page language="vb" EnableViewState="false" runat="server"%>
<script  runat=server>

Sub CountDown(sender As Object, e As System.EventArgs)
      dim i as Integer
      for i = CDbl(Text1.Text) to 1     Step -1
          OurLabel.Text += "Countdown: " + i.ToString() + "<br>"
      next
End Sub

Sub StringLength(sender As Object, e As System.EventArgs)
    OurLabel.Text = "The length of this string is: " + Text1.Text.Length.toString
End Sub

</script>
<html>
<head>
<title>What do you want?</title>
```

```
</head>
<body>
<form runat="server">
Either enter a word to find its length or a number to count down from<br>
<asp:TextBox id="Text1" runat="server"/>
<asp:Button id="btnCountDown" text="Count Down" onClick="CountDown"
➥runat="server"/>
<asp:Button id="btnLength" text="Get Length" onClick="StringLength"
➥runat="server"/>
<br><br>
<asp:label id="OurLabel" runat="server"/><br>
</form>
</body>
</html>
```

C#

```
<%@ page language="cs" EnableViewState="false" runat="server"%>
<script  runat=server>
void CountDown(object Source, System.EventArgs s){
    int i;
    for (i = Convert.ToInt16(Text1.Text);i >= 1;-i){
        OurLabel.Text += "Countdown: " + i.ToString() + "<br>";
    }
}

void StringLength(object Source, System.EventArgs s){
    OurLabel.Text = "The length of this string is: " +
    ➥Text1.Text.Length.ToString();
}

</script>
<html>
<head>
<title>What do you want?</title>
</head>
<body>
<form runat="server">
Either enter a word to find its length or a number to count down from<br>
<asp:TextBox id="Text1" runat="server"/>
<asp:Button id="btnCountDown" text="Count Down" onClick="CountDown"
➥runat="server"/>
<asp:Button id="btnLength" text="Get Length" onClick="StringLength"
➥runat="server"/>
<br><br>
<asp:label id="OurLabel" runat="server"/><br>
</form>
</body>
</html>
```

If you look at Figure 4.3 you can see that after the Count Down button was clicked, with the value of 10 in the text box, the CountDown function was executed and the code generated and displayed properly.

FIGURE 4.3

Clicking the Count Down button causes the CountDown function to execute.

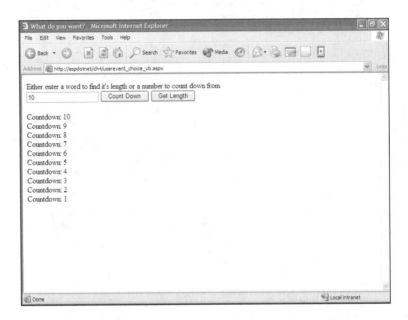

Now if you put a string such as "What is the length?" in the text box and click the Get Length button, you are executing the StringLength function.

N O T E

This example has a bit of hidden danger in that if someone enters a string in the text box and clicks the Count Down button, ASP.NET will cause an error. This is because it can't convert a String type to an Integer in this circumstance. But you don't need to worry about this in your real-world applications because ASP.NET provides some really, REALLY cool answers to validating input data (that we will be devoting an entire chapter to later). The validators would totally solve any issues like this—and more.

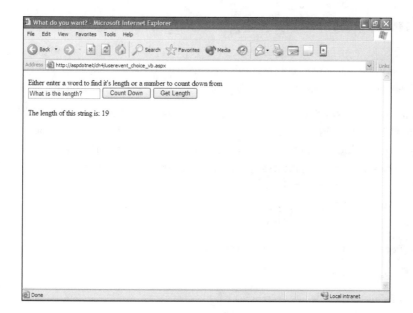

FIGURE 4.4

*Clicking the
Get Length
button causes the
StringLength
function to execute.*

As if all the objects and events covered earlier weren't enough, the concept of user-initiated events opens up a totally new way of thinking again about how you can handle and manipulate data, depending on how a user interacts with your web application.

Other events are also available that can help you manipulate data and objects, and I would encourage you again to go to the class browser located at the following link and look at what events you can use on each object:

```
http://samples.gotdotnet.com/quickstart/aspplus/
```

Now that we've touched on the different events, both default and user-initiated, let's move on to looking at some of the key properties of the Page object.

Understanding Page Properties

As I've said over and over and over and over again, ASP.NET is an object-oriented programming paradigm, and ASP.NET pages are no exception. They are objects, as well, and have properties and methods just like every other object.

Let's take some time to explore some of the key properties that the ASP.NET page object has. First, it is helpful to know where in the .NET Framework the `Page` object is. It is located in `System.Web.UI`. You can go there in the class browser that I mentioned in earlier chapters (`http://www.gotdotnet.com`) and investigate all the properties. In this book, however, we are going to cover the biggies, the heavyweights, the granddaddies. In other words, we're going to cover the ones that are used most commonly.

The `Page` object properties covered in this section are:

- `Application`

- `IsPostBack`

- `Request`

- `Response`

There are actually a few additional properties, such as `Session` and `Validation`, that are covered in other chapters and are pointed out as `Page` object properties then.

N O T E

If you come from a traditional ASP programming background, many of these probably look familiar to you. In traditional ASP, many of these ASP.NET Page properties were what made up the default objects in the language. You ask, "Why are they now properties of the page instead of remaining objects?" In reality they are still objects and can be found in the `System.Web` section of the .NET Framework. To simplify the use of objects, many properties of objects are really just instances of other objects. You will see this throughout the framework. Actually, just about every property is an instance of another object. For instance, any property that is a string is actually an instance of the `System.String` object. So properties in the .NET Framework are generally just instances of other objects.

Application

The `Application` property or `HttpApplicationState` object contains a collection of data that is available across the entire application during the life of the application. It is a shared variable among the users and is an easy-to-use place to store global information that will be needed across your application.

Setting an `Application` variable is a piece of cake:

Visual Basic .NET

```
Application("Publisher") = "New Riders"
OurLabel.Text = Application("Publisher")
```

C#

```
Application("Publisher") = "New Riders";
OurLabel.Text = Application("Publisher");
```

This would write the words "New Riders" to your browsers. You typically wouldn't go around setting an application variable all over the place every time a page loaded. Because it is an application-level variable, under most circumstances it really needs to be set only once during the life of an application. ASP.NET provides a way to set `Application` variables (in addition to many other things) within a file called the global.asax, which resides in the root folder of your application. On a web site, this is typically the folder that your domain points to, where your index or default home page is located. This example creates four application variables in the `Application_OnStart` event, which happens the first time a web page is requested from an application. This doesn't mean that web service on the server must be stopped and started if you make a change to anything in the `Application_OnStart`. ASP.NET is smart enough to recognize the change and reset the variable's value.

Visual Basic .NET—`global.asax`

```
<script language="vb" runat=server>
Sub Application_OnStart()
    Application("Publisher") = "New Riders"
    Application("BookTitle") = "ASP.NET for Web Designers"
    Application("Author") = "Peter"
    Application("Rating") = "5 Stars, WHAHOOO!!"
End Sub
</script>
```

C#—global.asax

```
<script language="c#" runat=server>
void Application_OnStart(){
    Application["Publisher"] = "New Riders";
    Application["BookTitle"] = "ASP.NET for Web Designers";
    Application["Author"] = "Peter";
    Application["Rating"] = "5 Stars, WHAHOOO!!";
}
</script>
```

Now, if you make a file that requests the application variables, you can see how they are retrieved.

Visual Basic .NET—page_application_vb.aspx

```
<%@ page language="vb" runat="server"%>
<script  runat=server>

Sub Page_Load()
    Title.Text = "<u>Title:</u> " + Application("BookTitle")
    Publisher.Text = "<u>Publisher:</u> " + Application("Publisher")
    Author.Text = "<u>Author:</u> " + Application("Author")
    BookRating.Text = "<u>Rating:</u> " + Application("Rating")
End Sub

</script>
<html>
<title>Application</title>
<body>
<asp:label id="Title" runat="server"/><br>
<asp:label id="Publisher" runat="server"/><br>
<asp:label id="Author" runat="server"/><br>
<asp:label id="BookRating" runat="server"/>
</body>
</html>
```

C#—page_application_cs.aspx

```
<%@ page language="cs" runat="server"%>
<script  runat=server>

void Page_Load(){
    Title.Text = "<u>Title:</u> " + Application["BookTitle"];
    Publisher.Text = "<u>Publisher:</u> " + Application["Publisher"];
    Author.Text = "<u>Author:</u> " + Application["Author"];
    BookRating.Text = "<u>Rating:</u> " + Application["Rating"];
}
```

```
</script>
<html>
<title>Application</title>
<body>
<asp:label id="Title" runat="server"/><br>
<asp:label id="Publisher" runat="server"/><br>
<asp:label id="Author" runat="server"/><br>
<asp:label id="BookRating" runat="server"/>
</body>
</html>
```

As you can see in Figure 4.5, the page requested these application variables and displayed them in the browser just as expected.

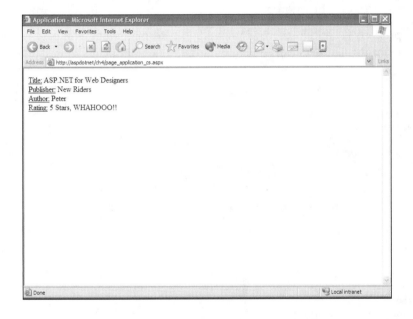

FIGURE 4.5

Application variables are a simple way to make routine and application-wide information available to you.

T I P

As I mentioned in Chapter 1, there is another file that can contain not only application variables but a ton of other information: the web.config file. This is an XML document that allows you to configure many elements of your web application and isn't limited to one file per application. You can add a web.config file to every folder in your application to set its configuration, rules, or variables. This file is a bit out of the scope of this book, but if you are looking for greater control over your application, the web.config file may be your answer. In addition, there are great performance advantages in using variables from within the web.config file over an application variable. You can learn more about configuring your web applications with the web.config file in the .NET Framework SDK at the following link:

```
ms-help://MS.NETFrameworkSDK/cpguidenf/html/
➥cpconaspnetconfiguration.htm
```

IsPostBack

You saw the IsPostBack property mentioned in one of the earlier examples. This is an incredibly useful property that you will find yourself using all the time when you are processing forms.

As a matter of fact, this property is at the core of some of the most powerful features in ASP.NET and its pages. ASP.NET web forms are built on the concept of making round trips to the server. It's a simple property whose value is either true or false. The property is set to true whenever you post a page to the server with a runat="server" directive in the form tag. Form tags with runat="server" directives always post back to themselves. If you put an action property in the tag, it will basically be ignored.

This property is basically used, as I've said, to determine whether a page is being loaded for the first time or is being posted back to itself. Take a look:

Visual Basic .NET—**page_postback_vb.aspx**

```
<%@ page language="vb" runat="server"%>
<script  runat=server>

Sub Page_Load()
    OurTitle.Text = "No this page wasn't posted back"

    If IsPostBack then
        OurTitle.Text = "Yes this page has been posted back"
    End If

End Sub
</script>
<html>
<title>Was this page posted back?</title>
<body>
<form runat="server">
<asp:label id="OurTitle" runat="server"/><br><br>
<asp:Button id="PostBack" text="Post this Form?"  runat="server"/>
</form>
</body>
</html>
```

C#—page_postback_cs.aspx

```
<%@ page language="cs" runat="server"%>
<script  runat=server>

void Page_Load(){
    OurTitle.Text = "No this page wasn't posted back";

    if (IsPostBack){
        OurTitle.Text = "Yes this page has been posted back";
    }
}

</script>
<html>
<title>Was this page posted back?</title>
<body>
<form runat="server">
<asp:label id="OurTitle" runat="server"/><br><br>
<asp:Button id="PostBack" text="Post this Form?"  runat="server"/>
</form>
</body>
</html>
```

You can see in Figure 4.6 that the first time you request this page, you are presented with the default message because the IsPostBack property is false on the initial load of that page, so the if branching statement doesn't execute its code.

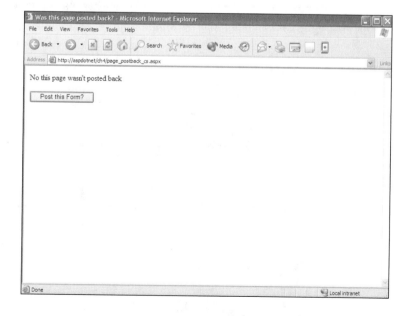

FIGURE 4.6

The first time the page is loaded, the page's IsPostBack *property is false.*

Now what happens if you click the button and post the form? In Figure 4.7 you can see that after you post the form, the label's text value is changed because `IsPostBack` is now true and the `if` block executes.

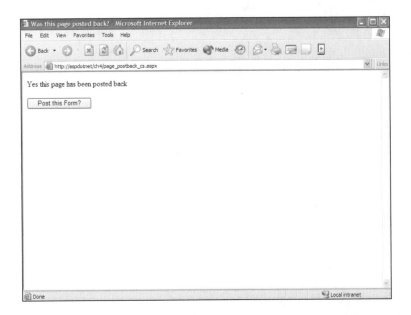

This technique will be used and demonstrated in abundance in later chapters, where you will be able to see it under many different circumstances. So hold your horses and don't get your undies in a twist.

Request and Response

I've always told people who ask me about the Internet that it's not a big mystical thing that can't be understood or pinned down. It's really very simple. It's a communication tool, just like a phone or even more simply a piece of paper and a pen. It's a way to say something to others and, thankfully, as dynamic languages have become so prolific, they can say stuff back and we can respond to what they said programmatically.

Picture two grandmothers sitting at a kitchen table enjoying a cup of tea and good conversation. The air is filled with the pleasing aroma of fresh baked apple pie so thick you can almost taste it.

Ethel: "Bernice, do you want to see my latest masterpiece? It's a deep dish apple pie done to perfection."

Bernice: "Certainly Ethel. Let me have a look see."

Ethel gets up from the table and saunters over to the window sill where the golden brown pie sits. She carefully slides it off the sill onto her toweled hand and returns with the same grace to the table. She approaches Bernice and lowers it in front of her so the waves of succulent aroma waft up to her nose.

Bernice: "Um Um!!!!! Can I have a piece of that?"

Ethel: "You sure can."

Ethel cuts and serves a slice of that delicious pie to Bernice, who proceeds to ravage it mercilessly. Whipped cream, crust, and apples fly as Bernice devours her prize. In between forkfuls, Bernice lifts her apple pie covered face and says:

Bernice: "Can I have the recipe? This is delicious!"

Ethel, also now covered in the remains of a once beautiful piece of apple pie from Bernice's frenzy, pulls the recipe from her recipe file and gives it to her dear friend...Bernice.

—The End—

Okay, a little too dramatic for you? I'm sorry. Sometimes I get carried away. I have behaved quite professionally so far this chapter, and I though it was time to get silly again.

Anyway, the point of my dramatic depiction of Ethel and Bernice was to demonstrate communication and to give an example that shows a bunch of different types of requests and responses. Later we will try to programmatically reproduce this scene and help you see it in action. First, though, it's a good idea to look a bit more into the Request and Response properties of your ASP.NET pages.

Request

If you can think of the Request as a question mark, you will quickly and easily understand what it does in concept. It's similar to Bernice asking whether she can have a piece of pie or have a copy of the recipe. It's also good for finding out what the response was to a question we ask just like Ethel asked whether Bernice wanted to see the pie. We find out the condition of things being sent to the server with the Request.

As I said with the `Application` property, the `Request` and `Response` properties are both actually objects in their own right and can be explored in the class browser I redundantly mention.

You can get tons of data by using the `Request` object, and I covered a few of them here. There are a handful that you will find yourself using over and over—such as `Request.Form`, `Request.Querystring`, and others—and that you will find yourself using as a very pointed tools for specific tasks. You won't use all the properties of the `Request` all the time, but they are powerful nonetheless.

For instance, let's take the `Request.IsSecureConnection` property. This is a nifty little tool that checks to see whether you are communicating via an HTTPS secure protocol or not. It returns a Boolean value of true or false, depending on whether the connection is secure. It's a neat gadget that will definitely come in handy in certain situations, but it's not something you're gonna use every day. Table 4.1 provides a list of some that you *will* use just about every day.

TABLE 4.1 Request Object Properties

Request Property	Description
Browser	An instance of the `HTTPBrowserCapabilites` object that is chock full of information about the client's browser and its capabilities.
Cookies	Enables you to store information on the client's machine and retrieve it at a later time.
Form	Retrieve the values of `form` elements submitted during a `form` post.
QueryString	Retrieve the values of name/value pairs stored in the requesting URL. These can be inserted directly or can be the result of a form being submitted via the `Get` method.
ServerVariables	An ocean full of variables about the request.

Now take a look at a few of these in action. The following is a code example that incorporates a few of these `Request` properties.

Visual Basic .NET—page_request_vb.aspx

```
<%@ page language="vb" runat="server"%>
<script  runat=server>

Sub Page_Load()
        OurLabel.Text = "Here are some of our Request properties in action<br>"
        OurLabel.Text += "My Browser is: " + Request.Browser.Browser + "<br>"
        OurLabel.Text += "Our Querystring Color is: " +
        ➡Request.QueryString("color") + "<br>"
        OurLabel.Text += "This file is located at: " +
        ➡Request.ServerVariables("Path_Translated")  + "<br>"

End Sub

</script>
<html>
<head>
<title>Page Request</title>
</head>
<body>
<asp:label id="OurLabel" runat="server"/>
</body>
</html>
```

C#—page_request_cs.aspx

```
<%@ page language="c#" runat="server"%>
<script  runat=server>

void Page_Load(){
        OurLabel.Text = "Here are some of our Request properties in action<br>";
        OurLabel.Text += "My Browser is: " + Request.Browser.Browser + "<br>";
        OurLabel.Text += "Our Querystring Color is: " +
        ➡Request.QueryString["color"] + "<br>";
        OurLabel.Text += "This file is located at: " +
        ➡Request.ServerVariables["Path_Translated"]  + "<br>";
}

</script>
<html>
<head>
<title>Page Request</title>
</head>
<body>
<asp:label id="OurLabel" runat="server"/>
</body>
</html>
```

> **N o t e**
>
> *Please note that whenever you are specifying an item in a collection, such as the* `Request.Form` *or* `Request.Querystring`, *the bracket types around the item are different in the two languages. In Visual Basic .NET, you use parentheses and quotes around the item name, whereas in C# you use square brackets and quotes. If you come from a traditional ASP/VBScript background and decide to use C# as your language, you will need to watch out for this.*

If you look at Figure 4.8, you can see we are requesting the value of the browser being used to view the ASP.NET page, a value in the `QueryString`—or in other words, name/value pairs passed in the URL of the page—and a `ServerVariable` called `"Path_Translated"`.

FIGURE 4.8

The `HTTPRequest` *object enables you to retrieve data either passed to a page or submitted by the user.*

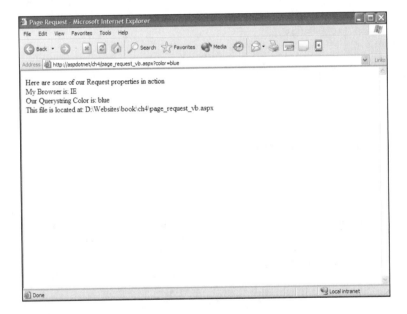

There are times when data that you request is a property like the `Request.Browser.Browser` property. This may look redundant with `Browser.Browser` being in the `Request`, but remember that you are dealing with an addressing system here, or a namespace. The first "Browser" is a property of the page and is an instance of the HTTPBrowserProperties object. That object has a property called Browser, and hence the Browser.Browser in the Request. It might have made more sense if I had written Request.Browser.JavaScript, which would have returned a Boolean true or false depending on whether a browser is JavaScript-enabled.

The second request type that you will see is called a *collection* and requires you to identify what you're looking for. With the QueryString, I knew I was looking for "color" and requested that from the QueryString collection. The Request.Form collection operates the same way. The contents of the Form and QueryString generally are determined by the programmers of the website, and you can pass whatever name/value pairs you would like through these methods.

With the ServerVariables, you need to specify the variable that you are requesting, but these aren't programmer-defined. The available variables are determined in ASP.NET and are a bit too numerous to list and describe in detail in this book. I would recommend that you investigate the .NET Framework SDK for more information on ServerVariables.

Now that you've seen how to get information from the user and how to request all types of different data, you need to be able to respond to those requests. ASP.NET has very generously provided an instance of the HTTPResponse object as a page property called Response.

Response

Every time that Bernice or Ethel asked a question or made a request, the other had a response. When Ethel asked:

> "Bernice, do you want to see my latest masterpiece? It's a deep dish apple pie done to perfection."

Bernice had a response:

> "Certainly Ethel. Let me have a look see."

There was a conversation. This is what the Request and its counterpart the Response allow us to do: carry on a conversation with the visitors of the web sites we create.

Table 4.2 lists a few of the common `Response` object's properties and methods.

TABLE 4.2 *Response* Object Properties and Methods

Response	Description
Buffer	This controls the flow of data from the server to the user's browser. When the buffer is set to true, which it is by default, data isn't sent to the browser until the server completely processes the page. When the buffer is set to false, data is sent to the browser as soon as it's processed and doesn't wait for the entire page to process.
Clear()	Use this when the buffer is set to true and you want to get rid of everything processed up to where the Clear() is.
End()	Use this when the buffer is set to true and you want to send to the browser what you've processed up to the point where the End() is and stop processing the page at that point.
Flush()	Use this when the buffer is set to true and you want to send to the browser what you've processed up to the point where the Clear() is.
Redirect()	Allows you to send the user to a new URL.
Write()	Allows you to write information into ASP.NET pages.
WriteFile()	Writes the specified file directly to an ASP.NET page.

I have this really great news; do you want to hear it? Nah. I'm not gonna tell you 'til I know everything. I want to wait 'til I know the whole story first before I let you know. Well...maybe I'll tell you what I know so far.

UGGHHHHHH!!! It's all over!! I don't want to talk about it anymore. I can't go on. I can't even face it anymore. I'm ruined...I'm ruined ......I'm ruined.

Dramatic, huh? In a feeble and yet to be determined successful manner I was trying to parallel how the `Buffer` and some of its methods would work in a practical application. If you want to hold back information from being delivered, you set the page's `Buffer` property to `True`. Then you can manipulate the page however you want as you progress. Look at an example of the `HttpResponse` object in action. You are using an object in the `System.Threading` namespace to pause the pages processing using a method called `Sleep`. You will hardly ever have need for this, but it helps me to demonstrate some of the `Buffer` features of the `HttpResponse` object.

Visual Basic .NET

```
<%@ page language="vb" runat="server" buffer="true"%>
<%@ import namespace="System.Threading"%>
<html>
<head>
<title>Hi</title>
</head>
<body>
<%
Response.Write(DateTime.Now + " The First Response.Write() has executed.<BR>" )
Response.Flush()
Thread.Sleep(5000)
Response.Write(DateTime.Now + " The Second Response.Write() has executed.<BR>" )
Response.Flush()
Thread.Sleep(5000)
Response.Write(DateTime.Now + " The Third Response.Write() has executed.<BR>" )
Response.Clear()
Thread.Sleep(5000)
Response.Write(DateTime.Now + " The Fourth Response.Write() has executed.<BR>" )
Response.End()
Response.Write("Where does this text go?")
%>
</body>
</html>
```

C#

```
<%@ page language="c#" runat="server" buffer="true"%>
<%@ import namespace="System.Threading"%>
<html>
<head>
<title>Hi</title>
</head>
<body>
<%
Response.Write(DateTime.Now + " The First Response.Write() has executed.<BR>" );
Response.Flush();
Thread.Sleep(5000);
Response.Write(DateTime.Now + " The Second Response.Write() has executed.<BR>" );
Response.Flush();
Thread.Sleep(5000);
Response.Write(DateTime.Now + " The Third Response.Write() has executed.<BR>" );
Response.Clear();
Thread.Sleep(5000);
Response.Write(DateTime.Now + " The Fourth Response.Write() has executed.<BR>" );
Response.End();
Response.Write("Where does this text go?");
%>
</body>
</html>
```

In Figure 4.9 you can see that three out of the five `Response.Write()` commands were rendered to the browser. Notice the times at which they were delivered to the browser. Can you see which two `Writes` are missing?

FIGURE 4.9

The `HTTPResponse`
*object offers several
ways to respond and
to control what is
output to ASP.NET
pages.*

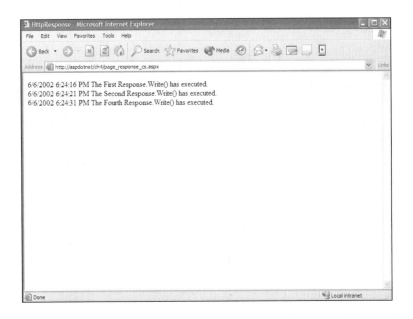

The first `Write` happens and is delivered to the browser when you execute the `Response.Flush()` method as is the second one with a lapse of five seconds between when the first and second `Write`. Notice that the third `Write` is missing from the browser window, but why? Simple. The `Response.Clear()` method disposed of everything that was still in the buffer. In other words, the buffer is like a container in which processed code is stored. If you use a flush, you dump the bucket to the browser. If you use a `Clear()`, you dump the bucket to the trash never to be seen again. Later, a `Response.End()` is used, which is just like a `clear()` except it completely stops page processing. Look at the generated HTML for this page. Do you notice anything peculiar about the tags that came after the `Response.End()`?

```
<html>
<head>
<title>HttpResponse</title>
</head>
<body>
2/6/2002 7:06:39 PM The First Response.Write() has executed.<BR>
2/6/2002 7:06:44 PM The Second Response.Write() has executed.<BR>
2/6/2002 7:06:54 PM The Fourth Response.Write() has executed.<BR>
```

The closing `</body>` and `</html>` tags are missing because the `Response.End()` isn't specific to stopping the processing of just ASP.NET but the entire HTTP stream of data. It basically dumps the bucket at that point and that's it. Nothing else gets processed.

What is a practical application for the buffer? One place we use it all the time and is a good example is on check-out pages of commerce applications we build. We have clients who send their credit card transactions to a third-party processing company and rely on this third-party processor's server to respond back to us indicating whether the card is accepted or declined. During this period of waiting, however, the visitor needs to be kept busy. Our technique is to build an HTML layer with a message that says "We're now processing your card." Then we flush the Buffer (dump the bucket) and send that message to the visitor's browser. Next, we send the credit card information to the third-party company and wait. When we get a reply from the transaction company we build code to hide the layer and do some fancy-schmancy stuff in the back end database depending on whether the card was accepted or declined. We either build a receipt page or a page with a message as to why the transaction was declined. Then we flush the buffer again and deliver the rest of what's in the bucket.

If we didn't have the buffer, the visitor would either be faced with a page that sat idle with no evidence of any activity and hope something was happening, or we'd be forced to jump through flaming hoops and redirect to different pages a bunch of times to accomplish the same thing. And visitors do not enjoy unexplained screen flashes and redirections. With the buffer, we can display a screen telling them what is happening and then deliver a response without any confusion.

I also want to add a thing or two about the `Response.Write` method. This was a highly used and abused method of writing data to traditional ASP pages. It was one of the only ways to dynamically write things into ASP pages.

This is not the case anymore, and with the proliferation of server controls such as the label used so far to display the example results, you will find yourself using `Response.Write` less and less. It is actually a bit out of place in the ASP.NET programming language because it really operates under the more traditional in-line, interpreted model than the event-oriented environment of ASP.NET. The `Response.Write` method doesn't allow you to affect other objects; it just does what it does, where it is, and that is that.

I must also mention the `Response.Redirect` method, as well. This is an oft-used method for transporting the user to another page or URL. The syntax for using this method is to simply place the desired location within the parentheses of the method call, enclosed in quotes if it is a string like the following example.

```
Response.Redirect("anotherpage.asp")
```

You can only use `Response.Redirect` if the HTML stream hasn't begun. In other words, if the buffer has begun to send HTML code to the browser, or if HTML code has been generated at all, using the `Response.Redirect` method causes an error.

As you can see, the `Request` and `Response` objects help you understand and carry on a conversation with the users of your web applications. These are critical tools in your toolbox and are objects you will be seeing over and over throughout the remainder of this book, as well as in your experience in programming in this wonderful language called ASP.NET.

Understanding Directives

ASP.NET directives can simply be described as instructions and settings used to describe how ASP.NET web form pages (.aspx) or User control (.ascx) pages will be processed by the .NET Framework. They are little do-dads that we insert in our ASP.NET pages to control how a page acts or the characteristics it has.

These directives aren't very different from a person's personality traits. Some people are shy, whereas others are outspoken. Some like loud, raucous music, whereas others enjoy the soft sounds of folk music. Some people can compute complicated math problems in their heads, and others can write wondrous stories that capture the imagination.

ASP.NET directives help you give your pages personality and capabilities. You can cause one page to behave in one fashion, whereas another page responds to the same stimulus in a totally different way. One page can have one set of skills or capabilities, whereas another has a totally different set. Directives give us this power.

Table 4.3 shows a list of directives that you will commonly use, but this isn't an exhaustive list. As is true with many aspects of the .NET Framework, the full scope of directives is beyond the scope of this book, but you can see the full list of directives, their functions and their players, in the .NET Framework SDK at the following link:

```
ms-help://MS.NETFrameworkSDK/cpgenref/html/cpconpagedirectives.htm
```

TABLE 4.3 Directives

Directive	Description
@Page	This defines page-specific attributes used in ASP.NET pages (.aspx).
@Control	This defines control-specific attributes used in ASP.NET User controls (.ascx).
@Import	Imports a namespace into a page or User control.
@Register	Creates an alias to User controls, allowing them to be rendered to the browser when they are included in a requested page.

@Page

@Page directives allow you to set attributes that directly affect your ASP.NET pages that end with the .aspx extension. There are 26 directives available, and you can explore the exhaustive list in the SDK at the link I provided a few paragraphs back, but Table 4.4 contains some of the more commonly used @page directives.

TABLE 4.4 @Page Directives

Directive	Description
Buffer	As seen in the previous section on the Response object, this sets whether the Buffer is enabled or not. This is true by default and would need to be set explicitly to false.
EnableSessionState	This defines Session-State requirements for the page. If this is set to true (default) then Session-State is enabled; if false Session-State is disabled; or if ReadOnly then Session state can be read but not changed.
EnableViewState	This direct controls whether ViewState (Maintain GUI state) is maintained across page requests. It is true by default.

continues

TABLE 4.4 Continued

Directive	Description
Explicit	Specifies whether all variables on a page must be declared using a `Dim`, `Private`, `Public`, or `ReDim` statement in Visual Basic .NET. The default is false.
Inherits	Defines a class from a code-behind page that a page should inherit. (Don't worry, this will be explained is a few short minutes.)
Language	Informs the .NET Framework of the language used for all inline(`<% %>`) and server-side script blocks within the ASP.NET page.
Src	This contains the name of the source file for an included code-behind page.
Trace	This indicates whether tracing is enabled or not. True is enabled; otherwise false. False is the default. Tracing is a debugging function in ASP.NET that allows you to see diagnostic and debug information about an ASP.NET page.

Some of these may seem a bit Greek to you, but you will be seeing many of them throughout the book, and they will be more clear to you then. For the time being, just keep this section in mind and look at it as a seed we're planting that will spring back to your memory later in the book.

The following is a small example of what an @Page directive looks like:

```
<%@ page language="c#" buffer="true" Explicit="true" runat="server" %>
```

@Control

The @Control directive operates in exactly the same way the @Page directive does, except that it is used specifically for User controls only. The next chapter discusses User controls in depth, but if you remember from Chapter 1, a User control is ASP.NET's answer to Server-Side Include files.

The @Control directive uses many of the same directives that the @Page directive uses. From the directives I included for @Page, @Control uses all of them except `Buffer`, `EnableSessionState`, and `Trace`. If you think about it, this makes perfect sense because these are attributes that affect an entire page and can't be applied to small sections of included documents, like a User control.

@Import

The `@Import` directive is used to allow you to import a namespace (group of class objects) into your ASP.NET page, making all its classes available for use on your page. You can use this function to import namespaces that are part of the .NET Framework, or you can also use it to import namespaces that are user-defined.

The following namespaces are automatically imported into your ASP.NET pages, so all the class objects within these namespaces are available without you having to explicitly import them.

- `System`
- `System.Collections`
- `System.Collections.Specialized`
- `System.Configuration`
- `System.IO`
- `System.Text`
- `System.Text.RegularExpressions`
- `System.Web`
- `System.Web.Caching`
- `System.Web.Security`
- `System.Web.SessionState`
- `System.Web.UI`
- `System.Web.UI.HtmlControls`
- `System.Web.UI.WebControls`

As I said before, the `@Import` directive can be used to import existing .NET Framework namespaces and user-defined namespaces as well. In an earlier chapter, you created a class (blueprint) for a ball. Also, I've outlined creating a user-defined class in Appendix B of this class in the namespace called `Peter.Toybox`. The following is an example of how to import this namespace, as well as of the .NET Framework namespace called `System.Data`.

```
<%@Import Namespace="Peter.Toybox" %>
<%@Import Namespace="System.Data" %>
```

@Register

The @Register directive is a powerful tool used for dynamically creating tags that represent your User controls.

WHAT? Can you repeat that in English?

First let me say that the next chapter shreds through User control in depth. We'll cover them from soup to nuts but for now try to remember that they are like Server-Side Includes except much cooler.

Let's imagine I create User controls for my site that will be used as my page's header and footer. These files will have an .ascx file extension to identify them as User controls. The @Register directive allows me to create a tag name and tag prefix with which my controls are associated, and it allows me to drop my User controls into my page with a single simple tag. I will call my header header.ascx and my footer footer.ascx for this example.

```
<%@Page Language="vb" runat="server"%>
<%@Register TagPrefix="OurTag" Tagname="Header" Src="header.ascx"%>
<%@Register TagPrefix="OurTag" Tagname="Footer" Src="footer.ascx"%>
<html>
<head>
<title>@Register</title>
</head>
<body>
<OurTag:Header id="OurHeader" runat="server"/>
Here is our pages content
<OurTag:Footer id="OurFooter" runat="server"/>
</body>
</html>
```

As you can see, I assign a TagPrefix, Tagname, and Src to define what file I'm attaching to TagPrefix:Tagname. As you can see, the TagPrefix and Tagname are separated by a colon. The TagPrefix can be used as many times as you want, and is set up this way so you can easily identify your own tags within your code. It's a simple yet powerful way to use User controls.

You can see how these different directives help you to shape and form your ASP.NET pages and control how they look, act and feel to your end user. We will be exploring and using in more abundance as time and this book progresses.

Code Separation and Using Code-Behind

As we've discussed before, ASP.NET has provided a really cool way to keep code separate by changing the paradigm from an inline, interpreted language to an object/event-oriented paradigm. But ASP.NET doesn't stop there. It provides another level of separation of code and content if you want to use it. It's called the *code-behind* technique.

This subject was mentioned briefly in Chapter 1 and also appeared in a little example, but here the code-behind technique is dissected so you can fully understand what's happening.

The following is an example of a typical ASP.NET page that doesn't utilize any code-behind techniques. It has an ASP:Label control that you're familiar with, a few server controls, and a button with a server-side function attached to its onClick event. It's nothing very complicated and its results are pretty predictable, as you can see in Figure 4.10.

Visual Basic .NET—**codebehind_not_vb.aspx**

```
<%@ page language="vb" runat="server"%>
<script runat="server">
Sub SubmitThis( s As Object, e As EventArgs )
    myLabel.Text = "You Selected: " + myList.SelectedItem.Text + " and " +
    ➥myDropdown.SelectedItem.Value
End Sub

Sub Page_Load
    myLabel.Text = ""
End Sub
</script>
<html>
<head><title>Not Codebehind</title></head>
<body>
<form Runat="Server">
<asp:Label ID="myLabel" forecolor="Red" font-bold="True" MaintainState="False"
➥Runat="Server" />
<br>
<asp:ListBox ID="myList" Runat="Server">
 <asp:ListItem Text="Red" />
 <asp:ListItem Text="Green" />
 <asp:ListItem Text="Blue" />
</asp:ListBox>
<br>
```

continues

Visual Basic .NET (continued)

```
<asp:DropDownList ID="myDropdown" Runat="Server">
 <asp:ListItem Text="One" />
 <asp:ListItem Text="Two" />
 <asp:ListItem Text="Three" />
</asp:DropDownList>
<br>
<asp:Button Text="Place Order" OnClick="SubmitThis" Runat="Server" />
</form>
</body>
</html>
```

C#—codebehind_not_cs.aspx

```
<%@ page language="c#" runat="server"%>
<script runat="server">

public void SubmitThis(object s, EventArgs e ){
        myLabel.Text = "You Selected: " + myList.SelectedItem.Text + " and " +
        ➥myDropdown.SelectedItem.Value;
    }
void Page_Load(){
        myLabel.Text = "";
    }
</script>

<html>
<head><title>Not Code Behind</title></head>
<body>
<form Runat="Server">

<asp:Label ID="myLabel" forecolor="Red" font-bold="True" MaintainState="False"
➥Runat="Server" />
<br>
<asp:ListBox ID="myList" Runat="Server">
 <asp:ListItem Text="Red" />
 <asp:ListItem Text="Green" />
 <asp:ListItem Text="Blue" />
</asp:ListBox>
<br>
<asp:DropDownList ID="myDropdown" Runat="Server">
 <asp:ListItem Text="One" />
 <asp:ListItem Text="Two" />
 <asp:ListItem Text="Three" />
</asp:DropDownList>
<br>
<asp:Button Text="Place Order" OnClick="SubmitThis" Runat="Server" />

</form>
</body>
</html>
```

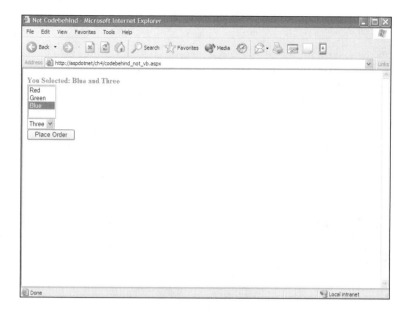

FIGURE 4.10

A predictable and typical ASP.NET page not utilizing any code-behind techniques.

The following is an example of the preceding page and function, but it uses the code-behind technique to separate logical or programming code from content or display code. The ASP.NET page ends with the .aspx extension. This is the content page. This simple example has the same label, a list box control, a drop-down list control, and a form button on the page. As you can see, there is no programming code on this page, with the exception of the @page directive that describes what class is inherited from the code-behind page and the name of the file that is the code-behind page.

Visual Basic .NET—`codebehind_vb.aspx`

```
<%@ page inherits="vbsamplecodebehind" src="codebehind_vb.vb" %>
<html>
<head><title>Code Behind</title></head>
<body>
<form Runat="Server">

<asp:Label ID="myLabel" forecolor="Red" font-bold="True" MaintainState="False"
➥Runat="Server" />

<asp:ListBox ID="myList" Runat="Server">
 <asp:ListItem Text="Red" />
 <asp:ListItem Text="Green" />
 <asp:ListItem Text="Blue" />
</asp:ListBox>
```

continues

Visual Basic .NET—(continued)

```
<br>
<asp:DropDownList ID="myDropdown" Runat="Server">
 <asp:ListItem Text="One" />
 <asp:ListItem Text="Two" />
 <asp:ListItem Text="Three" />
</asp:DropDownList>
<br>
<asp:Button Text="Place Order" OnClick="SubmitThis" Runat="Server" />
</form>
</body>
</html>
```

C#—codebehind_cs.aspx

```
<%@ page inherits="cssamplecodebehind" src="codebehind_cs.cs" %>
<html>
<head><title>Code Behind</title></head>
<body>
<form Runat="Server">

<asp:Label ID="myLabel" forecolor="Red" font-bold="True" MaintainState="False"
➥Runat="Server" />

<asp:ListBox ID="myList" Runat="Server">
 <asp:ListItem Text="Red" />
 <asp:ListItem Text="Green" />
 <asp:ListItem Text="Blue" />
</asp:ListBox>
<br>
<asp:DropDownList ID="myDropdown" Runat="Server">
 <asp:ListItem Text="One" />
 <asp:ListItem Text="Two" />
 <asp:ListItem Text="Three" />
</asp:DropDownList>
<br>

<asp:Button Text="Place Order" OnClick="SubmitThis" Runat="Server" />

</form>
</body>
</html>
```

The line highlighted in bold shows an example of the Inherits directive and Src directive in the @Page portion of the previously discussed directives. The source of the code-behind page is described in the Src value, and the value of inherits describes the class name that you will see in the following code-behind pages. Notice that the class name in the @Page directive is identical to the class name in the code-behind page.

Visual Basic .NET—codebehind_vb.vb

```vb
Imports System
Imports System.Web.UI
Imports System.Web.UI.WebControls
Imports System.Web.UI.HtmlControls


Public Class vbsamplecodebehind
    Inherits Page

    Protected WithEvents myLabel as Label
    Protected WithEvents myList as ListBox
    Protected WithEvents myDropdown as DropDownList

    Sub SubmitThis( s As Object, e As EventArgs )
        myLabel.Text = "You Selected: " + myList.SelectedItem.Text + " and " +
        ➥myDropdown.SelectedItem.Value

    End Sub

    Sub Page_Load
        myLabel.Text = ""
    End Sub
End Class
```

C#—codebehind_cs.cs

```csharp
using System;
using System.Web.UI;
using System.Web.UI.WebControls;
using System.Web.UI.HtmlControls;


public class cssamplecodebehind   : System.Web.UI.Page
    {
    protected Label myLabel;
    protected ListBox myList;
    protected DropDownList myDropdown;

    public void SubmitThis(object s, EventArgs e )
    {
        myLabel.Text = "You Selected: " + myList.SelectedItem.Text + " and " +
        ➥myDropdown.SelectedItem.Value;
    }


    void Page_Load()
    {
        myLabel.Text = "";
    }
}
```

You can see in Figure 4.11 that you will get the exact results you'd expect, and to the user the functionality of the page is identical to that of the page that doesn't use code-behind.

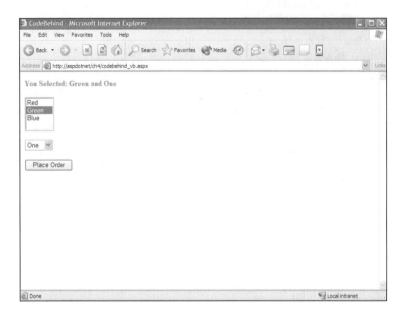

It is very cool that you can separate code out even further than just by having all the logic at the top of the page and the content or display aspects after that, but that doesn't come without a bit of a price.

Like every convenience, it comes at a cost, and with regard to code-behind the cost comes in the form of more typing. I explain as I go through the highlighted portions of the code-behind example.

First (though not part of the price) I'd like you to take notice of the classname called either vbsamplecodebehind or cssamplecodebehind, depending on the language you use. This is the class that is created in the code-behind page and what is inherited in the @page directive in the ASP.NET page with the .aspx extension.

Now on to the price you pay for the additional layer of separation provided by code-behind. First, code-behind pages don't automatically import any namespaces, as .aspx pages do, so you must explicitly include them into your code-behind pages. In Visual Basic .NET you use the `Imports` keyword to do this and in C# you use the `using` keyword.

Second, you must create a class to contain the logical code in your code-behind page so that you can inherit this class into your .aspx page.

And third, you must create instances of every object that is in your .aspx page that you will reference in your code-behind page. You do this in the same way that you would create any other object, but you must assure that the name of the object you create in your code-behind page is identical to the ID of your object on the .aspx page.

If your pages are very complex, the number of namespaces and objects you need to create in your code-behind pages can be extensive, and the extra work can outweigh the advantage of being able to separate out your code this way. You'll need to consider this, of course, as part of a personal or team decision on which method you'll use to create your ASP.NET pages, but it's nice to have the options.

Also note that the extension of the code-behind page is either .vb or .cs, depending on what language your code-behind page contains. This extension is what tells the .NET Framework what language your code-behind page contains. Another small nugget of code-behind is that you aren't forced to use the same language your .aspx file uses in your code-behind pages. In other words, you could have easily used a C# code-behind page in a Visual Basic .NET .aspx page or vice-versa. As long as the classname and source in the .aspx page's @page directive correctly match the class of our code-behind page, your page will work properly.

Summary

Now that you've explored ASP.NET pages and dug into some of their core functions, you can now move onto more of the tools provided by ASP.NET to simplify design features and aspects. (You didn't think this whole book was going to be about how to code in ASP.NET.) In the next chapter you're going to explore ASP.NET User controls and see how they open up a whole new world for you as a designer.

5

Understanding User Controls

It's better than your average Include!

"**Y**ou know, in the olden days we used to program pages for the web in classics like Notepad and SimpleText. We didn't have any of these new fangled editors with any of that code highlighting and stuff like that. And we were happy with our simple include files. So they were hard to use—but that's back when we understood the value of a dollar and a hard day's work. These kids today don't value nothing!! And they had to improve on our beloved include files. Huh, improved on my corns and bunions, that's what they shoulda done. Or figured out how to make my dentures stay in better. There was absolutely nothing wrong with include files. We used em, and these young whipper snappers ought to use em too!!"

Well, Clyde the classic web programmer might be having a hard time accepting that the beloved include file is on its way out, but you shouldn't.

What Are User Controls?

User controls are an answer to prayers we have been secretly been petitioning the web gods about. Include files have always been a semi-answer to simple code reuse in web pages, but there are several inherent problems with include files that have been powerfully addressed by User controls.

User controls are essentially reusable blocks of code focused for user interface purposes. They are available to reuse as common components across your web application. They aren't magic or really any different than ASP.NET pages, except that they are created and formatted in a particular way so that they may be reused across your application.

As Clyde said earlier, SSIs (or Server Side Include files) partially filled this gap and provided the most flexible solution for providing reusable blocks of code before ASP.NET, but they really had huge problems (better stated as *limitations*) associated with them as well.

The biggest difference between the two is again the biggest difference between traditional ASP and ASP.NET. User controls operate under the same object-oriented paradigm and are treated as objects in your ASP.NET pages. These User controls can contain properties and methods just like any other object. They can be manipulated programmatically, just like other server controls in ASP.NET. You can even use code behind techniques in User controls to further separate UI function from logical programming.

Another annoying characteristic of include files is that all paths to images must be full paths. If you tried to insert images with document-relative paths, you would run into broken links if the file you were inserting the include file into didn't have the exact path to the images folder that the include file did.

Now it may not sound like a big deal to have to insert fully qualified paths using full protocol and domain name or IP address as well as file structure, but let me point out where the hassle begins. What if you do development on one system and move the site into production on another? In development you would have to have your full paths point to a local IP address such as `http://192.168.1.100/ images/image.gif`, but when you were ready to go live into production all of these paths would need to be changed to replace the IP with your domain. Not only was this a big pain in the behind but it left tons of room for mishap and errors. Nothing like making sweeping changes to file paths just before you go live with a site without being able to test it thoroughly.

As I've said, User controls replace the function of SSIs and solve these problems, not by enhancing the function of SSIs, but by approaching it from a totally .NET point of view. ASP.NET does allow you to continue to use SSIs in the traditional sense, just as you have in the past, but after you are finished with this chapter I doubt you will see the point of that.

User Control Creation Techniques

User controls can be created in a method similar to the way you create your typical ASP.NET web form pages. The primary difference between ASP.NET web form pages and User controls is that User controls do not include `<html><body>` and `<form runat="server">` tags within them. These tags would already be included in your ASP.NET web form page.

ASP.NET pages can contain only one `<form runat="server">` tag per page. You can include as many standard `<form>` tags as you'd like, but there can be only one "web form" per ASP.NET page.

Creating User Controls

Let's start out with a simple example of a form box that asks what the password is and go from there. The following are the User control pages. Notice that a User control must have a file extension of .ascx.

Visual Basic .NET—`uc_simple_vb.ascx`

```vb
<script language="vb" runat=server>
Sub Btn_Click(Sender as Object, E as EventArgs)
    if thepassword.Text.ToLower = "holy grail" then
        OurLabel.Text = "You have chosen wisely!"
    else
        OurLabel.Text = "You have chosen poorly!"
    end if
End Sub
</script>
<table width="200" border="0" cellspacing="0" cellpadding="5">
<tr>
<td><div align="center">
<asp:Textbox TextBoxMode="password" id="thepassword" runat="server"/>
</div></td>
</tr>
<tr>
<td>
```

continues

Visual Basic .NET—(continued)

```
<div align="center">
<asp:Button id="Password_Btn" text="What's the password?"  OnClick="Btn_Click"
➥runat="server"/>
</div>
</td>
</tr>
<tr>
<td><div align="center">
<asp:Label id="OurLabel" runat="server"/>
</div></td>
</tr>
</table>
```

C#—uc_simple_cs.ascx

```
<script  language="c#" runat=server>
void Btn_Click(object Source, System.EventArgs s){
    if (thepassword.Text.ToLower() == "holy grail"){
        OurLabel.Text = "You have chosen wisely!";
    }else{
        OurLabel.Text = "You have chosen poorly!";
    }
}
</script>
<table width="200" border="0" cellspacing="0" cellpadding="5">
<tr>
<td><div align="center">
<asp:Textbox TextBoxMode="password" id="thepassword" runat="server"/>
</div></td>
</tr>
<tr>
<td>
<div align="center">
<asp:Button id="Password_Btn" text="What's the password?"  OnClick="Btn_Click"
➥runat="server"/>
</div>
</td>
</tr>
<tr>
<td><div align="center">
<asp:Label id="OurLabel" runat="server"/>
</div></td>
</tr>
</table>
```

As you can see, this page is really no different than a typical ASP.NET page with the exception of the tags mentioned earlier. We have some logical code and UI code that have some interplay when our button is clicked.

The following shows you the code of the ASP.NET web form page. Notice how the @Register directive that we explored in Chapter 5 is used to set up a custom tag name and tag prefix for the User control, and how it's plopped in wherever we want the User control inserted by referencing the custom tag created with this directive.

Visual Basic .NET—uc_simple_vb.aspx

```
<%@ page language="vb" EnableViewState="false" runat="server"%>
<%@Register TagPrefix="Peter" Tagname="PasswordTest" Src="uc_simple_vb.ascx"%>
<script runat="server">

Sub Page_Load()
    OurTitle.Text = "<u><b>What is your Quest?<br>I seek the . . . </b></u>"
End Sub

</script>
<html>
<title>User Controls - Simple</title>
<body>
<form id="passwordform" runat="server">
<table width="200" border="0" cellspacing="0" cellpadding="0">
<tr>
<td>
<div align="center">
<asp:label id="OurTitle" runat="server"/>
</div>
</td>
<tr>
<td>
<Peter:PasswordTest id="OurPassword" runat="server"/>
</td>
</tr>
</table>
</form>
</body>
</html>
```

C#—uc_simple_cs.aspx

```
<%@ page language="c#" EnableViewState="false" runat="server"%>
<%@Register TagPrefix="Peter" Tagname="PasswordTest" Src="uc_simple_cs.ascx"%>
<script runat="server">

void Page_Load(){
    OurTitle.Text = "<u><b>What is your Quest?<br>I seek the . . . </b></u>";
}

</script>
```

continues

C#—(continued)

```
<html>
<title>User Controls - Simple</title>
<body>
<form id="passwordform" runat="server">
<table width="200" border="0" cellspacing="0" cellpadding="0">
<tr>
<td>
<div align="center">
<asp:label id="OurTitle" runat="server"/>
</div>
</td>
<tr>
<td>
<Peter:PasswordTest id="OurPassword" runat="server"/>
</td>
</tr>
</table>
</form>
</body>
</html>
```

In Figure 5.1, you can see both what was in the .aspx page and also the content and functionality encapsulated inside the User control.

FIGURE 5.1

User controls offer a great tool for simple and effective code reuse.

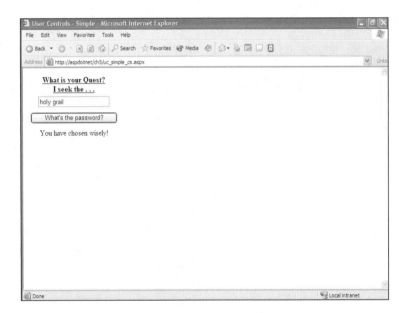

If you look at the rendered HTML you'll see that it's inserted the User control into the page seamlessly.

Generated HTML

```
<html>
<title>User Controls - Simple</title>
<body>
<form name="passwordform" method="post" action="uc_simple_vb.aspx"
➥id="passwordform">
<input type="hidden" name="__VIEWSTATE"
➥value="dDwtMzQyOTAzMjY2Ozs+sDEoFA1dlzcJtRzMTXy4Q/BrZJQ=" /><table width="200"
➥border="0" cellspacing="0" cellpadding="0">
<tr>
<td>
<div align="center">
<span id="OurTitle"><u><b>What is your Quest?<br>I seek the . . . </b></u></span>
</div>
</td>
<tr>
<td>
<table width="200" border="0" cellspacing="0" cellpadding="5">
<tr>
<td><div align="center">
<input name="OurPassword:thepassword" type="text" value="holy grail"
➥id="OurPassword_thepassword" TextBoxMode="password" />
</div></td>
</tr>
<tr>
<td>
<div align="center">
<input type="submit" name="OurPassword:Password_Btn" value="What's the password?"
➥id="OurPassword_Password_Btn" />
</div>
</td>
</tr>
<tr>
<td><div align="center">
<span id="OurPassword_OurLabel">You have chosen wisely!</span>
</div></td>
</tr>
</table>
</td>
</tr>
</table>
</form>
</body>
</html>
```

Sometimes (actually most times) it can be easier to create a User control by actually creating it first as a standard ASP.NET web form page and then converting it to a User control afterward. This gives you the flexibility to test it as a self-contained unit and debug it totally before you try including it in other pages where it can muddy the water and become difficult to debug. To convert an ASP.NET web form page into a User control, simply remove all the <html></html>, <body></body>, and <form runat="server"></form> tags from the page.

Using Code Behind in User Controls

Understanding that User controls are strikingly similar to standard ASP.NET web form pages, and that one of ASP.NET's goals is to help separate code from content, it only makes sense that you can utilize code behind techniques in User controls just like you do in ASP.NET pages.

Let's take the previous example and convert it to a user control that utilizes code behind. First, look at the code behind page.

Visual Basic .NET—uc_codebehind.vb

```
Imports System
Imports System.Web.UI
Imports System.Web.UI.WebControls

public class OurUCCodeBehind
    Inherits UserControl

    public thepassword as TextBox
    public OurLabel as Label

    Sub Btn_Click(Sender as Object, E as EventArgs)
    if thepassword.Text.ToLower = "holy grail" then
        OurLabel.Text = "You have chosen wisely!"
    else
        OurLabel.Text = "You have chosen poorly!"
    end if
    End Sub
End Class
```

C#—uc_codebehind.cs

```
using System;
using System.Web.UI;
using System.Web.UI.WebControls;

public class OurUCCodeBehind:UserControl{
```

```
public TextBox thepassword;
public Label OurLabel;

public void Btn_Click(object Source, System.EventArgs s){
    if (thepassword.Text.ToLower() == "holy grail"){
        OurLabel.Text = "You have chosen wisely!";
    }else{
        OurLabel.Text = "You have chosen poorly!";
    }
}
}
```

Notice again—just like in the discussion about code behind—that you must import the proper namespaces into your code behind page, as well as replicate instances of all needed objects as well. Now look at the User control.

Visual Basic .NET—`uc_codebehind_vb.ascx`

```
<%@control inherits="OurUCCodeBehind" src="uc_codebehind.vb" %>
<table width="200" border="0" cellspacing="0" cellpadding="5">
<tr>
<td><div align="center">
<asp:Textbox TextBoxMode="password" id="thepassword" runat="server"/>
</div></td>
</tr>
<tr>
<td>
<div align="center">
<asp:Button id="Password_Btn" text="What's the password?"  OnClick="Btn_Click"
➥runat="server"/>
</div>
</td>
</tr>
<tr>
<td><div align="center">
<asp:Label id="OurLabel" runat="server"/>
</div></td>
</tr>
</table>
```

C#—`uc_codebehind_cs.ascx`

```
<%@ control inherits = "OurUCCodeBehind" src = "uc_codebehind.cs" %>
<table width="200" border="0" cellspacing="0" cellpadding="5">
<tr>
<td><div align="center">
<asp:Textbox TextBoxMode="password" id="thepassword" runat="server"/>
</div></td>
</tr>
```

continues

C#—(continued)

```
<tr>
<td>
<div align="center">
<asp:Button id="Password_Btn" text="What's the password?"  OnClick="Btn_Click"
➥runat="server"/>
</div>
</td>
</tr>
<tr>
<td><div align="center">
<asp:Label id="OurLabel" runat="server"/>
</div></td>
</tr>
</table>
```

As you can see, the class name created in the code behind page is inherited into the User control the same way a code behind class is inherited into a standard ASP.NET web form page. Instead of this inheritance and source attribute being set in the @Page directive, it is set in the @Control directive. This is the User control's version of this directive (as discussed in Chapter 4). Just as you can have only one @Page directive on your ASP.NET page, you can have only one @Control directive on your User control pages.

Again, you are faced with the tradeoff that this layer of code separation requires: specifically, importing namespaces and initialization of objects in the code behind page. Again this comes down to personal or development team choice.

Exposing Properties and Methods to Your ASP.NET Pages

I've slipped and included some of what I am going to explain here in the previous example, but I didn't want to make the previous example too plain vanilla. I am trying to get the gears rolling in your head, and one way I like to do that is not giving examples that are so, well, *boring* when I introduce new concepts.

User controls are, as I've said at least twice if not three times, objects just like everything else in the .NET Framework, and because of this we can use them and their properties and methods in ASP.NET web form pages just like other objects. Here you'll investigate, explore, and uncover ways of using this stuff in your applications.

Properties

There are two different types of properties that are available for use in a User control. There is a public variable type, and there are properties that have explicit Get and Set functions that you can place logical code inside of, just like with the ball object you created in Chapter 2.

When you deal with the public variable type of property in User controls, you're dealing with a property just as you might deal with any server control or object. You can deal with them declaratively or programmatically. Take a look.

Visual Basic .NET—`uc_simple_property_vb.ascx`

```
<script  language="vb" runat=server>
Public OurLabelsText as String
Sub Page_Load()
    OurLabel.Text = OurLabelsText
End Sub
</script>
<asp:Label id="OurLabel" runat="server"/>
```

C#—`uc_ simple_property _cs.ascx`

```
<script  language="c#" runat=server>
public String OurLabelsText;
void Page_Load(){
    OurLabel.Text = OurLabelsText;
}
</script>
<asp:Label id="OurLabel" runat="server"/>
```

The first thing highlighted in this User control is the `public` variable. The `public` keyword is what makes it available outside of the code block in which it resides, hence exposing it for use in the ASP.NET page in which it's being included. The second thing that's highlighted is that the `Text` property of `OurLabel` is set to the value of this `public` variable. Now look at the ASP.NET web form page.

Visual Basic .NET —`uc_simple_property_vb.aspx`

```
<%@ page language="vb" EnableViewState="false" runat="server"%>
<%@Register TagPrefix="Peter" Tagname="PublicVariableExample"
➥Src="uc_simple_property_vb.ascx"%>
<script  runat=server>

Sub Page_Load()
    If Page.IsPostBack then
```

continues

Visual Basic .NET —(continued)

```
            OurPublicVariable.OurLabelsText = OurTextBox.Text
    End If
End Sub

</script>
<html>
<title>User Controls -  Public Variable</title>
<body>
<form id="publicvariableform" runat="server">
<table width="200" border="0" cellspacing="0" cellpadding="0">
<tr>
<td>
<div align="center">
<asp:Textbox id="OurTextbox" runat="server"/><br>
<asp:Button id="OurButton" text="Change Variable"  runat="server"/>
</div>
</td>
<tr>
<td>
<div align="center">
<Peter:PublicVariableExample OurLabelsText="It can't be this easy to access a
➥public variable" id="OurPublicVariable" runat="server"/>
</div>
</td>
</tr>
</table>
</form>
</body>
</html>
```

C#—uc_simple_property_cs.aspx

```
<%@ page language="cs" EnableViewState="false" runat="server"%>
<%@Register TagPrefix="Peter" Tagname="PublicVariableExample"
➥Src="uc_simple_property_cs.ascx"%>
<script  runat=server>

void Page_Load(){
    if (Page.IsPostBack){
        OurPublicVariable.OurLabelsText = OurTextbox.Text;
    }
}
</script>
<html>
<title>User Controls -  Public Variable</title>
<body>
```

```
<form id="publicvariableform" runat="server">
<table width="200" border="0" cellspacing="0" cellpadding="0">
<tr>
<td>
<div align="center">
<asp:Textbox id="OurTextbox" runat="server"/><br>
<asp:Button id="OurButton" text="Change Variable"  runat="server"/>
</div>
</td>
<tr>
<td>
<div align="center">
<Peter:PublicVariableExample OurLabelsText="It can't be this easy to access a
➥public variable" id="OurPublicVariable" runat="server"/>
</div>
</td>
</tr>
</table>
</form>
</body>
</html>
```

If you look at the two portions that I've highlighted in the ASP.NET pages, you will see two things. First, and actually farther down in the code, a value is declaratively set for the public variable when the OurLabelsText property of the custom tag is set. Then that value is programmatically changed up in the top of the page in the Page_Load event, where the Page's IsPostBack property is checked to see whether it is true. If it is, the OurLabelsText property is set to the value of the OurTextBox. This property passes the value to the public variable.

> **N o t e**
>
> Notice that we reference our User control as an object by referring to the ID value we set in the custom tag. In the preceding example, you see the Peter:PublicVariableExample tag has an ID of "OurPublicVariable". Then it and its OurLabelsText property are referenced the way you would any other object—by an object.property reference. To reference the Property of OurLabelsText, you would address it as OurPublicVariable .OurLabelsText (Object.Property). If you don't give your custom tag an ID, you won't be able to reference it like an object, and as a matter of fact, you won't be able to reference it at all.

In Figures 5.2 and 5.3, you can see the before and after results of this page's function and manipulation of this public variable.

FIGURE 5.2

On the initial page load, the public variable is set to the value that is declared in the custom tag.

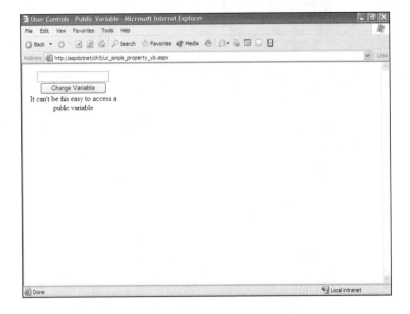

FIGURE 5.3

When you post back the page, the public variable is set to the value of the text box programmatically.

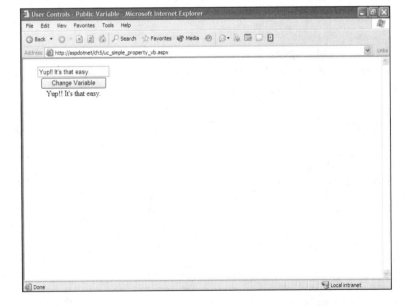

You can also manipulate properties in the User controls by creating get and set functions as a full blown property just like when you create properties for objects. You may want to do this to verify which type of data an individual put in a text box (although there are server controls that are much more powerful at this). The following is an example of using the set/get property method of using properties in User controls.

Visual Basic .NET User Control—uc_setget_property_vb.ascx

```vb
<script  language="vb" runat=server>
private DayOfWeek as String

public Property OurLabelsText as String
    get
        return OurLabel.Text
    end get
    set
        if (value.Length > 0) then
            Select(value.ToLower())
                case "monday"
                    DayOfWeek = "First day of the work week"
                case "tuesday"
                    DayOfWeek = "Second day of the work week"
                case "wednesday"
                    DayOfWeek = "Third day of the work week"
                case "thursday"
                    DayOfWeek = "Fourth day of the work week"
                case "friday"
                    DayOfWeek = "Last day of the work week"
                case "saturday"
                    DayOfWeek = "It's Saturday"
                case "sunday"
                    DayOfWeek = "It's Sunday"
                case else
                    DayOfWeek = "That doesn't appear to be an actual day."
            end Select
            OurLabel.Text = DayOfWeek
        else
            OurLabel.Text = "Please enter something in the textbox."
        end if
    end set
end property
</script>
<asp:Label id="OurLabel" runat="server"/>
```

Visual Basic .NET Web Form Page—uc_setget_property_vb.aspx

```
<%@ page language="vb" EnableViewState="false" runat="server"%>
<%@Register TagPrefix="Peter" Tagname="PublicVariableExample"
➥Src="uc_setget_property_vb.ascx"%>
<script  runat=server>

Sub Page_Load()
    if (Page.IsPostBack)
        SetProperty.OurLabelsText = OurTextbox.Text
    end if
end sub
</script>
<html>
<title>User Controls -  Public Variable</title>
<body>
<form id="propertyform" runat="server">
<table width="300" border="0" cellspacing="0" cellpadding="0">
<tr>
<td>
<div align="center">
Enter the name of a day (ie.Friday)<br>
<asp:Textbox id="OurTextbox" runat="server"/><br>
<asp:Button id="OurButton" text="Change Variable"  runat="server"/>
</div>
</td>
<tr>
<td>
<div align="center">
<Peter:PublicVariableExample id="SetProperty" runat="server"/>
</div>
</td>
</tr>
</table>
</form>
</body>
</html>
```

C# User Control Page—uc_setget_property_cs.ascx

```
<script  language="c#" runat=server>
private String DayOfWeek;

public String OurLabelsText{
    get{
        return OurLabel.Text;
        }
    set{
        if (value.Length > 0){
            switch(value.ToLower()){
                case "monday":
```

```
                DayOfWeek = "First day of the work week";
            break;

        case "tuesday":
            DayOfWeek = "Second day of the work week";
        break;

        case "wednesday":
            DayOfWeek = "Third day of the work week";
        break;

        case "thursday":
            DayOfWeek = "Fourth day of the work week";
        break;

        case "friday":
            DayOfWeek = "Last day of the work week";
        break;

        case "saturday":
            DayOfWeek = "It's Saturday";
        break;

        case "sunday":
            DayOfWeek = "It's Sunday";
        break;

        default:
            DayOfWeek = "That doesn't appear to be an actual day.";
        break;
        }
        OurLabel.Text = DayOfWeek;
    }else{
        OurLabel.Text = "Please enter something in the textbox.";
    }
    }
}
</script>
<asp:Label id="OurLabel" runat="server"/>
```

C# Web Form Page—uc_setget_property_cs.aspx

```
<%@ page language="cs" EnableViewState="false" runat="server"%>
<%@Register TagPrefix="Peter" Tagname="PublicVariableExample"
➥Src="uc_setget_property_cs.ascx"%>
<script  runat=server>

void Page_Load(){
    if (Page.IsPostBack){
        SetProperty.OurLabelsText = OurTextbox.Text;
    }
```

continues

C# Web Form Page—(continued)

```
}
</script>
<html>
<title>User Controls -  Public Variable</title>
<body>
<form id="propertyform" runat="server">
<table width="300" border="0" cellspacing="0" cellpadding="0">
<tr>
<td>
<div align="center">
Enter the name of a day (ie.Friday)<br>
<asp:Textbox id="OurTextbox" runat="server"/><br>
<asp:Button id="OurButton" text="Change Variable"  runat="server"/>
</div>
</td>
<tr>
<td>
<div align="center">
<Peter:PublicVariableExample id="SetProperty" runat="server"/>
</div>
</td>
</tr>
</table>
</form>
</body>
</html>
```

As you can see in Figure 5.4, the User control works without a hitch. If you look at the ASP.NET web form page, you can see that we check to see whether we are posting back using the Page's `IsPostBack` property.

In a postback, you set the value of the `OurLabelText` property to the value of the text box, just like you would with any other object. Then it runs through the `if` statement to check whether you entered anything in the box. It does so by seeing whether the property has any characters. If you entered anything in the box, the Length property will be greater than 0. What was entered then goes through the `Select`/`switch` statement to find out what day it matches, or if it doesn't match one of the cases, it defaults to tell you it didn't match. If the Length of the property returns as `0` (empty text box), then we tell you "Hey put somethin' in the box, willya."

This opens up some very interesting avenues for interaction between your ASP.NET web form pages and your User controls.

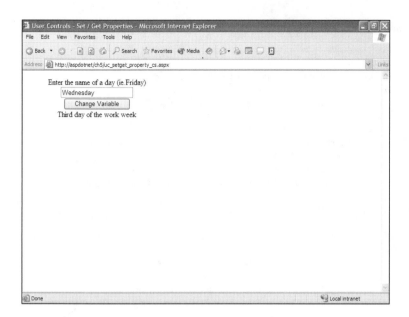

FIGURE 5.4

User controls also allow you to set and get properties just as you can with full featured objects.

Methods

Remember, the User control is an object, and objects can have methods, so it is safe to say that User controls can have methods. And is there a method to my madness or an end to this grief? One can never tell, but we hope against hope that the gods in heaven or the mother of all mankind will be kind and have mercy on our fragile souls that we may once again see the sun rise and be glad that another day has been granted us.

Huh?…whatever.

A User control exposes any public sub or function as a method of a User control object. So what's the difference between using a programmatic property (as we did in the previous example) and a method, you ask? Simple. You get to require multiple parameters being passed to a method instead of just the property's value, and you can overload a method as well. Remember that overloading a method is just a way of allowing different "signatures" or combinations of parameters and parameter types to be sent to a method.

Let's look at an example where you send can send a different number of parameters to a sub/function by overloading the method. Again, a parameter with a set/get can deal with delivering only one value to the User control, which is the value of the parameter. With methods, the number and combinations are limited only by your desire to limit the method.

Visual Basic .NET User Control—uc_method_vb.ascx

```
<script language="vb" runat=server>

public Sub OurMessage(Message as Integer)
    if (Message = 0) then
        OurLabel.Text = "You don't want a message"
    elseif (Message = 1) then
        OurLabel.Text = "You want the default message"
        OurOtherLabel.Text = "The default message is BLAHHHH!!!"
    elseif (Message = 2) then
        OurLabel.Text = "You want your own message"
        OurOtherLabel.Text = "But you didn't include a message"
    end if
end sub

public Sub OurMessage(Message as Integer,TheMessage as String)
    if (Message = 0) then
        OurLabel.Text = "You don't want a message"
    elseif (Message = 1) then
        OurLabel.Text = "You want the default message"
        OurOtherLabel.Text = "The default message is BLAHHHH!!! and we ignore your
➥message"
    elseif (Message = 2)
        OurLabel.Text = "You want your own message"
        OurOtherLabel.Text = TheMessage
    end if
end sub
</script>
<asp:Label id="OurLabel" runat="server"/><br>
<asp:Label id="OurOtherLabel" runat="server"/>
```

Visual Basic .NET Web Form—uc_method_vb.aspx

```
<%@ page language="vb" EnableViewState="false" runat="server"%>
<%@Register TagPrefix="Peter" Tagname="MethodExample" Src="uc_method_vb.ascx"%>
<script runat=server>

Sub Page_Load()
    if (Page.IsPostBack) then
        if (OurMessage.Text.Length > 0) then
            UCMethod.OurMessage(MessageType.SelectedIndex,OurMessage.Text)
        else
            UCMethod.OurMessage(MessageType.SelectedIndex)
        end if
    end if
end sub
</script>
<html>
<title>User Controls - Methods</title>
<body>
```

```
<form id="methodform" runat="server">
<table width="300" border="0" cellspacing="0" cellpadding="0">
<tr>
<td>
<div align="center">
Select the type of message.<br>
<asp:DropDownList id="MessageType" runat="server">
<asp:ListItem  text="No Message" />
<asp:ListItem  text="Default Message" />
<asp:ListItem  text="My Own Message" />
</asp:DropDownList>
<br>
Enter your message. .  if you dare!!!<br>
<asp:Textbox id="OurMessage" runat="server"/><br>
<asp:Button id="OurButton" text="Send Message"  runat="server"/>
</div>
</td>
<tr>
<td>
<div align="center">
<Peter:MethodExample id="UCMethod" runat="server"/>
</div>
</td>
</tr>
</table>
</form>
</body>
</html>
```

C# User Control—uc_method_cs.ascx

```
<script  language="c#" runat=server>

public void OurMessage(int Message){
    if (Message == 0){
        OurLabel.Text = "You don't want a message";
    }else if (Message == 1){
        OurLabel.Text = "You want the default message";
        OurOtherLabel.Text = "The default message is BLAHHHH!!!";
    }else if (Message == 2){
        OurLabel.Text = "You want your own message";
        OurOtherLabel.Text = "But you didn't include a message";
    }
}

public void OurMessage(int Message, string TheMessage){
    if (Message == 0){
        OurLabel.Text = "You don't want a message";
    }else if (Message == 1){
        OurLabel.Text = "You want the default message";
```

continues

C# User Control—(continued)

```
        OurOtherLabel.Text = "The default message is BLAHHHH!!! and we ignore your
➡message";
    }else if (Message == 2){
        OurLabel.Text = "You want your own message";
        OurOtherLabel.Text = TheMessage;
    }
}
</script>
<asp:Label id="OurLabel" runat="server"/><br>
<asp:Label id="OurOtherLabel" runat="server"/>
```

C# Web Form—uc_method_cs.aspx

```
<%@ page language="cs" EnableViewState="false" runat="server"%>
<%@Register TagPrefix="Peter" Tagname="MethodExample" Src="uc_method_cs.ascx"%>
<script  runat=server>

void Page_Load(){
    if (Page.IsPostBack){
        if (OurMessage.Text.Length > 0){
            UCMethod.OurMessage(MessageType.SelectedIndex,OurMessage.Text);
        }else{
            UCMethod.OurMessage(MessageType.SelectedIndex);
        }
    }
}
</script>
<html>
<title>User Controls -  Methods</title>
<body>
<form id="methodform" runat="server">
<table width="300" border="0" cellspacing="0" cellpadding="0">
<tr>
<td>
<div align="center">
Select the type of message.<br>
<asp:DropDownList id="MessageType" runat="server">
<asp:ListItem  text="No Message" />
<asp:ListItem  text="Default Message" />
<asp:ListItem  text="My Own Message" />
</asp:DropDownList>
<br>
Enter your message. .  if you dare!!!<br>
<asp:Textbox id="OurMessage" runat="server"/><br>
<asp:Button id="OurButton" text="Send Message"  runat="server"/>
</div>
</td>
<tr>
<td>
```

```
<div align="center">
<Peter:MethodExample id="UCMethod" runat="server"/>
</div>
</td>
</tr>
</table>
</form>
</body>
</html>
```

In the results in Figure 5.5, you can see that you can pass either one or two parameters to the method. The first version is executed when you leave the text box empty, because it triggers the first branch of the `if` statement contained in your `IsPostBack` check. The text box length is zero, so you call your method and send a single parameter.

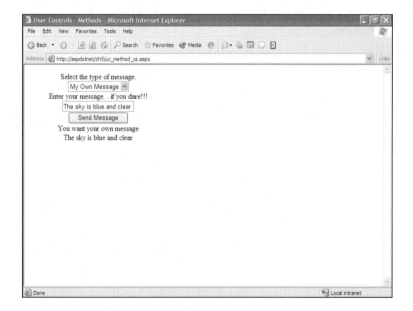

FIGURE 5.5

Exposing Methods in User controls opens up a lot of possibilities over just manipulating properties.

If there is something in the text box, then the `else` branch is triggered in the `if` statement contained in the `IsPostBack` check. This sends a method call with two parameters to the User control.

Notice that as with our parameters, we call our methods just like any other object by *objectname.methodname(parameters)*. Multiple parameters are separated by commas in User control methods, as well, like other objects.

Using the *LoadControl* Method

One more very cool feature of User controls (and a major yucky of SSIs) is that they can be dynamically loaded with logic. This isn't to say that you can't dynamically execute the code in SSIs. This you can do as follows:

```
<%if var = 1 then%>
<!--#include file="file1.inc" -->
<%else%>
<!--#include file="file2.inc" -->
<%end if%>
```

If var is equal to 1, then the code that is in file1.inc executes; otherwise the code in file2.inc executes. The thing to remember is that all the contents of both files will be included in the file, though. So if you have 10 include files with 200 lines of code each on your page, and only one of these will execute, you have a total of 2000 lines of code, 1800 of which aren't needed and just bog down your server.

The Loadcontrol method allows you to truly load User controls dynamically and treat them as objects and plop them on the page wherever you see fit.

In the following example, the value of an item in the QueryString is requested, and, based on that value, one control or another is loaded. This example demonstrates how you might dynamically load menus to different types of users. You would probably never use the QueryString to pass security or user information like this, but it is simple and easy to see for this example.

Following are two User controls, which are simply an HTML table containing different menu items. A known user will receive two more items than an anonymous user does. We control this by maintaining two different User controls that have this specific HTML in them. I am going to display the User control example code only once because it is identical for both languages.

Anonymous User—`uc_loadcontrol_au_vb.ascx` / `uc_loadcontrol_au_cs.ascx`

```
<table width="200" border="0" cellspacing="0" cellpadding="0">
<tr>
<td bgcolor="#000000">
<div align="center" style="color:#FFFFFF">Anonymous User</div>
</td>
</tr>
<tr>
<td bgcolor="#CCCCCC">
```

```
<div align="center"><a href="#">Menu Item 1</a></div>
</td>
</tr>
<tr>
<td bgcolor="#CCCCCC">
<div align="center"><a href="#">Menu Item 2</a></div>
</td>
</tr>
<tr>
<td bgcolor="#CCCCCC">
<div align="center"><a href="#">Menu Item 3</a></div>
</td>
</tr>
</table>
```

Known User—uc_loadcontrol_ku_vb.ascx / uc_loadcontrol_ku_cs.ascx

```
<table width="200" border="0" cellspacing="0" cellpadding="0">
<tr>
<td bgcolor="#000000">
<div align="center" style="color:#FFFFFF">Known User</div>
</td>
</tr>
<tr>
<td bgcolor="#CCCCCC">
<div align="center"><a href="#">Menu Item 1</a></div>
</td>
</tr>
<tr>
<td bgcolor="#CCCCCC">
<div align="center"><a href="#">Menu Item 2</a></div>
</td>
</tr>
<tr>
<td bgcolor="#CCCCCC">
<div align="center"><a href="#">Menu Item 3</a></div>
</td>
</tr>
<tr>
<td bgcolor="#CCCCCC">
<div align="center"><a href="#">Menu Item 4</a></div>
</td>
</tr>
<tr>
<td bgcolor="#CCCCCC">
<div align="center"><a href="#">Menu Item 5</a></div>
</td>
</tr>
</table>
```

Visual Basic .NET—`uc_loadcontrol_vb.aspx`

```
<%@ page language="vb" EnableViewState="false" runat="server"%>
<script runat=server>
Sub Page_Load()
    dim myControl as Control
    If lcase(Request.Params("user")) = "known" then
        myControl = Page.LoadControl("uc_loadcontrol_ku_vb.ascx")
    else
        myControl = Page.LoadControl("uc_loadcontrol_au_vb.ascx")
    end if
    myPlaceHolder.Controls.Add(myControl)
end sub
</script>
<html>
<title>User Controls -  Load Control</title>
<body>
<asp:PlaceHolder runat="server" id="myPlaceHolder" />
</body>
</html>
```

C#—`uc_loadcontrol_cs.aspx`

```
<%@ page language="cs" EnableViewState="false" runat="server"%>
<script runat=server>
void Page_Load(){
    Control myControl;
    if (Request.Params["user"] == "known"){
        myControl = Page.LoadControl("uc_loadcontrol_ku_vb.ascx");
    }else{
        myControl = Page.LoadControl("uc_loadcontrol_au_vb.ascx");
    }
    myPlaceHolder.Controls.Add(myControl);
}
</script>
<html>
<title>User Controls -  Load Control</title>
<body>
<asp:PlaceHolder runat="server" id="myPlaceHolder" />
</body>
</html>
```

As you can see in Figures 5.6 and 5.7, the correct menu was loaded for the appropriate users. This is one simple example of how using the LoadControl for User controls can give you additional power to deliver user-specific content in your ASP.NET web applications. And power is good, I always say.

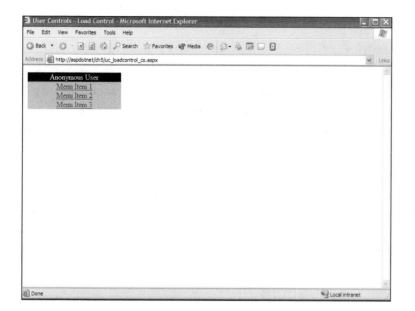

FIGURE 5.6

When there is no QueryString value, the User control for Anonymous Users is loaded.

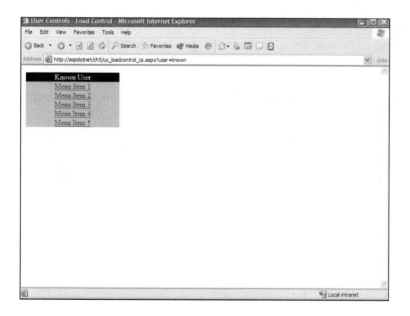

FIGURE 5.7

When you identify the user as known, the User control for Known Users is delivered and loaded.

Now look at the line of code that reads as follows:

```
myControl = Page.LoadControl("uc_loadcontrol_ku_vb.ascx");
```

This line uses the `Page.LoadControl` method to create a User control object named `myControl`. Two of these statements populate `myControl` with one of the two files, based on a value in the QueryString called `user`. If user=known, then we load for known users; otherwise, we load the User control for anonymous users. Look at the next relevant line:

```
myPlaceHolder.Controls.Add(myControl);
```

Down in the body of the .aspx page is a generic placeholder object that is just waiting for something to be added to it. You do just that with the preceding line of code by using the `Control.Add()` method. This is a great way of dynamically controlling what control, or even whether a control, should be displayed.

Summary

We have gone through a bunch of the building blocks that make ASP.NET applications possible, and up to this point you have been given a good foundation. Starting with the next chapter, you can really dig deeper into the meat of ASP.NET. You'll start off by learning about different controls, then progress through to the cool form validators, data access, state management, and security, and finally even touch on XML.

By the time you're through with this book, I'll have to worry whether I'll get to do a follow-up title to this book or New Riders will be calling you to write it. (P.S. Writing a book is a lot harder than you'd think, especially for a lughead like me.)

<Part> **II**

DESIGNING WITH ASP.NET

chapter 6

HTML Server Controls

Can we demonstrate a little HTML
control here?

Ahhhh!!! Now that we are through building a foundation, we can really sink
our teeth into ASP.NET and all the great stuff it has to offer. Microsoft has put
a lot of thought into ASP.NET—three years plus. They've done two incredible
things for web developers like you and me: They've built a framework (remember
skeleton) that is built of great objects that cover the gamut of typical web design
needs, and they have made a platform of extensibility that gives developers the
ability to fill in the gaps and dream up crazy outside-the-box objects that can do
just about anything you can imagine.

You are going to spend the next few chapters checking out the key objects that
are part of the .NET Framework. We'll poke, prod, and stretch these objects to
really see what they can do. This chapter starts with HTML server controls.

Working with HTML Server Controls

As you go through this section, you may begin to think, "These things look kinda familiar, Peter, and they ain't so innovative." But don't be deceived by their initial appearance; server controls are much more powerful than you think they are.

You see, HTML server controls are very much like the familiar HTML tags, with one difference: RUNAT="SERVER". That beautiful phrase, those lovely 14 characters change average HTML tags into SUPER TAGS with magical mystical powers. Well, not quite, but they do become…OBJECTS!! Yeah! Oh baby, oh baby. Objects are so cool, and HTML server controls are objects. What does that mean? They have all the advantages of being approachable from an event/object-oriented programming paradigm.

This means that you can manipulate the attributes, retrieve information, and affect with events standard HTML tags like you never could before. This group of objects has been assembled in the System.Web.UI.HtmlControls namespace (remember, a namespace is simply a location system). There are 22 objects in this namespace, but not all of them are for use on your ASP.NET pages. This brings up a topic that I'm going explain really briefly, but in reality we could spend much more time on it. That's the topic of inheritance.

We are not going to do an exhaustive study on inheritance here or anywhere in this book, for that matter, but I'm sure you understand the basics of inheritance from your everyday life experience.

I have green eyes and brown hair. These are traits, or, if you look at me as an object, *properties* that were given to me by my parents. I'm also left-handed, as are both my parents. I'm involved in computers just like my father. I have certain ways that I do things, or maybe you could call them *methods* of doing things, to better parallel an object. All these attributes, mannerisms, and traits are things that I inherited from my parents.

Objects have parents, too. The .NET Framework is full of inheritance that you just don't see. In the .NET Framework, all objects—yup, all of them—inherit methods from the System.Object class.

Some of the traits that I have gotten from my father probably came from my grandfather, or his grandfather. Inheritance as a concept travels across generations and generations. Each person through the years has also had personal traits that made him or her an individual, and with people inheritance is by chance. With .NET, inheritance is absolute. If an object is a parent of another object, the child object gets all the properties and methods of the parent.

HTML Control Classes

We aren't going to examine the entire family tree or hierarchy of an object's inheritance in this book, but you will learn about three objects in the `System.Web.UI.HtmlControls` namespace that are parents to the other remaining `HtmlControls`. The three parents are

- `HtmlControl`
- `HtmlContainerControl`
- `HtmlInput`

HtmlControl

The `HtmlControl` object is pretty important to HTML server controls. Why, you ask? Because every property and method it has is inherited by every HTML server control, that's why. If you learn the properties and methods of the `HtmlControl` class, you have learned about 80% of the properties and methods of all the objects in the `System.Web.UI.HtmlControls` namespace. This makes it pretty simple to understand the rest.

The HTML server controls have their own properties and methods, as well, but they all have the properties and methods contained in the `HtmlControl` object.

This isn't a complete or exhaustive list, but a list of the properties and methods you will most commonly use. I again encourage you to investigate the class browser located at `http://www.gotdotnet.com`.

I'm also going to show you a few tricks that inheritance allows and that you will be able to use to your advantage in coding your ASP.NET pages and having them deliver the code to the browser that you want. First take a look at the HtmlControl object's properties in Table 6.1

TABLE 6.1 *HtmlControl* Object Properties

Property	Description	Readonly
Attribute	Returns the object's attributes collection.	Yes
Disabled	A Boolean (true or false) value that you can get or set that indicates whether a control is disabled.	No
EnableViewState	A Boolean (true or false) value that you can get or set that indicates whether a control should maintain its viewstate.	No
ID	A string that you can get or set that defines the Identifier for the control.	No
Style	Returns the CSSStyleCollection for a control.	Yes
TagName	Returns the tag name of an element such as input or div.	Yes
Visible	A Boolean (true or false) value that you can get or set that indicates whether a control is rendered to HTML for delivery to the client's browser.	No

Most of these properties are self explanatory, but take a look at the Attribute and Style properties because they both might seem a bit mysterious to you at this point without a little explaination. I'm also going to show you a few tricks with these properties, as well.

Both of these properties may seem a bit odd to you, especially if you try to use them in your ASP.NET pages like this:

```
Response.Write(MyObject.Attributes) + "<br>"
Response.Write(MyObject.Styles)
```

This returns something that may also look a bit odd to you. This is what you'd get returned to your browser:

```
<html>
<head>
<title>HtmlControl</title>
</head>
<body>
System.Web.UI.AttributeCollection
<br>
System.Web.UI.CssStyleCollection
</body>
</html>
```

That doesn't seem very useful. What would you ever need to see that for? You really wouldn't, but what that shows is that these properties are a collection just like the form collection and the QueryString collection that was discussed in Chapter 4 on ASP.NET pages. This collection contains a name/value pair for every attribute or style belonging to the object in question. Take a look:

Visual Basic .NET—**control_collection_vb.aspx**

```
<%@ page language="vb" runat="server"%>
<script  runat=server>
Sub Page_Load()
    OurDiv.InnerHTML = "Our align attribute = " +
    ➥OurDiv.Attributes("align") + "<br>"
    OurDiv.InnerHTML += "Our font-size style = " +
    ➥OurDiv.Style("font-size")
End Sub
</script>
<html>
<head>
<title>HtmlControl Collections</title>
</head>
<body>
<div id="OurDiv" align="center" style="font-size:14px;
➥font-weight:bold" runat="server"/>
</body>
</html>
```

C#—`control_collection_cs.aspx`

```
<%@ page language="cs" runat="server"%>
<script  runat=server>
void Page_Load(){
    OurDiv.InnerHtml = "Our align attribute = " +
    ➥OurDiv.Attributes["align"] + "<br>";
    OurDiv.InnerHtml += "Our font-size style = " +
    ➥OurDiv.Style["font-size"];
}
</script>
<html>
<head>
<title>HtmlControl Collections</title>
</head>
<body>
<div id="OurDiv" align="center" style="font-size:14px;
➥font-weight:bold" runat="server"/>
</body>
</html>
```

As you can see in Figure 6.1, specific items are now being retrieved in the `AttributeCollection` and `StyleCollection`. As Chapter 4 described, the `Response` and `Request` properties of the page are really just instances of other objects. You can also say that `Attribute` and `Style` are instances of the `System.Web.UI.AttributeCollection` and `System.Web.UI.StyleCollection`. This is inheritance, as well.

FIGURE 6.1

You can retrieve the values of specific attributes and styles within the Attributes *and* Styles *collection.*

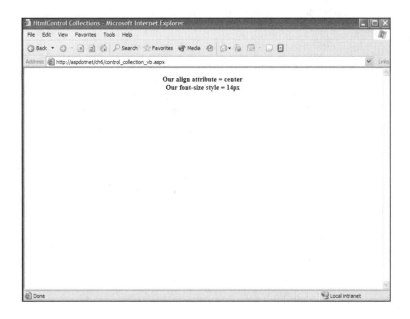

This is where you can do some fun stuff now that you understand inheritance a bit better. You know that you are really accessing different classes with both the `Attributes` and `Styles` properties. In the `HtmlControl`, these properties are read-only. It appears that you can't set an attribute or a style to any of the HTML server controls because they are read-only properties. This is true, but only if you look at it on the surface. But because `Attribute` and `Style` are really instances of the `AttributeCollection` and the `StyleCollection`, you can use its properties and methods, too.

There are two ways you can approach these collections. You can set the value of a specified item as part of the collection, or you can call a method. To set the value of a specific item of the collection, do the reverse of getting the item as you did in the previous code example.

Both these collections also have an `Add()` method that take two arguments, like this: `Add("Name","Value")`. You can use this method to add attributes and styles to all your `HtmlControl`'s tags. Look at these two different approaches in action.

Visual Basic .NET—`control_addattstyle_vb.aspx`

```
<%@ page language="vb" runat="server"%>
<script  runat=server>
Sub Page_Load()
    OurDiv.InnerHtml = "This is the displayed text"
    OurDiv.Attributes("align")= "center"
    OurDiv.Style.Add("font-size","14px")
End Sub
</script>
<html>
<head>
<title>HtmlControl Collections</title>
</head>
<body>
<div id="OurDiv" style="font-weight:bold" runat="server"/>
</body>
</html>
```

C#—`control_addattstyle_cs.aspx`

```
<%@ page language="cs" runat="server"%>
<script  runat=server>
void Page_Load(){
    OurDiv.InnerHtml = "This is the displayed text";
    OurDiv.Attributes["align"] = "center";
    OurDiv.Style.Add("font-size","14px");
}
</script>
<html>
<head>
<title>HtmlControl Collections</title>
</head>
<body>
<div id="OurDiv" style="font-weight:bold" runat="server"/>
</body>
</html>
```

N O T E

Notice again that when you refer to a specific item in a collection of items like this that C# uses square brackets around the item name and Visual Basic .NET uses parentheses.

In the preceding code example, I used the "set item value" approach to add an attribute to the tag. I used the `Add()` method in these examples to add a style to the tag.

Following is the resulting HTML. You can see that the attribute and the style have been added to the `Div` tag. Notice also that .NET is smart enough to know that a style tag already exists, so it simply appended the `font-size:14px` to the already existing `font-weight:bold` style and separated them with a semicolon.

```
<html>
<head>
<title>HtmlControl Collections</title>
</head>
<body>
<div id="OurDiv" style="font-weight:bold;font-size:14px;"
➥align="center">This is the displayed text</div>
</body>
</html>
```

This comes in handy and gives you another tool for manipulating and programming in your ASP.NET applications. Keep this in the back of your mind because I'm sure it will be a handy solution for you at some time during ASP.NET development.

HtmlContainerControl

HtmlContainerControl is used as the parent for any HTML control that requires a closing tag, such as div, form, or select. This class actually inherits all its properties and methods from the HtmlControl class and adds a few of its own. So to clarify, any object that is a container-type object doesn't directly inherit from the HtmlControl class we just discussed. The HtmlContainerControl actually inherits the HtmlControl, and then when a container-type object uses the HtmlContainerControl it gets the HtmlControl class's objects that way.

The two properties that an HtmlContainerControl bring to the party are InnerText and InnerHtml. These properties basically do the same thing. They stick stuff between the open and closing tags of the container-type tag. They just handle the way it's inserted differently. Take a look.

Visual Basic .NET—**html_container_vb.aspx**

```
<%@ page language="vb" runat="server"%>
<script  runat=server>
Sub Page_Load()
    dim OurText as String = "<b>Wow!!</b> This is really <i>Cool!</i>"
    OurDiv.InnerHtml = OurText
    OurDiv2.InnerText = OurText
End Sub
</script>
<html>
<head>
<title>HtmlControl InnerStuff</title>
</head>
<body>
<div id="OurDiv" style="font-size:14px" runat="server"/>
<div id="OurDiv2" style="font-size:14px" runat="server"/>
</body>
</html>
```

C#—html_container_cs.aspx

```
<%@ page language="cs" runat="server"%>
<script  runat=server>
void Page_Load(){
    string OurText = "<b>Wow!!</b> This is really <i>Cool!</i>";
    OurDiv.InnerHtml = OurText;
    OurDiv2.InnerText = OurText;
}
</script>
<html>
<head>
<title>HtmlControl InnerStuff</title>
</head>
<body>
<div id="OurDiv" style="font-size:14px" runat="server"/>
<div id="OurDiv2" style="font-size:14px" runat="server"/>
</body>
</html>
```

FIGURE 6.2

InnerHtml *and*
InnerText *give
you two different
ways to insert text
into a container-
type object.*

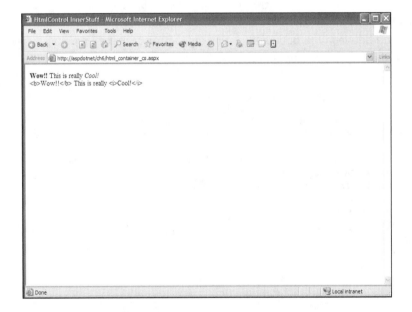

As you can see in Figure 6.2, `InnerHtml` and `InnerText` deal with the same exact string in two totally different ways. `OurDiv` is displaying the text and rendering it to the browser just the way you'd expect, but what happened to the text in `OurDiv2`? Look at the delivered file and try to figure it out.

```
<html>
<head>
<title>HtmlControl InnerStuff</title>
</head>
<body>
<div id="OurDiv" style="font-size:14px"><b>Wow!!</b> This is really
➡<i>Cool!</i></div>
<div id="OurDiv2" style="font-size:14px">&lt;b&gt;Wow!!&lt;/b&gt;
➡This is really &lt;i&gt;Cool!&lt;/i&gt;</div>
</body>
</html>
```

You can see that `OurDiv2` contains some wacky characters. What ASP.NET does when you set the `InnerText` property is it interprets all characters in your string into the format in which the character will actually be displayed in the browser. For instance, in this example, `&lt;` is what you would use to produce a less than sign (<) in a browser. ASP.NET interpreted all the characters to their displayable equivalent when using `InnerText`.

When using `InnerHtml`, it delivers your text to the HTML document with any HTML tags you used being properly interpreted. This is why when you used `InnerHtml`, the string of text appeared exactly as you'd expect in a browser.

HtmlInput

Just like the `HtmlContainerControl`, the `HtmlInput` inherits from the `HtmlControl` and adds a few properties of its own for the different object that live off it. It brings three additional properties to the table, as described in Table 6.2.

TABLE 6.2 *HtmlInput* Object Properties

Property	Description
Name	Gets or sets the unique name for the `HtmlInput` control.
Type	Determines what kind of `Input` element the `HtmlInput` control is.
Value	Gets or sets the value of the content of the `HtmlInput` object.

The `Name` and `Value` properties are pretty self-explanatory, but I think it might be helpful to list the potential types of `HtmlInput` controls that inherit from this class. All these are covered later in this chapter with explanations and examples. The list in Table 6.3 is just in preparation.

TABLE 6.3 *HtmlInput* Object Types

Type	Html Server Control	Tag
Button	HtmlInputButton	`<input type="button" runat="server">`
CheckBox	HtmlInputCheckBox	`<input type="checkbox" runat="server">`
File	HtmlInputFile	`<input type="file" runat="server">`
Hidden	HtmlInputHidden	`<input type="hidden" runat="server">`
Image	HtmlInputImage	`<input type="image" runat="server">`
Password	HtmlInputText	`<input type="password" runat="server">`
Radio	HtmlInputRadioButton	`<input type="radio" runat="server">`
Reset	HtmlInputButton	`<input type="reset" runat="server">`
Submit	HtmlInputButton	`<input type="submit" runat="server">`
Text	HtmlInputText	`<input type="text" runat="server">`

This covers the three parent or base classes for the objects in the `System.Web.UI.HtmlControls` namespace. Now let's start looking at them individually.

HTML Server Controls

Now that we've laid that ground work, you can begin to look at the specific HTML server controls. As I've said before, they are going to look very familiar because they are basically ASP.NET versions of existing HTML tags. Let's look at the HTML server controls.

HtmlAnchor

The HtmlAnchor is based off the HTML <a> tag and has the properties listed in Table 6.4 in addition to the HtmlContainerControl.

TABLE 6.4 *HtmlAnchor* Object Properties

Property	Description
Href	Gets or sets the URL to which the encapsulated item will link.
Name	Gets or sets the Name of the anchor element.
Target	Gets or sets the target frame or window in which the link will load. As with the HTML <a> tag, this is _self by default.
Title	Gets or sets the tooltip attribute of the <a> tag that is shown when you mouse over a text link.

The HtmlAnchor also raises the OnServerClick event, so you can use this server control to trigger subs and functions with this event. Take a look at some of these properties and this event in action. Notice in the following code that for the HtmlAnchor OnServerClick event to work, there must be a form tag with a runat="server" attribute surrounding the anchor.

Visual Basic .NET—**html_anchor_vb.aspx**

```
<%@ page language="vb" runat="server"%>
<script  runat=server>
Sub Page_Load()
    OurAnchor1.InnerText = "This will open a new window"
    OurAnchor2.InnerText = "This will link back to this page and run
    ➥a function"
    OurAnchor1.Href = "newpage.htm"
    OurAnchor1.Target = "_blank"
End Sub

Sub SetLabelText(sender As Object, e As System.EventArgs)
    OurLabel.Text = "You have clicked and triggered the
    ➥OnServerClick event"
```

continues

Visual Basic .NET—(continued)

```
End Sub
</script>
<html>
<head>
<title>HtmlControl Anchor</title>
</head>
<body>
<form runat="server">
<a id="OurAnchor1" runat="server"/>
<br>
<a id="OurAnchor2" onserverclick="SetLabelText" runat="server"/>
<br>
<ASP:Label id="OurLabel" runat="server"/>
</form>
</body>
</html>
```

C#—html_anchor_cs.aspx

```
<%@ page language="cs" runat="server"%>
<script  runat=server>
void Page_Load(){
    OurAnchor1.InnerText = "This will open a new window";
    OurAnchor2.InnerText = "This will link back to this page and run
    ➥a function";
    OurAnchor1.HRef = "newpage.htm";
    OurAnchor1.Target = "_blank";
}

void SetLabelText(object o, System.EventArgs s){
    OurLabel.Text = "You have clicked and triggered the
    ➥OnServerClick event";
}
</script>
<html>
<head>
<title>HtmlControl Anchor</title>
</head>
<body>
<form runat="server">
<a id="OurAnchor1" runat="server"/>
<br>
<a id="OurAnchor2" onserverclick="SetLabelText" runat="server"/>
<br>
<ASP:Label id="OurLabel" runat="server"/>
</form>
</body>
</html>
```

Resulting HTML

```
<a href="/ch6/newpage.htm" id="OurAnchor1" target="_blank">This will
➥open a new window</a>
<a id="OurAnchor2" href="javascript:__doPostBack('OurAnchor2','')"
➥>This will link back to this page and run a function</a>
```

Notice in the resulting HTML that OurAnchor1 has a target and href attribute as set in the Page_Load event. Because my browser is JavaScript-enabled, ASP.NET uses a JavaScript function to perform the OnServerClick event.

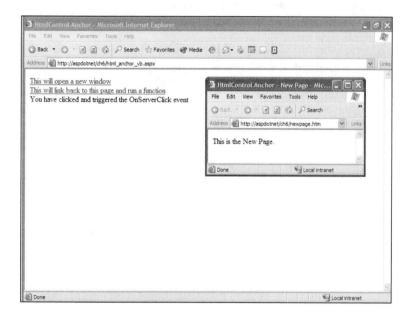

FIGURE 6.3

You can set attributes and raise events in <a> tags using the HtmlAnchor control.

HtmlButton

The HtmlButton class is based on the <button> tag. Take caution when you are using this HTML control. It is fully supported in Internet Explorer version 4 and later, but isn't supported in Netscape Navigator 4.x at all. Netscape Navigator 6 supports this tag, but I can't say I'm completely thrilled at its implementation. The only time we use button tags at our firm is when we know we are in a controlled environment in which Internet Explorer is being used.

This is a container tag that can hold HTML, such as <img> tags and the like. In the following example, I have created two buttons—one good and one naughty. These buttons have all the physical attributes of an <input> type form button except they can contain HTML.

The HtmlButton control also has an OnServerClick event that is used on both buttons in the following example. Notice that I set the content of the buttons and the styles of the two buttons in different ways. The "good" button has an image set as its InnerHtml property, whereas text is explicitly inserted between the opening and closing tags on the "naughty" button.

I also set the styles through the StyleCollection on the "good" button, but explicitly set the styles directly in the tag of the "naughty" button.

Visual Basic .NET—**html_button_vb.aspx**

```
<%@ page language="vb" runat="server"%>
<script  runat=server>
Sub Page_Load()
    OurButton.InnerHtml = "<img src=""images/our_button.gif"">"
    OurButton.Style("background-color")="#DDDDDD"
    OurButton.Style("border-color")="#000000"
    OurButton.Style("width")="150"
    OurButton.Style("height")="35"
End Sub

Sub SetLabelText(sender As Object, e As System.EventArgs)
    OurLabel.Text = "You have clicked the correct button. Very good"
End Sub
Sub SetLabelText2(sender As Object, e As System.EventArgs)
    OurLabel.Text = "You just couldn't resist, could you.<br> Now I've
    ➥got to take the bad button away.<br><b>Click the one that is
    ➥left, will ya?</b>"
    OurButton2.visible=false
End Sub
</script>
<html>
<head>
<title>HtmlControl Button</title>
</head>
<body>
<form runat="server">
<button id="OurButton" onServerClick="SetLabelText" runat="server"/> 
<button id="OurButton2" onServerClick="SetLabelText2"
➥style="background-color:#DDDDDD;border-color:
➥#000000;width:150;height:35" runat="server">Don't click
➥this button</button>
<br><br>
<ASP:Label id="OurLabel" runat="server"/>
</form>
</body>
</html>
```

C#—html_button_cs.aspx

```
<%@ page language="cs" runat="server"%>
<script  runat=server>
void Page_Load(){
    OurButton.InnerHtml = "<img src=images/our_button.gif>";
    OurButton.Style["background-color"]="#DDDDDD";
    OurButton.Style["border-color"]="#000000";
    OurButton.Style["width"]="150";
    OurButton.Style["height"]="35";
}

void SetLabelText(object o, System.EventArgs e){
    OurLabel.Text = "You have clicked the correct button. Very good";
}
void SetLabelText2(object o, System.EventArgs e){
    OurLabel.Text = "You just couldn't resist, could you.<br> Now I've
    got to take the bad button away.<br><b>Click the one that is left,
    will ya?</b>";
    OurButton2.Visible=false;
}
</script>
<html>
<head>
<title>HtmlControl Button</title>
</head>
<body>
<form runat="server">
<button id="OurButton" onServerClick="SetLabelText"
➡runat="server"/> 
<button id="OurButton2" onServerClick="SetLabelText2"
➡style="background-color:#DDDDDD;border-color:
➡#000000;width:150;height:35" runat="server">Don't click
➡this button</button>
<br><br>
<ASP:Label id="OurLabel" runat="server"/>
</form>
</body>
</html>
```

Resulting HTML

```
<button language="javascript" onclick="__doPostBack('OurButton','')" id="OurButton"
➡style="background-color:#DDDDDD;border-color:#000000;width:150;height:35;"><img
➡src="images/our_button.gif"></button>

<button language="javascript" onclick="__doPostBack('OurButton2','')"
➡id="OurButton2" style="background-color:#DDDDDD;
➡border-color:#000000;width:150;height:35">Don't click is button</button>
```

Notice in Figure 6.4 that there are two buttons, as expected. The first contains an image as its HTML between the opening and closing <button> tags, whereas the other button contains just text.

FIGURE 6.4

These are the rendered buttons on the page's first load. Notice that the button on the left contains an image as its content.

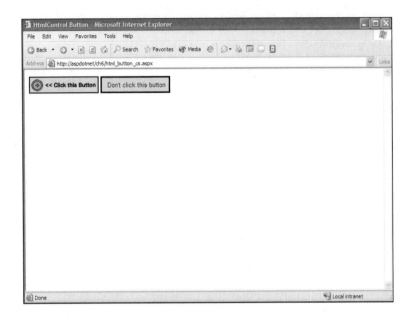

Also notice in Figure 6.5 that after clicking the "naughty" button we trigger the SetLabelText2 function with the OnServerClick event and set this button's Visible property to false. When the page is returned to the browser, the "naughty" button is gone and you get a tongue lashing.

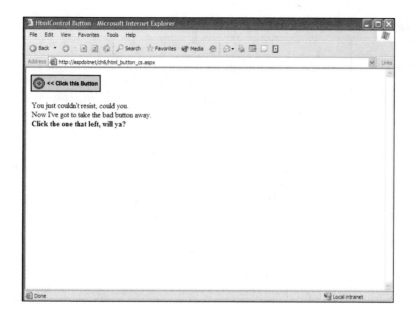

FIGURE 6.5

The button page after clicking the "Naughty" button and executing the SetLabelText2 *function. You get scolded and hide the "Naughty" button.*

HtmlForm

The HtmlForm class is the core of ASP.NET (see Table 6.5). It is what makes all the funky event-driven stuff we've been seeing like OnServerclick. The HtmlForm object is not a whole lot different from a standard HTML form, with two exceptions. First…you guessed it, runat="server"; and second, there is no accessible action attribute. An HtmlForm MUST post back to itself. This is at the root of ASP.NET web forms and their entrenched nature of using PostBack as a programming paradigm. Trust me—it is a good choice and the fact that you can't post your pages to other pages makes many other things such as server events and advanced form validation possible.

TABLE 6.5 *HtmlForm* Object Properties

Property	Description
EncType	This property instructs the browser on what encoding type to use when posting form data to the server. By default this is application/x-www-form-urlencoded, but if you are using an HtmlInputFile object for browsing and uploading files, you will need to change this property to multipart/form-data.
Method	This instructs the browser in what collection to send the form data. The Post() method places the form data in the form collection in the HTTP headers and can contain file attachments (such as files you want to upload). The Get() method places the form data in the QueryString (URL) collection, cannot have attachments, and is limited to 4Kb of data.
Name	This sets the name attribute of the <form> tag.
Target	Gets or sets the target frame or window to which the form will be posted. As with the HTML <form> tag, this is _self by default.

HtmlGenericControl

The HtmlGenericControl is available for providing properties and methods for HTML tags that the .NET Framework doesn't address with a specific object class. Examples of this would be the <body>, <span>, and <div>. None of these tags have their own dedicated HTML server control.

This object has a single exception to the other HTML server controls in that its TagName property is Read/Write instead of Readonly. Of course, if you think about this a little it makes sense, because you need to set the tag's Tagname to whatever generic element you want to runat="server".

You can set any available property or method available to the HtmlContainerControl to any HtmlGenericControl. In the following examples I am reiterating some things we've already covered with regard to setting properties and using methods to reinforce their use with the HtmlGenericControl.

Visual Basic .NET—html_generic_vb.aspx

```
<%@ page language="vb" runat="server"%>
<script  runat=server>
Sub Page_Load()
    OurBody.Attributes("bgcolor")="#CCCCCC"
    OurDiv.InnerHtml = "This text will be <b>Centered</b>"
    OurDiv.Attributes.Add("align","center")
    OurSpan.InnerText = "This is our span"
    OurSpan.Style("font-family")="arial,helvetica,sanserif"
End Sub
</script>
<html>
<head>
<title>HtmlControl Generic</title>
</head>
<body id="OurBody" runat="server">
<div id="OurDiv" runat="server"/>
<span id="OurSpan" runat="server"/>
</body>
</html>
```

C#—html_generic_cs.aspx

```
<%@ page language="cs" runat="server"%>
<script  runat=server>
void Page_Load(){
    OurBody.Attributes["bgcolor"]="#CCCCCC";
    OurDiv.InnerHtml = "This text will be <b>Centered</b>";
    OurDiv.Attributes.Add("align","center");
    OurSpan.InnerText = "This is our span";
    OurSpan.Style["font-family"]="arial,helvetica,sanserif";
}
</script>
<html>
<head>
<title>HtmlControl Button</title>
</head>
<body id="OurBody" runat="server">
<div id="OurDiv" runat="server"/>
<span id="OurSpan" runat="server"/>
</body>
</html>
```

As you can see in Figure 6.6, the <body> tag's bgcolor attribute was set to #CCCCCC, the <div> tag's align attribute was added through the AttributeCollection's Add method and set to align="center", and the <span> tag's font-family style was set to us sanserif fonts. This was all done by affecting these HtmlGenericControls programmatically during the Page_Load event.

FIGURE 6.6

The HtmlGenericControl allows you to manipulate properties and methods of HTML tags that don't have explicit corresponding HTML server controls.

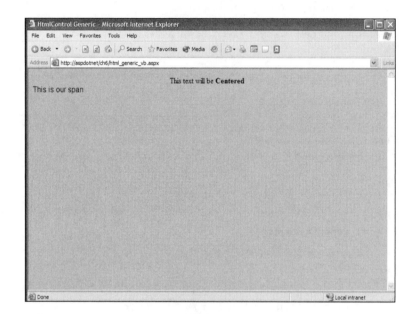

HtmlImage

The HtmlImage control, as you probably have guessed, is associated with the <img> tag in HTML. Table 6.6 describes the properties associated with the HtmlImage control.

TABLE 6.6 *HtmlImage* Object Properties

Property	Description
Align	Gets or sets the align property of the image object. This property affects where an image is rendered in relation to its surrounding content.
Alt	Gets or sets the text that displays when an image is moused over or delivered to voice HTML readers.
Border	Gets or sets the border width of a image in pixels.
Height	Gets or sets the height of the image in pixels.
Src	Gets or sets the path and image name that is the source of the image.
Width	Gets or sets the width of the image in pixels.

Let's take a look at manipulating the properties of the `HtmlImage` control.

Visual Basic .NET—`html_image_vb.aspx`

```
<%@ page language="vb" runat="server"%>
<script  runat=server>
Sub Page_Load()
    ProductImage.Src = "images/brown_jeans.jpg"
    ProductImage.Width = 176
    ProductImage.Height = 320
    ProductImage.Border = 1
End Sub

Sub ShowBrownJeans(sender As Object, e As System.EventArgs)
    ProductImage.Src = "images/brown_jeans.jpg"
End Sub

Sub ShowBlueJeans(sender As Object, e As System.EventArgs)
    ProductImage.Src = "images/blue_jeans.jpg"
End Sub
</script>
<html>
<head>
<title>HtmlControl Generic</title>
</head>
<body bgcolor="#FFFFFF" text="#000000">
<form runat="server">
<table width="500" border="0" cellspacing="0" cellpadding="2">
<tr bgcolor="#999999">
<td colspan="2">Peter's Denim Emporium</td>
</tr>
<tr>
<td width="150" bgcolor="#CCCCCC"> </td>
<td width="350">Product: Peter Jeans</td>
```

continues

Visual Basic .NET—(continued)

```
</tr>
<tr>
<td width="150" valign="top" align="center" bgcolor="#CCCCCC">
<u>Available Colors</u><br>
<a OnServerClick="ShowBrownJeans" runat="server">Brown</a><br>
<a OnServerClick="ShowBlueJeans" runat="server">Blue</a>
</td>
<td width="350" align="center">
<img id="ProductImage" runat="server"/>
</td>
</tr>
</table>
</form>
</body>
</html>
```

C#—html_image_cs.aspx

```
<%@ page language="cs" runat="server"%>
<script  runat=server>
void Page_Load(){
    ProductImage.Src = "images/brown_jeans.jpg";
    ProductImage.Width = 176;
    ProductImage.Height = 320;
    ProductImage.Border = 1;
}

void ShowBrownJeans(object o, System.EventArgs s){
    ProductImage.Src = "images/brown_jeans.jpg";
}

void ShowBlueJeans(object o, System.EventArgs s){
    ProductImage.Src = "images/blue_jeans.jpg";
}
</script>
<html>
<head>
<title>HtmlControl Generic</title>
</head>
<body bgcolor="#FFFFFF" text="#000000">
<form runat="server">
<table width="500" border="0" cellspacing="0" cellpadding="2">
<tr bgcolor="#999999">
<td colspan="2">Peter's Denim Emporium</td>
</tr>
<tr>
<td width="150" bgcolor="#CCCCCC"> </td>
<td width="350">Product: Peter Jeans</td>
</tr>
```

```
<tr>
<td width="150" valign="top" align="center" bgcolor="#CCCCCC">
<u>Available Colors</u><br>
<a OnServerClick="ShowBrownJeans" runat="server">Brown</a><br>
<a OnServerClick="ShowBlueJeans" runat="server">Blue</a>
</td>
<td width="350" align="center">
<img id="ProductImage" runat="server"/>
</td>
</tr>
</table>
</form>
</body>
</html>
```

You can see the result of this example in Figure 6.7. On Page_Load many of the properties of the HtmlImage object are set, but visitors are given the ability to see different colors of jeans based on their selections, and through functions the Src property of the HtmlImage object on the page is changed.

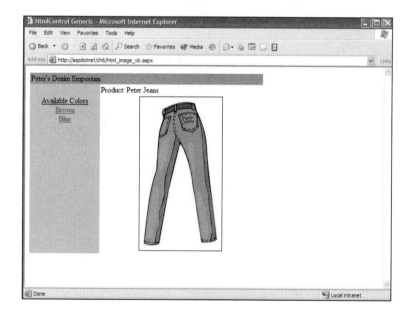

FIGURE 6.7

You can program-matically manipulate an HtmlImage *object's properties.*

HtmlInputButton

The HtmlInputButton object supports three different types of HTML input elements: Button, Submit, and Reset. These are parallel to their HTML counterparts and have all the same properties with the exception of one additional one.

The additional property is called CauseValidation, a Boolean value that is true by default. You would utilize this property only if you wanted to set it to false and override the processing of any validation you may be performing in your HtmlForm.

The HtmlInputButton can use the OnServerClick event for all three types. Take a look at some examples.

Visual Basic .NET—**html_inputbutton_vb.aspx**

```
<%@ page language="vb" runat="server"%>
<script  runat=server>
dim TextBox1Text as string  = "Insert your First Name"
dim TextBox2Text as string  = "Insert your Last Name"

Sub Page_Load()
    if (Page.IsPostBack)then
        OurSpan.InnerText = "Your Name is " + TextBox1.Value + " " +
        ➡ TextBox2.Value
    else
        TextBox1.Value = TextBox1Text
        TextBox2.Value = TextBox2Text
    end if
End Sub

Sub ReInitPage(sender As Object, e As System.EventArgs)
        TextBox1.Value = TextBox1Text
        TextBox2.Value = TextBox2Text
        OurSpan.InnerText = ""
End Sub
</script>
<html>
<head>
<title>HtmlControl Generic</title>
</head>
<body bgcolor="#FFFFFF" text="#000000">
<form runat="server">
<input type="text" id="TextBox1" runat="server"><br>
<input type="text" id="TextBox2" runat="server"><br>
<input type="submit" id="BtnSubmit" value="Submit Form" runat="server">
<input type="reset" id="BtnReset" value="Reset Values"
➡runat="server"><br>
```

```
<input type="button" id="BtnButton" OnServerClick="ReInitPage"
➥ value="Set Page to Original Settings" runat="server">
<br><br>
<span id="OurSpan" runat="server"/>
</form>
</body>
</html>
```

C#—html_inputbutton_cs.aspx

```
<%@ page language="cs" runat="server"%>
<script  runat=server>
string TextBox1Text = "Insert your First Name";
string TextBox2Text = "Insert your Last Name";

void Page_Load(){
    if (Page.IsPostBack){
        OurSpan.InnerText = "Your Name is " + TextBox1.Value + " " +
        ➥ TextBox2.Value;
    }else{
        TextBox1.Value = TextBox1Text;
        TextBox2.Value = TextBox2Text;
    }
}

void ReInitPage(object o, System.EventArgs s){
        TextBox1.Value = TextBox1Text;
        TextBox2.Value = TextBox2Text;
        OurSpan.InnerText = "";
}
</script>
<html>
<head>
<title>HtmlControl Generic</title>
</head>
<body bgcolor="#FFFFFF" text="#000000">
<form runat="server">
<input type="text" id="TextBox1" runat="server"><br>
<input type="text" id="TextBox2" runat="server"><br>
<input type="submit" id="BtnSubmit" value="Submit Form" runat="server">
<input type="reset" id="BtnReset" value="Reset Values"
➥runat="server"><br>
<input type="button" id="BtnButton" OnServerClick="ReInitPage"
➥value="Set Page to Original Settings" runat="server">
<br><br>
<span id="OurSpan" runat="server"/>
</form>
</body>
</html>
```

You can see the result of this example in Figure 6.8, where the three types of `HtmlInputButton` objects are rendered. The Submit type does a standard form submit, which will cause the `Page` object's `IsPostBack` property to be true and so that that branch will execute. The Reset type sets the form back to its original state when it was rendered to the browser. In this particular instance, this will either be the values set by the global variables, or `TextBox1Text` and `TextBox2Text` the first time the page has loaded, or whatever value you posted from the previous page.

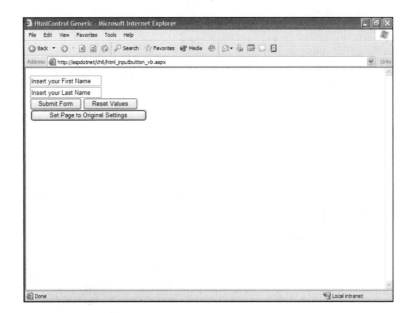

The Button type does whatever you tell it to through the `OnServerClick` event; in this case it sets the text boxes back to the value of the global variables and set the span's `InnerText` value to nothing. The Button type is similar to the `HtmlButton` in function. It is fortunately cross-browser-compatible, but unfortunately doesn't contain an `InnerHtml` property, so inserting images and other HTML elements isn't possible.

HtmlInputCheckBox

The `HtmlInputCheckBox` allows you to access and manipulate the property's `<input type="checkbox">`. This HTML server control has a property called `Checked` that you may Get or Set, and uses a different server event that you haven't seen yet, called `OnServerChange`.

OnServerChange can recognize whether the state of a check box has changed between posts. This doesn't submit the form or trigger the event immediately, but it lies in wait for the form to be posted by another means; then the event is fired.

Visual Basic .NET—**html1_inputcheckbox_vb.aspx**

```
<%@ page language="vb" runat="server"%>
<script  runat=server>

Sub InspectCheckBoxes(sender As Object, e As System.EventArgs)
    if CheckBox1.Checked = true then
        if CheckBox2.Checked = true then
            OurSpan.InnerText = "Both CheckBoxes are Checked"
        else
            OurSpan.InnerText = "Just CheckBox 1 is Checked"
        end if
    elseif CheckBox2.Checked = true then
            OurSpan.InnerText = "Just CheckBox 2 is Checked"
    else
            OurSpan.InnerText = "No CheckBoxes are Checked"
    end if
End Sub

Sub CheckBoxChanged(sender As Object, e As System.EventArgs)
    OurSpan2.InnerText = "You changed one of the CheckBoxes between
    submits"
End Sub
</script>
<html>
<head>
<title>HtmlControl InputCheckbox</title>
</head>
<body bgcolor="#FFFFFF" text="#000000">
<form runat="server">
CheckBox 1
<input type="checkbox" id="CheckBox1" OnServerChange="CheckBoxChanged"
➡ runat="server"><br>
CheckBox 2
<input type="checkbox" id="CheckBox2" OnServerChange="CheckBoxChanged"
➡ runat="server"><br>
<input type="submit" id="btn_submit" OnServerClick="InspectCheckBoxes"
➡runat="server">
<br><br>
<span id="OurSpan" runat="server"/><br>
<span id="OurSpan2" enableviewstate="false" runat="server"/>
</form>
</body>
</html>
```

C#—html_inputcheckbox_cs.aspx

```
<%@ page language="cs" runat="server"%>
<script  runat=server>

void InspectCheckBoxes(object o, System.EventArgs s){
    if (CheckBox1.Checked == true){
        if(CheckBox2.Checked == true){
            OurSpan.InnerText = "Both CheckBoxes are Checked";
        }else{
            OurSpan.InnerText = "Just CheckBox 1 is Checked";
        }
    }else if (CheckBox2.Checked == true){
            OurSpan.InnerText = "Just CheckBox 2 is Checked";
    }else{
            OurSpan.InnerText = "No CheckBoxes are Checked";
    }
}
void CheckBoxChanged(object o, System.EventArgs s){
    OurSpan2.InnerText = "You changed one of the CheckBoxes between
    submits";
}
</script>
<html>
<head>
<title>HtmlControl InputCheckbox</title>
</head>
<body bgcolor="#FFFFFF" text="#000000">
<form runat="server">
CheckBox 1
<input type="checkbox" id="CheckBox1" OnServerChange="CheckBoxChanged"
➥runat="server"><br>
CheckBox 2
<input type="checkbox" id="CheckBox2" OnServerChange="CheckBoxChanged"
➥runat="server"><br>
<input type="submit" id="btn_submit" OnServerClick="InspectCheckBoxes"
➥runat="server">
<br><br>
<span id="OurSpan" runat="server"/><br>
<span id="OurSpan2" enableviewstate="false" runat="server"/>
</form>
</body>
</html>
```

You can see the results of the preceding code in Figure 6.9.

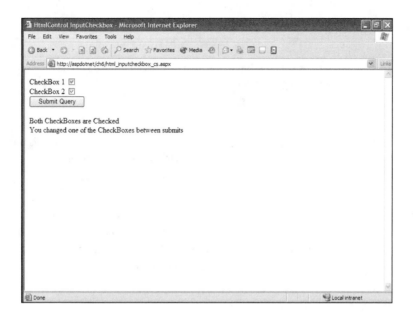

FIGURE 6.9

The `HtmlInputCheck Box` *has a* checked *property and an* `OnServerChange` *event at its disposal.*

HtmlInputFile

Yahoooeeee!!!!! This is another *huge improvement* in ASP.NET. Before, with traditional ASP, when you needed to provide a way for someone to upload a file, you generally needed to use a third-party component to provide the functionality, although there were a few other more complicated ways to do it without one. But these weren't always available, either, depending on what your hosting situation was and whether you were allowed to install components on your web server.

The .NET Framework has made a way. Can I hear a hallelujah? How about an amen? No matter what your religious beliefs you should shout out a big thank you because this is a REALLY AWESOME THING!!! The `HtmlInputFile` control has all you need to cure your uploading ills. It's got the properties. It's got the methods. It's got all that and more. Check out Table 6.7 for a look-see.

TABLE 6.7 *HtmlInputFile* Object Properties

Property	Description
Accept	Gets or sets the MIME encodings that can be used in the HtmlInputFile control.
MaxLength	Gets or sets the maximum length of the path statement for the file selected for upload.
PostFile	This is the magic property. It's really an instance of another class that is called HttpPostedFile, located in System.Web namespace.
Size	Gets or sets the size of the file textbox in the browser.

The Accept, MaxLength, and Size properties don't need to be addressed, but let's dig in a bit to the PostFile property. Like it says in the table, this is an instance of the HttpPostedFile class located in the System.Web namespace. It has three properties you can see in Table 6.8, and one magic method.

TABLE 6.8 *HttpPostedFile* Object Properties

Property	Description
ContentLength	Gets the size in bytes of an uploaded file.
ContentType	Gets the MIME content type of a uploaded file.
FileName	Gets the full path and filename for the upload file on the client's machine (example: c:\mydocuments\file.jpg).

The magical method is the SaveAs method. This saves an uploaded file to the server and bypasses the need for third-party components. The next code block demonstrates these properties and methods. I use the ContentType property to check and allow only JPEG images to be uploaded. I also use the ContentLength property to restrict the file size to allow only files that are under 20Kb to be uploaded.

Another thing to notice, and something you may remember from the HtmlForm section of this chapter, is that the form must contain the enctype= "multipart/form-data"; otherwise, it won't work.

Look for comments in the UploadFile function that will explain what stuff is going on and when. This may seem a bit complicated, but just follow the comments (Visual Basic .NET comment line starts with a single quote (') and a C# comment line starts with two forward slashes(//)).

Visual Basic .NET—**html_inputfile_vb.aspx**

```
<%@ Import Namespace="System.IO" %>
<script language="VB" runat="server">

Sub UploadFile(sender As Object, e As EventArgs)
    dim TheFile as String = FileBox.PostedFile.FileName
    If TheFile.Length > 0 Then
        dim FileType as String = FileBox.PostedFile.ContentType
        dim FileSize as Integer = FileBox.PostedFile.ContentLength

        'Check to see if the file is a JPEG
        if  FileType <> "image/jpeg" AND FileType <> "image/pjpeg" then
            OurSpan.InnerHtml = "You can <b>Only Upload Jpegs.</b> Got It?"
        'Check to see if file is larger than 20k
        elseif FileSize > 20000 then
            OurSpan.InnerHtml = "You can't upload a file bigger than
            20k. Yours was bigger."
        'if we pass both tests,proceed to try to upload file
        else
                'Build file path
            dim filepath as String = Mappath("") + "\uploadedfiles\"
                dim filename as String = TheFile.SubString
                ➥(TheFile.LastIndexOf("\")+1)
                dim fullpath = filepath + filename
                'Try to upload file
            Try

                    FileBox.PostedFile.SaveAs(fullpath)
                    OurSpan.InnerHtml = "A file named <b>" + filename
                    ➥+ "</b> was uploaded successfully<br>"
                    OurSpan.InnerHtml += "It was uploaded to the <b>"
                    ➥ + filepath + "</b> directory"
                Catch Exc As Exception
                    OurSpan.InnerHtml = "Error saving file <b>" &
                    ➥filename & "</b><br>" & Exc.ToString
                End Try
            end if
    Else
            OurSpan.InnerText = "Please specify a file to upload"
    End If
End Sub
</script>
<html>
<head>
<title>Html InputFile</title>
</head>
<body>
<form enctype="multipart/form-data" runat="server">
Upload a JPEG Image under 20k<br>
<input id="FileBox" type="file" runat="server"><br>
<input type=button id="btn_Submit" value="Upload"
➥OnServerClick="UploadFile" runat="server">
```

continues

Visual Basic .NET—(continued)

```
<br><span id="OurSpan" runat="server" />
</form>
</body>
</html>
```

C#—html_inputfile_cs.aspx

```vb
<%@ Import Namespace="System.IO" %>
<script language="VB" runat="server">

Sub UploadFile(sender As Object, e As EventArgs)
    dim TheFile as String = FileBox.PostedFile.FileName
    If TheFile.Length > 0 Then
        dim FileType as String = FileBox.PostedFile.ContentType
        dim FileSize as Integer = FileBox.PostedFile.ContentLength

        //Check to see if the file is a JPEG
        if  FileType <> "image/jpeg" AND FileType <> "image/pjpeg" then
            OurSpan.InnerHtml = "You can <b>Only Upload Jpegs.</b> Got It?"
        //Check to see if file is larger than 20k
        elseif FileSize > 20000 then
            OurSpan.InnerHtml = "You can't upload a file bigger than
            ➥ 20k. Yours was bigger."
        //if we pass both tests,proceed to try to upload file
        else
                //Build file path
            dim filepath as String = Mappath("") + "\uploadedfiles\"
                dim filename as String = TheFile.SubString
                ➥(TheFile.LastIndexOf("\")+1)
                dim fullpath = filepath + filename
                //Try to upload file
            Try
                    FileBox.PostedFile.SaveAs(fullpath)
                OurSpan.InnerHtml = "A file named <b>" + filename
                ➥+ "</b> was uploaded successfully<br>"
                OurSpan.InnerHtml += "It was uploaded to the <b>"
                ➥+ filepath + "</b> directory"
            Catch Exc As Exception
                OurSpan.InnerHtml = "Error saving file <b>" &
                ➥filename & "</b><br>" & Exc.ToString
            End Try
          end if
    Else
            OurSpan.InnerText = "Please specify a file to upload"
    End If
```

```
End Sub
</script>
<html>
<head>
<title>Html InputFile</title>
</head>
<body>
<form enctype="multipart/form-data" runat="server">
Upload a JPEG Image under 20k<br>
<input id="FileBox" type="file" runat="server"><br>
<input type=button id="btn_Submit" value="Upload"
➥OnServerClick="UploadFile" runat="server">
<br><span id="OurSpan" runat="server" />
</form>
</body>
</html>
```

In Figure 6.10 you can see the results of a successful JPEG file being uploaded to the server.

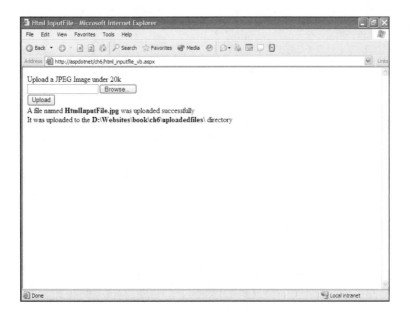

FIGURE 6.10

The .NET Framework supplies a way for you to upload files to a server without using any third-party components.

HtmlInputHidden

An HtmlInputHidden object allows access to properties of the <input type= "hidden"> object. This element is an intricate part of how ASP.NET maintains information from page to page and also how ASP.NET pages pass server event variables back to the server in a JavaScript enabled browser.

In the past, with traditional ASP, hidden form boxes were one way of persisting data from page to page. This needed to be done manually by the programmer. Now, thankfully, ASP.NET does this for you with ViewState and the use of hidden form boxes.

There still may be practical uses for this control in instances where you wish to pass data back to the server without it being visible or editable by the user.

The HtmlInputHidden control has no properties or methods of its own and simply inherits them from the HtmlInputControl.

A simple example of the code necessary for this control, which is applicable in both languages, looks like the following:

```
<input type="hidden" runat="server">
```

HtmlInputImage

The HtmlInputImage object is kinda like the best of all worlds to me when it comes to things that act like buttons. The HtmlButton object lets you insert an image into its content, but it isn't cross-browser compatible. The HtmlInputButton is kinda kludgy and homely without some cascading style sheet intervention. The HtmlInputImage object has all the function of an <input type="submit">, except that the image is visibly offset when you click it, and the great advantage of being able to use an image in the first place is so that your Submit buttons can look the way you'd like.

The HtmlInputImage object actually has all the same properties and methods that an HtmlImage has, with two nifty advantages. First, as I said, it submits the form in which it is contained, and second, it sends X,Y coordinates of the position where the image was clicked. This can be quite handy for a number of different situations in which knowing where a user clicked on an image might be helpful, such as a map. Notice that I use the ImageClickEventArgs from the System.Web.UI namespace in place of the standard EventArgs. This gives me access to the X,Y coordinates that are properties of this class.

Visual Basic .NET—**html_inputimage_vb.aspx**

```
<%@ page language="vb" runat="server"%>
<script  runat=server>

Sub PickDessert(o as object , e as ImageClickEventArgs)
    OurSpan.InnerText = "You picked "
      if e.X < 135 then
          if e.Y < 125 then
              OurSpan.InnerText += "Pumpkin Pie"
          else
              OurSpan.InnerText += "Ice Cream Sundae"
          end if
      else
          if e.Y < 125 then
              OurSpan.InnerText += "Cheesecake"
          else
              OurSpan.InnerText += "Cookies, These are my favorite too!"
          end if
      end if
end Sub
</script>
<html>
<head>
<title>HtmlControl InputImage</title>
</head>
<body bgcolor="#FFFFFF" text="#000000">
<form runat="server">
<div align="center">
<h2>What is your favorite dessert?</h2>
<input type="image" id="FavDessert" OnServerClick="PickDessert"
➥src="images/favorite_dessert.gif" runat="server">
<br><br>
<span id="OurSpan" runat="server"/>
</div>
</form>
</body>
</html>
```

C#—html_inputimage_cs.aspx

```
<%@ page language="cs" runat="server"%>
<script  runat=server>

void PickDessert(object o, ImageClickEventArgs e){
    OurSpan.InnerText = "You picked ";
    if (e.X < 135){
        if (e.Y < 125){
            OurSpan.InnerText += "Pumpkin Pie";
        }else{
            OurSpan.InnerText += "Ice Cream Sundae";
        }
    }else{
        if (e.Y < 125){
            OurSpan.InnerText += "Cheesecake";
        }else{
            OurSpan.InnerText += "Cookies, These are my favorite too!";
        }
    }
}
</script>
<html>
<head>
<title>HtmlControl InputImage</title>
</head>
<body bgcolor="#FFFFFF" text="#000000">
<form runat="server">
<div align="center">
<h2>What is your favorite dessert?</h2>
<input type="image" id="FavDessert" OnServerClick="PickDessert"
➥src="images/favorite_dessert.gif" runat="server">
<br><br>
<span id="OurSpan" runat="server"/>
</div>
</form>
</body>
</html>
```

You can see the results of these (and learn what my favorite dessert is, as well) in Figure 6.11.

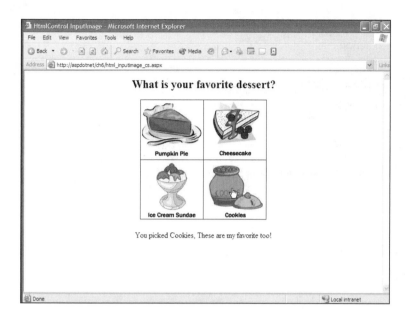

FIGURE 6.11

HtmlInputImage
*gives you access to
the X,Y coordinates
of where a user
clicked and acts like
a form submit as
well.*

HtmlInputRadioButton

The HtmlInputRadioButton is the server control counterpart to the HTML radio button (as if you couldn't figure that out). As if it weren't totally obvious that every single HTML server control has a matching HTML tag, and as if you're not smart enough to figure that out. Heck. Maybe I don't even need to write the rest of this chapter. Maybe nobody will notice if I just jump to the next chapter and forget about the rest of the server controls.

Anywho, the HtmlInputRadioButton has three additional properties that need to be mentioned, which are described in Table 6.9.

TABLE 6.9 *HtmlInputRadioButton* Object Properties

Property	Description
Checked	Gets or sets whether a radio button is the selected one in its group.
Name	Allows you to group radio buttons.
Value	Gets or sets the value of a radio button.

This control also has the `OnServerChange` event available for use. Now look at this control in action.

Visual Basic .NET—`html_radiobutton_vb.aspx`

```
<%@ page language="vb" runat="server"%>
<script  runat=server>

Sub InspectRadioButton(o as object, s as System.EventArgs)
    OurSpan.InnerText = "You picked " + Request.Form("Dessert")
    if Radio4.Checked then OurSpan.InnerText += ", That's my favorite too!"
End Sub

Sub CheckBoxChanged(o as object, s as System.EventArgs)
    OurSpan2.InnerText = "You changed your selection this time"
End Sub
</script>
<html>
<head>
<title>HtmlControl InputRadioButton</title>
</head>
<body bgcolor="#FFFFFF" text="#000000">
<form runat="server">
<h2>What is your favorite dessert?"</h2>
<input type="radio" id="Radio1" Name="Dessert" value="Pumpkin Pie"
➥OnServerChange="CheckBoxChanged" runat="server">
Pumpkin Pie<br>
<input type="radio" id="Radio2" Name="Dessert" value="Cheesecake"
➥OnServerChange="CheckBoxChanged" runat="server">➥
Cheesecake<br>
<input type="radio" id="Radio3" Name="Dessert" value="Ice Cream"
➥OnServerChange="CheckBoxChanged" runat="server">
Ice Cream<br>
<input type="radio" id="Radio4" Name="Dessert" value="Cookies"
➥OnServerChange="CheckBoxChanged" runat="server">
Cookies<br><br>
<input type="submit" id="btn_submit" OnServerClick="InspectRadioButton"
➥runat="server">
<br><br>
<span id="OurSpan" runat="server"/><br>
<span id="OurSpan2" enableviewstate="false" runat="server"/>
</form>
</body>
</html>
```

C#—html_radiobutton_cs.aspx

```
<%@ page language="cs" runat="server"%>
<script runat=server>

void InspectRadioButton(object o, System.EventArgs s){
    OurSpan.InnerText = "You picked " + Request.Form["Dessert"];
    if (Radio4.Checked)
        OurSpan.InnerText += ", That's my favorite too!";
}
void CheckBoxChanged(object o, System.EventArgs s){
    OurSpan2.InnerText = "You changed your selection this time";
}
</script>
<html>
<head>
<title>HtmlControl InputRadioButton</title>
</head>
<body bgcolor="#FFFFFF" text="#000000">
<form runat="server">
<h2>What is your favorite dessert?"</h2>
<input type="radio" id="Radio1" Name="Dessert" value="Pumpkin Pie"
➥OnServerChange="CheckBoxChanged" runat="server">
Pumpkin Pie<br>
<input type="radio" id="Radio2" Name="Dessert" value="Cheesecake"
➥OnServerChange="CheckBoxChanged" runat="server">-
Cheesecake<br>
<input type="radio" id="Radio3" Name="Dessert" value="Ice Cream"
➥OnServerChange="CheckBoxChanged" runat="server">
Ice Cream<br>
<input type="radio" id="Radio4" Name="Dessert" value="Cookies"
➥OnServerChange="CheckBoxChanged" runat="server">
Cookies<br><br>
<input type="submit" id="btn_submit" OnServerClick="InspectRadioButton"
➥runat="server">
<br><br>
<span id="OurSpan" runat="server"/><br>
<span id="OurSpan2" enableviewstate="false" runat="server"/>
</form>
</body>
</html>
```

You can see the results of this code in Figure 6.11. Notice in the code that I used
`Request.Form` to retrieve the value of which radio button was checked. This is a
time when programmatically finding out what a user selected is a bit more work
than reverting to using `Request.Form`. If I wanted to figure out which one of
the group was picked by the user by inspecting the `Checked` property, I'd have
to write a loop for each control in the group. In this way I get the value with a
simple request.

It is important to note that the Name property of the HtmlInputRadioButton must be the same for all HtmlInputRadioButtons that you'd like to group together.

I still use the checked property to see whether the user picked my favorite dessert, so both the more traditional way and the ASP.NET object way are useful and valid here.

FIGURE 6.12

The HtmlInputRadio-Button provides a way to manipulate and control radio buttons in ASP.NET.

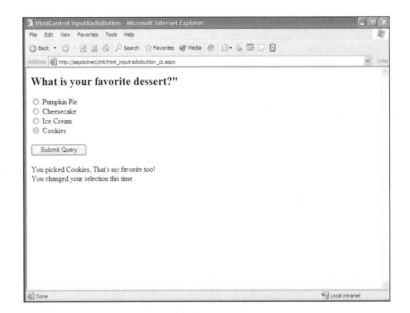

HtmlInputText

This server control takes care of both the <input type="text"> and <input type="password"> text box types. This server control has three additional properties available, described in Table 6.10.

TABLE 6.10 *HtmlInputText Object Properties*

Property	Description
MaxLength	Gets or sets the maximum allowable number of characters that a user can put in the text box or password box.
Size	Gets or sets how many characters wide the text box or password box is.
Value	Gets or sets the value of the text box or password box.

Both the text box and password box also make the OnServerChange event
available for programmatic use.

Visual Basic .NET—html_inputtext_vb.aspx

```vb
<%@ page language="vb" runat="server"%>
<script runat=server>

Sub Page_Load()
    if Page.IsPostBack then
        if Password.Value.ToLower() = "cookies" then
            OurSpan.InnerHtml = "<b>Hey " + Name.Value + ", You're In!!!"
        else
            if Password.Value <> Failed.Value then
                OurSpan.InnerHtml = "No dice " + Name.Value + ". Think,
                ➥what's my favorite dessert?"
                Failed.Value = Password.Value
            else
                OurSpan.InnerHtml = "Yo" + Name.Value + ", Did you
                ➥think the password magically changed from what
                ➥you put in last time?"
            end if
        end if
    end if
end sub
</script>
<html>
<head>
<title>HtmlControl TextBox</title>
</head>
<body bgcolor="#FFFFFF" text="#000000">
<form runat="server">
<input type="text" id="Name" runat="server"> What's Your Name?<br>
<input type="password" id="Password" runat="server"> What's the
➥Password? (hint:My Favorite Dessert)<br>
<input type="submit" id="BtnSubmit" value="Submit Form" runat="server">
<input type="hidden" id="Failed" runat="server">
<br><br>
<span id="OurSpan" runat="server"/>
</form>
</body>
</html>
```

C#—html_inputtext_cs.aspx

```
<%@ page language="cs" runat="server"%>
<script  runat=server>

void Page_Load(){
    if (Page.IsPostBack){
        if (Password.Value.ToLower() == "cookies"){
            OurSpan.InnerHtml = "<b>Hey " + Name.Value + ", You're In!!!";
        }else{
            if(Password.Value != Failed.Value){
                OurSpan.InnerHtml = "No dice " + Name.Value + ". Think,
                ➥what's my favorite dessert?";
                Failed.Value = Password.Value;
            }else{
                OurSpan.InnerHtml = "Yo" + Name.Value + ", Did you
                ➥think the password magically changed from what you
                ➥put in last time?";
            }
        }
    }
}
</script>
<html>
<head>
<title>HtmlControl TextBox</title>
</head>
<body bgcolor="#FFFFFF" text="#000000">
<form runat="server">
<input type="text" id="Name" runat="server"> What's Your Name?<br>
<input type="password" id="Password" runat="server"> What's the
➥Password? (hint:My Favorite Dessert)<br>
<input type="submit" id="BtnSubmit" value="Submit Form" runat="server">
<input type="hidden" id="Failed" runat="server">
<br><br>
<span id="OurSpan" runat="server"/>
</form>
</body>
</html>
```

The results for this example can be seen in Figure 6.12. Notice the HtmlInputHidden control on the page. Here is a situation where I want to maintain a value and pass it across page posts. If the user login fails I store the failing password in the box. Then on the user's next try, if he fails again, I check to see whether the newly submitted password is identical to the last failed password. If so, I give him a nasty message about not changing the password and submitting again.

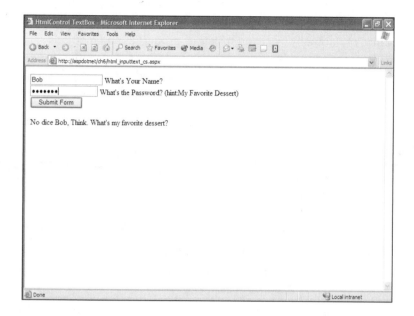

FIGURE 6.13

The
`HtmlInputText`
*control handles both
the standard text
box and the
password box.*

HtmlSelect

The `HtmlSelect` object allows you to access and affect the properties and
methods of the `<select runat="server">` tag. This object has several additional
properties and some inherited methods as well. Have a look in Table 6.11.

TABLE 6.11   *HtmlSelect* Object Properties

Property	Description
Datasource	Gets or sets the value of what is being used as a datasource for the `HtmlSelect` options.
DataTextField	Gets or sets the field in a table or hashtable that will populate the text portion of a `HtmlSelect` object's items.
DataValueField	Gets or sets the field in a table or hashtable that will populate the value portion of an `HtmlSelect` object's items.
Items	Gets or sets the option item's value.
Multiple	Gets or sets a Boolean value declaring whether a select box will allow the user to pick multiple values in the box.
SelectedIndex	Gets or sets the index value of the selected option. The index start at 0 and increments by 1 through the number of options.
Size	Gets or sets how many lines of the select box are displayed. If you select Multiple, it defaults to multiple lines. You can specify how many lines with this property.
Value	Gets or sets the value of the Select box.

The `Items` property, as with so many other things I've mentioned before, is an instance of another object and makes its properties and methods available. The `Items` property is an instance of `ListItemCollection` in the `System.Web.UI.WebControls` namespace. It has a boatload of properties and methods that will be useful for manipulating your `HtmlSelect` control, which are described in Table 6.12.

TABLE 6.12   *ListItemCollection* Object Properties

Property/Method	Description
Add (M)	Provides a way to add a new option to the `HtmlSelect` control.
Count (P)	Returns the number of `Items` in the `HtmlSelect` control.
Clear (M)	Empties the entire `HtmlSelect` control.
Insert (M)	Inserts an `Item` into the `HtmlSelect` control at the specified `Index`.
Remove (M)	Removes the specified `Item` from the `HtmlSelect` control at the specified `Index`.

Visual Basic .NET—**html_select_vb.aspx**

```
<%@ page language="vb" runat="server"%>
<script runat=server>
Sub Page_Load(sender As Object, e As EventArgs)
    dim myArray() as String = {"Pumpkin Pie", "Cheesecake", "Ice Cream
    ➥Sundae", "Cookies"}
    if not IsPostBack
        Dessert.DataSource = myArray
        Dessert.DataBind()
    end if
end sub

Sub PickDessert(sender As Object, e As EventArgs)
    OurSpan.InnerText = "You chose: " + Dessert.Value
    if Dessert.Value = "Cookies" Then
        OurSpan.InnerText += ". These are my favorite too."
    end if
End Sub

Sub AddNewDessert(sender As Object, e As EventArgs)
    if NewDessert.Value <> "" Then
        Dessert.Items.Add(NewDessert.Value)
    end if
End Sub
</script>
<html>
```

```
<head>
<title>HtmlControl Select</title>
</head>
<body>
<form runat=server>
Select a dessert:<br>
<select id="Dessert" runat="server" />
<input type="button" runat="server" Value="Submit" OnServerClick="PickDessert">
<br><br>
If you don't see <b>your</b> favorite dessert in the list, you can add it:<br>
<input type="text" id="NewDessert" runat="server">
<input type="button" runat="server" Value="Add" OnServerClick="AddNewDessert">
<br><br>
<span id="OurSpan" runat="server"></span>
</form>
</body>
</html>
```

C#—html_select_cs.aspx

```
<%@ page language="cs" runat="server"%>
<script runat=server>
void Page_Load(object sender, EventArgs e) {
    string[] myArray = {"Pumpkin Pie", "Cheesecake", "Ice Cream
    ➡Sundae", "Cookies"};
    if (!IsPostBack) {
        Dessert.DataSource = myArray;
        Dessert.DataBind();
    }
}


void PickDessert(object sender, EventArgs e) {
    OurSpan.InnerText = "You chose: " + Dessert.Value;
    if (Dessert.Value == "Cookies") {
        OurSpan.InnerText += ". These are my favorite too.";
    }
}


void AddNewDessert(object sender, EventArgs e) {
    if (NewDessert.Value != "") {
        Dessert.Items.Add(NewDessert.Value);
    }
}
</script>
<html>
<head>
<title>HtmlControl Select</title>
</head>
<body>
<form runat=server>
```

continues

C#—(continued)

```
Select a dessert:<br>
<select id="Dessert" runat="server" />
<input type="button" runat="server" Value="Submit" OnServerClick="PickDessert">
<p>
If you don't see <b>your</b> favorite dessert in the list, you can add it:<br>
<input type="text" id="NewDessert" runat="server">
<input type="button" runat="server" Value="Add" OnServerClick="AddNewDessert">
<p>
<span id="OurSpan" runat="server"></span>
</form>
</body>
</html>
```

In Figure 6.14, you will see that you can select an option from the Select box, and if you don't see an option that suits you, you can add whatever value you want to the Select box. You do so by using an `OnServerClick` event and the `Item.Add()` method discussed earlier.

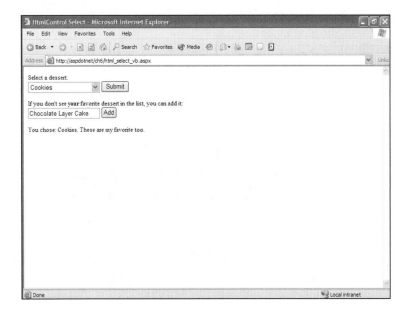

FIGURE 6.14

The `HtmlSelect` *control gives you a way to manipulate Select boxes programmatically.*

HtmlTable, HtmlTableRow, HtmlTableCell

These controls are a gas. You can do just about anything to adjust all the properties of a table, table row, or table cell with these three controls. What I'm going to do is provide you with all the properties and a few of the methods of these controls (in Tables 6.13, 6.14, and 6.15), and then give you a big, fat example and let you have at it.

TABLE 6.13   *HtmlTable* Object Properties

Property	Description
Align	Gets or Sets the value of the align attribute (that is, align="center").
BgColor	Gets or Sets the table's Background color.
Border	Gets or Sets how wide a table's border is in pixels.
BorderColor	Gets or Sets the color of the table's border.
CellPadding	Gets or Sets the value of the table's cellpadding attribute.
CellSpacing	Gets or Sets the value of the table's cellspacing attribute.
Height	Gets or Sets the value of the table's height attribute.
Rows	Instance of the HtmlTableRowCollection, exposing its properties and methods.
Width	Gets or Sets the value of the table's width attribute.

TABLE 6.14   *HtmlTableRow* Object Properties

Property	Description
Align	Gets or Sets the value of the row's align attribute (that is, align="center").
BgColor	Gets or Sets the background color of the row.
BorderColor	Gets or Sets the color of the row's border.
Cells	Instance of the HtmlTableCellCollection, exposing its properties and methods.
Height	Gets or Sets the value of the row's height attribute.
VAlign	Gets or Sets the vertical alignment of the contents of the cells of the row.

TABLE 6.15 *HtmlTableCell* Object Properties

Property	Description
Align	Gets or Sets the value of the cell's align attribute (that is, align="center").
BgColor	Gets or Sets the background color of the cell.
BorderColor	Gets or Sets the color of the cell's border.
ColSpan	Gets or Sets how many columns the cell spans across.
Height	Gets or Sets the value of the row's height attribute.
NoWrap	Gets or Sets a Boolean value that defines whether text within a cell should wrap. False is the default.
RowSpan	Gets or Sets how many rows the cell spans across.
VAlign	Gets or Sets the vertical alignment of the contents of a cell.
Width	Gets or Sets the value of the row's width attribute.

These properties and methods are exposed through HtmlTable's row property. The HtmlTableRows cell property gives you a golf bag full of clubs to create and manipulate tables. Manipulating a table this way isn't a method I use often, but it's nice to have for situations where complete programmatic control over a table solves problems.

The following is an example of creating a table, then manipulating its properties programmatically. You can also create a table programmatically with the methods and properties available through the HtmlTable's row property and the HtmlTableRows cell property, but I don't do that here. I do use the Add() method to dynamically add a row of cells to the table if the Add Row check box is checked.

Visual Basic .NET—**html_table_vb.aspx**

```
<%@ page language="vb" runat="server"%>
<script  runat=server>
sub Page_Load(sender As Object, e As EventArgs)
    dim OurArray() as Integer = {0,1,2,3,5,6,7,8,9,10}
    dim OurColorArray() as String = {"Red", "Blue", "Green", "Orange", "Cyan"}
    if not IsPostBack
        OurCellPaddingSelect.DataSource = OurArray
        OurCellSpacingSelect.DataSource = OurArray
        OurBorderSelect.DataSource = OurArray
        OurBGColorSelect.DataSource = OurColorArray
        OurBorderColorSelect.DataSource = OurColorArray
        DataBind()
```

```
        else
            OurTable.CellSpacing = CInt(OurCellSpacingSelect.Value)
            OurTable.CellPadding = CInt(OurCellPaddingSelect.Value)
            OurTable.Border = Cint(OurBorderSelect.Value)
            OurTable.BGColor = OurBGColorSelect.Value
            OurTable.BorderColor = OurBorderColorSelect.Value
            if (OurCheckBox.Checked) then
                dim cell as HtmlTableCell
                dim row as HtmlTableRow
                row = new HtmlTableRow()
                cell = new HtmlTableCell()
                cell.InnerText = "Pie"
                row.Cells.Add(cell)
                cell = new HtmlTableCell()
                cell.InnerText = "Cookies"
                row.Cells.Add(cell)
                cell = new HtmlTableCell()
                cell.InnerText = "Ice Cream"
                row.Cells.Add(cell)
                OurTable.Rows.Add(row)
            end if
        end if
end sub

</script>
<html>
<head>
<title>HtmlControl Table</title>
</head>
<body>
<form runat=server>
<table>
<tr>
<td>Table Cell Padding:</td>
<td><select id="OurCellPaddingSelect" runat="server" /></td>
</tr>
<tr>
<td>Table Cell Spacing:</td>
<td><select id="OurCellSpacingSelect" runat="server" /></td>
</tr>
<tr>
<td>Table Borders:</td>
<td><select id="OurBorderSelect" runat="server" /></td>
</tr>
<tr>
<td>Table BG Color:</td>
<td><select id="OurBgColorSelect" runat="server" /></td>
</tr>
<tr>
<td>Table Border Color:</td>
<td><select id="OurBorderColorSelect" runat="server" /></td>
</tr>
```

continues

Visual Basic .NET—(continued)

```
<tr>
<td>Insert Row:</td>
<td><input type="checkbox" runat="server" id="OurCheckBox" /></td>
</tr>
<tr>
<td colspan="2"><input type="submit" value="Submit" runat="server" /></td>
</tr>
</table>
<br><br>
<table id="OurTable" runat="server">
<tr>
<td>Cell 1</td>
<td>Cell 2</td>
<td>Cell 3</td>
</tr>
<tr>
<td>Cell 4</td>
<td>Cell 5</td>
<td>Cell 6</td>
</tr>
<tr>
<td>Cell 7</td>
<td>Cell 8</td>
<td>Cell 9</td>
</tr>
</table>
</font>
</form>
</body>
</html>
```

C#—html_table_cs.aspx

```
<%@ page language="c#" runat="server"%>
<script  runat=server>
void Page_Load(object sender, EventArgs e)
{
    int[] OurArray  = {0,1,2,3,5,6,7,8,9,10};
    string[] OurColorArray = {"Red", "Blue", "Green", "Orange", "Cyan"};
    if (!IsPostBack) {
        OurCellPaddingSelect.DataSource = OurArray;
        OurCellSpacingSelect.DataSource = OurArray;
        OurBorderSelect.DataSource = OurArray;
        OurBgColorSelect.DataSource = OurColorArray;
        OurBorderColorSelect.DataSource = OurColorArray;
        DataBind();
    }
    else {
        OurTable.CellSpacing = int.Parse(OurCellSpacingSelect.Value);
```

```
        OurTable.CellPadding = int.Parse(OurCellPaddingSelect.Value);
        OurTable.Border = int.Parse(OurBorderSelect.Value);
        OurTable.BgColor = OurBgColorSelect.Value;
        OurTable.BorderColor = OurBorderColorSelect.Value;
        if (OurCheckBox.Checked) {
            HtmlTableCell cell;
            HtmlTableRow row;
            row = new HtmlTableRow();
            cell = new HtmlTableCell();
            cell.InnerText = "Pie";
            row.Cells.Add(cell);
            cell = new HtmlTableCell();
            cell.InnerText = "Cookies";
            row.Cells.Add(cell);
            cell = new HtmlTableCell();
            cell.InnerText = "Ice Cream";
            row.Cells.Add(cell);
            OurTable.Rows.Add(row);
        }


    }
}

</script>
<html>
<head>
<title>HtmlControl Table</title>
</head>
<body>
<form runat=server>
<table>
<tr>
<td>Table Cell Padding:</td>
<td><select id="OurCellPaddingSelect" runat="server" /></td>
</tr>
<tr>
<td>Table Cell Spacing:</td>
<td><select id="OurCellSpacingSelect" runat="server" /></td>
</tr>
<tr>
<td>Table Borders:</td>
<td><select id="OurBorderSelect" runat="server" /></td>
</tr>
<tr>
<td>Table BG Color:</td>
<td><select id="OurBgColorSelect" runat="server" /></td>
</tr>
<tr>
<td>Table Border Color:</td>
<td><select id="OurBorderColorSelect" runat="server" /></td>
</tr>
```

continues

C#—(continued)

```
<tr>
<td>Insert Row:</td>
<td><input type="checkbox" runat="server" id="OurCheckBox" /></td>
</tr>
<tr>
<td colspan="2"><input type="submit" value="Submit" runat="server" /></td>
</tr>
</table>
<br><br>
<table id="OurTable" runat="server">
<tr>
<td>Cell 1</td>
<td>Cell 2</td>
<td>Cell 3</td>
</tr>
<tr>
<td>Cell 4</td>
<td>Cell 5</td>
<td>Cell 6</td>
</tr>
<tr>
<td>Cell 7</td>
<td>Cell 8</td>
<td>Cell 9</td>
</tr>
</table>
</font>
</form>
</body>
</html>
```

In Figure 6.15, you will see a stunningly attractive HTML table (ah? yeah!) that demonstrates how to manipulate your HtmlTable control. I also used the Add() method to add both rows and cells (and my favorite dessert) to the table.

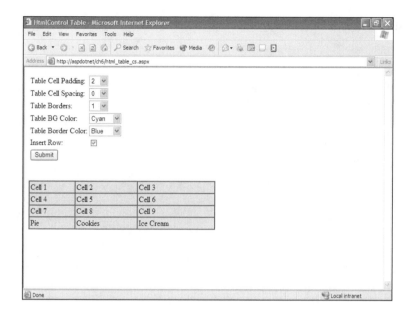

FIGURE 6.15

The HtmlTable, HtmlTableRow, *and* HtmlTableCell *give you the ability to treat a table as an object and manipulate its properties.*

HtmlTextArea

The HtmlTextArea is pretty darn similar to the HtmlTextBox, except that it has properties to control the size of the box. Table 6.16 lists the HtmlTextArea's additional properties.

TABLE 6.16 *HtmlTextArea* Object Properties

Property	Description
Cols	Gets or Sets the width in characters of a textarea.
Name	Gets or Sets the unique identifier name of the textarea.
Rows	Gets or Sets the number of rows based on the character height of a textarea.
Value	Gets or Sets the text entered into the textarea.

Visual Basic .NET—**html_textarea_vb.aspx**

```
<%@ page language="vb" runat="server"%>
<script runat=server>
sub Page_Load(Sender as Object, e as EventArgs)
    if Not IsPostBack Then
        OurTextArea.Rows = 5
        OurTextArea.Cols = 50
    else
        OurSpan.InnerHtml = "<b>You Wrote:</b> <i>" + OurTextArea.Value + "</i>"
    end if
end sub
</script>
<html>
<head>
<title>HtmlControl TextArea</title>
</head>
<body bgcolor="#FFFFFF" text="#000000">
<form runat="server">
<h2>In 250 words or less, please describe why your favorite dessert is the
➥best.</h2>
<textarea id="OurTextArea" runat="server" />
<br><br>
<input type="Submit" value="Submit">
<br><br>
<span id="OurSpan" runat="server"/>
</form>
</body>
</html>
```

C#—**html_textarea_cs.aspx**

```
<%@ page language="cs" runat="server"%>
<script runat=server>
void Page_Load(object o, EventArgs e){
    if (!IsPostBack) {
        OurTextArea.Rows = 5;
        OurTextArea.Cols = 50;
    }
    else {
        OurSpan.InnerHtml = "<b>You Wrote:</b> <i>" + OurTextArea.Value
        ➥+ "</i>";
    }
}
</script>
<html>
<head>
<title>HtmlControl TextArea</title>
</head>
<body bgcolor="#FFFFFF" text="#000000">
<form runat="server">
```

```
<div align="center">
<h2>In 250 words or less, please describe why your favorite dessert is the
➥best.</h2>
<textarea id="OurTextArea" runat="server" />
<br><br>
<input type="Submit" value="Submit">
<br><br>
<span id="OurSpan" runat="server"/>
</div>
</form>
</body>
</html>
```

You can see the results of this example is Figure 6.16. The Cols and Rows
properties are set during the Page_Load event, and then the textarea's value
is retrieved when the page is posted back.

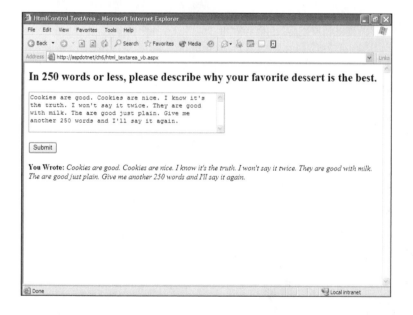

Summary

We've reached a part of this chapter that I guess can be summed up in a song sung by one of my heroes. Decked out in top hat, coat, and tail, Bugs Bunny struts on the stage swinging his cane and sings like a beautiful song bird:

> "Overture, dim the lights!
>
> This is it, the night of nights!
>
> No more rehearsing and versing the parts! We know every part by Heart!
>
> Overture, dim the lights!
>
> This is it, we'll hit the heights!
>
> And, oh what heights we'll hit!
>
> ON WITH THE SHOW, THIS IS IT!!!"

Exit stage left and on to Web controls.

7

Web Server Controls

Oh, what a tangled web server control we weave!

Y ou might ask yourself, "Self, why do we need more controls than the ones we just covered in the chapter on HtmlControl? I can do just about everything I can think of in designing web sites with these controls. What do I need more for? And to be honest, some of them look repetitive."

First I would say, "Very observant." Then I would say, "There is a very good reason for what appears to be redundancy, but isn't." Remember that the development of the .NET Framework wasn't haphazard or flagrant but very well thought out. The issue of programming paradigms also comes into play here. HTML server controls are nothing more than standard HTML tags dressed in .NET clothing. Web server controls are the real Elvis.

What Is a Web Server Control?

First let me tell you where they are, and then we'll address what they are. Web server controls are located in the `System.Web.UI.WebControls` namespace. There are other *very* cool objects in there that are covered in the next two chapters. They are created from a clean slate and don't need to conform to any legacy thinking or models. The creators of ASP.NET created these controls from the ground up, and this gave them the ability to shape and form these controls without rule or guide outside of those they generated themselves.

This gave them the opportunity to build a single base class that serves as the foundation for all Web server controls, giving them a base uniform set of properties and methods. All Web server controls also are addressed the same way, which makes them easier to locate within your code—for example:

```
<asp:Image runat="server"/>
<asp:CheckBox runat="server"/>
<asp:Label runat="server"/>
```

As you can see, all Web server controls are identified with an opening `asp:`, which is followed by the control's type or name. This makes them very easy to spot within your code blocks.

Why Use Web Server Controls?

You should use Web server controls for three simple reasons:

- Simplicity
- Uniformity
- Productivity

Where each of these begins and ends is hard to define. I find that because of the uniform properties and methods across the base class, Web server controls are much simpler to use than HTML server controls. For instance, across all Web server controls the `width` property determines the width of the Web server control. This isn't so with HTML server controls. For instance, with the `HtmlInputText` control you set the width of the control with the `size` property, but with the `HtmlTextArea` you set the width of the control with the `Cols` property. This can at the very least lead to confusion, which hampers productivity.

Additional areas of productivity will become more apparent in the next few chapters, where you will investigate two other types of server controls that I've mentioned several times and that you've seen in a few of the examples. They are the validation controls and ASP.NET list controls. These are equally a big deal, a time saver, and besides that, they are totally awesome objects.

Web Form Server Controls

Let's dig in again by investigating the base class from which all the objects in the System.Web.UI.WebControls namespace are created. This is a big part of the excitement in these controls as well as the others in the two following chapters. The primary properties are uniform because they are inherited from the base WebControl object.

WebControl

This is the name of the base object for all...ah? Yeah, Web server controls. As you look at its properties in Table 7.1, you can see that Microsoft has done a good job on this object and supplied all the meaty things necessary for programming with WebControl in a nice, neat way.

TABLE 7.1   *WebControl* Object Properties

Property	Description
Attribute	Returns the attributes collection of the object.
BackColor	Gets or sets the background color of the Web server control.
BorderColor	Gets or sets the border color of the Web server control.
BorderStyle	Gets or sets the border style of the Web server control, for instance Dotted, Dashed, Solid, and so on.
BorderWidth	Gets or sets the border width of the Web server control.
CssClass	Gets or sets the Cascading Style Sheet (CSS) class rendered by the Web server control on the client.
EnableViewState	A Boolean (true or false) value that you can get or set that indicates whether a control should maintain its viewstate.
Enabled	A Boolean (true or false) value that you can get or set that indicates whether a control is enabled.

continues

TABLE 7.1   continued

Property	Description
Font	Gets the font properties associated with the Web server control.
ForeColor	Gets or sets the foreground color (typically the color of the text) of the Web server control.
Height	Gets or sets the height of the Web server control.
ID	A string that you can get or set that defines the identifier for the control.
Style	Returns the CSSStyleCollection for a control.
TabIndex	Gets or sets the tab index of the Web server control
ToolTip	Gets or sets the text displayed when the mouse pointer hovers over the Web server control.
Visible	Gets or sets a value that indicates whether a Web server control is rendered as UI on the page.
Width	Gets or sets the width of the Web server control.

Remember that just like the HTML server controls, the attribute and style properties are instances of collections, and you can get and set particular attributes and styles the same way that I described in Chapter 6, either through setting the value of a particular named attribute or style or through using the Add() method of the collection. I've included the following example as a refresher.

Visual Basic .NET

```
Getting Attributes and Styles
var1 = OurDiv.Attributes("align")
var2 = OurDiv.Style("width")

Setting Attributes and Styles
OurDiv.Attributes("align")= "center"
OurDiv.Style.Add("font-size","14px")
```

C#

```
Getting Attributes and Styles
var1 = OurDiv.Attributes["align"];
var2 = OurDiv.Style["width"];

Setting Attributes and Styles
OurDiv.Attributes["align"]= "center";
OurDiv.Style.Add("font-size","14px");
```

This is a pretty rich bunch of properties and creates a very solid base class from which the other Web server controls are built. Let's move forward and investigate the Web server controls themselves. The remainder of this chapter looks at Web server controls that generate some basic familiar HTML function such as check boxes, images, and text boxes, as well as some more exotic and mysterious Web server controls such as the panel and placeholder. Let's check it out.

Button

The Button Web server control renders an `<input type="submit">` to the browser. It has some pretty interesting properties (see Table 7.2) and two useful methods called OnClick and onCommand, which you'll learn more about in a bit.

TABLE 7.2 Button Object Properties

Property	Description
CausesValidation	A Boolean (true or false) that gets or sets whether validation is performed when the Button control is clicked. Default is true.
CommandArgument	Gets or sets an optional parameter passed to the Command event along with the associated CommandName.
CommandName	Gets or sets the command name associated with the Button control that is passed to the Command event.
Text	Gets or sets the text on the button.

The two properties that I'd like to touch on are CommandArgument and CommandName. The two properties are associated and available with an event that the asp:button fires called onCommand. This button also fires the onClick event as well, but you've seen this event a bunch of times already, so I'll focus on the onCommand instead.

The onCommand event works in pretty much the same way as the onClick event, except you can include the two required properties of the button, CommandName and CommandArgument. You can use these as a way of identifying which button was clicked and use that information programmatically to figure out what branch of code to process.

Notably, if you don't include the CommandName and CommandArgument, the button is of the Submit type and will submit the form and cause the page to post back. An onCommand event doesn't cause postback and allows you to manipulate your ASP.NET page without executing a postback as far as .NET is concerned. Look at this example:

Visual Basic .NET—**web_button_vb.aspx**

```vb
<%@ page language="vb" runat="server"%>
<script runat="server">
    sub Page_Load(sender as Object, e as CommandEventArgs)
        if IsPostBack then
            ourLabel1.Text = "This text will never appear on the page"
        end if
    end sub

    sub CommandButton_Click(sender as Object, e as CommandEventArgs)
        select case e.CommandArgument
            case "OurCommandArgument1"
                ourLabel2.Text = "You clicked Our First Button"
            case "OurCommandArgument2"
                ourLabel3.Text = "You clicked Our Second Button"
            case else
        end select
    end sub
</script>

<html>
<head>
<title>Web Controls - Button</title>
</head>
<body bgcolor="#FFFFFF" text="#000000">
<form runat="server">
<asp:Button id="ourButton1"
    runat="server"
    text="Our First Button"
    CommandName="ourButtonCommand"
    CommandArgument="OurCommandArgument1"
    onCommand="CommandButton_Click" />

<asp:Button id="ourButton2"
    runat="server"
    text="Our Second Button"
    CommandName="ourButtomCommand"
    CommandArgument="OurCommandArgument2"
    onCommand="CommandButton_Click" />

<br>
```

```
<asp:label id="ourLabel1" runat="server" /><br>
<asp:label id="ourLabel2" runat="server" /><br>
<asp:label id="ourLabel3" runat="server" /><br><br>
Note that neither of those fired the "if IsPostBack" block of code.
</form>
</body>
</html>
```

C#—control_button_cs.aspx

```
<%@ page language="cs" runat="server"%>
<script runat="server">
    void Page_Load(Object sender, CommandEventArgs e) {
        if (IsPostBack) {
            ourLabel1.Text = "This text will never appear on the page";
        }
    }

    void CommandButton_Click(Object sender, CommandEventArgs e) {
        switch (Int32.Parse(e.CommandArgument.ToString())) {
            case 1:
                ourLabel2.Text = "You clicked Our First Button";
                break;
            case 2:
                ourLabel3.Text = "You clicked Our Second Button";
                break;
            default:
                break;
        }
    }
</script>

<html>
<head>
<title></title>
</head>
<body bgcolor="#FFFFFF" text="#000000">
<form runat="server">

<asp:Button id="ourButton1"
    runat="server"
    text="Our First Button"
    CommandName="ourButtonCommand"
    CommandArgument="1"
    onCommand="CommandButton_Click" />

<asp:Button id="ourButton2"
    runat="server"
    text="Our Second Button"
```

continues

C#—(continued)

```
        CommandName="ourButtomCommand"
        CommandArgument="2"
        onCommand="CommandButton_Click" />

    <br>
    <asp:label id="ourLabel1" runat="server" /><br>
    <asp:label id="ourLabel2" runat="server" /><br>
    <asp:label id="ourLabel3" runat="server" /><br><br>
     Note that neither of those fired the "if IsPostBack" block of code.
    </form>
    </body>
    </html>
```

As you can see in Figure 7.1, the two different buttons cause different branches of the CommandButton_Click to fire, but the IsPostBack portion of the code never executes.

FIGURE 7.1

Using the command event prevents the IsPostBack event from firing while enabling you to programmatically manipulate the ASP.NET page.

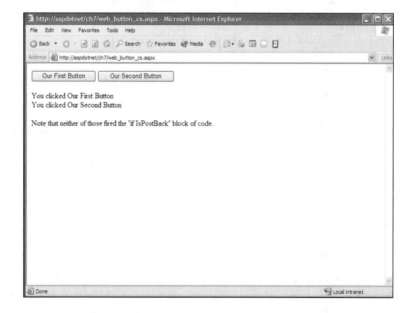

CheckBox

The CheckBox Web server control will render an `<input type="checkbox">` to the browser. It has additional properties worth mentioning and a great method called OnCheckChanged that we can use to fire functions and subs.

TABLE 7.3 *Checkbox* Object Properties

Property	Description
AutoPostBack	Gets or sets the value that determines whether the check box causes a form to post back to the server.
Checked	Gets or sets the value indicating whether a check box is checked or not.
Text	Gets or sets the text that is displayed as a label for the check box
TextAlign	Gets or sets whether the text label is displayed on the right or left of the check box.

The interesting property here is the AutoPostBack property. If this property is set to true, it causes the form in which the check box is contained to post back to the server.

There is also an event similar to the onServerChanged event of the HTMLInputCheckBox control that you saw in Chapter 6. It is called onCheckedChanged, and it performs in the same manner. What basically happens is the server keeps track of the asp:checkbox's checked property. If it is different from the last time it dealt with the object, it fires the onCheckedChanged events. Take a look.

Visual Basic .NET—web_checkbox_vb.aspx

```
<%@ page language="vb" runat="server"%>
<script runat=server>
    Sub OurCheckBoxClick(sender as Object, e as EventArgs)
        if OurCheckBox1.Checked Then
            OurLabel1.Text = "OurCheckBox1 is checked."
        else
            OurLabel1.Text = "OurCheckBox1 is not checked."
        end if
        if OurCheckBox2.Checked Then
            OurLabel2.Text = "OurCheckBox2 is checked."
        else
            OurLabel2.Text = "OurCheckBox2 is not checked."
        end if
    end sub
```

continues

Visual Basic .NET—(continued)

```
</script>

<html>
<head>
<title></title>
</head>
<body bgcolor="#FFFFFF" text="#000000">
<form runat="server">
<asp:CheckBox id="OurCheckBox1"
    Text="No AutoPostBack"
    TextAlign="right"
    OnCheckedChanged="OurCheckBoxClick"
    runat="server" />
<br>
<asp:CheckBox id="OurCheckBox2"
    Text="With AutoPostBack"
    TextAlign="right"
    OnCheckedChanged="OurCheckBoxClick"
    AutoPostBack="True"
    runat="server"/>
<br>
<asp:Button runat="server" text="Submit" /><br><br>
<asp:Label id="OurLabel1" runat="server" /><br>
<asp:Label id="OurLabel2" runat="server" />
</form>
</body>
</html>
```

C#—web_checkbox_cs.aspx

```
<%@ page language="c#" runat="server"%>
<script runat=server>
    void OurCheckBoxClick(Object sender, EventArgs e) {
        if (OurCheckBox1.Checked) {
            OurLabel1.Text = "OurCheckBox1 is checked.";
        }
        else {
            OurLabel1.Text = "OurCheckBox1 is not checked.";
        }
        if (OurCheckBox2.Checked) {
            OurLabel2.Text = "OurCheckBox2 is checked.";
        }
        else {
            OurLabel2.Text = "OurCheckBox2 is not checked.";
        }
    }
</script>

<html>
```

```
<head>
<title></title>
</head>
<body bgcolor="#FFFFFF" text="#000000">
<form runat="server">
<asp:CheckBox id="OurCheckBox1"
    Text="No AutoPostBack"
    TextAlign="right"
    OnCheckedChanged="OurCheckBoxClick"
    runat="server" />
<br>
<asp:CheckBox id="OurCheckBox2"
    Text="With AutoPostBack"
    TextAlign="right"
    OnCheckedChanged="OurCheckBoxClick"
    AutoPostBack="True"
    runat="server"/>
<br>
<asp:Button runat="server" text="Submit" /><br><br>
<asp:Label id="OurLabel1" runat="server" /><br>
<asp:Label id="OurLabel2" runat="server" />
</form>
</body>
</html>
```

In Figure 7.2 you can see two different CheckBox Web server controls. The first doesn't have an AutoPostBack set to true, but the second does. They both have an OnCheckedChanged event that fires whenever the Checked property of the control changes between posts.

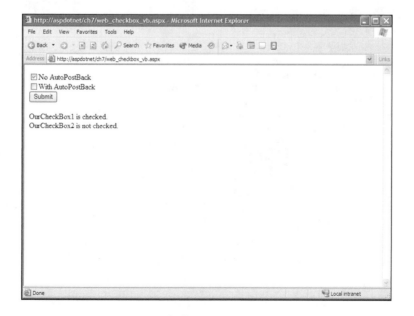

FIGURE 7.2

The AutoPostBack *property allows you to post a form by checking a check box. The* OnChecked-Changed *event fires whenever a check box's checked property is changed between posts.*

Hyperlink

The Hyperlink Web server control renders an <a></a> tag to the web browser and has 4 additional properties that you can see in Table 7.4 and are used in the code example.

TABLE 7.4 *Hyperlink* Object Properties

Property	Description
ImageURL	Gets or sets the path location if you want an image to be placed inside the <a> tag.
NavigateURL	Gets or sets the URL that the hyperlink goes to if it is clicked.
Target	Gets or sets the target where the NavigateURL property will be loaded, such as _blank, _parent, _self, _top, or the name of a frame in a frameset.
Text	Gets or sets the text that appears as the hyperlink if the ImageURL property isn't set, or sets the Alt property of the image if there is an ImageURL.

The Hyperlink Web server control has no special events associated with it, but because you can programmatically control it, you can do many interesting things with it, as demonstrated in the following example.

Visual Basic .NET—**web_hyperlink_vb.aspx**

```
<%@ page language="vb" runat="server"%>
<script runat=server>
sub Page_Load(sender as Object, e as EventArgs)
    if IsPostBack then
        OurHyperLink.ImageUrl = "images/nr_logo.gif"
        OurHyperLink.Target = "_blank"
        OurHyperLink.NavigateURL = "http://www.newriders.com"
        OurHyperLink.Text = "Exciting Link"
        OurLabel.Text = "There, that's much better."
        OurButton.Visible = false
    end if
end sub
</script>

<html>
<head>
<title>Web Controls - Hyperlink</title>
</head>
<body bgcolor="#FFFFFF" text="#000000">
<form runat="server">
```

```
<asp:HyperLink id="OurHyperLink"
NavigateURL="http://www.bored.com"
text="Boring Link" runat="server" />
<br><br>
<asp:label id="OurLabel" runat="server" text="That link is pretty useless. Click
the button to fix it." /><br>
<asp:button id="OurButton" runat="server" text="Submit" />
</form>
</body>
</html>
```

C#—web_hyperlink_cs.aspx

```
<%@ page language="cs" runat="server"%>
<script runat=server>
void Page_Load(Object sender, EventArgs e) {
    if (IsPostBack) {
        OurHyperLink.ImageUrl = "something.gif";
        OurHyperLink.Target = "_blank";
        OurHyperLink.NavigateUrl = "http://www.newriders.com";
        OurHyperLink.Text = "Exciting Link";
        OurLabel.Text = "There, that's much better.";
        OurButton.Visible = false;
    }
}
</script>

<html>
<head>
<title>Web Controls - Hyperlink</title>
</head>
<body bgcolor="#FFFFFF" text="#000000">
<form runat="server">
<asp:HyperLink id="OurHyperLink"
NavigateURL="http://www.bored.com"
text="Boring Link" runat="server" />
<br><br>
<asp:label id="OurLabel" runat="server"
text="That link is pretty useless. Click the button to fix it." />
<br>
<asp:button id="OurButton" runat="server" text="Submit" />
</form>
</body>
</html>
```

Figure 7.3 shows that the hyperlink has been changed programmatically to contain an image rather than text. This isn't the only way to use this, but being able to set a hyperlink's property programmatically has endless possibilities.

FIGURE 7.3

The AutoPostBack *property allows you to post a form by checking a check box, and the* OnChecked- Changed *event fires whenever a check box's checked prop- erty is changed between posts.*

Image

The Image Web server control renders the <img> tag to the browser and has a few properties all its own, listed in Table 7.5.

TABLE 7.5 *Image Object Properties*

Property	Description
AlternateText	Gets or sets the alternate text displayed in the Image control when the image is unavailable. Browsers that support the ToolTips feature display this text as a ToolTip.
ImageAlign	Gets or sets the alignment property of the image in relation to its surrounding content. The options are Left, Right, Baseline, Top, Middle, Bottom, AbsBottom, AbsMiddle, and TextTop.
ImageURL	Gets or sets the path location of the image you want to display.

There is nothing particularly exciting about this Web server control, but the following is a copy of the object for both languages so you can see how it appears.

```
<asp:Image id="OurImage"
    ImageUrl="image.gif"
    AlternateText="This is Alt Text"
    ImageAlign="Left"
    runat="server" />
```

ImageButton

The ImageButton Web control renders the <input type="image"> tag to the browser. Three of its properties are identical to the Image Web server control, and for good reason. The ImageButton Web server control inherits these properties from the Image Web server control. The three remaining properties and two methods are identical to the Button Web server control and perform in exactly the same way as they do for the Button control. Look at Table 7.6 for a description of the properties.

TABLE 7.6 *ImageButton* Object Properties

Property	Description
AlternateText	Gets or sets the alternate text displayed in the Image control when the image is unavailable. Browsers that support the ToolTips feature display this text as a ToolTip.
CausesValidation	A Boolean (true or false) that gets or sets whether validation is performed when the Button control is clicked. Default is true.
CommandArgument	Gets or sets an optional parameter passed to the Command event along with the associated CommandName.
CommandName	Gets or sets the command name associated with the Button control that is passed to the Command event.
ImageAlign	Gets or sets the alignment property of the image in relation to its surrounding content. The options are Left, Right, Baseline, Top, Middle, Bottom, AbsBottom, AbsMiddle, and TextTop.
ImageURL	Gets or sets the path location of the image you want to display.

The two events I mentioned are OnClick and OnCommand. They operate just as they do with the Button Web server control.

As with the Image Web server control, there isn't anything here that you haven't seen before, and in an effort to not be redundant, not be redundant, not be redundant, I will just show the object in raw form and leave tinkering with this control to your imagination at this point.

```
<asp:ImageButton id="OurImage"
    ImageUrl="image.gif"
    AlternateText="This is Alt Text"
    ImageAlign="Left"
    CommandName="ourCommand"
    CommandArgument="OurArgument"
    onCommand="Command_Click" />
```

Label

Man, we have used and abused this Web server control since somewhere around page 2 of this book. It has a single property of text, but in case you missed it, it looks like this:

```
<asp:Label text="This is the text that will display" runat="server" />
```

Not too difficult. It renders a <span> tag to the browser, and you can manipulate its contents visibly by changing the inherited properties of the WebControl object discussed in the beginning of this chapter, such as CssClass, the style collection, or the attribute collection of the <span> tag. Remember: This isn't exclusive to this Web server control—you can manipulate these things on all the Web server controls.

LinkButton

The LinkButton Web server control renders an <a> tag to the browser and basically gives a hyperlink the same function as the Button Web server control, which can either trigger a command event or submit a form. It has the same four properties as the Button Web server control (see Table 7.7) and the same two events, which are OnClick and OnCommand.

TABLE 7.7 *LinkButton* Object Properties

Property	Description
CausesValidation	A Boolean (true or false) that gets or sets whether validation is performed when the LinkButton control is clicked. Default is true.
CommandArgument	Gets or sets an optional parameter passed to the Command event along with the associated CommandName.
CommandName	Gets or sets the command name associated with the Button control that is passed to the Command event.
Text	Gets or set the text that is displayed for the LinkButton.

Visual Basic .NET—**web_linkbutton_vb.aspx**

```
<%@ page language="vb" runat="server"%>
<script runat=server>
sub Page_Load(sender as Object, e as EventArgs)
    if IsPostBack then
        OurLabel.Text = "Form Submitted Successfully"
    end if
end sub
</script>

<html>
<head>
<title>Web Controls - LinkButton</title>
</head>
<body bgcolor="#FFFFFF" text="#000000">
<form runat="server">
<asp:LinkButton id="OurLinkButton"
    text="Click the link to submit this form"
    runat="server" />
    <br>
<asp:label id="OurLabel" runat="server" />
</form>
</body>
</html>
```

C#—**web_linkbutton_cs.aspx**

```
<%@ page language="c#" runat="server"%>
<script runat=server>
void Page_Load(Object sender, EventArgs e) {
    if (IsPostBack) {
        OurLabel.Text = "Form Submitted Successfully";
    }
}
</script>

<html>
<head>
<title>Web Controls - LinkButton</title>
</head>
<body bgcolor="#FFFFFF" text="#000000">
<form runat="server">
<asp:LinkButton id="OurLinkButton"
    text="Click the link to submit this form"
    runat="server" />
<br>
<asp:label id="OurLabel" runat="server" /><br>
</form>
</body>
</html>
```

As you can see in Figure 7.4, when you click the hyperlink on the page, the IsPostBack of the page returns true, which means that you have successfully submitted the form. The LinkButton gives you another option for creating Submit button functionality, as well as another avenue for firing the OnClick and OnCommand events. This can be very useful when an image or a traditional Submit button doesn't lend itself to the design of the user interface. In this situation, you can use the LinkButton to submit the form or fire these events.

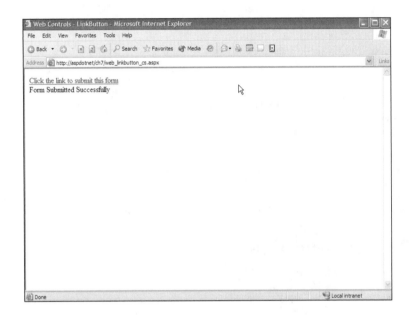

Literal

Okay, I lied. I just lied to you and I feel horrible. I just got through rambling about how you could manipulate all these different things on all the Web server controls, and it's just a big fat lie.

It's a lie because unlike the other Web server controls, the Literal control doesn't inherit the WebControl class and is an exception to the rule that all objects in the System.Web.UI.WebControl namespace inherit the WebControl class. I'm sorry, and I'd like to make amends and set the record straight.

The Literal Web server control is literally what you'd think it literally is in the most literal sense. It is a control that literally writes its text property directly to the HTML stream. (The Literal Web server controls only property outside of what every control gets from the Control object.) For instance:

Visual Basic .NET—web_literal_vb.aspx

```
<%@ page language="vb" runat="server"%>
<script runat=server>
Sub Page_Load(sender as Object, e as EventArgs)
    OurTitle.Text="<title>Web Controls - Literal</title>"
end Sub
</script>
<html>
<head>
<asp:Literal id="OurTitle" runat="server" />
</head>
<body bgcolor="#FFFFFF" text="#000000">
<asp:Literal id="OurBody"
    Text="Literally just this text will appear."
    runat="server" />
</body>
</html>
```

C#—web_literal_cs.aspx

```
<%@ page language="cs" runat="server"%>
<script runat=server>
void Page_Load(){
    OurTitle.Text="<title>Web Controls - Literal</title>";
}
</script>
<html>
<head>
<asp:Literal id="OurTitle" runat="server" />
</head>
<body bgcolor="#FFFFFF" text="#000000">
<asp:Literal id="OurBody"
    Text="Literally just this text will appear."
    runat="server" />
</body>
</html>
```

The Resulting HTML

```
<html>
<head>
<title>Web Controls - Literal</title>
</head>
<body bgcolor="#FFFFFF" text="#000000">
Literally just this text will appear.
</body>
</html>
```

As you can see, the `Literal` Web server control simply writes the exact contents of its text property to the page without mucking with it one bit. This comes in handy in a lot of situations when you need to dynamically set things, such as the page's `<title>` tag, but there isn't an exact matching control for the code or tags you want to produce.

Panel

The `Panel` Web server control renders a `<div>` container tag to the web browser, and you can basically do anything you want with it. You can set styles and attributes to set absolute positioning, or play with the visibility properties. It can contain any type of HTML, `HTMLControl`, or `WebControl`. It presents a whole host of possibilities.

The `Panel` Web server control has three properties all its own and no methods or events (see Table 7.8).

TABLE 7.8 *Panel* Web Server Control Properties

Property	Description
BackImageURL	Gets or sets the URL of the background image that the panel will have.
HorizontalAlign	Gets or sets the horizontal alignment of the contents of the panel.
Wrap	A Boolean value (true or false) that gets or sets whether the contents within the panel will wrap or not.

Next we play around with the `Panel` Web server control's `visible` property to determine whether `Panel` and its contents will be visible in the browser.

The `visible` property doesn't control the `<div>` tag's visibility through the visibility property that you might be familiar with in cascading style sheets that you might have manipulated via JavaScript in the past. The Web server controls `visible` property actually prevents the `<div>` from being inserted in the HTML if it is set to false.

Visual Basic .NET—web_panel_vb.aspx

```
<%@ page language="vb" runat="server"%>
<script runat=server>
Sub OurCheckBoxClick(sender as Object, e as EventArgs)
    if OurCheckBox1.Checked Then
        OurPanel.Visible = "True"
    else
        OurPanel.Visible = "False"
    end if
End Sub

Sub Move_Panel(sender as Object, e as EventArgs)
    OurPanel.Style("position")="absolute"
    OurPanel.Style("left")="250"
    OurPanel.Style("top")="150"
    OurLabel.Text="The panel is a Left = 250, Top = 150"
End Sub
</script>

<html>
<head>
<title>Web Controls - Panel</title>
</head>
<body bgcolor="#FFFFFF" text="#000000">
<form runat="server">
<asp:CheckBox id="OurCheckBox1" runat="server" OnCheckedChanged="OurCheckBoxClick"
➥Checked="true" AutoPostBack="true" /> Display Panel<br>
<asp:Button Text="Move Panel" OnClick="Move_Panel" runat="server" />
Move the panel to the middle of the screen.<br>
<asp:Panel id="OurPanel"
    BorderStyle="Double"
    BorderColor="#000000"
    BackColor="#CCCCCC"
    HorizontalAlign="Center"
    Height="100"
    Width="250"
    runat="server" >
<asp:Label id="OurLabel" runat="server" /><br>
<b>This is some text that I've written into the panel.</b>
</asp:Panel>
</form>
</body>
</html>
```

C#—web_panel_cs.aspx

```
<%@ page language="cs" runat="server"%>
<script runat=server>
void OurCheckBoxClick(Object sender,EventArgs e){
    if (OurCheckBox1.Checked){
        OurPanel.Visible = true;
    }else{
        OurPanel.Visible = false;
    }
}

void Move_Panel(Object sender,EventArgs e){
    OurPanel.Style["position"]="absolute";
    OurPanel.Style["left"]="250";
    OurPanel.Style["top"]="150";
    OurLabel.Text="The panel is a Left = 250, Top = 150";
}
</script>

<html>
<head>
<title>Web Controls - Panel</title>
</head>
<body bgcolor="#FFFFFF" text="#000000">
<form runat="server">
<asp:CheckBox id="OurCheckBox1" runat="server" OnCheckedChanged="OurCheckBoxClick"
➥Checked="true" AutoPostBack="true" /> Display Panel<br>
<asp:Button Text="Move Panel" OnClick="Move_Panel" runat="server" />
Move the panel to the middle of the screen.<br>
<asp:Panel id="OurPanel"
    BorderStyle="Double"
    BorderColor="#000000"
    BackColor="#CCCCCC"
    HorizontalAlign="Center"
    Height="100"
    Width="250"
    runat="server" >
<asp:Label id="OurLabel" runat="server" /><br>
<b>This is some text that I've written into the panel.</b>
</asp:Panel>
</form>
</body>
</html>
```

As you can see in Figure 7.5, we programmatically set the Panel's visible property and also added some style attributes to it when the button was clicked that allowed absolute positioning of the <div>.

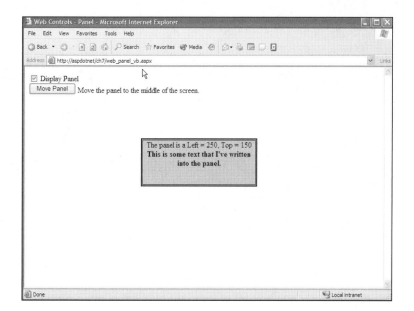

FIGURE 7.5

The Panel *web server control creates a <div> tag that can be manipulated with style sheets for positioning.*

PlaceHolder

The PlaceHolder Web server control holds a spot for you to programmatically add or remove controls in its place. For instance, say you want to provide a drop-down list if a certain condition is true. You can add or remove as many controls to the PlaceHolder as you would like. This way you can dynamically build forms, or as we noted in an earlier chapter, dynamically load User controls to customize the user's interface.

In the following example, the Control property of the PlaceHolder is really an instance of the ControlCollection object located in the System.Web.UI.Control namespace. You use the ControlCollection's Add() method to add Controls to the PlaceHolder. A bunch of other methods are available to manipulate what the PlaceHolder contains, and I suggest you check out this object in the Class Browser located at http://www.gotdotnet.com or in the .NET Framework SDK.

Visual Basic .NET—web_placeholder_vb.aspx

```
<%@ page language="vb" runat="server"%>
<script runat=server>
sub OurCheckBoxClick(sender as Object, e as EventArgs)
    if OurCheckBox.Checked then
        dim OurArrayList as new ArrayList()
        dim OurDropDown as new DropDownList()
        OurArrayList.Add("Cake")
        OurArrayList.Add("Cookies")
        OurArrayList.Add("Ice Cream")
        OurArrayList.Add("Pie")
        OurDropDown.DataSource = OurArrayList
        OurDropDown.DataBind()
        OurPlaceholder.Controls.Add(OurDropDown)
    end if
end sub
</script>


<html>
<title>Web Controls -  PlaceHolder</title>
<body>
<form runat="server">
<asp:CheckBox id="OurCheckBox"
    OnCheckedChanged="OurCheckBoxClick"
    Checked="false" AutoPostBack="true"
    runat="server" />
Populate Placeholder with Dropdown<br>
<asp:PlaceHolder runat="server" id="OurPlaceHolder" /> <br>
</form>
</body>
</html>
```

C#—web_placeholder_cs.aspx

```
<%@ page language="c#" runat="server"%>
<script runat=server>
void OurCheckBoxClick(Object sender, EventArgs e) {
    if (OurCheckBox.Checked) {
        ArrayList OurArrayList = new ArrayList();
        DropDownList OurDropDown = new DropDownList();
        OurArrayList.Add("Cake");
        OurArrayList.Add("Cookies");
        OurArrayList.Add("Ice Cream");
        OurArrayList.Add("Pie");
        OurDropDown.DataSource = OurArrayList;
        OurDropDown.DataBind();
        OurPlaceHolder.Controls.Add(OurDropDown);
```

```
      }
}
</script>


<html>
<title>Web Controls -  PlaceHolder</title>
<body>
<form runat="server">
<asp:CheckBox id="OurCheckBox"
    OnCheckedChanged="OurCheckBoxClick"
        Checked="false" AutoPostBack="true"
        runat="server" />
Populate Placeholder with Dropdown<br>
<asp:PlaceHolder runat="server" id="OurPlaceHolder" /> <br>
</form>
</body>
</html>
```

As Figure 7.6 shows, after you click the check box, the PlaceHolder tag is replaced with the drop-down list. You might also programmatically decide between two different dropdowns or multiple text boxes or whatever controls you'd like to add or remove from the PlaceHolder. The only limitation is your imagination! (Sci-Fi music fades up and camera zooms in and disappears in Mad Scientist's pupil).

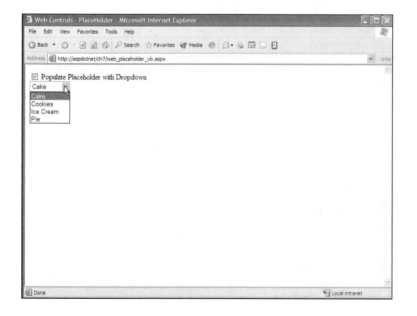

FIGURE 7.6

The PlaceHolder *enables you to dynamically add or remove controls and render them where the* Placeholder *tag appears in your code.*

RadioButton

The RadioButton Web server control renders the `<input type="radio">` to the web browser. It inherits all the properties and methods of the CheckBox Web server control and has a single additional property (see Table 7.9).

TABLE 7.9 *RadioButton* Web Server Control Properties

Property	Description
AutoPostBack	Gets or sets the value that determines whether the check box causes a form to post back to the server.
Checked	Gets or sets the value indicating whether a check box is checked or not.
GroupName	Gets or sets the name of the group of radio buttons to which the control belongs.
Text	Gets or sets the text that is displayed as the label for the check box.
TextAlign	Gets or sets whether the Text label is displayed to the right or left of the check box.

Visual Basic .NET—`web_radiobutton_vb.aspx`

```
<%@ page language="vb" runat="server"%>
<script runat=server>
sub Radio_Click(sender as Object, e as EventArgs)
    OurLabel.Text = "You Selected: " & Request.Params("OurRadioButtonGroup")
end sub

</script>

<html>
<head>
<title>Web Control - RadioButton</title>
</head>
<body bgcolor="#FFFFFF" text="#000000">
<form runat="server">
<asp:RadioButton id="OurRadioButton1"
    AutoPostBack="true"
    Text="Radio Button 1"
    GroupName="OurRadioButtonGroup"
    OnCheckedChanged="Radio_Click"
    value="Radio Button Number 1"
    runat="server" Checked = "true"  />
```

```
<br>
<asp:RadioButton id="OurRadioButton2"
    AutoPostBack="true"
    Text="Radio Button 2"
    GroupName="OurRadioButtonGroup"
    value="Radio Button Number 2"
    OnCheckedChanged="Radio_Click" runat="server" />
<br>
<asp:label id="OurLabel" Text="Button 1 is preselected" runat="server" />
</form>
</body>
</html>
```

C#—web_radiobutton_cs.aspx

```
<%@ page language="cs" runat="server"%>
<script runat=server>
void Radio_Click(Object sender, EventArgs e) {
    OurLabel.Text = "You Selected: " + Request.Params["OurRadioButtonGroup"];
}
</script>

<html>
<head>
<title>Web Control - RadioButton</title>
</head>
<body bgcolor="#FFFFFF" text="#000000">
<form runat="server">
<asp:RadioButton id="OurRadioButton1"
    AutoPostBack="true"
    Text="Radio Button 1"
    GroupName="OurRadioButtonGroup"
    OnCheckedChanged="Radio_Click"
    value="Radio Button Number 1"
    runat="server" Checked = "true"  />
<br>
<asp:RadioButton id="OurRadioButton2"
    AutoPostBack="true"
    Text="Radio Button 2"
    GroupName="OurRadioButtonGroup"
    value="Radio Button Number 2"
    OnCheckedChanged="Radio_Click" runat="server" />
<br>
<asp:label id="OurLabel" Text="Button 1 is preselected" runat="server" />
</form>
</body>
</html>
```

In Figure 7.7 you can see that the OnCheckChanged event of the radio button was fired and the Text property of OurLabel was set. Also notice how the value of the radio button was retrieved through the Page object's Request.Params collection, which is a combined collection of all Querystring, Form, ServerVariables, and Cookies items for the Page.

FIGURE 7.7

The RadioButton web server control allows you to programmatically manipulate and retrieve information from a radio button or group of radio buttons.

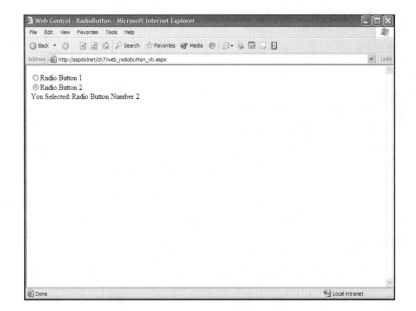

Table, TableRow, TableCell

The table Web server controls render their corresponding table elements to the web browser: <table></table>, <tr></tr>, and <td></td>. These have many properties, listed in Tables 7.10, 7.11, and 7.12.

TABLE 7.10 *Table* Object Properties

Property	Description
BackImageURL	Gets or sets the URL of the background image that panel will have.
CellPadding	Gets or sets the value of the table's cellpadding attribute.
CellSpacing	Gets or sets the value of the table's cellspacing attribute.
GridLines	Gets or sets the value that determines the grid line style of the table control. Options are None, Horizontal, Vertical, or Both.
HorizontalAlign	Gets or sets the horizontal alignment of the table within its container, which could be the page or could be nested in a table or a div.
Rows	Instance of the TableRowCollection, exposing its properties and methods.

TABLE 7.11 *TableRow* Object Properties

Property	Description
Cells	Instance of the TableCellCollection, exposing its properties and methods.
HorizontalAlign	Gets or sets the horizontal alignment of the contents in the row.
VerticalAlign	Gets or sets the vertical alignment of the contents in the row.

TABLE 7.12 *TableCell* Object Properties

Property	Description
ColumnSpan	Gets or sets across how many columns the cell spans.
HorizontalAlign	Gets or sets the horizontal alignment of the contents in the cell.
RowSpan	Gets or sets down how many rows the cell extends.
Text	Gets or sets the text contents of the cell.
VerticalAlign	Gets or sets the vertical alignment of the contents in the cell.
Wrap	Gets or sets a Boolean value that defines whether the contents within a cell should wrap. True is the default.

In the `HTMLControl` example of the `HTMLTable`, you manipulated a bunch of the properties programmatically, but here you'll do something different. The following code builds a table programmatically.

Visual Basic .NET—**web_buildtable_vb.aspx**

```
<%@ page language="vb" runat="server"%>
<script  runat=server>
sub Page_Load(sender As Object, e As EventArgs)
    dim OurArray() as Integer = {1,2,3,4,5,6,7,8,9,10}
    if not IsPostBack
        OurCells.DataSource = OurArray
        OurRows.DataSource = OurArray
        DataBind()
    end if
end sub

Sub Build_Table(sender As Object, e As System.EventArgs)
    dim NumRows As Integer
    dim NumCells As Integer
    dim iCell As Integer
    dim iRow As Integer
    dim R As TableRow
    dim C As TableCell
    NumRows = CInt(OurRows.SelectedItem.Value)
    NumCells = CInt(OurCells.SelectedItem.Value)

    For iRow = 1 To NumRows
        r = new TableRow()
        For iCell = 1  To NumCells
                c = new TableCell()
                c.Controls.Add(new LiteralControl("row " &
                [ccc]iRow & ", cell " & iCell))
                r.Cells.Add(c)
            Next iCell
        OurTable.Rows.Add(r)
      Next iRow
End Sub
</script>
<html>
<head>
<title>Web Control Table</title>
</head>
<body>
<form runat=server>
<asp:Table id="OurTable"
    GridLines="Both"
    CellPadding="3"
    CellSpacing="0"
    BorderWidth="1"
    BorderColor="#000000"
    runat="server" />
```

```
<br><br>
<asp:DropDownList id="OurCells" runat="server" /> Cells<br>
<asp:DropDownList id="OurRows" runat="server" /> Rows<br>
<asp:Button id="OurButton" Text="Build Table" OnClick="Build_Table" runat=
➥"server" />
</form>
</body>
</html>
```

C#—web_buildtable_cs.aspx

```
<%@ page language="cs" runat="server"%>
<script  runat=server>
void Page_Load(){
    int[] OurArray = {1,2,3,4,5,6,7,8,9,10};
    if (!IsPostBack) {
        OurCells.DataSource = OurArray;
        OurRows.DataSource = OurArray;
        DataBind();
    }
}

void Build_Table(object s,System.EventArgs e){
    int NumRows;
    int NumCells;
    int iCell;
    int iRow;
    TableRow R;
    TableCell C;
    NumRows = int.Parse(OurRows.SelectedItem.Value);
        NumCells = int.Parse(OurCells.SelectedItem.Value);

    for (iRow = 1;iRow <= NumRows;iRow++){
        R = new TableRow();
        for (iCell = 1;iCell <= NumCells;iCell++){
                C = new TableCell();
                C.Controls.Add(new LiteralControl("row " + iRow.ToString() + ",
                ➥cell " + iCell.ToString()));
                R.Cells.Add(C);
            }
        OurTable.Rows.Add(R);
        }
}
</script>
<html>
<head>
<title>Web Control Table</title>
</head>
<body>
<form runat=server>
<asp:Table id="OurTable"
```

continues

C#—(continued)

```
        GridLines="Both"
        CellPadding="3"
        CellSpacing="0"
        BorderWidth="1"
        BorderColor="#000000"
        runat="server" />
<br><br>
<asp:DropDownList id="OurCells" runat="server" /> Cells<br>
<asp:DropDownList id="OurRows" runat="server" /> Rows<br>
<asp:Button id="OurButton" Text="Build Table" OnClick="Build_Table" runat=
➥"server" />
</form>
</body>
</html>
```

Here some of the looping you learned in an earlier chapter is used, and it dynamically creates and adds `TableCells` to `TableRows`, and the `TableRows` are added dynamically to the `Table`, as you can see in Figure 7.8.

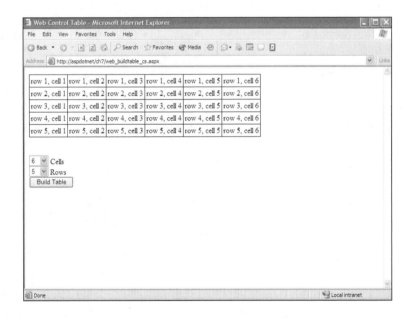

FIGURE 7.8

The `Table`, `TableRow`, *and* `TableCell` *Web server controls give you the ability to programmatically build and manipulate tables.*

Don't be intimidated by this code block. If I can understand it, you can understand it. Let me break it down. The piece of code that reads R = new TableRow() is creating a new instance of a `TableRow` object. Then there's a loop where you see C = New TableCell(), which is creating a new `TableCell` object. You fill its contents with a `Literal` control and loop through the number of cells you want, adding them to the `TableRow` that was created with `R.Cells.Add(C)`. The `C` specifies the `TableCell` just created. After the `Row` has all the specified cells, you add that `TableRow` instance to the table with `OurTable.Rows.Add(R)` (the `R` specifies the `TableRow` just created), and then loop back and do it again until all the rows are created and added to the table. For those who would benefit from a visual of that explanation, look at this:

```
Outer Loop Generates Row
    Inner Loop Generates Cell
        Create Cell
    End Inner Loop
End Outer Loop
```

TextBox

The `TextBox` Web server control can be rendered as three different things depending on the `TextMode` property; `<input type="text">`, `<input type="password">`, or `<textarea>`. It has a bunch of other properties (see Table 7.13), as well as a single method of its own called `OnTextChanged`.

TABLE 7.13 *TextBox* Object Properties

Property	Description
AutoPostBack	Gets or sets the value that determines whether the `TextBox` causes a form to post back to the server.
Columns	Gets or sets the display width of the text box in characters.
MaxLength	Gets or sets the maximum number of characters a user can enter into a `TextBox`.
ReadOnly	Gets or sets whether the contents of the `TextBox` can be changed.
Rows	Gets or sets the height of the `TextBox` if the `TextMode` property is set to `Multiline`.
Text	Gets or sets the contents of the `TextBox`.
TextMode	Gets or sets the kind of `TextBox` that is rendered. Available options are `SingleLine` (default), `Multiline`, and `Password`.
Wrap	Gets or sets the value indicating whether the text contents wrap inside the `TextBox`.

Let's take a look at the `TextBox` Web server control in action. You'll use the `AutoPostBack` property to post the form and trigger the `OnTextChanged` event if you have changed the contents of the `TextBox`. This example also programmatically manipulates what type of `TextBox` it is, although you may never do this. I did it…because we can!

Visual Basic .NET—`web_textbox_vb.aspx`

```vb
<%@ page language="vb" runat="server"%>
<script runat=server>
sub Radio_Click(sender as Object, e as EventArgs)
    if OurRadioButton1.Checked Then
        OurTextBox.TextMode = TextBoxMode.SingleLine
    elseif OurRadioButton2.Checked then
        OurTextBox.TextMode = TextBoxMode.MultiLine
        OurTextBox.Rows = 5
    elseif OurRadioButton3.Checked Then
        OurTextBox.TextMode = TextBoxMode.Password
    end if
end sub

sub Text_Changed(s as Object,e as EventArgs)
    OurLabel.Text="You have changed the text in the " +
    ➥OurTextBox.TextMode.ToString() + " box"
end sub
</script>

<html>
<head>
<title>Web Controls - TextBox</title>
</head>
<body bgcolor="#FFFFFF" text="#000000">
<form runat="server">
Pick what kind of textbox you would like this to be:<br>
<asp:RadioButton id="OurRadioButton1"
    AutoPostBack="true"
    Text="Single Line"
    GroupName="OurRadioButtonGroup"
    OnCheckedChanged="Radio_Click"
    runat="server"
    Checked="true" />
<br>
<asp:RadioButton id="OurRadioButton2"
    AutoPostBack="true"
    Text="Multi Line"
    GroupName="OurRadioButtonGroup"
    OnCheckedChanged="Radio_Click"
    runat="server" />
<br>
<asp:RadioButton id="OurRadioButton3"
    AutoPostBack="true"
    Text="Password"
```

```
        GroupName="OurRadioButtonGroup"
        OnCheckedChanged="Radio_Click"
        runat="server" />
<br>
<asp:TextBox id="ourTextBox"
    AutoPostBack="true"
    TextMode = "SingleLine"
    OnTextChanged="Text_Changed"
    runat="server" />
<br>
<asp:Label id="OurLabel" EnableViewState="false" runat="Server" />
</form>
</body>
</html>
```

C#—web_textbox_cs.aspx

```
<%@ page language="cs" runat="server"%>
<script runat=server>
void Radio_Click(Object sender,EventArgs e){
    if (OurRadioButton1.Checked){
        OurTextBox.TextMode = TextBoxMode.SingleLine;
    }else if (OurRadioButton2.Checked){
        OurTextBox.TextMode = TextBoxMode.MultiLine;
        OurTextBox.Rows = 5;
    }else if (OurRadioButton3.Checked){
        OurTextBox.TextMode = TextBoxMode.Password;
    }
}

void Text_Changed(Object sender,EventArgs e){
    OurLabel.Text="You have changed the text in the " +
    ➥OurTextBox.TextMode.ToString() + " box";
}
</script>

<html>
<head>
<title>Web Controls - TextBox</title>
</head>
<body bgcolor="#FFFFFF" text="#000000">
<form runat="server">
Pick what kind of textbox you would like this to be:<br>
<asp:RadioButton id="OurRadioButton1"
    AutoPostBack="true"
    Text="Single Line"
    GroupName="OurRadioButtonGroup"
    OnCheckedChanged="Radio_Click"
    runat="server"
    Checked="true" />
<br>
<asp:RadioButton id="OurRadioButton2"
```

continues

C#—(continued)

```
        AutoPostBack="true"
        Text="Multi Line"
        GroupName="OurRadioButtonGroup"
        OnCheckedChanged="Radio_Click"
        runat="server" />
<br>
<asp:RadioButton id="OurRadioButton3"
        AutoPostBack="true"
        Text="Password"
        GroupName="OurRadioButtonGroup"
        OnCheckedChanged="Radio_Click"
        runat="server" />
<br>
<asp:TextBox id="OurTextBox"
        AutoPostBack="true"
        TextMode = "SingleLine"
        OnTextChanged="Text_Changed"
        runat="server" />
<br>
<asp:Label id="OurLabel" EnableViewState="false" runat="Server" />
</form>
</body>
</html>
```

As you can see in Figure 7.9, changing the contents of the TextBox has caused the OnTextChanged event. I have also set the TextBox Web server control's TextMode property to Multiline and set the Rows property to 5 to show multiple lines.

FIGURE 7.9

The TextBox web server control can produce three different types of Text form elements; a standard text box, a multi-line text area, and a password text box.

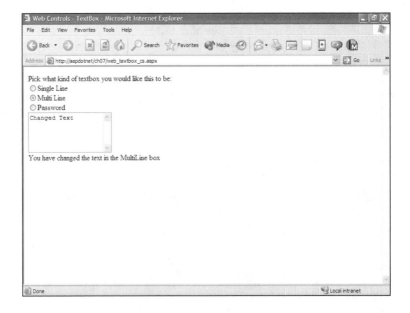

Now That's Cool! Rich Server Controls

ASP.NET provides a few very rich Web server controls that create form and produce function that would take tons of code in any other environment. But in ASP.NET they can be achieved with a single tag. Chapter 1 touched on the `Calendar` Web server control; in this section you'll see that and the `AdRotator` Web server control, as well.

AdRotator

Anyone who has had to manage banner ads will love ASP.NET's `AdRotator` object. This Web server control enables you to deliver and maintain banner ad campaigns, filter what ads are delivered, and control how many times they are delivered, all through the use of a controlling XML file. Table 7.14 lists and describes its properties.

TABLE 7.14 *AdRotator* Object Properties

Property	Description
AdvertisementFile	Gets or sets the path to an XML file that contains advertisement information.
KeywordFilter	Gets or sets a category keyword to filter for specific types of advertisements in the XML advertisement file.
Target	Gets or sets the target where the page displayed by clicking the banner will be loaded, such as _blank, _parent, _self, _top, or the name of a frame in a frameset.

Now you're gonna get your first taste of XML, at least in this book. Don't be alarmed or overwhelmed with the concept of XML. If you take a look at the OurAds.xml file (in a few paragraphs) you will see it is quite simple to understand what's going on in this file. XML works a lot like HTML, using delimiters to define and contain information.

When you deal with HTML, if you want to put a Title into a page with HTML, you use a predefined tag such as `<title>This is the title</title>`. There is an opening delimiter and a closing delimiter for the predefined tag.

XML works in a similar manner, except the delimiters are not predefined. They are self-defining. Instead of me explaining, take a look at the example.

The XML file that defines the AdRotator information includes five necessary elements: ImageURL, NavigateURL, AlternateText, Keyword, and Impressions. The XML document identifies this through its tag delimiters.

OurAds.xml

```
<Advertisements>
    <Ad>
            <ImageUrl>images/nr_ad.gif</ImageUrl>
             <NavigateUrl>http://www.newriders.com</NavigateUrl>
              <AlternateText>New Riders</AlternateText>
              <Keyword>Publishers</Keyword>
              <Impressions>100</Impressions>
    </Ad>
        <Ad>
              <ImageUrl>images/peter_ad.gif</ImageUrl>
              <NavigateUrl>http://www.nexusmediagroup.com</NavigateUrl>
              <AlternateText>It's Peter</AlternateText>
              <Keyword>Authors</Keyword>
              <Impressions>150</Impressions>
        </Ad>
</Advertisements>
```

Notice that there are tags that delimit where the advertisements are, where the ads begin and end, and where the attributes of each ad begin and end in this document. Not too hard to follow, right? Now look at the AdRotator in action. Even though there are only two ads in the XML file, I want to demonstrate the KeywordFilter property to limit the ads to be displayed to only those with a keyword of Authors. If there were many ads with this keyword, they would be randomly displayed.

Visual Basic .NET—**web_adrotator_vb.aspx**

```
<%@ page language="vb" runat="server"%>
<html>
<head>
<title>Web Controls - Ad Rotator</title>
</head>
<body bgcolor="#FFFFFF" text="#000000">
<form runat="server">
<asp:AdRotator id="OurAdRotator"
    KeywordFilter="Authors"
    AdvertisementFile  = "OurAds.xml"
    runat=server />
</form>
</body>
</html>
```

C#—web_adrotator_cs.aspx

```
<%@ page language="c#" runat="server"%>
<html>
<head>
<title>Web Controls - AdRotator</title>
</head>
<body bgcolor="#FFFFFF" text="#000000">
<form runat="server">
<asp:AdRotator id="OurAdRotator"
    KeywordFilter="Authors"
    AdvertisementFile  = "OurAds.xml"
    runat=server />
</form>
</body>
</html>
```

As you can see in Figure 7.10, the "Author that Blabbers" ad was delivered to the web page as expected. This control also has an event called AdCreate, which has its own set of event arguments. One of these arguments, called AdProperties, enables you to access any name-value pair within the XML document for the specific delivered ad.

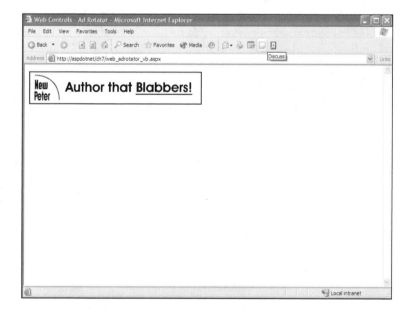

FIGURE 7.10

The AdRotator *web server control is a blessing for programmers that must create and manage banner ad campaigns.*

So imagine that you had an additional entry in your ads called <message>Here is your message</message>. You could call a function when you create the ad through the AdCreate event and maybe set a label's text value to the value of <message> in your XML document.

Visual Basic .NET

```
Sub AdCreated_Event(sender As Object, e As AdCreatedEventArgs)
       OurLabel.Text = e.AdProperties("Message")
    End Sub
```

C#

```
void AdCreated_Event(Object sender, AdCreatedEventArgs e){
       OurLabel.Text = e.AdProperties["Message"];
    }
```

Calendar

Lordy, Lordy. The Calendar control sure does have a lot of properties all its own. Table 7.15 is one big table…but, as I describe briefly in Chapter 1, this control would take loads more time to code by hand than you need to learn and understand its properties.

TABLE 7.15 *Calendar* Object Properties

Property	Description
CellPadding	Gets or sets the amount of space between the contents of a cell and the cell's border.
CellSpacing	Gets or sets the amount of space between cells.
DayHeaderStyle	Gets the style properties for the section that displays the day of the week.
DayNameFormat	Gets or sets the name format of days of the week.
DayStyle	Gets the style properties for the days in the displayed month.
FirstDayOfWeek	Gets or sets the day of the week to display in the first day column of the Calendar control.
NextMonthText	Gets or sets the text displayed for the next month's navigation control.
NextPrevFormat	Gets or sets the format of the Next and Previous Month navigation elements in the title section of the Calendar control.

Property	Description
NextPrevStyle	Gets the style properties for the Next and Previous Month navigation elements.
OtherMonthDayStyle	Gets the style properties for the days on the Calendar control that are not in the displayed month.
PrevMonthText	Gets or sets the text displayed for the Previous Month navigation control.
SelectedDate	Gets or sets the selected date.
SelectedDates	Gets a collection of System.DateTime objects that represent the selected dates on the Calendar control.
SelectedDayStyle	Gets the style properties for the selected dates.
SelectionMode	Gets or sets the date selection mode on the Calendar control that specifies whether the user can select a single day, a week, or an entire month.
SelectMonthText	Gets or sets the text displayed for the month selection element in the selector column.
SelectorStyle	Gets the style properties for the week and month selector column.
SelectWeekText	Gets or sets the text displayed for the week selection element in the selector column.
ShowDayHeader	Gets or sets a value indicating whether the heading for the days of the week is displayed.
ShowGridLines	Gets or sets a value indicating whether the days on the Calendar control are separated with grid lines.
ShowNextPrevMonth	Gets or sets a value indicating whether the Calendar control displays the Next and Previous Month navigation elements in the title section.
ShowTitle	Gets or sets a value indicating whether the title section is displayed.
TitleFormat	Gets or sets the title format for the title section.
TitleStyle	Gets the style properties of the title heading for the Calendar control.
TodayDayStyle	Gets the style properties for today's date on the Calendar control.
TodaysDate	Gets or sets the value for today's date.
VisibleDate	Gets or sets the date that specifies the month to display on the Calendar control.
WeekendDayStyle	Gets the style properties for the weekend dates on the Calendar control.

Phewwwww!! Yes, there are a lot of properties. No, it's not that complicated. If you read the properties in Table 7.14, they are all very understandable. If you need additional information, refer to the SDK, where you can get an exhaustive amount of information about every little nook and cranny of every property the `Calendar` Web server control possesses.

N O T E

I know that I've mentioned this before, but it's worth repeating. Whenever you need information about anything having to do with the .NET Framework, your best bet is to go to the SDK. It's as thorough a set of documents as you are going to find on the .NET Framework, and its navigation is intuitive and logical. Whenever you need to dig deeper into an object or control, you can always find links that will take you where you need to go. Want to find out about the `Calendar` object's properties? Navigate to the `Calendar` object and click to see its "Members." Want to know about the `DayNameFormat` property? Click its name, which is a link to a document about it. Want to see allowable values for this property? Click the `DayNameFormat` Value link. Dig deep. You can spend days digging through here.

Now look at an example that plays around with a bunch of the properties. You will see some of the properties hyphenated with what looks like properties from other classes. You can do this because these are actually instances of other objects and you can directly manipulate these instances' properties through this hyphenated system. This gives you awesome amounts of control over how Web server controls—and, particularly in this example, calendars—will look and act.

Visual Basic .NET—**web_calendar_vb.aspx**

```
<%@ page language="vb" runat="server"%>
<script runat=server>
Sub SelectionChange(sender as Object, e as EventArgs)
    OurLabel.Text = "The date you selected is " &
    ➥OurCalendar.SelectedDate.ToShortDateString()
end sub
</script>
<html>
<head>
<title>Web Control - Calendar</title>
</head>
<body bgcolor="#FFFFFF" text="#000000">
<form runat="server">
    <asp:Calendar id="OurCalendar"
        CellPadding="2"
        Font-Name="verdana"
        Font-Size="12px"
        FirstDayOfWeek="Monday"
        TitleStyle-Font-Size="14px"
        TitleStyle-BackColor="#CCCCCC"
        NextMonthText=">>"
        PrevMonthText="<<"
```

```
            NextPrevStyle-Font-Bold="false"
            DayHeaderStyle-BackColor="#000000"
            DayHeaderStyle-ForeColor="#FFFFFF"
            SelectedDayStyle-BackColor="#000000"
            ShowGridLines="true"
            SelectionMode="Day"
            OnSelectionChanged="SelectionChange"
            BorderColor="#000000"
            runat="server" />
<br><br>
<asp:Label id="OurLabel" runat="server" />
</form>
</body>
</html>
```

C#—web_calendar_cs.aspx

```
<%@ page language="cs" runat="server"%>
<script runat=server>
void SelectionChange(Object sender,EventArgs e){
    OurLabel.Text = "The date you selected is " +
    ➥OurCalendar.SelectedDate.ToShortDateString();
}
</script>
<html>
<head>
<title>Web Control - Calendar</title>
</head>
<body bgcolor="#FFFFFF" text="#000000">
<form runat="server">
    <asp:Calendar id="OurCalendar"
        CellPadding="2"
        Font-Name="verdana"
        Font-Size="12px"
        FirstDayOfWeek="Monday"
        TitleStyle-Font-Size="14px"
        TitleStyle-BackColor="#CCCCCC"
        NextMonthText=">>"
        PrevMonthText="<<"
        NextPrevStyle-Font-Bold="false"
        DayHeaderStyle-BackColor="#000000"
        DayHeaderStyle-ForeColor="#FFFFFF"
        SelectedDayStyle-BackColor="#000000"
        ShowGridLines="true"
        SelectionMode="Day"
        OnSelectionChanged="SelectionChange"
        BorderColor="#000000"
        runat="server" />
<br><br>
<asp:Label id="OurLabel" runat="server" />
</form>
</body>
</html>
```

In Figure 7.11 you can see that this code has formatted the tar out of the calendar, and this is just the tip of the iceberg. Experiment with the properties and you will quickly see that you can make this control do just about anything you'd like it to and make it look any way you'd like.

FIGURE 7.11

The Calendar control emits code that would take hours and hours to code by hand with the setting of some simple properties.

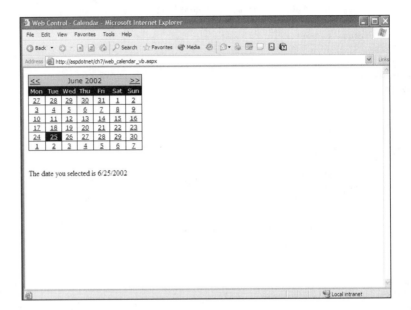

Summary

This chapter has gone over some of the standard Web server controls and two of the rich Web server controls, and as you can see, these controls add a dynamic to ASP.NET that the HTML server controls don't have. As you just saw in the Calendar control, many of the properties are actually instances of other objects that expose multiple levels of properties and methods, giving you the opportunity to build very powerful applications.

Because the Web server controls are built around the same core parent objects across the board, after you master and understand these building blocks you can powerfully manipulate all the Web server controls, including both the validators that you'll explore in the next chapter, and the list objects and DataGrids that are discussed in the chapter after that.

8

Web Form Validators

Oh, you'd better be telling the
truth...cause i'm gonna check!

For anyone who's ever validated a user's input on an HTML form using either
client-side JavaScript or using round-trip server-side validation, you're going to *love*
this chapter. And I mean *LOVE!*

Microsoft has done an immeasurable kindness to web designers with this group
of Web server controls. They have basically reduced what could be hours and
hours and hours and hours of work into a few basic lines of code.

Form Validation

If you've ever really dealt with form validation in a serious manner, where a user's input must be validated to the *nth* degree, you know that it can be a very daunting task. In critical situations, it was generally necessary to use round trips to the server in conjunction with client-side JavaScript as a preliminary check. In these situations, you needed to perform server-side validation because you couldn't guarantee that an individual had a JavaScript-enabled browser. Even users who did have capable browser possibly could disable the JavaScript functionality.

But you would generally develop both strategies to save from making trips to the server if you could prevent them through client-side JavaScript. If you had many form elements, your validation code could run into hundreds of lines of code for both server-side and client-side validation.

Enter ASP.NET! (Can't you hear the collective cheers of web programmers around the world?) ASP.NET provides a bunch of validators for which you will be thanking a higher power (I'm not talking about Bill Gates) for years to come. These validators are Power Tools with a capital P and T.

I'm gonna throw you a baited hook and I know you're going to bite. I did a test today and wrote from scratch two different web pages: A traditional ASP page and an ASP.NET web form. They both have identical form fields for the user to fill out. I have timed my development time and lines of code to show you how cool these ASP.NET validators are.

In Figure 8.1 you can see a basic form requesting a name, address, city, state, zip code, phone number, and e-mail address. What I did was create this form by hand in traditional ASP and in ASP.NET with full client-side and server-side form validation.

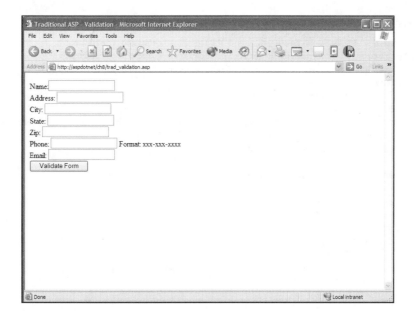

FIGURE 8.1

Validating forms in traditional ASP was at the very least a nightmare.

The following is the traditional ASP page:

Traditional ASP—`trad_validation.asp`

```
<%
dim vName,vAddress,vCity,vState,vZip,vPhone,vEmail,vError
vName=""
vAddress=""
vCity=""
vState=""
vZip=""
vPhone=""
vEmail=""
vError=""

If Request.Form("Submit") <> "" then
vName = Request.Form("Name")
vAddress = Request.Form("Address")
vCity = Request.Form("City")
vState = Request.Form("State")
vZip = Request.Form("Zip")
vPhone = Request.Form("Phone")
vEmail = Request.Form("Email")


if vName = "" then vError = vError & "Name is a required field<br>"
if vAddress = "" then vError = vError & "Address is a required
➥field<br>"
```

continues

Traditional ASP—(continued)

```
if vCity = "" then vError = vError & "City is a required field<br>"
if vState = "" then vError = vError & "State is a required field<br>"
if SSisZipCode(vZip) = False then vError = vError & "Enter a valid Zip
➥Code<br>"
if SSisPhoneNum(vPhone) = False then vError = vError & "Enter a valid Phone
➥Number<br>"
if SSisEmail(vEmail) = False then vError = vError & "Enter a valid Email<br>"
If vError = "" then
    vError = "You have filled in the form successfully!!!"
Else
    vError = "There are problems with your form:<br>" & vError
End If
End If
Function SSisEmail(theField)
    SSisEMail = false
    Dim regExMail, retValMail
    Set regExMail = New RegExp
    regExMail.Pattern ="^[\w-\.]{1,}\@([\da-zA-Z-]{1,}\.){1,}
    ➥ [\da-zA-Z-]{2,3}$"
    regExMail.IgnoreCase = true
    retValMail = regExMail.Test(theField)
    Set regExpMail = Nothing
    If not retValMail Then
        exit function
    End If
    SSisEmail = true
End Function

Function SSisPhoneNum(theField)
    SSisPhoneNum = false
    Dim regExPh, retValPh
    Set regExPh = New RegExp
    regExPh.Pattern ="[0-9]{3}-[0-9]{3}-[0-9]{4}"
    retValPh = regExPh.Test(theField)
    Set regExPh = Nothing
    If not retValPh Then
        exit function
    End If
    SSisPhoneNum = true
End Function

Function SSisZipCode(theField)
    SSisZipCode = false
    Dim regExZip, retValZip
    Set regExZip = New RegExp
    regExZip.Pattern ="^([0-9]{5}(( |-)[0-9]{4})?)"
    retValZip = regExZip.Test(theField)
    Set regExZip = Nothing
    If not retValZip Then
        exit function
    End If
```

```
        SSisZipCode   = true
End Function
%>
<head>
<title>Traditional ASP - Validation</title>
<script language="JavaScript1.2">

function ValidForm(form){
    var valid = true
    var message="There are problems with your form:";
    if (!isRequired(form.elements["Name"])){
        message += "\n Name is a required field"
        valid= false;
        }
    if (!isRequired(form.elements["Address"])){
        message += "\n Address is a required field"
        valid= false;
    }
    if (!isRequired(form.elements["City"])){
        message += "\n City is a required field"
        valid= false;
    }
     if (!isRequired(form.elements["State"])){
        message += "\n State is a required field"
        valid= false;
    }
    if (!isZIPCode(form.elements["Zip"])){
        message += "\n Insert a valid Zip code"
        valid= false;
    }
    if (!isPhoneNum(form.elements["Phone"])){
        message += "\n Insert a valid Phone Number"
        valid= false;
    }
    if (!isEmail(form.elements["Email"])){
        message += "\n Insert a valid Email"
        valid= false;
    }
    if (!valid){
        alert(message)
        return false
    }
return true
}

function isEmail(theField){
    if (!isRequired(theField)) return false;
    var filter=/^([a-zA-Z0-9_\.\-])+\@(([a-zA-Z0-9\-])+\.)+
    ➥ ([a-zA-Z0-9])+$/;
    if (filter.test(theField.value)){
        return true;
    }else{
```

continues

Traditional ASP—(continued)

```
                return false;
        }
}

function isPhoneNum(theField){
    if (!isRequired(theField)) return false;
    var filter=/\(?\d{3}\)?([-\/\.])\d{3}\1\d{4}/;
        if (filter.test(theField.value)){
            return true;
    }else{
            return false;
    }
}

function isZIPCode(theField){
    if (!isRequired(theField)) return false;
    var filter=/^\d{5}$|^\d{5}[\-\s]?\d{4}$/;
    if (filter.test(theField.value)){
        return true;
    }else{
        return false;
    }
}

function isRequired(theField){
    return (!theField.value == "")
}
</script>
</head>
<body bgcolor="#FFFFFF" text="#000000">
<%if vError <> "" then Response.Write vError%>
<form name="form1" method="post" action="trad_validation.asp" >
Name:<input type="text" name="Name" value="<%=vName%>"><br>
Address: <input type="text" name="Address" value="<%=vAddress%>"><br>
City: <input type="text" name="City" value="<%=vCity%>"><br>
State: <input type="text" name="State" value="<%=vState%>"><br>
Zip: <input type="text" name="Zip" value="<%=vZip%>"><br>
Phone: <input type="text" name="Phone" value="<%=vPhone%>">
➥Format: xxx-xxx-xxxx<br>
Email: <input type="text" name="Email" value="<%=vEmail%>"><br>
<input type="Submit" name="Submit" value="Validate Form" onClick="return
➥ValidForm(this.form)"><br>
</form>
</body>
</html>
```

And the results were 168 lines of code and 2 hours and 15 minutes to code by hand. Whew! (I must confess, my JavaScript isn't what it used to be, and I spent a bit of time debugging my pitiful client-side validation.) Now here's the part of the book where I get mean, but it's for your own good because I want you to get all you can out of this chapter.

I'm not going to show you the results 'til the end of the chapter. (Don't even think of flipping forward…HEY!!! YOU HEARD ME…DON'T FLIP FORWARD!) There you will find out all the details of how cool, exciting, efficient and, did I say, exciting ASP.NET really is.

Validating Input Controls

Now let's look at the specific ASP.NET Web server control validators. Remember that these controls all reside in the `System.Web.UI.WebControls` namespace and they inherit the `WebControl` base class.

They also have another class called `BaseValidator` from which they inherit. This class has properties and methods that are common to all validator controls (see Table 8.1).

N O T E
Remember—and it's worth repeating—that inheritance isn't a big word to be afraid of. It's easily understandable. If one object class inherits from another, it gets all of its properties and methods from that class. Each inherited object is a building block that brings its pieces to the receiving object. All methods and properties within an object have either been inherited or have been defined uniquely within the object.

TABLE 8.1 *BaseValidator* Object Properties

Property	Description
ControlToValidate	Gets or sets the input web control that the validator is assigned to.
Display	Gets or sets whether the validation control is displayed and whether its place is held in the HTML. The options are none, static, or dynamic.
EnableClientScript	Gets or sets a value indicating whether client-side validation is enabled.
Enabled	Gets or sets a value indicating whether the validator is enabled.
ErrorMessage	Gets or sets the text for the error message.
ForeColor	Gets or sets the color of the error message text. The default color is red.
IsValid	Gets or sets a value that indicates whether the associated input control validates.

The BaseValidator also has one method called Validate(), which performs the validation on the control. This is handy, and I will show you how to use this method to bring added control to your validation plans.

There is also another class of validators that compare values inherited from an object called the BaseCompareValidator. It only has one additional property called Type, which is described in Table 8.2.

TABLE 8.2 *BaseCompareValidator* Object Properties

Property	Description
Type	Gets or sets the data type that the values being compared are converted to before the comparison is made. The default is String.

This property enables you to tell the validator what data type you want to compare. Table 8.3 provides a list of data types that this property can use.

TABLE 8.3 Data Types for *BaseCompareValidator* Type Property

Data Type	Description
String	Specifies a string data type.
Integer	Specifies a 32-bit signed integer data type.
Double	Specifies a double precision floating point number data type.
Date	Specifies a date data type.
Currency	Specifies a monetary data type.

Now let's look at the validators themselves. There are very simple validators, such as a RequiredFieldValidator, that just force any type of information to be inserted to more complex validators—such as the custom validator that allows you to create custom validation controls.

RequiredFieldValidator

The RequiredFieldValidator does exactly what you'd expect. It requires something to be input into a field. It has one property, described in Table 8.4.

TABLE 8.4 *RequiredFieldValidator* Object Properties

Property	Description
InitialValue	Gets or sets the value with which the input field is compared. By default it compares to an empty string or nothing, but setting this property causes the validator to compare against the InitialValue property.

The RequiredFieldValidator has no methods of its own. The following example sets the EnableClientScript="False", which forces server-side validation.

Visual Basic .NET—**web_requiredfieldvalidator_vb.aspx**

```
<%@ page language="vb" runat="server"%>
<script runat=server>
sub Page_Load(sender as Object, e as EventARgs)
    if (IsPostBack) then
        Validate()
    end if
end sub
</script>
<html>
<head>
<title></title>
```

continues

Visual Basic .NET—(continued)

```
</head>
<body bgcolor="#FFFFFF" text="#000000">
<form runat="server">
<asp:TextBox id="OurTextBox" runat="server" />
<asp:RequiredFieldValidator
    id="OurRequiredFieldValidator"
    EnableClientScript="false"
    ControlToValidate="OurTextBox"
    ErrorMessage="This is a Required Field"
    runat="server" /> <br>
<asp:Button runat="server" text="Submit" /><br>
</form>
</body>
</html>
```

C#—web_requiredfieldvalidator_cs.aspx

```
<%@ page language="c#" runat="server"%>
<script runat=server>
void Page_Load(Object sender, EventArgs e) {
    if (IsPostBack) {
        Validate();
    }
}
</script>

<html>
<head>
<title></title>
</head>
<body bgcolor="#FFFFFF" text="#000000">
<form runat="server">
<asp:TextBox id="OurTextBox" runat="server" />
<asp:RequiredFieldValidator
    id="OurRequiredFieldValidator"
    EnableClientScript="false"
    ControlToValidate="OurTextBox"
    ErrorMessage="This is a Required Field"
    runat="server" /><br>
<asp:Button runat="server" text="Submit" /><br>
<asp:label id="OurLabel" runat="server" />
</form>
</body>
</html>
```

RangeValidator

The RangeValidator allows you to compare the input data and validate whether it falls between two values. The two values make up the additional properties of the range validator (see Table 8.5).

> **N O T E**
>
> The RangeValidator *fails only if the entered data doesn't fit into the range provided. If the field is left blank, this validator will not create an error. If the field being validated is a required field, you must use a* RequiredFieldValidator *in conjunction with the* RangeValidator *as well.*

TABLE 8.5 *RangeValidator* Object Properties

Property	Description
MinimumValue	Gets or sets the minimum value of the validation range.
MaximumValue	Gets or sets the maximum value of the validation range.

Remember the Type property from the BaseValidator object? We are going to use that here to change what kind of data is being validated. One text box validates a range based on an integer and the other validates a date range.

Visual Basic .NET—**web_rangevalidator_vb.aspx**

```
<%@ page language="vb" runat="server"%>
<script runat=server>
sub Page_Load(sender as Object, e as EventArgs)
    if (IsPostBack) then
        Validate()
    end if
end sub
</script>
<html>
<head>
<title>Validators - Range</title>
</head>
<body bgcolor="#FFFFFF" text="#000000">
<form runat="server">
<h1>Bulk Ticket Offer</h1>
How many tickets (between 20 and 100)<br>
<asp:RangeValidator
    id="NumRange"
    ControlToValidate="OurNumBox"
    Type="Integer"
    MinimumValue="20"
```

continues

Visual Basic .NET—(continued)

```
    MaximumValue="100"
    ErrorMessage="You must pick between 20 and 100"
runat="server" /><br>
<asp:TextBox id="OurNumBox" runat="server" /><br>
Dates: July 1, 2002 - December 31,2002<br>
<asp:RangeValidator
    id="DateRange"
    ControlToValidate="OurDateBox"
    Type="Date"
    MinimumValue="7/1/2002"
    MaximumValue="12/31/2002"
    ErrorMessage="Show isn't offered on that date."
    runat="server" /><br>
<asp:TextBox id="OurDateBox" runat="server" /> Format: xx/xx/xxxx<br>
<asp:Button runat="server" text="Submit" />
</form>
</body>
</html>
```

C#—web_rangevalidator_cs.aspx

```
<%@ page language="c#" runat="server"%>
<script runat=server>
void Page_Load(Object sender, EventArgs e) {
    if (IsPostBack) {
        Validate();
    }
}
</script>
<html>
<head>
<title>Validators - Range</title>
</head>
<body bgcolor="#FFFFFF" text="#000000">
<form runat="server">
<h1>Bulk Ticket Offer</h1>
How many tickets (between 20 and 100)<br>
<asp:RangeValidator
    id="NumRange"
    ControlToValidate="OurNumBox"
    Type="Integer"
    MinimumValue="20"
    MaximumValue="100"
    ErrorMessage="You must pick between 20 and 100"
    runat="server" /><br>
<asp:TextBox id="OurNumBox" runat="server" /><br>
Dates: July 1, 2002 - December 31,2002<br>
<asp:RangeValidator
    id="DateRange"
```

```
          ControlToValidate="OurDateBox"
          Type="Date"
          MinimumValue="7/1/2002"
          MaximumValue="12/31/2002"
          ErrorMessage="Show isn't offered on that date."
          runat="server" /><br>
  <asp:TextBox id="OurDateBox" runat="server" /> Format: xx/xx/xxxx<br>
  <asp:Button runat="server" text="Submit" />
  </form>
  </body>
  </html>
```

As you can see in Figure 8.2, I have used the RangeValidator to validate two different text boxes containing two different data types.

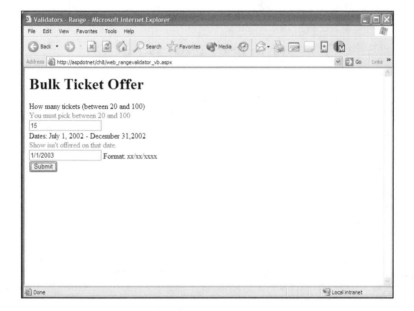

FIGURE 8.2

The RangeValidator *control makes it possible to check whether a value of data falls between a minimum and maximum value. This can be checked against several data types.*

CompareValidator

The CompareValidator can serve two purposes. It can compare the value of a input control against a defined value with a variety of comparison operators. For instance, you can restrict that the input value be less than an certain number. It can also compare the value of two controls against each other. Table 8.6 lists the properties that let you do this.

TABLE 8.6 *CompareValidator* Object Properties

Property	Description
ControlToCompare	Gets or sets the input control to compare with the input control being validated.
Operator	Gets or sets the comparison operation to perform. The default is Equal, with additional options being NotEqual, GreaterThan, GreatThanEqual (greater than or equal to), LessThan, and LessThanEqual (less than or equal to).
ValueToCompare	Gets or sets a constant value to compare with the value entered by the user into the input control being validated.

The following example compares two text boxes against each other. You can just as easily test to see whether a single box matches a specific set of criteria, as well.

Visual Basic .NET—**web_comparevalidator_vb.aspx**

```
<%@ page language="vb" runat="server"%>
<script runat=server>
sub Page_Load(sender as Object, e as EventArgs)
    if (IsPostBack) then
        Validate()
    end if
end sub
</script>
<html>
<head>
<title>Validators - Compare</title>
</head>
<body bgcolor="#FFFFFF" text="#000000">
<form runat="server">
<h3>Set Up User Account</h3>
Username: <asp:TextBox id="UserName" runat="server" /><br>
Password:
<asp:TextBox id="Password"
    TextMode = "Password"
    runat="server" /><br>
Confirm:    
<asp:TextBox id="PasswordConfirm"
    TextMode = "Password"
    runat="server" /><br>
<asp:CompareValidator
    id="ComparePasswords"
    ControlToValidate="PasswordConfirm"
    ControlToCompare="Password"
    ErrorMessage="Hey, They don't Match"
```

```
    runat="server" /><br>
<asp:Button runat="server" text="Submit" /><br>
</form>
</body>
</html>
```

C#—web_comparevalidator_cs.aspx

```
<%@ page language="cs" runat="server"%>
<script runat=server>
void Page_Load(Object sender, EventArgs e) {
    if (IsPostBack) {
        Validate();
    }
}
</script>
<html>
<head>
<title>Validators - Compare</title>
</head>
<body bgcolor="#FFFFFF" text="#000000">
<form runat="server">
<h3>Set Up User Account</h3>
Username: <asp:TextBox id="UserName" runat="server" /><br>
Password:
<asp:TextBox id="Password"
    TextMode = "Password"
    runat="server" /><br>
Confirm:    
<asp:TextBox id="PasswordConfirm"
    TextMode = "Password"
    runat="server" /><br>
<asp:CompareValidator
    id="ComparePasswords"
    ControlToValidate="PasswordConfirm"
    ControlToCompare="Password"
    ErrorMessage="Hey, They don't Match"
    runat="server" /><br>
<asp:Button runat="server" text="Submit" /><br>
</form>
</body>
</html>
```

In Figure 8.3, the CompareValidator checks the contents of the two text boxes and throws an error. As I said before, you can also use the ValueToCompare property to compare the CompareValidator against a defined value.

FIGURE 8.3

FIGURE 8.3

The CompareValidator *allows you to compare a control against a defined value, or to compare two input controls against one another.*

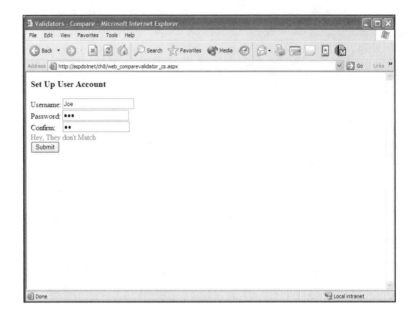

RegularExpressionValidator

The RegularExpressionValidator allows you to compare the value of an input control against a regular expression. This provides a way to verify different types of data input against predictable patterns.

> **NOTE**
>
> *The regular expression is a powerful tool that allows you to match character patterns in blocks of text. For instance, all e-mail addresses contain a specific pattern that can vary in many ways, depending on how the prefix is formatted or what domain extension it contains. Regular expressions give you a way to pattern-match this type of data so you can verify that the user has input an email address that matches that pattern. The* RegularExpressionValidator *is one place where you will use regular expressions, but there are also some objects—particularly the* RegEx *object, in the* System.Text.RegularExpression *namespace—that will allow you to use regular expressions in any coding situation. For instance, you might want to find, replace, or edit a particular pattern of data as you retrieve it from a database.*

The RegularExpressionValidator has a single additional property and no additional methods (see Table 8.7).

TABLE 8.7   *RegularExpressionValidator* Object Properties

Property	Description
`ValidationExpression`	Gets or sets the regular expression that determines the pattern used to validate a field.

Regular expressions can be quite a complex subject and are *way* beyond the scope of this book. I've included a couple of things so that you can take advantage of the `RegularExpressionValidator` as well as learn more about regular expressions.

First, I've included two URLs for pages in the .NET Framework SDK. The first link takes you to the root page on .NET regular expressions. This provides links to other pertinent information on regular expressions. The second URL is for one of the specific links in the first page. It is a page with links to all the specific elements of regular expressions in the .NET Framework.

```
ms-help://MS.NETFrameworkSDK/cpguidenf/html/
➥cpconcomregularexpressions.htm
```

```
ms-help://MS.NETFrameworkSDK/cpgenref/html/
➥cpconregularexpressionslanguageelements.htm
```

Table 8.8 includes some regular expressions that you will find yourself using often. It gives you a jump start on using the `RegularExpressionValidator` as a foundation to build on. Some very good libraries of regular expressions for the .NET Framework are also available on the web and I would encourage you to search the web for these resources. Note that the expressions in Table 8.8 are simple versions and aren't the only ways to pattern-match these types of data. After you investigate, you will see that there are a million ways to skin a cat with regular expressions.

TABLE 8.8   Common Regular Expressions

Data Type	Regular Expression
Date xx/xx/xxxx	`^\d{1,2}\/\d{1,2}\/\d{4}$`
Email Address	`^[\w\.=-]+@[\w\.-]+\.[a-z]{2,4}$`
Phone Number (xxx)xxx-xxxx	`^(\d{10}|\d{3}-\d{3}-\d{4}|\(\d{3}\)\s*\d{3}-\d{4})$`
Zip Code xxxxx or xxxxx-xxxx	`(^\d{5}$)|(^\d{5}-\d{4}$)`

The following code examples validate both an email address and a phone number. Let's take a look.

Visual Basic .NET—`web_regex_vb.aspx`

```
<%@ page language="vb" runat="server"%>
<script runat=server>
sub Page_Load()
    if (IsPostBack) then
        Validate()
    end if
end sub
</script>
<html>
<head>
<title>Validators - Regular Expression</title>
</head>
<body bgcolor="#FFFFFF" text="#000000">
<form runat="server">
Email Address:<br>
<asp:TextBox id="OurEmail" runat="server" />
<asp:RegularExpressionValidator
    id="ValidEmail"
    ControlToValidate="OurEmail"
    ValidationExpression="^([a-zA-Z0-9_\-\.]+)@((\[[0-9]{1,3}\.
    ➥[0-9]{1,3}\.[0-9]{1,3}\.)|(([a-zA-Z0-9\-]+\.)+))
    ➥([a-zA-Z]{2,4}|[0-9]{1,3})(\]?)$"
    ErrorMessage="Invalid Email Entry"
    runat="server" /><br>
Phone Number:<br>
<asp:TextBox id="OurPhone" runat="server" />
<asp:RegularExpressionValidator
    id="ValidPhone"
    ControlToValidate="OurPhone"
    ValidationExpression="^\([0-9]{3}\)[0-9]{3}-[0-9]{4}$"
    ErrorMessage="Invalid Phone Number"
    runat="server"  /><br>
<asp:Button runat="server" text="Submit" /><br>
</form>
</body>
</html>
```

C#—web_regex_cs.aspx

```
<%@ page language="c#" runat="server"%>
<script runat=server>
void Page_Load(Object sender, EventArgs e) {
    if (IsPostBack) {
        Validate();
    }
}
</script>

<html>
<head>
<title>Validators - Regular Expression</title>
</head>
<body bgcolor="#FFFFFF" text="#000000">
<form runat="server">
Email Address:<br>
<asp:TextBox id="OurEmail" runat="server" />
<asp:RegularExpressionValidator
    id="ValidEmail"
    ControlToValidate="OurEmail"
    ValidationExpression="^([a-zA-Z0-9_\-\.]+)@((\[[0-9]{1,3}\.
 ➡ [0-9]{1,3}\.[0-9]{1,3}\.)|(([a-zA-Z0-9\-]+\.)+))
 ➡ ([a-zA-Z]{2,4}|[0-9]{1,3})(\]?)$"
    ErrorMessage="Invalid Email Entry"
    runat="server" /><br>
Phone Number:<br>
<asp:TextBox id="OurPhone" runat="server" />
<asp:RegularExpressionValidator
    id="ValidPhone"
    ControlToValidate="OurPhone"
    ValidationExpression="^\([0-9]{3}\) [0-9]{3}-[0-9]{4}$"
    ErrorMessage="Invalid Phone Number"
    runat="server"   /><br>
<asp:Button runat="server" text="Submit" /><br>
</form>
</body>
</html>
```

You can see the results of this experiment in Figure 8.4. Regular expression and specifically the RegularExpressionValidator will come in quite handy when you need to control the patterns of data that a user is allowed to input.

FIGURE 8.4

The Regular- Expression- Validator *allows you to match patterns of data such as e-mails, phone numbers, and zip codes.*

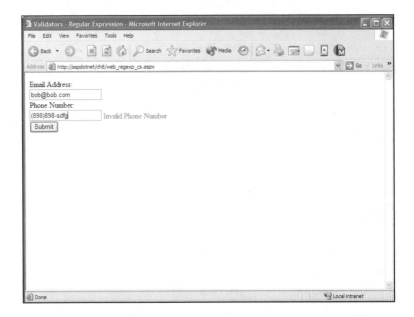

CustomValidator

The CustomValidator provides a method to validate input data when none of the other validators can do the job. It provides a way for you to define custom functions, both client-side and server-side, against which to validate data. It has a single property called ClientValidationFunction (see Table 8.9) and an event called ServerValidate, which you call with the OnServerValidate method. This method specifies what function to use for server-side validation.

TABLE 8.9 *CustomValidator* Properties

Property	Description
ClientValidationFunction	Gets or sets the name of the custom client-side script function to be used for validation.

In the following example I've included only a server-side validation example, but if you want both types of validation present to prevent unnecessary server-side processing, you can easily create a JavaScript function and place its name in the ClientValidationFunction property as well.

Visual Basic .NET—`web_customvalidator_vb.aspx`

```
<%@ page language="vb" runat="server"%>
<script runat=server>
sub Page_Load(sender as Object, e as EventArgs)
    if (IsPostBack) then
        Validate()
        if (Page.IsValid) Then
    OurLabel.Text = "Wahooo!!! You entered a valid number<br>"
        end if
    end if
end sub
sub SSValidate(source as Object, value as ServerValidateEventArgs)
    value.IsValid =((CInt(OurTextBox.Text) mod 3 = 0) or
    ➡(CInt(OurTextBox.Text) mod 5 = 0))
end sub
</script>
<html>
<head>
<title>Validators - CustomValidator</title>
</head>
<body bgcolor="#FFFFFF" text="#000000">
<form runat="server">
<h2>Please insert a multiple of 3 or 5 </h2>
<asp:Label id="OurLabel" EnableViewState="false" runat="server" />
<asp:TextBox id="OurTextBox" runat="server" />
<asp:CustomValidator
    id="OurCustomValidator"
    ControlToValidate="OurTextBox"
    OnServerValidate="SSValidate"
    ErrorMessage="Entry must be a multiple of 3 or 5"
    runat="server"  /><br>
<asp:Button runat="server" text="Submit" /><br>
</form>
</body>
</html>
```

C#—`web_customervalidator_cs.aspx`

```
<%@ page language="c#" runat="server"%>
<script runat=server>
void Page_Load(Object sender, EventArgs e) {
    if (IsPostBack) {
        Validate();
        if (Page.IsValid){
    OurLabel.Text = "Wahooo!!! You entered a valid number<br>";
        }
    }
}

void SSValidate(Object source, ServerValidateEventArgs value) {
```

continues

C#—(continued)

```
        value.IsValid = (Int32.Parse(OurTextBox.Text) % 3 == 0 ||
        ➡Int32.Parse(OurTextBox.Text) % 5 == 0);
}
</script>
<html>
<head>
<title>Validators - CustomValidator</title>
</head>
<body bgcolor="#FFFFFF" text="#000000">
<form runat="server">
<h2>Please insert a multiple of 3 or 5 </h2>
<asp:Label id="OurLabel" EnableViewState="false" runat="server" />
<asp:TextBox id="OurTextBox" runat="server" />
<asp:CustomValidator
    id="OurCustomValidator"
    ControlToValidate="OurTextBox"
    OnServerValidate="SSValidate"
    ErrorMessage="Entry must be a multiple of 3 or 5"
    runat="server"  /><br>
<asp:Button runat="server" text="Submit" /><br>
</form>
</body>
</html>
```

As you can see in Figure 8.5, I have designated through the CustomValidator that a multiple of 3 or 5 must be entered into the text box and the SSValidate process determines whether the IsValid property is set to true or false.

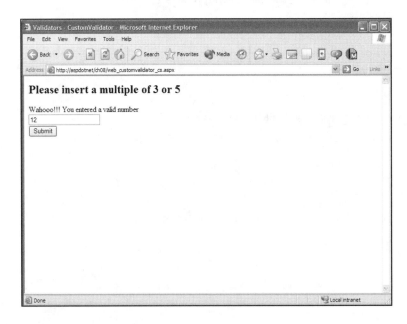

FIGURE 8.5

The CustomValidator allows you to create a function by which you validate the input data.

ValidationSummary

There are many times where you don't want the validation error messages inline with your text boxes, but would like the errors grouped together somewhere on the page. You could do this by putting all of the validation controls in the same place on the page, but this makes programming a bit more difficult to organize. It's easier to have the validators near the controls they validate. There is also a neat little trick that you can pull off using a validator's text property to place a highlight next to the input control and have the error message appear in the summary.

The ValidationSummary has a few properties that can help you control exactly how it behaves with regard to both client-side and server-side validation (see Table 8.10).

TABLE 8.10   *ValidationSummary* Properties

Property	Description
DisplayMode	Gets or sets the display mode of the validation summary. The valid possibilities are BulletList, List, and SingleParagraph. BulletList is the default.
EnableClientScript	Gets or sets a value indicating whether the ValidationSummary control updates itself using client-side script.
ForeColor	Gets or sets the color of the ErrorMessage text.
HeaderText	Gets or sets the text that appears in the header of the summary.
ShowMessageBox	Gets or sets a value indicating whether the validation summary is displayed in a client-side message box. If the EnableClientScript is set to false, this property has no effect.
ShowSummary	Gets or sets a value indicating whether the validation summary is displayed inline.

The following code sample sets EnableClientScript and ShowMessageBox to true so that any possible client-side verification is performed and the user is presented with an alert box if he tries to submit the page and the input data still isn't valid.

Visual Basic .NET—**web_validationsummary_vb.aspx**

```
<%@ page language="vb" runat="server"%>
<script runat=server>
sub Page_Load(sender as Object, e as EventARgs)
    if (IsPostBack) then
        Validate()
        if (IsValid) then
            response.redirect("thankyou.aspx")
        end if
    end if
end sub
</script>

<html>
<head>
<title>Validators Summary</title>
</head>
<body bgcolor="#FFFFFF" text="#000000">
<form runat="server">
<h3>What's your name and how many widgets do you want?</h3>
You can buy between 1 and 10 widgets.<br>
<table>
<tr><td colspan="2">
<asp:ValidationSummary
    id="OurValidator"
    HeaderText="The following errors were found:"
    DisplayMode="List"
    ShowMessageBox="true"
    runat="server" />
</td></tr>
<tr><td>Name:</td>
<td><asp:TextBox id="Name" runat="server" />
<asp:RequiredFieldValidator
    id="NameValidator"
    ControlToValidate="Name"
    Text="*"
    ErrorMessage="Name is a required field"
    runat="server" />
</td></tr>
<tr><td># of Widgets</td>
<td><asp:TextBox id="Widgets" runat="server" />
<asp:RequiredFieldValidator
    id="WidgetReqdValidator"
    ControlToValidate="Widgets"
    Text="*"
    ErrorMessage="Widgets is a required field"
    runat="server" />
<asp:RangeValidator
    id="WidgetValidator"
    ControlToValidate="Widgets"
    Type="Integer"
```

```
        MinimumValue="1"
        MaximumValue="10"
        Text="*"
        ErrorMessage="# of Widgets must be between 1 and 10"
        runat="server"/></td>
</tr>
<tr>
<td> </td>
<td><asp:Button runat="server" text="Submit" /></td>
</tr>
</table>
</form>
</body>
</html>
```

C#—web_validationsummary_cs.aspx

```
<%@ page language="c#" runat="server"%>
<script runat=server>
void Page_Load(Object sender, EventArgs e) {
    if (IsPostBack) {
        Validate();
        if (IsValid) {
            Response.Redirect("thankyou.aspx");
        }
    }
}
</script>

<html>
<head>
<title>Validators Summary</title>
</head>
<body bgcolor="#FFFFFF" text="#000000">
<form runat="server">
<h3>What's your name and how many widgets do you want?</h3>
You can buy between 1 and 10 widgets.<br>
<table>
<tr><td colspan="2">
<asp:ValidationSummary
    id="OurValidator"
    HeaderText="The following errors were found:"
    DisplayMode="List"
    ShowMessageBox="true"
    runat="server" />
</td></tr>
<tr><td>Name:</td>
<td><asp:TextBox id="Name" runat="server" />
<asp:RequiredFieldValidator
    id="NameValidator"
    ControlToValidate="Name"
```

continues

C#—(continued)

```
        Text="*"
        ErrorMessage="Name is a required field"
        runat="server" />
</td></tr>
<tr><td># of Widgets</td>
<td><asp:TextBox id="Widgets" runat="server" />
<asp:RequiredFieldValidator
    id="WidgetReqdValidator"
    ControlToValidate="Widgets"
    Text="*"
    ErrorMessage="Widgets is a required field"
    runat="server" />
<asp:RangeValidator
    id="WidgetValidator"
    ControlToValidate="Widgets"
    Type="Integer"
    MinimumValue="1"
    MaximumValue="10"
    Text="*"
    ErrorMessage="# of Widgets must be between 1 and 10"
    runat="server"/></td>
</tr>
<tr>
<td> </td>
<td><asp:Button runat="server" text="Submit" /></td>
</tr>
</table>
</form>
</body>
</html>
```

As you can see in Figure 8.6, the user received errors for entering bad data and was presented with an alert box to make the problem even more apparent.

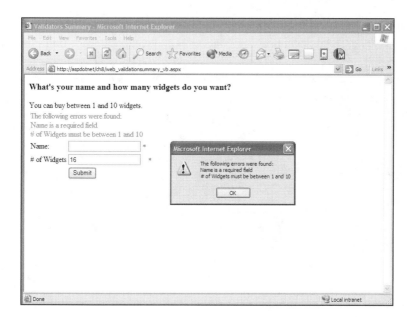

FIGURE 8.6

The
ValidationSummary
collects the invalid controls' ErrorMessage
*properties and displays
them in a single location. It can also pop up
an alert box to identify
the problems.*

Multi-Browser Support and Validation

This is an area that could afford some investigation on how ASP.NET delivers different code to different browsers depending on their capabilities. As I've said, ASP.NET is pretty smart about handling browser capabilities and rendering code that different browsers can handle.

By default, ASP.NET lumps browsers together as uplevel and downlevel browsers.

- **Uplevel**. Internet Explorer 4.x and up
- **Downlevel**. Basically everything else, including Netscape 6.x

These aren't hard and fast rules for all Web server controls, but where validators are concerned, the uplevel browsers deliver both JavaScript client-side validation and server-side validation, and downlevel browsers are restricted to server-side validation. Take a look at the code generated for CompareValidator in both an uplevel and downlevel browser.

Uplevel Browser

```
<html>
<head>
<title>Validators - Compare</title>
</head>
<body bgcolor="#FFFFFF" text="#000000">
<form name="_ctl0" method="post" action="web_comparevalidator_vb.aspx"
➥language="javascript" onsubmit="ValidatorOnSubmit();" id="_ctl0">
<input type="hidden" name="__VIEWSTATE" value=
➥"dDwtMTI1OTcyOTYwNzs7Pv8j9BzKw7eb4mzYMNwlwPYrQl1R" />

<script language="javascript" src="/aspnet_client/system_web/
➥1_0_3705_0/WebUIValidation.js"></script>


<h3>Set Up User Account</h3>
Username: <input name="UserName" type="text" id="UserName" /><br>
Password: <input name="Password" type="password" id="Password" /><br>
Confirm:    <input name="PasswordConfirm" type="password"
➥id="PasswordConfirm" /><br>
<span id="ComparePasswords" controltovalidate="PasswordConfirm"
➥errormessage="Hey, They don't Match"
evaluationfunction="CompareValidatorEvaluateIsValid"
➥controltocompare="Password" controlhookup="Password"
➥style="color:Red;visibility:hidden;">Hey, They don't Match</span><br>
<input type="submit" name="_ctl1" value="Submit" onclick="if
➥(typeof(Page_ClientValidate) == 'function') Page_ClientValidate(); "
➥language="javascript" /><br>

<script language="javascript">
<!-
    var Page_Validators =  new Array(document.all["ComparePasswords"]);
// ->
</script>

<script language="javascript">
<!-
var Page_ValidationActive = false;
if (typeof(clientInformation) != "undefined" &&
➥clientInformation.appName.indexOf("Explorer") != -1) {
    if (typeof(Page_ValidationVer) == "undefined")
        alert("Unable to find script library '/aspnet_client/system_web/
        ➥1_0_3705_0/WebUIValidation.js'. Try placing this file
        ➥manually, or reinstall by running 'aspnet_regiis -c'.");
```

```
        else if (Page_ValidationVer != "125")
            alert("This page uses an incorrect version of
            ➥WebUIValidation.js. The page expects version 125.
            ➥The script library is " + Page_ValidationVer + ".");
        else
            ValidatorOnLoad();
}

function ValidatorOnSubmit() {
    if (Page_ValidationActive) {
        ValidatorCommonOnSubmit();
    }
}
}
// -->
</script>
</form>
</body>
</html>
```

Downlevel Browser

```
<html>
<head>
<title>Validators - Compare</title>
</head>
<body bgcolor="#FFFFFF" text="#000000">
<form name="_ctl0" method="post" action="web_comparevalidator_vb.aspx"
➥id="_ctl0">
<input type="hidden" name="__VIEWSTATE" value=
➥"dDwtMTI1OTcyOTYwNzs7Pv8j9BzKw7eb4mzYMNwlwPYrQl1R" />

<h3>Set Up User Account</h3>
Username: <input name="UserName" type="text" id="UserName" /><br>
Password: <input name="Password" type="password" id="Password" /><br>
Confirm:    <input name="PasswordConfirm" type="password"
➥id="PasswordConfirm" /><br>
 <br>
<input type="submit" name="_ctl1" value="Submit" onclick="if
➥(typeof(Page_ClientValidate) == 'function') Page_ClientValidate(); "
➥ language="javascript" /><br>
</form>
</body>
</html>
```

The downlevel code block doesn't have the weight of the JavaScript, but remember that it must make a round trip to the server to validate the data, whereas the uplevel browser can handle client-side validation.

To investigate more about the function of ASP.NET and browser capabilities, check out the following URL for the .NET Framework SDK. It will supply you with a lot of information on how ASP.NET handles browsers and how you can manipulate what code is delivered to the browser through the `HTTPBrowserCapabilites` object.

```
ms-help://MS.NETFrameworkSDK/cpguidenf/html/
➥cpconWebFormsControlsBrowserCapabilities.htm
```

ASP.NET Web Form Validation Example

Now it's finally time to compare the traditional ASP version to my ASP.NET version of the same page. If you remember, I decided to develop two pages, one in traditional ASP and one in ASP.NET. Just for a refresher, the traditional ASP page took me 2 hours and 15 minutes to code and contained 168 lines of code.

I develop an ASP.NET page with similar function and it contained—are you ready?—35 lines of code and took me 34 minutes to program. Just 35 lines of code. And it took less than 25% of the time to develop. Granted, this will vary depending on what your core skills are, but you can see how ASP.NET will massively reduce the amount of coding you need to do and the time it takes you to code.

The following is the code for the ASP.NET page. It may look like more than 35 lines, but this is only because I needed to format it in a way that it would display correctly in the book's format. And still, take notice that even though every property of every validation object gets a single line to itself in the example, it is *still* only 95 lines—a whopping 73 lines shorter than the traditional example.

Validation ASP.NET Style—`aspx_validation.aspx`

```
<%@ page language="vb" runat="server"%>
<script runat=server>
sub Page_Load(sender as Object, e as EventARgs)
if (IsPostBack) then
Validate()
if (IsValid) then
OurLabel.Text = "CONGRADULATIONS!!! The form is valid."
end if
end if
end sub
</script>
<html>
```

```
<head
<title></title>
</head>
<body bgcolor="#FFFFFF" text="#000000">
<form id="validateform" runat="server" >
<asp:Label id="OurLabel" runat="server" /><br>
<asp:ValidationSummary id="ValidatorSummary"
Runat="server"
ShowMessageBox="true"
HeaderText="The following errors were found:"
DisplayMode="BulletList" />
Name:<asp:TextBox id="Name" runat="server" />
<asp:RequiredFieldValidator
id="ValidName"
ControlToValidate="Name"
Text="*"
ErrorMessage="Name is a Required Field"
runat="server" /> <br>
Address: <asp:TextBox id="Address" runat="server" />
<asp:RequiredFieldValidator
id="ValidAddress"
ControlToValidate="Address"
Text="*"
ErrorMessage="Address is a Required Field"
runat="server" /><br>
City: <asp:TextBox id="City" runat="server" />
<asp:RequiredFieldValidator
id="ValidCity"
ControlToValidate="City"
Text="*"
ErrorMessage="City is a Required Field"
runat="server" /><br>
State: <asp:TextBox id="State" runat="server" />
<asp:RequiredFieldValidator
id="ValidState"
ControlToValidate="State"
Text="*"
ErrorMessage="State is a Required Field"
runat="server" /><br>
Zip: <asp:TextBox id="Zip" runat="server" />
<asp:RequiredFieldValidator
id="ValidZip"
ControlToValidate="Zip"
Text="*"
ErrorMessage="Zip is a Required Field"
runat="server" />
<asp:RegularExpressionValidator
id="ValidZipExp"
ControlToValidate="Zip"
Text="*"
ErrorMessage="Enter a Valid Zip Code"
ValidationExpression= "^([0-9]{5}(( |-)[0-9]{4})?)"
```

continues

Validation ASP.NET Style—(continued)

```
runat="server" /><br>
Phone: <asp:TextBox id="Phone" runat="server" /> Format: xxx-xxx-xxxx
<asp:RequiredFieldValidator
id="Validphone"
ControlToValidate="Phone"
Text="*"
ErrorMessage="Phone is a Required Field"
runat="server" />
<asp:RegularExpressionValidator
id="ValidPhoneExp"
ControlToValidate="Phone"
Text="*"
ErrorMessage="Enter a Valid Phone Number"
ValidationExpression= "[0-9]{3}-[0-9]{3}-[0-9]{4}"
runat="server" /><br>
Email:<asp:TextBox id="Email" runat="server" />
<asp:RequiredFieldValidator
id="ValidEmail"
ControlToValidate="Email"
Text="*"
ErrorMessage="Email is a Required Field"
runat="server" />
<asp:RegularExpressionValidator
id="ValidEmailExp"
ControlToValidate="Email"
Text="*"
ErrorMessage="Enter a Valid Email"
ValidationExpression= "^[\w-\.]{1,}\@([\da-zA-Z-]{1,}\.){1,}
➥ [\da-zA-Z-]{2,3}$"
runat="server" /><br>
<asp:Button id="OurButton" runat="server" text="Validate Form" /><br>
</form>
</body>
</html>
```

That rocks!!! This is just one example of how ASP.NET will enable you to be more productive, write less code, and maybe go home for dinner like a normal person at a normal hour occasionally. (I know this will never happen because there will always be more code to write, but it's nice to dream.)

Summary

Validators make it possible to control the data that users input into web forms. ASP.NET also delivers the proper validation function based on a browser's capabilities. This provides power for controlling the interaction between the user and your web applications.

Now with the validators in the bag, you are 2/3 of the way through the Web server controls. In the next chapter, you're going to be playing with the list controls, which enable you to display collections of data as simply as the validators allow you to validate data.

chapter 9

Displaying Data with Server Controls

Let me see what you've got…ah, yes…it's fabulous!

If you've spent any time building web applications (and I assume that many of you have), you've learned one of the biggest parts of this is displaying lists and tabular data.

Let me set this chapter up a bit before I dig into these topics so you can be clear on what you're about to investigate. I was a little torn when deciding on the structure of this book and what to write about first. I was really dealing with a chicken-and-egg kind of quandary.

See, there is no need for displaying data if there is no data, and data doesn't really do you any good if you can't display it. So I had to decide "Do I write about manipulating and retrieving data first?" or "Do I write about how to display the data first?" Here is the big reason behind my thinking and what is at the core of my decision.

Talking about data display first helps keep all the server controls together in Part II of this book. If I had handled data manipulation first, the book's continuity would have been compromised and server controls wouldn't have been together or progressed in a logical fashion. But this left me with another problem that really turned out not to be a problem at all. This meant that you have to do some work to ignore the data portions of this chapter. I promise I will focus on these with great depth in the next chapter.

The reason why this isn't a problem is because you were smart enough to buy this wonderful publication. (This proves your superior intelligence, common sense, royal descent, and striking good looks.) Someone of your outstanding character, beauty, and intellect can certainly control the temptation and craving to understand the data aspects first and patiently wait for those explanations until later. So you, in your infinite wisdom, have made my decision for me.

In most examples, I am going to use the Northwind database. (Not the blasted Northwind database, that's as bad a starting the book with "Hello World.") Yes, the Northwind database; and I'll tell you why. Because Microsoft distributes this database with everything, including Microsoft Kitchen Sink XP. Chances are you have it in one form or another somewhere. So remember, continue to ignore everything about retrieving data and focus on the server controls.

What Are List Controls?

Now back to displaying data in ASP.NET. I can sum it up like this: It's fun for the whole family. Well, at least it's fun for you and anyone else working in ASP.NET.

In the past, with traditional interpreted scripting languages, displaying data was one of the big creators of spaghetti code's abundance. To display data you could either jump in and out of HTML code or you could write HTML code using ASP's `Response` object's `Write()` method.

Below is an example of a page written with traditional ASP. The `<select box>` in this page is created by having its option tags written by the `Response` object. The table that follows uses a example of spaghetti code where what is called "context switching" occurs. Context switching is just a fancy word for switching back and forth between HTML and ASP.

Traditional ASP—`trad_spaghetti.asp`

```
<%
dim arrSelectBox(3)
arrSelectBox(0)="Cake"
arrSelectBox(1)="Cookies"
arrSelectBox(2)="Ice Cream"
arrSelectBox(3)="Pie"
%>

<html>
<head>
<title>Traditional Example</title>
</head>

<body bgcolor="#FFFFFF" text="#000000">
This is a select box created by writing HTML through the Response.Write method.
<br>
<Select name="select">
<%
i=0
for i=0 to Ubound(arrSelectBox)
    Response.Write "<option value=""" & arrSelectBox(i) & """>"
    Response.Write arrSelectBox(i)
    Response.Write "</option>"
next
%>
</Select>
<br><br>
This is building a table with more spagetti code<br>
<table border="1">
<%for i=0 to Ubound(arrSelectBox)%>
<tr><td><%=arrSelectBox(i)%></td></tr>
<%next%>
</table>
</body>
</html>
```

Now that you've gone through many examples of the advantages of objects and server controls, you can see that this method of displaying lists of data is a bit antiquated. ASP.NET has to have a better answer for this, right?

Let me assure you that ASP.NET has a much, much, much better answer than this for displaying lists and tables of data. These server controls let you do just about anything you want with this type of data, including formatting, displaying, listing, paging through large amounts of data, and even editing data without much effort at all.

The server controls can pretty much be broken down into two categories. These aren't official categories, but I think it makes it easier to group them into these three categories:

- **Simple List Controls**. CheckBoxList, DropDownList, ListBox, RadioButtonList

- **Repeater Control**. Repeater

- **Complex List Controls**. DataList, DataGrid

The controls provide you with just about every possible control you could need to display listed and tabular data, with the DataGrid in particular being able to just about butter your toast in the morning.

List Controls

As with every other group of server controls, it pays for us to first take a look at the parent of all these controls. This group's Mama and Dada is the ListControl class, which is located in the System.Web.UI.WebControls namespace. Table 9.1 displays the ListControl's properties. It also has one method that the other list controls will inherit.

TABLE 9.1 *ListControl* Object Properties

Property	Description
AutoPostBack	Gets or sets a value indicating whether a postback to the server automatically occurs when the user changes the list selection.
DataMember	Gets or sets the specific table in the datasource to bind to the control.
DataSource	Gets or sets the data source that is used to populate the items of the list control.
DataTextField	Gets or sets what field in the data source provides the text content of the list items.
DataTextFormatString	Gets or sets the formatting string that controls the format of the data bound to the list control.
DataValueField	Gets or sets what field in the data source provides the value of each list item.

Property	Description
Items	Gets the collection of items in the list control.
SelectedIndex	Gets or sets the lowest index of the items selected in the list.
SelectedItem	Gets the item selected with the lowest index in the list control.

The event that I'd like to mention is the OnSelectedIndexChanged. The method is called whenever the selection of the list control changes and is posted back to the server. I'll show you a few examples in this section so that you understand it.

CheckBoxList

The CheckBoxList server control is an object that allows you to bind data to it; it dynamically generates a group of check boxes either in a table or just listed out, depending on how you want it to appear.

N o t e

Binding data is a concept that I haven't mentioned yet but is semi-self-explanatory. Each of the simple list controls, the repeater, and the complex list controls has a magical property called DataSource *and a magical method called* DataBind() *that...well...binds data in the* DataSource *to the control.*

Table 9.2 describes the CheckBoxList's properties.

TABLE 9.2 *CheckBoxList* Object Properties

Property	Description
CellPadding	Gets or sets the distance (in pixels) between the border and contents of the cell.
CellSpacing	Gets or sets the distance (in pixels) between cells.
RepeatColumns	Gets or sets how many columns to display in the CheckBoxList control.
RepeatDirection	Gets or sets a value that indicates whether the control displays vertically or horizontally. Values are Vertical or Horizontal. Vertical is default.
RepeatLayout	Gets or sets the layout of the check boxes. Flow or Table are valid; Table is the default. Flow displays items without table structure.
TextAlign	Gets or sets the text alignment for the check boxes within the group. Left or Right are valid; Right is the default.

Check out this control in action. I'm going to use a check box to change the `RepeatDirection` so I can control and set how this `CheckBoxList` is displayed in the browser.

Visual Basic .NET—**web_checkboxlist_vb.aspx**

```
<%@ page language="vb" runat="server"%>
<script runat="server">
Sub Page_Load(sender as Object, e as EventArgs)
    dim OurArray() as String = {"Item 1", "Item 2", "Item 3", "Item 4", "Item 5"}
    if Not IsPostBack Then
        OurCheckBoxList.DataSource = OurArray
        DataBind()
    end if

End Sub


Sub OurButton_Click(sender As Object, e As EventArgs)

    Dim OurString As String = "You Selected:<br>"
    Dim OurCounter As Integer
    For OurCounter = 0 to OurCheckBoxList.Items.Count-1
      If OurCheckBoxList.Items(OurCounter).Selected Then
          OurString += OurCheckBoxList.Items(OurCounter).Text
          OurString += "<br>"
      End If
    Next
       OurLabel.Text = OurString
End Sub


Sub OurCheckBox_CheckedChanged(sender As Object, e As EventArgs)
    If OurCheckBox.Checked Then
        OurCheckBoxList.RepeatDirection = RepeatDirection.Vertical
    Else
        OurCheckBoxList.RepeatDirection = RepeatDirection.Horizontal
    End If
End Sub

</script>

<html>
<head>
<title>Simple List Controls - CheckBoxList</title>
</head>
<body bgcolor="#FFFFFF" text="#000000">
<form runat="server">
<asp:CheckBoxList
    id="OurCheckBoxList"
    BorderColor="#000000"
    BorderWidth="1"
    BackColor="#EEEEEE"
```

```
            CellPadding="1"
            CellSpacing="1"
            runat="server" />
<br>
<asp:CheckBox
        id="OurCheckBox"
        OnCheckedChanged="OurCheckBox_CheckedChanged"
        Text="Display Vertically"
        AutoPostBack="true"
        Checked="True"
        runat="server" />
<br>
<asp:Button id="OurButton" Text="Submit" onclick="OurButton_Click" runat="server"/>
<br><br>
<asp:Label id="OurLabel" runat="server"/>
</form>
</body>
</html>
```

C#—web_checkboxlist_cs.aspx

```
<%@ page language="cs" runat="server"%>
<script runat="server">
void Page_Load(Object sender, EventArgs e) {
    String[] OurArray = {"Item 1", "Item 2", "Item 3", "Item 4", "Item 5"};
    if (!IsPostBack) {
        OurCheckBoxList.DataSource = OurArray;
        DataBind();
    }

}

void OurButton_Click(Object sender, EventArgs e) {
   String OurString = "You Selected:<br>";
   int OurCounter;
   for(OurCounter = 0; OurCounter < OurCheckBoxList.Items.Count; OurCounter++) {
      if (OurCheckBoxList.Items[OurCounter].Selected) {
         OurString = OurString + OurCheckBoxList.Items[OurCounter].Text;
         OurString = OurString + "<br>";
      }
   }
   OurLabel.Text = OurString;
}

void OurCheckBox_CheckedChanged(Object sender, EventArgs e) {
    if (OurCheckBox.Checked) {
        OurCheckBoxList.RepeatDirection = RepeatDirection.Vertical;
    }
    else {
```

continues

C#—(continued)

```
            OurCheckBoxList.RepeatDirection = RepeatDirection.Horizontal;

    }
}

</script>

<html>
<head>
<title>Simple List Controls - CheckBoxList</title>
</head>
<body bgcolor="#FFFFFF" text="#000000">
<form runat="server">
<asp:CheckBoxList
    id="OurCheckBoxList"
    BorderColor="#000000"
    BorderWidth="1"
    BackColor="#EEEEEE"
    CellPadding="1"
    CellSpacing="1"
    runat="server" />
<br>
<asp:CheckBox
    id="OurCheckBox"
    OnCheckedChanged="OurCheckBox_CheckedChanged"
    Text="Display Vertically"
    AutoPostBack="true"
    Checked="True"
    runat="server" />
<br>
<asp:Button id="OurButton" Text="Submit" onclick="OurButton_Click"
runat="server"/>
<br><br>
<asp:Label id="OurLabel" runat="server"/>
</form>
</body>
</html>
```

You can see the results of this ASP.NET page in Figure 9.1. This page changes the RepeatDirection property when the check box is checked and also inspects to see which items in the CheckBoxList are checked when the button is clicked.

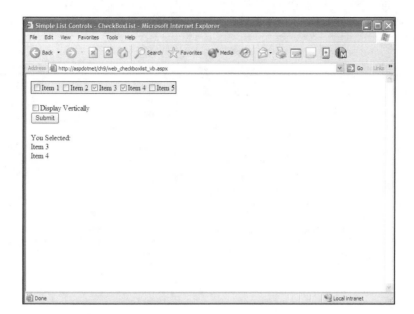

FIGURE 9.1

The `CheckBoxList` *enables you to easily create a collection of check boxes.*

You can also see that the values were used in an array, and that this array was bound as the list's contents through its `DataSource` property and `DataBind()` method.

Notice that when the `"Display Vertically"` check box is changed, it calls a function called `OurCheckBox_CheckedChanged`. In this function the `RepeatDirection` property of the `CheckBoxList` is set with a strange value called either `RepeatDirection.Vertical` or `RepeatDirection.Horizontal`. The `RepeatDirection` property is really an integer as far as the .NET Framework is concerned. The Framework will only know what the words "Vertical" or "Horizontal" mean when they are associated with the proper property. So the .NET Framework actually sees `RepeatDirection.Vertical` or `RepeatDirection.Horizontal` as a number and not a String such as "Vertical" or "Horizontal".

DropDownList

I have snuck a few of these controls into this book to this point while demonstrating other aspects of ASP.NET. Now it's time to take a look at the `DropDownList` in more depth. It has only one additional property beyond what it inherits from the `ListControl`, as shown in Table 9.3.

TABLE 9.3 *DropDownList* Object Property

Property	Description
SelectedIndex	Gets or sets the index of the item selected in the DropDownList.

Visual Basic .NET—**web_dropdownlist_vb.aspx**

```
<%@ page language="vb" runat="server"%>
<script runat=server>
Sub Page_Load(sender As Object, e As EventArgs)
    if IsPostBack then
        if OurDropDown.SelectedIndex = 0 then
            OurLabel.Text = "This isn't a dessert"
        Else
            OurLabel.Text = "Text: " & OurDropDown.SelectedItem.Text & "<br>"
            OurLabel.Text += "Value: " & OurDropDown.SelectedItem.Value & "<br>"
            OurLabel.Text += "SelectedIndex: " & OurDropDown.SelectedIndex
        end if
    end if
end sub
</script>

<html>
<head>
<title>Simple List Controls - DropDownList</title>
</head>
<body bgcolor="#FFFFFF" text="#000000">
<form runat="server">
<asp:DropDownList
    id="OurDropDown"
    AutoPostBack="True"
    runat="server">
<asp:ListItem value="" text="Pick your Favorite Dessert"/>
<asp:ListItem value="Cake's Value" text="Cake"/>
<asp:ListItem value="Cookies' Value" text="Cookies"/>
<asp:ListItem value="Ice Cream's Value" text="Ice Cream"/>
<asp:ListItem value="Pie's Value" text="Pie"/>
</asp:DropDownList>
<br>
<asp:label id="OurLabel" runat="server" />
</form>
</body>
</html>
```

C#—**web_dropdownlist_cs.aspx**

```
<%@ page language="cs" runat="server"%>
<script runat=server>
void Page_Load(Object sender, EventArgs e){
    if (IsPostBack){
        if (OurDropDown.SelectedIndex == 0){
            OurLabel.Text = "This isn't a dessert";
        }else{
            OurLabel.Text = "Text: " + OurDropDown.SelectedItem.Text + "<br>";
            OurLabel.Text += "Value: " + OurDropDown.SelectedItem.Value + "<br>";
            OurLabel.Text += "SelectedIndex: " + OurDropDown.SelectedIndex;
        }
    }
}
</script>

<html>
<head>
<title>Simple List Controls - DropDownList</title>
</head>
<body bgcolor="#FFFFFF" text="#000000">
<form runat="server">
<asp:DropDownList
    id="OurDropDown"
    AutoPostBack="True"
    runat="server">
<asp:ListItem value="" text="Pick your Favorite Dessert"/>
<asp:ListItem value="Cake's Value" text="Cake"/>
<asp:ListItem value="Cookies' Value" text="Cookies"/>
<asp:ListItem value="Ice Cream's Value" text="Ice Cream"/>
<asp:ListItem value="Pie's Value" text="Pie"/>
</asp:DropDownList>
<br>
<asp:label id="OurLabel" runat="server" />
</form>
</body>
</html>
```

In Figure 9.2 you can see that the DropDownList posts back to the server whenever its value changes. Also notice that I used a different way of populating the DropDownList than I did with the CheckBoxList. This time I used a ListItem control, which will work with all simple list controls and will allow you to create items within the list individually.

FIGURE 9.2

The
DropDownList
allows you the
programmatically
control and access
the <Select> input
type as a
single object.

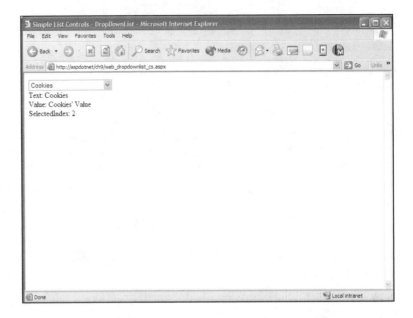

Also notice that you can access not only the item's SelectedItems.Value, but you can also retrieve the SelectedItems.Text, as well, which is a beautiful thing. If you've ever had to try to get a drop-down box's text value before in traditional ASP, you know it was always quite a feat. Now it couldn't be simpler.

ListBox

The ListBox is pretty similar to the DropDownBox, with a few exceptions. First, ListBox can display multiple rows in the browser window, and second, it gives the user the ability to select multiple values from the ListBox. This multiple selection behavior parallels the behavior of the CheckBoxList, in that a user can select multiple values from the list control. Table 9.4 describes the two additional properties the ListBox has that make this possible.

TABLE 9.4 *ListBox* Object Properties

Property	Description
Rows	Gets or sets how many rows are to be displayed in the ListBox.
SelectionMode	Gets or sets the selection mode of the ListBox, either Single or Multiple. Default is Single.

The following example pulls data out of the Northwind database from the Categories table that can be seen in Figure 9.3. It sets the DataValueField property to the CategoryID column and the DataTextField to the CategoryName column. These will populate the <select> option's value property and populate the text property between the <option></option> tags, which will become the displayed text in the list box.

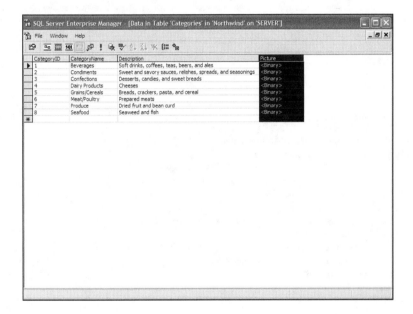

FIGURE 9.3

The Northwind database Categories table.

Visual Basic .NET—`web_listbox_vb.aspx`

```
<%@ page language="vb" runat="server"%>
<%@ Import Namespace="System.Data"%>
<%@ Import Namespace="System.Data.SQLClient"%>
<script runat=server>
Sub Page_Load(sender As Object, e As EventArgs)
    if IsPostBack then
        if OurListBox.SelectedIndex > -1 then
            dim i as Integer
            for i = 0 to OurListBox.Items.Count - 1
                if OurListBox.Items(i).Selected Then
                    OurText.Text += OurListBox.Items(i).Text & "<br>"
                    OurValues.Text +=OurListBox.Items(i).Value & "<br>"
                end if
            next
            OurText.Text = "<u>Selected Text:</u><br> " & OurText.Text
            OurValues.Text = "<u>Selected Values:</u><br> " & OurValues.Text
        end if
    else
        DataSub
    end if
end sub

Sub DataSub()
    dim OurCommand as SQLCommand
    dim OurConnection as SQLConnection
    dim OurDataAdapter as SQLDataAdapter
    dim OurDataSet as New DataSet()
    OurConnection = New SQLConnection("Server=server;
    ↦uid=newriders;pwd=password;database=Northwind")
    OurCommand = New SQLCommand("Select CategoryID,CategoryName from
    ↦Categories",OurConnection)
    OurDataAdapter = New SQLDataAdapter(OurCommand)
    OurDataAdapter.Fill(OurDataSet, "Categories")
    dim OurDataTable as New DataView(OurDataSet.Tables("Categories"))
    OurListBox.DataSource = OurDataTable
    OurListBox.DataBind()
End Sub
</script>
<html>
<head>
<title>Simple List Controls - ListBox</title>
</head>
<body bgcolor="#FFFFFF" text="#000000">
<form runat="server">
Please select the Categories you want.<br>
<asp:ListBox
    id="OurListBox"
    DataTextField="CategoryName"
    DataValueField="CategoryID"
    Rows="6"
```

```
        SelectionMode="Multiple"
        runat="server" />
<asp:button text="Click Me" runat="server" />
<br><br>
<asp:label id="OurText" EnableViewState="false" runat="server" /><br>
<asp:label id="OurValues" EnableViewState="false" runat="server" /><br>
</form>
</body>
</html>
```

C#—web_listbox_cs.aspx

```
<%@ page language="cs" runat="server"%>
<%@ Import Namespace="System.Data"%>
<%@ Import Namespace="System.Data.SqlClient"%>
<script runat=server>
void Page_Load(Object sender, EventArgs e) {
    if (IsPostBack){
        if (OurListBox.SelectedIndex > -1){
            int i;
            for (i = 0; i < OurListBox.Items.Count;i++){
                if (OurListBox.Items[i].Selected){
                    OurText.Text += OurListBox.Items[i].Text + "<br>";
                    OurValues.Text +=OurListBox.Items[i].Value + "<br>";
                }
            }
            OurText.Text = "<u>Selected Text:</u><br> " + OurText.Text;
            OurValues.Text = "<u>Selected Values:</u><br> " + OurValues.Text;
        }
    }else{
        DataSub();
    }
}

void DataSub(){
    SqlCommand OurCommand;
    SqlConnection OurConnection;
    SqlDataAdapter OurDataAdapter;
    DataSet OurDataSet;
    OurDataSet = new DataSet();
    OurConnection = new
SqlConnection("Server=server;uid=newriders;pwd=password;database=Northwind");
    OurCommand = new SqlCommand("Select CategoryID,CategoryName from
    ➥Categories",OurConnection);
    OurDataAdapter = new SqlDataAdapter(OurCommand);
    OurDataAdapter.Fill(OurDataSet, "Categories");
    DataView OurDataTable = new DataView(OurDataSet.Tables["Categories"]);
    OurListBox.DataSource = OurDataTable;
    OurListBox.DataBind();
}
</script>
```

continues

C#—(continued)

```
<html>
<head>
<title>Simple List Controls - ListBox</title>
</head>
<body bgcolor="#FFFFFF" text="#000000">
<form runat="server">
Please select the Categories you want.<br>
<asp:ListBox
    id="OurListBox"
    DataTextField="CategoryName"
    DataValueField="CategoryID"
    Rows="6"
    SelectionMode="Multiple"
    runat="server" />
<asp:button text="Click Me" runat="server" />
<br><br>
<asp:label id="OurText" EnableViewState="false" runat="server" /><br>
<asp:label id="OurValues" EnableViewState="false" runat="server" /><br>
</form>
</body>
</html>
```

You can see in Figure 9.4 how the ListBox enables a user to select multiple options from with the ListBox's options. If you look at the code examples, you can see that, as with the DropDownList, you can retrieve both the text and value properties of the ListBox.

FIGURE 9.4

The ListBox server control gives you a tool that enables the user to select multiple options from a list of items.

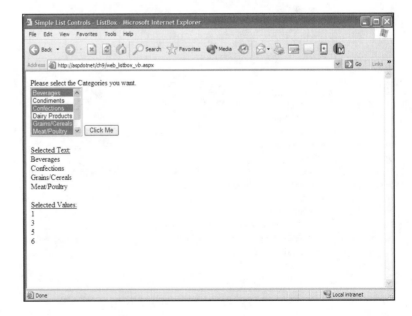

RadioButtonList

If the ListBox and the CheckBoxList behave similarly in allowing multiple selections from their respective lists, the RadioButtonList is similar to the DropDownList in that they both allow only a single selection from their lists. In the appearance arena, the RadioButtonList acts similarly to the CheckBoxList in that it has all the same additional properties. It can be displayed either in a table or inline, and you can control how the list repeats itself, as well.

TABLE 9.5 *RadioButtonList* Object Properties

Property	Description
CellPadding	Gets or sets the distance (in pixels) between the border and contents of the cell.
CellSpacing	Gets or sets the distance (in pixels) between cells.
RepeatColumns	Gets or sets how many columns to display in the CheckBoxList control.
RepeatDirection	Gets or sets a value that indicates whether the control displays vertically or horizontally. Values are Vertical or Horizontal; Vertical is default.
RepeatLayout	Gets or sets the layout of the check boxes. Flow or Table are valid; Table is default. Flow displays items without table structure.
TextAlign	Gets or sets the text alignment for the check boxes within the group. Left or Right are valid; Right is the default.

Visual Basic .NET—web_radiobuttonlist_vb.aspx

```vb
<%@ page language="vb" runat="server"%>
<%@ Import Namespace="System.Data"%>
<%@ Import Namespace="System.Data.SQLClient"%>
<script runat=server>
Sub Page_Load(sender As Object, e As EventArgs)
    if Not IsPostBack then
        DataSub
    end if
end sub

Sub Select_Shipper(sender As Object, e As EventArgs)
    OurText.Text = "Selected Shipper: " + OurRadioList.SelectedItem.Text
    OurValue.Text = "Their ShipperID: " + OurRadioList.SelectedItem.Value
End Sub

Sub DataSub()
    dim OurCommand as SQLCommand
```

continues

Visual Basic .NET—(continued)

```
    dim OurConnection as SQLConnection
    dim OurDataAdapter as SQLDataAdapter
    dim OurDataSet as New DataSet()
    OurConnection = New SQLConnection("Server=server;
    ➥uid=newriders;pwd=password;database=Northwind")
    OurCommand = New SQLCommand("Select ShipperID,CompanyName from
    ➥Shippers",OurConnection)
    OurDataAdapter = New SQLDataAdapter(OurCommand)
    OurDataAdapter.Fill(OurDataSet, "Categories")
    dim OurDataTable as New DataView(OurDataSet.Tables("Categories"))
    OurRadioList.DataSource = OurDataTable
    OurRadioList.DataBind()
End Sub
</script>
<html>
<head>
<title>Simple List Controls - RadioButtonList</title>
</head>
<body bgcolor="#FFFFFF" text="#000000">
<form runat="server">
<h3>Please select your shipper.</h3>
<asp:RadioButtonList
    id="OurRadioList"
    DataTextField="CompanyName"
    DataValueField="ShipperID"
    BorderColor="#000000"
    BorderWidth="1"
    BackColor="#EEEEEE"
    CellPadding="1"
    CellSpacing="1"
    AutoPostBack="true"
    OnSelectedIndexChanged="Select_Shipper"
    runat="server" />
<br><br>
<asp:label id="OurText" runat="server" /><br>
<asp:label id="OurValue" runat="server" /><br>
</form>
</body>
</html>
```

C#—web_radiobuttonlist_cs.aspx

```
<%@ page language="cs" runat="server"%>
<%@ Import Namespace="System.Data"%>
<%@ Import Namespace="System.Data.SqlClient"%>
<script runat=server>
void Page_Load(Object sender, EventArgs e) {
    if (!IsPostBack){
        DataSub();
```

```
        }
}

void Select_Shipper(Object sender, EventArgs e){
    OurText.Text = "Selected Shipper: " + OurRadioList.SelectedItem.Text;
    OurValue.Text = "Their ShipperID: " + OurRadioList.SelectedItem.Value;
}

void DataSub(){
    SqlCommand OurCommand;
    SqlConnection OurConnection;
    SqlDataAdapter OurDataAdapter;
    DataSet OurDataSet;
    OurDataSet = new DataSet();
    OurConnection = new SqlConnection("Server=server;
    ➥uid=newriders;pwd=password;database=Northwind");
    OurCommand = new SqlCommand("Select ShipperID,CompanyName from
    ➥Shippers",OurConnection);
    OurDataAdapter = new SqlDataAdapter(OurCommand);
    OurDataAdapter.Fill(OurDataSet, "Categories");
    DataView OurDataTable = new DataView(OurDataSet.Tables["Categories"]);
    OurRadioList.DataSource = OurDataTable;
    OurRadioList.DataBind();
}
</script>
<html>
<head>
<title>Simple List Controls - RadioButtonList</title>
</head>
<body bgcolor="#FFFFFF" text="#000000">
<form runat="server">
<h3>Please select your shipper.</h3>
<asp:RadioButtonList
    id="OurRadioList"
    DataTextField="CompanyName"
    DataValueField="ShipperID"
    BorderColor="#000000"
    BorderWidth="1"
    BackColor="#EEEEEE"
    CellPadding="1"
    CellSpacing="1"
    AutoPostBack="true"
    OnSelectedIndexChanged="Select_Shipper"
    runat="server" />
<br><br>
<asp:label id="OurText" runat="server" /><br>
<asp:label id="OurValue" runat="server" /><br>
</form>
</body>
</html>
```

As you can see in Figure 9.5, the RadioButtonList can be controlled and displayed in a similar way to the CheckBoxList. Through the SelectedItem property, you can retrieve both the text and value of the selected option.

This example also uses data binding to populated the RadioButtonList's text and value properties. I also have the RadiobuttonList's AutoPostBack property set to true, so that when a user changes a selection the form posts back.

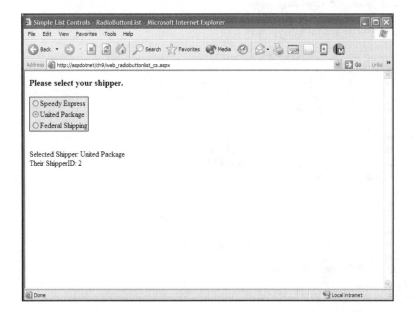

Repeater Control

The Repeater control is a very flexible server control. It also may appear to be like a small regression back to a spaghetti coding situation, but looks can be deceiving. Look at the Repeater's properties first, and then I'll pull back the veil and show you how the Repeater isn't really spaghetti code at all.

TABLE 9.6   *Repeater* Object Properties

Property	Description
DataMember	Gets or sets the table in the data source that will be bound to the control. (Note: In .NET, there are ways that data sources can have multiple tables, and that's what this property is for.)
DataSource	Gets or sets which data source provides the data that the Repeater will contain.

You might be thinking, "What the heck can I do with so few properties?" and to some degree you are correct. There isn't much you can do with just those. Truthfully, according to the .NET Framework, there are more properties than this, but I am going to deal with these specific type of properties in a different way for the rest of this chapter. These properties all fall under a family of properties known as *templates*.

Using Templates

Truthfully, the Repeater control is the first control where I introduce templates. These templates are what give you the control you need to make bound data appear the way you want.

Templates enable you to format how different components of these objects appear and operate and what they contain. The templates become more abundant and possess greater function as you progress through the next three controls.

I started with the Repeater because it is the simplest of the controls that contain templates. In a nutshell, the Repeater control contains no structure whatsoever. There is no inherent HTML formatting, and you are required to place all form within the Repeater yourself.

This is what may make the Repeater appear that it is similar to spaghetti-type code, but it has all the advantages of being an object. When you populate these templates with code, you are actually setting a property. Get it? You aren't writing spaghetti code; you are populating the related property, which exposes the Repeater to manipulation just like any other object. Table 9.7 looks at the templates available to the Repeater control. All these templates are technically properties of the same name.

TABLE 9.7 *Repeater* Object Templates

Template	Description
HeaderTemplate	If specified, rendered one time before anything in any of the other templates.
ItemTemplate	Required; renders once for each item within the bound datasource.
AlternatingItemTemplate	If specified, rendered alternately with ItemTemplate through the items within the bound datasource.
SeparatorTemplate	If specified, renders between each item in the bound datasource.
FooterTemplate	If specified, renders once after all the items of the datasource have been rendered.

Now take a look at a simple example of the Repeater control being used to display and format data.

Visual Basic .NET—web_repeater_vb.aspx

```
<%@ page language="vb" runat="server"%>
<%@ Import Namespace="System.Data"%>
<%@ Import Namespace="System.Data.SQLClient"%>
<script runat=server>
Sub Page_Load(sender As Object, e As EventArgs)
    if Not IsPostBack then
        DataSub
    end if
end sub

Sub DataSub()
    dim OurCommand as SQLCommand
    dim OurConnection as SQLConnection
    dim OurDataAdapter as SQLDataAdapter
    dim OurDataSet as New DataSet()
    OurConnection = New SQLConnection("Server=server;
    ➥uid=newriders;pwd=password;database=Northwind")
    OurCommand = New SQLCommand("Select CompanyName,Phone from
    ➥Shippers",OurConnection)
    OurDataAdapter = New SQLDataAdapter(OurCommand)
    OurDataAdapter.Fill(OurDataSet, "Categories")
    dim OurDataTable as New DataView(OurDataSet.Tables("Categories"))
    OurRepeater.DataSource = OurDataTable
    OurRepeater.DataBind()
End Sub
</script>

<html>
```

```
<head>
<title>Web Repeater</title>
</head>
<body bgcolor="#FFFFFF" text="#000000">
<form runat="server">
<asp:Repeater id="OurRepeater" runat="server">
<HeaderTemplate>
    <u><b>Shippers and PhoneNumbers</b></u><br>
</HeaderTemplate>
<ItemTemplate>
    <%# DataBinder.Eval(Container.DataItem, "CompanyName") %>:
    <%# DataBinder.Eval(Container.DataItem, "Phone") %><br>
</ItemTemplate>
<FooterTemplate>
This is the end of the phone numbers
</FooterTemplate>
</asp:Repeater>
</form>
</body>
</html>
```

C#—web_repeater_cs.aspx

```
<%@ page language="cs" runat="server"%>
<%@ Import Namespace="System.Data"%>
<%@ Import Namespace="System.Data.SqlClient"%>
<script runat=server>
void Page_Load(Object sender, EventArgs e) {
    if (!IsPostBack){
        DataSub();
    }
}
void DataSub(){
    SqlCommand OurCommand;
    SqlConnection OurConnection;
    SqlDataAdapter OurDataAdapter;
    DataSet OurDataSet;
    OurDataSet = new DataSet();
    OurConnection = new SqlConnection("Server=server;
    ➥uid=newriders;pwd=password;database=Northwind");
    OurCommand = new SqlCommand("Select CompanyName, Phone from
    ➥Shippers",OurConnection);
    OurDataAdapter = new SqlDataAdapter(OurCommand);
    OurDataAdapter.Fill(OurDataSet, "Categories");
    DataView OurDataTable = new DataView(OurDataSet.Tables["Categories"]);
    OurRepeater.DataSource = OurDataTable;
    OurRepeater.DataBind();
}
</script>
<html>
<head>
```

continues

C#—(continued)

```
<title>Web Repeater</title>
</head>
<body bgcolor="#FFFFFF" text="#000000">
<form runat="server">
<asp:Repeater id="OurRepeater" runat="server">
<HeaderTemplate>
    <u><b>Shippers and PhoneNumbers</b></u><br>
</HeaderTemplate>
<ItemTemplate>
    <%# DataBinder.Eval(Container.DataItem, "CompanyName") %>:
    <%# DataBinder.Eval(Container.DataItem, "Phone") %><br>
</ItemTemplate>
<FooterTemplate>
This is the end of the phone numbers
</FooterTemplate>
</asp:Repeater>
</form>
</body>
</html>
```

Looking at Figure 9.6, you can see that the Repeater operates just like a Literal control, except it has different players in the different templates. It basically dumps the HTML just as you wrote it to the page.

FIGURE 9.6

The Repeater *allows you to bind data sources to it, and, through the use of templates, display that data.*

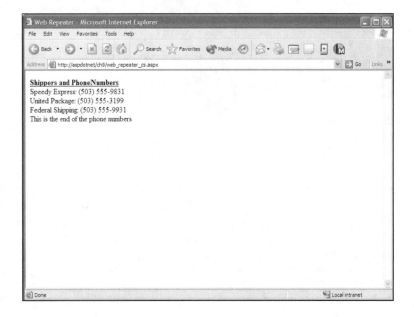

Building a Complex *Repeater*

As you can see in the preceding example, the Repeater object simply places the HTML in the templates in the order we want over into the HTML output. This means as far as template creation is concerned, you can go hog wild with what is inside the Repeater. Now look at a much more complicated Repeater with a table with multiple rows per item and a separator, to boot.

Visual Basic .NET—`web_complexrepeater_vb.aspx`

```
<%@ page language="vb" runat="server"%>
<%@ Import Namespace="System.Data"%>
<%@ Import Namespace="System.Data.SQLClient"%>
<script runat=server>
Sub Page_Load(sender As Object, e As EventArgs)
    if Not IsPostBack then
        DataSub
    end if
end sub

Sub DataSub()
    dim OurCommand as SQLCommand
    dim OurConnection as SQLConnection
    dim OurDataAdapter as SQLDataAdapter
    dim OurDataSet as New DataSet()
    OurConnection = New SQLConnection("Server=server;
    ➥uid=newriders;pwd=password;database=Northwind")
    OurCommand = New SQLCommand("Select Top 3
    ➥TitleOfCourtesy,FirstName,LastName,Title,HireDate,Address,City,Region,
    ➥PostalCode,Country from Employees",OurConnection)
    OurDataAdapter = New SQLDataAdapter(OurCommand)
    OurDataAdapter.Fill(OurDataSet, "Categories")
    dim OurDataTable as New DataView(OurDataSet.Tables("Categories"))
    OurRepeater.DataSource = OurDataTable
    OurRepeater.DataBind()
End Sub
</script>

<html>
<head>
<title>Web Repeater</title>
</head>
<body bgcolor="#FFFFFF" text="#000000">
<form runat="server">
<asp:Repeater id="OurRepeater" runat="server">
<HeaderTemplate>
    <table width="700" cellpadding="2" cellspacing="1" border="0">
    <tr><td colspan="3"><h3>Employees for Northwind</h3></td></tr>
</HeaderTemplate>
<ItemTemplate>
```

continues

Visual Basic .NET—(continued)

```
    <tr bgcolor="#AAAAAA"><td><b>Name</b></td>
    <td><b>Title</b></td>
    <td><b>Hire Date</b></td></tr>
    <tr bgcolor="#EEEEEE"><td>
    <%# DataBinder.Eval(Container.DataItem, "TitleOfCourtesy") %>
    <%# DataBinder.Eval(Container.DataItem, "FirstName") %>
    <%# DataBinder.Eval(Container.DataItem, "LastName") %>
    </td><td>
    <%# DataBinder.Eval(Container.DataItem, "Title") %>
    </td><td>
    <%# DataBinder.Eval(Container.DataItem, "HireDate") %>
    </td></tr>
    <tr bgcolor="#AAAAAA"><td><b>Address</b></td>
    <td><b>City</b></td>
    <td><b>Region, Postal Code, Country</b></td></tr>
    <tr bgcolor="#EEEEEE"><td>
    <%# DataBinder.Eval(Container.DataItem, "Address") %>
    </td><td>
    <%# DataBinder.Eval(Container.DataItem, "City") %>
    </td><td>
    <%# DataBinder.Eval(Container.DataItem, "Region") %>
    <%# DataBinder.Eval(Container.DataItem, "PostalCode") %>
    <%# DataBinder.Eval(Container.DataItem, "Country") %>
    </td></tr>
</ItemTemplate>
<SeparatorTemplate>
<tr><td colspan="3"><hr></td></tr>
</SeparatorTemplate>
<FooterTemplate>
</table>
</FooterTemplate>
</asp:Repeater>
</form>
</body>
</html>
```

C#—web_complexrepeater_cs.aspx

```
<%@ page language="cs" runat="server"%>
<%@ Import Namespace="System.Data"%>
<%@ Import Namespace="System.Data.SqlClient"%>
<script runat=server>
void Page_Load(Object sender, EventArgs e) {
    if (!IsPostBack){
        DataSub();
    }
}
void DataSub(){
    SqlCommand OurCommand;
```

```
    SqlConnection OurConnection;
    SqlDataAdapter OurDataAdapter;
    DataSet OurDataSet;
    OurDataSet = new DataSet();
    OurConnection = new SqlConnection("Server=server;
    ➥uid=newriders;pwd=password;database=Northwind");
    OurCommand = new SqlCommand("Select Top 3
    ➥TitleOfCourtesy,FirstName,LastName,Title,HireDate,Address,City,Region,
    ➥PostalCode,Country from Employees",OurConnection);
    OurDataAdapter = new SqlDataAdapter(OurCommand);
    OurDataAdapter.Fill(OurDataSet, "Categories");
    DataView OurDataTable = new DataView(OurDataSet.Tables["Categories"]);
    OurRepeater.DataSource = OurDataTable;
    OurRepeater.DataBind();
}
</script>
<html>
<head>
<title>Web Repeater</title>
</head>
<body bgcolor="#FFFFFF" text="#000000">
<form runat="server">
<asp:Repeater id="OurRepeater" runat="server">
<HeaderTemplate>
    <table width="700" cellpadding="2" cellspacing="1" border="0">
    <tr><td colspan="3"><h3>Employees for Northwind</h3></td></tr>
</HeaderTemplate>
<ItemTemplate>
    <tr bgcolor="#AAAAAA"><td><b>Name</b></td>
    <td><b>Title</b></td>
    <td><b>Hire Date</b></td></tr>
    <tr bgcolor="#EEEEEE"><td>
    <%# DataBinder.Eval(Container.DataItem, "TitleOfCourtesy") %>
    <%# DataBinder.Eval(Container.DataItem, "FirstName") %>
    <%# DataBinder.Eval(Container.DataItem, "LastName") %>
    </td><td>
    <%# DataBinder.Eval(Container.DataItem, "Title") %>
    </td><td>
    <%# DataBinder.Eval(Container.DataItem, "HireDate") %>
    </td></tr>
    <tr bgcolor="#AAAAAA"><td><b>Address</b></td>
    <td><b>City</b></td>
    <td><b>Region, Postal Code, Country</b></td></tr>
    <tr bgcolor="#EEEEEE"><td>
    <%# DataBinder.Eval(Container.DataItem, "Address") %>
    </td><td>
    <%# DataBinder.Eval(Container.DataItem, "City") %>
    </td><td>
    <%# DataBinder.Eval(Container.DataItem, "Region") %>
    <%# DataBinder.Eval(Container.DataItem, "PostalCode") %>
    <%# DataBinder.Eval(Container.DataItem, "Country") %>
    </td></tr>
```

continues

C#—(continued)

```
</ItemTemplate>
<SeparatorTemplate>
<tr><td colspan="3"><hr></td></tr>
</SeparatorTemplate>
<FooterTemplate>
</table>
</FooterTemplate>
</asp:Repeater>
</form>
</body>
</html>
```

As you can see in the results displayed in Figure 9.7, the only real limitation as to what you can have a `Repeater` do is you. You can place any valid HTML in the `Repeater`, and it will render it to the browser.

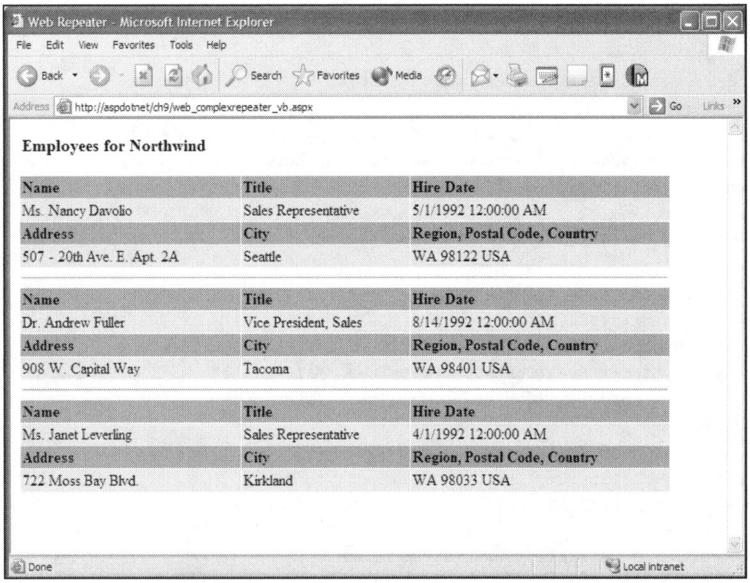

FIGURE 9.7

You can build very complex HTML databound objects with the Repeater *control.*

> **T IP**
>
> *One thing to watch out for, as with the literal control, is that the* `Repeater` *renders to the browser what it contains. If you are delivering anything from a data source that might be interpreted as HTML, such as arrows (< or >), this will cause the browser to flake out and not give you the desired results. Any time you might be delivering data to a* `Repeater` *that might contain confusing characters such as these, I recommend that you HTMLEncode it this way:*
>
> `Server.HTMLEncode(DataBinder.Eval(Container.DataItem, "Address"))`

Don't be afraid to experiment and see what interesting things you can come up with when using the `Repeater`. Although it does require you to code the templates, it also provides an abundance of freedom in displaying bound data.

Complex List Controls

Now it's time to investigate some of the more complex beasts that ASP.NET has to offer for displaying list and bound tabular data. The `DataList` and `DataGrid` offer a lot more structure for the data that is bound to them. They also offer tons of control over how the data is displayed and what it can do with the addition of more powerful templates that handle column formatting and as well as function.

DataList Server Control

Because the `DataList` control has HTML formatting and additional function, it has a few more properties than the `Repeater` control.

TABLE 9.8 *DataList* Object Properties

Property	Description
AlternatingItemStyle	Gets the style properties for alternating items in the `DataList` control.
EditItemIndex	Gets or sets the index number of the item selected for editing in the `DataList` control.
EditItemStyle	Gets the style properties for the item selected for editing in the `DataList` control.

continues

TABLE 9.8 Continued

Property	Description
ExtractTemplateRows	Gets or sets a value that indicates whether the rows of a Table control, defined in each template of a DataList control, are extracted and displayed. In other words, if you want to control the layout of each Repeater, insert an asp:table object into the ItemTemplate and set this to true. Then the data list will use the rows and layout from the table object rather than the DataList itself.
FooterStyle	Gets the style properties of the footer section in the DataGrid control.
GridLines	Gets or sets what the style of the gridline are for the DataList control when the RepeatLayout property is set to RepeatLayout.Table.
HeaderStyle	Gets the style properties for the heading section of the DataList control.
Items	Gets a collection of DataListItem objects representing the individual items within the control.
ItemStyle	Gets the style properties for the items in the DataList control.
RepeatColumns	Gets or sets the number of columns to display in the DataList control.
RepeatDirection	Gets or sets whether the DataList control displays vertically or horizontally.
RepeatLayout	Gets or sets whether the control is displayed in a table or flow layout.
SelectedIndex	Gets or sets the index of the selected item in the DataList control.
SelectedItem	Gets the selected item in the DataList control.
SelectedItemStyle	Gets the style properties for the selected item in the DataList control.
SeparatorStyle	Gets the style properties of the separator between each item in the DataList control.
ShowFooter	Gets or sets a value indicating whether the footer section is displayed in the DataList control.
ShowHeader	Gets or sets a value indicating whether the header section is displayed in the DataList control.

The DataList possesses all the templates that the Repeater has (see Table 9.9), plus one additional template called the EditItemTemplate, which is used to control the layout and function of an item that has been selected for editing.

TABLE 9.9 *DataList* Object Templates

Template	Description
HeaderTemplate	If specified, rendered one time before anything in any of the other templates.
ItemTemplate	Required; renders once for each item within the bound data source.
EditItemTemplate	If specified, renders for the item selected for editing in the DataList control.
AlternatingItemTemplate	If specified, rendered alternately with ItemTemplate through the items within the bound data source.
SeparatorTemplate	If specified, renders between each item in the bound data source.
FooterTemplate	If specified, renders once after all the items of the datasource have been rendered.

As you can see, there are a whole bunch more toys to play with in the DataList. I could take up 20 pages just describing and giving examples of the forms and functions of the DataList, but I'm not going to do that. What I am going to show you is some of the power function of the DataList, including its capability to define the visual aspect of the data, as well as some functions of the DataList.

One of the functions I'd like to demonstrate is how to use the control to edit data directly. In the following example there is a whole heckuvalotta stuff going on, and again I stress that you should focus on the DataList control in this example. In a nutshell, this example builds a table of employee names, displays them in a DataList control, and enables the user to update and delete employees from the table.

Visual Basic .NET—web_datalist_vb.aspx

```
<%@ page language="vb" runat="server"%>
<%@ Import Namespace="System.Data" %>
<script language="VB" runat="server">
Dim Employees As DataTable
Dim EmployeesView As DataView

Sub Page_Load(sender As Object, e As EventArgs)
    If Session("Employees") Is Nothing Then
        Employees = New DataTable()
        Employees.Columns.Add(New DataColumn("ID", GetType(String)))
        Employees.Columns.Add(New DataColumn("FirstName", GetType(String)))
        Employees.Columns.Add(New DataColumn("LastName", GetType(String)))
        Session("Employees") = Employees

        dim OurArray(,) as String = {{"1","Nancy","Davolio"},
        ➡{"54","Andrew","Fuller"},{"138","Janet","Leverling"}}

        dim i As Integer
        For i = 0 To 2
            Dim dr As DataRow = Employees.NewRow()
            dr(0) = OurArray(i,0)
            dr(1) = OurArray(i,1)
            dr(2) = OurArray(i,2)
            Employees.Rows.Add(dr)
        Next i
    Else
        Employees = CType(Session("Employees"), DataTable)
        End If
        EmployeesView = New DataView(Employees)
        EmployeesView.Sort = "ID"
        If Not IsPostBack Then
            BindList()
        End If
End Sub

Sub BindList()
    OurDataList.DataSource = EmployeesView
    OurDataList.DataBind()
End Sub

Sub DataList_EditCommand(sender As Object, e As DataListCommandEventArgs)
    OurDataList.EditItemIndex = CInt(e.Item.ItemIndex)
    BindList()
End Sub

Sub DataList_CancelCommand(sender As Object, e As DataListCommandEventArgs)
    OurDataList.EditItemIndex = - 1
    BindList()
End Sub

Sub DataList_DeleteCommand(sender As Object, e As DataListCommandEventArgs)
```

```
        Dim ID As String = CType(e.Item.FindControl("OurLabel"), Label).Text
        EmployeesView.RowFilter = "ID='" & ID & "'"
        If EmployeesView.Count > 0 Then
            EmployeesView.Delete(0)
        End If
        EmployeesView.RowFilter = ""
        OurDataList.EditItemIndex = - 1
        BindList()
End Sub

Sub DataList_UpdateCommand(sender As Object, e As DataListCommandEventArgs)
        Dim ID As String = CType(e.Item.FindControl("OurLabel"), Label).Text
        Dim FirstName As String = CType(e.Item.FindControl("FirstNameText"),
        ➥TextBox).Text
        Dim LastName As String = CType(e.Item.FindControl("LastNameText"),
        ➥TextBox).Text
        EmployeesView.RowFilter = "ID='" & ID & "'"
        If EmployeesView.Count > 0 Then
            EmployeesView.Delete(0)
        End If
        EmployeesView.RowFilter = ""
        Dim dr As DataRow = Employees.NewRow()
        dr(0) = ID
        dr(1) = FirstName
        dr(2) = LastName
        Employees.Rows.Add(dr)
        OurDataList.EditItemIndex = - 1
        BindList()
End Sub
</script>
<html>
<head>
<title>Edit DataList</title>
</head>
<body>
<form runat=server>
<asp:DataList id="OurDataList" runat="server"
    BorderWidth="1"
    BorderColor="#000000"
    CellPadding="3"
    CellSpacing="1"
    HeaderStyle-BackColor="#AAAAAA"
    ItemStyle-BackColor="#EEEEEE"
    EditItemStyle-BackColor="#CCCCCC"
    OnEditCommand="DataList_EditCommand"
    OnUpdateCommand="DataList_UpdateCommand"
    OnDeleteCommand="DataList_DeleteCommand"
    OnCancelCommand="DataList_CancelCommand">
<HeaderTemplate><b>Employees</b></HeaderTemplate>
<ItemTemplate>
    <u>ID:</u>
    <%# (CType(Container.DataItem, DataRowView))("ID")%><br>
```

continues

Visual Basic .NET—(continued)

```
                <u>Name:</u>
                <%# (CType(Container.DataItem, DataRowView))("FirstName")%>
                <%# (CType(Container.DataItem, DataRowView))("LastName")%><br>
                <asp:LinkButton
                    id="button1"
                    Text="Edit"
                    CommandName="edit"
                    runat="server"/>
        </ItemTemplate>
        <EditItemTemplate>
        ID:
        <asp:Label id="OurLabel"
            Text='<%# (CType(Container.DataItem, DataRowView))("ID") %>'
            runat="server"/><br>
        FirstName:
        <asp:TextBox id="FirstNameText"
            Text='<%# (CType(Container.DataItem, DataRowView))("FirstName") %>'
            Size="5"
            runat="server"/><br>
        LastName:
        <asp:TextBox id="LastNameText"
            Text='<%# DataBinder.Eval(Container.DataItem, "LastName") %>'
        Size="5"
            runat="server"/> <br>
        <asp:LinkButton id="button2"
            Text="Update"
            CommandName="update"
            runat="server"/>
        <asp:LinkButton id="button3"
            Text="Delete"
            CommandName="delete"
            runat="server"/>
        <asp:LinkButton id="button4"
            Text="Cancel"
            CommandName="cancel"
            runat="server"/>
        </EditItemTemplate>
        </asp:DataList>
        </form>
        </body>
        </html>
```

C#—web_datalist_cs.aspx

```
<%@ page language="cs" runat="server"%>
<%@ Import Namespace="System.Data" %>
<script runat="server">
DataTable Employees;
DataView EmployeesView;
void Page_Load(Object sender, EventArgs e){
    if (Session["Employees"] == null){
            Employees = new DataTable();
        Employees.Columns.Add(new DataColumn("ID", typeof(string)));
        Employees.Columns.Add(new DataColumn("FirstName", typeof(string)));
        Employees.Columns.Add(new DataColumn("LastName", typeof(string)));
        Session["Employees"] = Employees;

        String[,] OurArray = {{"1","Nancy","Davolio"},{"54","Andrew","Fuller"}
        ,{"138","Janet","Leverling"}};

        for (int i = 0;i<=2;i++){
            DataRow dr = Employees.NewRow();
            dr[0] = OurArray[i,0];
            dr[1] = OurArray[i,1];
            dr[2] = OurArray[i,2];
            Employees.Rows.Add(dr);
        }
    }else{
        Employees = (DataTable)Session["Employees"];
    }
    EmployeesView = new DataView(Employees);
    EmployeesView.Sort = "ID";
    if (!IsPostBack){
        BindList();
    }
}


void BindList(){
    OurDataList.DataSource = EmployeesView;
    OurDataList.DataBind();
}

void DataList_EditCommand(Object sender,DataListCommandEventArgs e){
    OurDataList.EditItemIndex = (int)e.Item.ItemIndex;
    BindList();
}

void DataList_CancelCommand(Object sender,DataListCommandEventArgs e){
    OurDataList.EditItemIndex = - 1;
    BindList();
}

void DataList_DeleteCommand(Object sender,DataListCommandEventArgs e){
    String ID = ((Label) e.Item.FindControl("OurLabel")).Text;
```

continues

C#—(continued)

```
    EmployeesView.RowFilter = "ID='" + ID + "'";
    if (EmployeesView.Count > 0){
        EmployeesView.Delete(0);
    }
    EmployeesView.RowFilter = "";
        OurDataList.EditItemIndex = - 1;
            BindList();
}

void DataList_UpdateCommand(Object sender,DataListCommandEventArgs e){
    String ID = ((Label)e.Item.FindControl("OurLabel")).Text;
    String FirstName = ((TextBox)e.Item.FindControl("FirstNameText")).Text;
    String LastName = ((TextBox)e.Item.FindControl("LastNameText")).Text;
    EmployeesView.RowFilter = "ID='" + ID + "'";
    if (EmployeesView.Count > 0){
        EmployeesView.Delete(0);
    }
    EmployeesView.RowFilter = "";
    DataRow dr = Employees.NewRow();
    dr[0] = ID;
    dr[1] = FirstName;
    dr[2] = LastName;
    Employees.Rows.Add(dr);
    OurDataList.EditItemIndex = - 1;
    BindList();
}

</script>
<html>
<head>
<title>Edit DataList</title>
</head>
<body>
<form runat=server>
<asp:DataList id="OurDataList" runat="server"
    BorderWidth="1"
    BorderColor="#000000"
    CellPadding="3"
    CellSpacing="1"
    HeaderStyle-BackColor="#AAAAAA"
    ItemStyle-BackColor="#EEEEEE"
    EditItemStyle-BackColor="#CCCCCC"
    OnEditCommand="DataList_EditCommand"
    OnUpdateCommand="DataList_UpdateCommand"
    OnDeleteCommand="DataList_DeleteCommand"
    OnCancelCommand="DataList_CancelCommand">
<HeaderTemplate><b>Employees</b></HeaderTemplate>
<ItemTemplate>
    <u>ID:</u>
    <%# ((DataRowView)Container.DataItem)["ID"]%><br>
    <u>Name:</u>
```

```
<%# ((DataRowView)Container.DataItem)["FirstName"]%>
<%# ((DataRowView)Container.DataItem)["LastName"]%><br>
<asp:LinkButton
    id="button1"
    Text="Edit"
    CommandName="edit"
runat="server"/>
</ItemTemplate>
<EditItemTemplate>
ID:
<asp:Label id="OurLabel"
    Text='<%# ((DataRowView)Container.DataItem)["ID"]%>'
    runat="server"/><br>
FirstName:
<asp:TextBox id="FirstNameText"
    Text='<%# ((DataRowView)Container.DataItem)["FirstName"]%>'
    Size="5"
    runat="server"/><br>
LastName:
<asp:TextBox id="LastNameText"
    Text='<%# ((DataRowView)Container.DataItem)["LastName"]%>'
    Size="5"
    runat="server"/> <br>
<asp:LinkButton id="button2"
    Text="Update"
    CommandName="update"
    runat="server"/>
<asp:LinkButton id="button3"
    Text="Delete"
    CommandName="delete"
    runat="server"/>
<asp:LinkButton id="button4"
    Text="Cancel"
    CommandName="cancel"
    runat="server"/>
</EditItemTemplate>
</asp:DataList>
</form>
</body>
</html>
```

As you can see in Figure 9.8, the DataList provides a powerful interface control for listing and editing data. After you move into the chapter on handling database and manipulating data, I will show you how to leverage these feature of the DataList—and the DataGrid, for that matter.

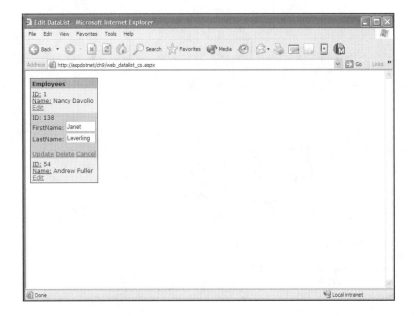

The DataList basically provides one table cell per Item Row in the data source; the DataGrid provides a cell for each Item in the data source's row.

DataGrid Control

Let me be honest with you. It's currently 1:00 a.m. and looking at the DataGrid now is like looking at Mount Everest. The DataGrid is the granddaddy of all controls. This thing slices, dices, whips, purrees, chops, blends, and dices data-sources in just about every way that you can think.

If you want to display tabular data, this is it—the be-all, end-all, you ain't gonna need anything else to do the job, control. You want properties, it's got properties. You want templates, it's got templates. I'd love to meet the guys who built this monster because it does it all.

Properties and methods and templates and their properties and methods and on and on and on. So buckle your seatbelts; I just got a fresh cup of coffee, we're going for a ride.

Table 9.10 lists the DataGrid object properties.

TABLE 9.10 *DataGrid* Object Properties

Property	Description
AllowCustomPaging	Gets or sets a Boolean value indicating whether custom paging is enabled.
AllowPaging	Gets or sets a Boolean value indicating whether paging is enabled.
AllowSorting	Gets or sets a Boolean value indicating whether sorting is enabled.
AlternatingItemStyle	Gets the style properties for the alternating items in the DataGrid.
AutoGenerateColumns	Gets or sets a Boolean value indicating whether BoundColumn objects are created automatically and displayed in the DataGrid for each field in the datasource.
BackImageURL	Gets or sets the URL for the image that is to be displayed in the background of the DataGrid.
Columns	Gets a collection of objects of the columns in the DataGrid.
CurrentPageIndex	Gets or sets the index of the currently displayed page.
EditItemIndex	Gets or sets the index of the item to be edited in the DataGrid.
EditItemStyle	Gets the style properties of the item selected to be edited in the DataGrid.
FooterStyle	Gets the style properties of the footer in the DataGrid.
HeaderStyle	Gets the style properties of the header in the DataGrid.
Items	Gets a collection of the DataGridItem objects in the DataGrid. This represents each individual item in the DataGrid.
ItemStyle	Gets the style properties of the items in the DataGrid.
PageCount	Gets the total number of pages that is required to display all the items in the DataGrid.
PagerStyle	Gets the style property of the paging elements of the DataGrid.
PageSize	Gets or sets how many items are to be displayed on each page of the DataGrid.
SelectedIndex	Gets or sets the index of the item selected in the DataGrid.

continues

TABLE 9.10 Continued

Property	Description
SelectedItem	Gets a DataGridItem object that contains the selected item in the DataGrid.
SelectedItemStyle	Gets the style properties of the currently selected item in the DataGrid.
ShowFooter	Gets or sets a Boolean value that determines whether the footer of the DataGrid is displayed.
ShowHeader	Gets or sets a Boolean value that determines whether the header of the DataGrid is displayed.
VirtualItemCount	Gets or sets the virtual number of items in the DataGrid control when custom paging is used.

That's a lot of properties, isn't it? Well, that's not the end of it. Just like the DataList, the DataGrid provides a lot of powerful individual controls for the display and function of the data in the DataGrid. They differ, though. The DataList and Repeater are definitely focused on controlling the contents of each row of items. The DataGrid gives much more power by the addition of column templates that handle different types of function (see Table 9.11).

TABLE 9.11 *DataGrid* Column Templates

Template	Description
BoundColumn	Creates a column that is populated with data from a specific field in the data source.
ButtonColumn	Creates a column that is populated with a command button for each item in the column.
EditCommandColumn	Displays common edit commands such as Edit, Update, and Cancel.
HyperlinkColumn	Creates a column of hyperlinks created from data from the data source.
TemplateColumn	Creates a column that enables you to create templates within the column to control the HTML the column contains.

The column templates all share a base set of properties, plus they have properties all their own, as well. Table 9.12 shows you the base properties first.

TABLE 9.12   *DataGridColumn* Base Properties

Property	Description
FooterStyle	Gets the style properties for the footer section of the column.
FooterText	This is the text that is displayed in the bottom cell after all the items to be displayed.
HeaderImageURL	The URL of the image that is rendered in the column heading. This overrides the HeaderText property.
HeaderStyle	Gets the style properties for the header section of the column.
HeaderText	This is the text that is displayed in the column heading.
ItemStyle	Gets the style properties for the item cells of the column.
SortExpression	The name of the field by which to sort the data source.
Visible	A Boolean value that determines whether the column is displayed.

As I said, each column template not only has the previous properties, but they also have unique properties that give them their individual function, as described in Tables 9.13–9.17.

TABLE 9.13   *BoundColumn* Properties

Property	Description
DataField	Identifies the field in the data source that is the source for the column.
DataFormatString	A formatting expression string that describes how to display the data in the column.
ReadOnly	A Boolean value that determines whether the field can be edited if the row enters edit mode.

N O T E

The DataFormatString and the DataTextFormatString properties in later columns are powerful properties that allow you to set formatting for data that appears in a columns, such as formatting currency, dates, or numbers. This subject is pretty lengthy for discussion here but the .NET Framework SDK has an exhaustive amount of data on this subject, which you can start to investigate at the following URL:

ms-help://MS.NETFrameworkSDK/cpguidenf/html/
cpconformattingoverview.htm

TABLE 9.14 *ButtonColumn* Properties

Property	Description
ButtonType	The type of button used when rendered. The valid options are LinkButton and PushButton.
CommandName	Gets or sets the name of the command to perform if the button is clicked.
DataTextField	The name of the field in the data source that will be bound to the button's text property.
DataTextFormatString	Formatting expression string that describes how to display the data in the column.
Text	Gets or sets the text property of the button in the column. If the DataTextField is set, this property is overridden.

TABLE 9.15 *EditCommandColumn* Properties

Property	Description
ButtonType	The type of button used when rendered. The valid options are LinkButton and PushButton.
EditText	Gets or sets the text displayed as the Edit LinkButton or PushButton.
UpdateText	Gets or sets the text displayed as the Update LinkButton or PushButton.
CancelText	Gets or sets the text displayed as the Delete LinkButton or PushButton.

TABLE 9.16 *HyperLinkColumn* Properties

Property	Description
DataNavigateURLField	Identifies the field in the data source that provides the URL of what page to go to.
DataNavigateURLFormatString	A formatting expression string that describes how to display the URL portion of the HyperlinkColumn of the data in the column.
DataTextField	The name of the field in the data source that will be bound to the column's text property.
DataTextFormatString	A formatting expression string that describes how to display the text in the column.
NavigateURL	Gets or sets the URL of the page to move to.
Target	Gets or sets the target window that the URL in NavigateURL is loaded.
Text	Gets or sets the text of the hyperlink.

TABLE 9.17 *TemplateColumn* Properties

Template	Description
HeaderTemplate	If specified, rendered one time before anything in any of the other templates.
ItemTemplate	Required; renders once for each item within the bound data source.
EditItemTemplate	If specified, renders for the item selected for editing in the DataList control.
FooterTemplate	If specified, renders once after all the items of the datasource have been rendered.

With all these different elements, you can begin to see that the sky's the limit with regard to the control you can exercise when using the DataGrid control. We are going to go over a bunch of examples that cover much of the different functionality of the DataGrid. Of course, you could write a short (maybe even long) book to cover and build examples of what the DataGrid can do, but what I will cover here will give you solid examples of using the most common functions that the DataGrid provides. Look first at a simple example of just populating a DataGrid with information.

Visual Basic .NET—**web_datagridsimple_vb.aspx**

```
<%@ page language="vb" runat="server"%>
<%@ Import Namespace="System.Data"%>
<%@ Import Namespace="System.Data.SQLClient"%>
<script runat=server>
Sub Page_Load(sender As Object, e As EventArgs)
    if Not IsPostBack then
        DataSub
    end if
end sub

Sub DataSub()
    dim OurCommand as SQLCommand
    dim OurConnection as SQLConnection
    dim OurDataAdapter as SQLDataAdapter
    dim OurDataSet as New DataSet()
    OurConnection = New
SQLConnection("Server=server;uid=newriders;pwd=password;database=Northwind")
    OurCommand = New SQLCommand("Select Top 10 ProductName, QuantityPerUnit,
    ➥UnitPrice, UnitsInStock From Products",OurConnection)
    OurDataAdapter = New SQLDataAdapter(OurCommand)
    OurDataAdapter.Fill(OurDataSet, "Products")
    dim OurDataTable as New DataView(OurDataSet.Tables("Products"))
    OurDataGrid.DataSource = OurDataTable
    OurDataGrid.DataBind()
End Sub
</script>

<html>
<head>
<title>Web Datagrid</title>
</head>
<body bgcolor="#FFFFFF" text="#000000">
<h3 style="font-family:Verdana">Our Products</h3>
<asp:DataGrid
id="OurDataGrid"
    BorderWidth="1"
    BorderColor="#000000"
    CellPadding="3"
    CellSpacing="0"
    Font-Name="Verdana"
```

```
        HeaderStyle-BackColor="#AAAAAA"
        ItemStyle-BackColor="#EEEEEE"
        runat="server" />
</body>
</html>
```

C#—web_datagridsimple_cs.aspx

```
<%@ page language="c#" runat="server"%>
<%@ Import Namespace="System.Data"%>
<%@ Import Namespace="System.Data.SqlClient"%>
<script runat=server>
void Page_Load(Object sender, EventArgs e) {
    if (!IsPostBack) {
        DataSub();
    }
}

void DataSub() {
    SqlCommand OurCommand;
    SqlConnection OurConnection;
    SqlDataAdapter OurDataAdapter;
    DataSet OurDataSet;
    OurDataSet = new DataSet();
    OurConnection = new
SqlConnection("Server=server;uid=newriders;pwd=password;database=Northwind");
    OurCommand = new SqlCommand("Select Top 10 ProductName, QuantityPerUnit,
    ➥UnitPrice, UnitsInStock From Products",OurConnection);
    OurDataAdapter = new SqlDataAdapter(OurCommand);
    OurDataAdapter.Fill(OurDataSet, "Products");
    DataView OurDataTable = new DataView(OurDataSet.Tables["Products"]);
    OurDataGrid.DataSource = OurDataTable;
    OurDataGrid.DataBind();
}
</script>
<html>
<head>
<title>Web Datagrid</title>
</head>
<body bgcolor="#FFFFFF" text="#000000">
<h3 style="font-family:Verdana">Our Products</h3>
<asp:DataGrid
    id="OurDataGrid"
    BorderWidth="1"
    BorderColor="#000000"
        CellPadding="3"
        CellSpacing="0"
        Font-Name="Verdana"
        HeaderStyle-BackColor="#AAAAAA"
        ItemStyle-BackColor="#EEEEEE"
    runat="server" />
</body>
</html>
```

If you look at Figure 9.9, you can see that displaying the contents of products in `DataGrid` is quite simple. The data source pulls information out of the Northwind database and binds it to the `DataGrid`. In this simple example, the `DataGrid`, without intervention, creates the proper number of columns and populates the table cells with the data. Just set a few properties and we've got a hot-looking table of data delivered to the browser.

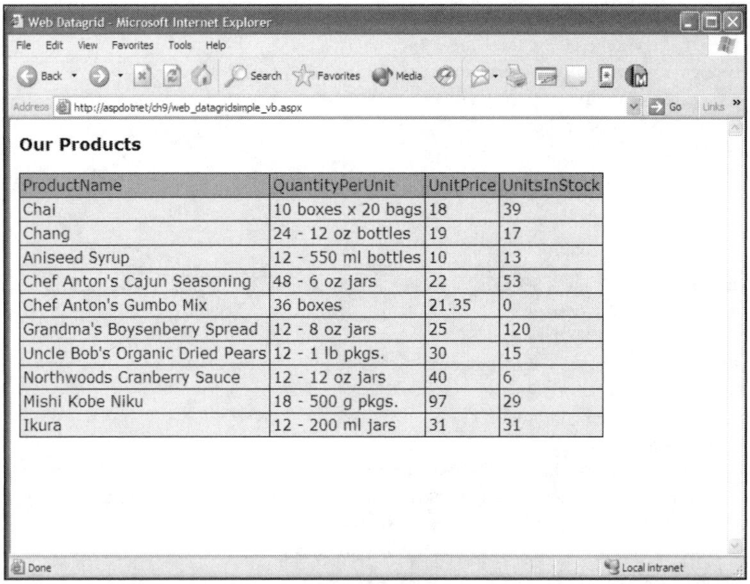

ProductName	QuantityPerUnit	UnitPrice	UnitsInStock
Chai	10 boxes x 20 bags	18	39
Chang	24 - 12 oz bottles	19	17
Aniseed Syrup	12 - 550 ml bottles	10	13
Chef Anton's Cajun Seasoning	48 - 6 oz jars	22	53
Chef Anton's Gumbo Mix	36 boxes	21.35	0
Grandma's Boysenberry Spread	12 - 8 oz jars	25	120
Uncle Bob's Organic Dried Pears	12 - 1 lb pkgs.	30	15
Northwoods Cranberry Sauce	12 - 12 oz jars	40	6
Mishi Kobe Niku	18 - 500 g pkgs.	97	29
Ikura	12 - 200 ml jars	31	31

FIGURE 9.9

The `DataGrid` *provides a power tool for displaying tabular data in ASP.NET pages.*

As I described earlier, the column templates give you a lot of power over formatting data within specific columns. Look at a few of the column types in action. Take notice that the `AutoGenerateColumns` property is set to false in the `DataGrid`'s opening tag, because the columns will be created manually with column templates.

Visual Basic .NET—`web_datagridcolumns_vb.aspx`

```
<%@ page language="vb" runat="server"%>
<%@ Import Namespace="System.Data"%>
<%@ Import Namespace="System.Data.SQLClient"%>
<script runat=server>
Sub Page_Load(sender As Object, e As EventArgs)
    if Not IsPostBack then
        DataSub
    end if
    If Request.Params("Product") <> "" Then
```

```
            OurLabel.Text = "You Chose: " & Request.Params("Product")
        end if
    end sub

    Sub DataSub()
        dim OurCommand as SQLCommand
        dim OurConnection as SQLConnection
        dim OurDataAdapter as SQLDataAdapter
        dim OurDataSet as New DataSet()
        OurConnection = New SQLConnection("Server=server;
    ➥uid=newriders;pwd=password;database=Northwind")
        OurCommand = New SQLCommand("Select Top 10 ProductName, QuantityPerUnit,
    ➥UnitPrice, UnitsInStock From Products",OurConnection)
        OurDataAdapter = New SQLDataAdapter(OurCommand)
        OurDataAdapter.Fill(OurDataSet, "Products")
        dim OurDataTable as New DataView(OurDataSet.Tables("Products"))
        OurDataGrid.DataSource = OurDataTable
        OurDataGrid.DataBind()
    End Sub
    </script>

    <html>
    <head>
    <title>Web Datagrid</title>
    </head>
    <body bgcolor="#FFFFFF" text="#000000">
    <h3 style="font-family:Verdana">Our Products</h3>
    <asp:DataGrid id="OurDataGrid"
        BorderWidth="1"
        BorderColor="#000000"
        CellPadding="3"
        CellSpacing="0"
        Font-Name="Verdana"
        Font-Size="12px"
        HeaderStyle-BackColor="#AAAAAA"
        ItemStyle-BackColor="#EEEEEE"
        AutoGenerateColumns="false"
        runat="server">
        <Columns>
            <asp:HyperLinkColumn
                HeaderText="Product Name"
    DataNavigateUrlFormatString="web_datagridcolumns_vb.aspx?Product={0}"
                DataNavigateUrlField="ProductName"
                DataTextField="ProductName" />
            <asp:BoundColumn
                HeaderText="Quantity Per Unit"
                DataField="QuantityPerUnit" />
            <asp:BoundColumn
                HeaderText="Unit Price"
                DataField="UnitPrice"
                DataFormatString="{0:c}"
                ItemStyle-HorizontalAlign="Center"  />
```

continues

Visual Basic .NET—(continued)

```
        <asp:BoundColumn
            HeaderText="Stock"
            DataField="UnitsInStock"
            ItemStyle-HorizontalAlign="Center" />
    </Columns>
</asp:DataGrid>
<asp:Label id="OurLabel" runat="server" />
</body>
</html>
```

C#—web_datagridcolumns_cs.aspx

```
<%@ page language="c#" runat="server"%>
<%@ Import Namespace="System.Data"%>
<%@ Import Namespace="System.Data.SqlClient"%>
<script runat=server>
void Page_Load(Object sender, EventArgs e) {
    if (!IsPostBack) {
        DataSub();
    }
    if (Request.Params["Product"] != null) {
        OurLabel.Text = "You Chose: " + Request.Params["Product"];
    }
}

void DataSub() {
    SqlCommand OurCommand;
    SqlConnection OurConnection;
    SqlDataAdapter OurDataAdapter;
    DataSet OurDataSet;
    OurDataSet = new DataSet();
    OurConnection = new SqlConnection("Server=server;
    ➥uid=newriders;pwd=password;database=Northwind");
    OurCommand = new SqlCommand("Select Top 10 ProductName, QuantityPerUnit,
    ➥UnitPrice, UnitsInStock From Products",OurConnection);
    OurDataAdapter = new SqlDataAdapter(OurCommand);
    OurDataAdapter.Fill(OurDataSet, "Products");
    DataView OurDataTable = new DataView(OurDataSet.Tables["Products"]);
    OurDataGrid.DataSource = OurDataTable;
    OurDataGrid.DataBind();
}
</script>

<html>
<head>
```

```
<title>Web Datagrid</title>
</head>
<body bgcolor="#FFFFFF" text="#000000">
<h3 style="font-family:Verdana">Our Products</h3>
<asp:DataGrid id="OurDataGrid"
    BorderWidth="1"
    BorderColor="#000000"
    CellPadding="3"
    CellSpacing="0"
    Font-Name="Verdana"
    Font-Size="12px"
    HeaderStyle-BackColor="#AAAAAA"
    ItemStyle-BackColor="#EEEEEE"
    AutoGenerateColumns="false"
    runat="server">
    <Columns>
        <asp:HyperLinkColumn
            HeaderText="Product Name"
            DataNavigateUrlFormatString="web_datagridcolumns_cs.aspx?Product={0}"
            DataNavigateUrlField="ProductName"
            DataTextField="ProductName" />
        <asp:BoundColumn
            HeaderText="Quantity Per Unit"
            DataField="QuantityPerUnit" />
        <asp:BoundColumn
            HeaderText="Unit Price"
            DataField="UnitPrice"
            DataFormatString="{0:c}"
            ItemStyle-HorizontalAlign="Center"  />
        <asp:BoundColumn
            HeaderText="Stock"
            DataField="UnitsInStock"
            ItemStyle-HorizontalAlign="Center" />
    </Columns>
</asp:DataGrid>
<asp:Label id="OurLabel" runat="server" />
</body>
</html>
```

In Figure 9.10, you can see the result of using column templates such as
the BoundColumn and HyperLinkColumn. Notice the different properties in the
HyperLinkColumn that allow you to link to where you want, as well as add item-
specific data to the URL. Also look at how I formatted the currency datatype in
the 3rd column and centered the alignment of the contents of the 3rd and 4th
columns with the ItemStyle-HorizontalAlign property.

FIGURE 9.10

FIGURE 9.10

Using column templates in your DataGrid *adds multiple levels of control to how data appears and functions in your* DataGrids.

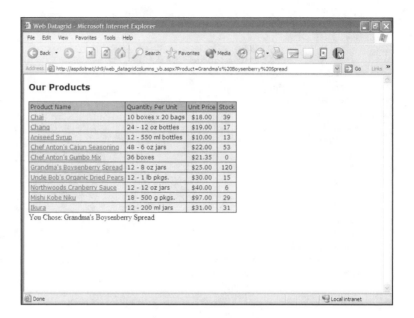

I want to move on to some of the built-in functionality in the DataGrid control. Sorting the contents of tabular data is a very useful function, and the DataGrid control isn't shy about sorting by any means.

Visual Basic .NET—**web_datagridsort_vb.aspx**

```vb
<%@ page language="vb" runat="server"%>
<%@ Import Namespace="System.Data"%>
<%@ Import Namespace="System.Data.SQLClient"%>
<script runat=server>

dim OurSortField as string

Sub Page_Load(sender As Object, e As EventArgs)
    if Not IsPostBack then
        DataSub
    end if
end sub

Sub DataSub()
    dim OurCommand as SQLCommand
    dim OurConnection as SQLConnection
    dim OurDataAdapter as SQLDataAdapter
    dim OurDataSet as New DataSet()
    OurConnection = New SQLConnection("Server=server;
    ➥uid=newriders;pwd=password;database=Northwind")
```

```
        OurCommand = New SQLCommand("Select Top 10 ProductName, QuantityPerUnit,
        ➥UnitPrice, UnitsInStock From Products",OurConnection)
        OurDataAdapter = New SQLDataAdapter(OurCommand)
        OurDataAdapter.Fill(OurDataSet, "Products")
        dim OurDataTable as New DataView(OurDataSet.Tables("Products"))
        if OurSortField <> "" Then
            OurDataTable.Sort = OurSortField
        end if
        OurDataGrid.DataSource = OurDataTable
        OurDataGrid.DataBind()
End Sub

Sub DataSort(sender As Object, e As DataGridSortCommandEventArgs)
    OurLabel.Text= "You sorted by " + e.SortExpression.ToString()
    OurSortField = e.SortExpression
    DataSub
End Sub

</script>

<html>
<head>
<title>Web Datagrid</title>
</head>
<body bgcolor="#FFFFFF" text="#000000">
<form runat="server">
<h3 style="font-family:Verdana">Our Products</h3>
<asp:DataGrid id="OurDataGrid"
    BorderWidth="1"
    BorderColor="#000000"
    CellPadding="3"
    CellSpacing="0"
    Font-Name="Verdana"
    Font-Size="12px"
    HeaderStyle-BackColor="#AAAAAA"
    ItemStyle-BackColor="#EEEEEE"
    AutoGenerateColumns="false"
    AllowSorting="True"
    OnSortCommand="DataSort"
    runat="server" >
    <Columns>
        <asp:BoundColumn
            HeaderText="Product Name"
            DataField="ProductName"
            SortExpression="ProductName" />
        <asp:BoundColumn
            HeaderText="Quantity Per Unit"
            DataField="QuantityPerUnit" />
        <asp:BoundColumn
            HeaderText="Unit Price"
            DataField="UnitPrice"
            DataFormatString="{0:c}"
```

continues

Visual Basic .NET—(continued)

```
            SortExpression="UnitPrice" />
        <asp:BoundColumn
            HeaderText="Stock"
            DataField="UnitsInStock"
            SortExpression="UnitsInStock" />
    </Columns>
</asp:DataGrid>
<asp:Label id="OurLabel" runat="server" />
</form>
</body>
</html>
```

C#—web_datagridsort_cs.aspx

```
<%@ page language="c#" runat="server"%>
<%@ Import Namespace="System.Data"%>
<%@ Import Namespace="System.Data.SqlClient"%>
<script runat=server>

String OurSortField;

void Page_Load(Object sender, EventArgs e) {
    if (!IsPostBack) {
        DataSub();
    }
}

void DataSub() {
    SqlCommand OurCommand;
    SqlConnection OurConnection;
    SqlDataAdapter OurDataAdapter;
    DataSet OurDataSet;
    OurDataSet = new DataSet();
    OurConnection = new SqlConnection("Server=server;
    ➥uid=newriders;pwd=password;database=Northwind");
    OurCommand = new SqlCommand("Select Top 10 ProductName, QuantityPerUnit,
    ➥UnitPrice, UnitsInStock From Products",OurConnection);
    OurDataAdapter = new SqlDataAdapter(OurCommand);
    OurDataAdapter.Fill(OurDataSet, "Products");
    DataView OurDataTable = new DataView(OurDataSet.Tables["Products"]);
    if (OurSortField != null ) {
        OurDataTable.Sort = OurSortField;
    }
    OurDataGrid.DataSource = OurDataTable;
    OurDataGrid.DataBind();
}

void DataSort(Object sender, DataGridSortCommandEventArgs e) {
```

```
        OurLabel.Text= "You sorted by " + e.SortExpression.ToString();
        OurSortField = e.SortExpression;
        DataSub();
}

</script>

<html>
<head>
<title>Web Datagrid</title>
</head>
<body bgcolor="#FFFFFF" text="#000000">
<form runat="server">
<h3 style="font-family:Verdana">Our Products</h3>
<asp:DataGrid id="OurDataGrid"
    BorderWidth="1"
    BorderColor="#000000"
    CellPadding="3"
    CellSpacing="0"
    Font-Name="Verdana"
    Font-Size="12px"
    HeaderStyle-BackColor="#AAAAAA"
    ItemStyle-BackColor="#EEEEEE"
    AutoGenerateColumns="false"
    AllowSorting="True"
    OnSortCommand="DataSort"
    runat="server" >
    <Columns>
        <asp:BoundColumn
            HeaderText="Product Name"
            DataField="ProductName"
            SortExpression="ProductName" />
        <asp:BoundColumn
            HeaderText="Quantity Per Unit"
            DataField="QuantityPerUnit" />
        <asp:BoundColumn
            HeaderText="Unit Price"
            DataField="UnitPrice"
            DataFormatString="{0:c}"
            SortExpression="UnitPrice" />
        <asp:BoundColumn
            HeaderText="Stock"
            DataField="UnitsInStock"
            SortExpression="UnitsInStock" />
    </Columns>
</asp:DataGrid>
<asp:Label id="OurLabel" runat="server" />
</form>
</body>
</html>
```

As you can see in Figure 9.11, the `DataGrid` control makes sorting the bound data easy by allowing you to pass an expression, which is the column's name in the data source, to the `SortCommand`, which is a function that sets a `sort` property on the data source.

FIGURE 9.11

The `DataGrid` provides you with a powerful way to sort the data in your `DataGrids`.

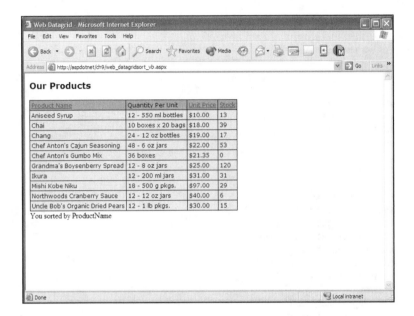

With the sort functions, you can sort the data on the page, but what if you have more data in your data source than you want to display on your page? You have to give the user the ability to page through this data. As a note, doing this in traditional ASP was not fun.

ASP.NET's `DataGrid` control now makes this a total piece of cake. Look first at one method that works well for smaller amounts of data.

Visual Basic .NET—**web_datagridbasicpaging_vb.aspx**

```
<%@ page language="vb" runat="server"%>
<%@ Import Namespace="System.Data"%>
<%@ Import Namespace="System.Data.SQLClient"%>
<script runat=server>

Sub Page_Load(sender As Object, e As EventArgs)
    if Not IsPostBack then
        DataSub
    end if
```

```
end sub

Sub DataSub()
    dim OurCommand as SQLCommand
    dim OurConnection as SQLConnection
    dim OurDataAdapter as SQLDataAdapter
    dim OurDataSet as New DataSet()
    OurConnection = New SQLConnection("Server=server;
    ➥uid=newriders;pwd=password;database=Northwind")
    OurCommand = New SQLCommand("Select ProductName, QuantityPerUnit, UnitPrice,
    ➥UnitsInStock From Products",OurConnection)
    OurDataAdapter = New SQLDataAdapter(OurCommand)
    OurDataAdapter.Fill(OurDataSet, "Products")
    dim OurDataTable as New DataView(OurDataSet.Tables("Products"))
    OurDataGrid.DataSource = OurDataTable
    OurDataGrid.DataBind()
    OurLabel.Text = "Page " & (OurDataGrid.CurrentPageIndex + 1) & " of " &
    ➥(OurDataGrid.PageCount)
End Sub

Sub OurPager(sender As Object, e As DataGridPageChangedEventArgs)
    OurDataGrid.CurrentPageIndex = e.NewPageIndex
    DataSub()
end sub

</script>

<html>
<head>
<title>Web Datagrid</title>
</head>
<body bgcolor="#FFFFFF" text="#000000">
<form runat="server">
<h3 style="font-family:Verdana">Our Products</h3>
<asp:DataGrid id="OurDataGrid"
    BorderWidth="1"
    BorderColor="#000000"
    CellPadding="3"
    CellSpacing="0"
    Font-Name="Verdana"
    Font-Size="12px"
    HeaderStyle-BackColor="#AAAAAA"
    ItemStyle-BackColor="#EEEEEE"
    AutoGenerateColumns="false"
    AllowPaging="true"
    OnPageIndexChanged="OurPager"
    PageSize="10"
    PagerStyle-NextPageText="Next"
    PagerStyle-PrevPageText="Prev"
    PagerStyle-HorizontalAlign="Right"
    runat="server">
    <Columns>
```

continues

Visual Basic .NET—(continued)

```
        <asp:BoundColumn
            HeaderText="Product Name"
            DataField="ProductName" />
        <asp:BoundColumn
            HeaderText="Quantity Per Unit"
            DataField="QuantityPerUnit" />
        <asp:BoundColumn
            HeaderText="Unit Price"
            DataField="UnitPrice" DataFormatString="{0:c}"
            ItemStyle-HorizontalAlign="right"  />
        <asp:BoundColumn
            HeaderText="Stock"
            DataField="UnitsInStock"
            ItemStyle-HorizontalAlign="center" />
    </Columns>
</asp:DataGrid>
<asp:Label id="OurLabel" runat="server" />
</form>
</body>
</html>
```

C#—web_datagridbasicpaging_cs.aspx

```
<%@ page language="c#" runat="server"%>
<%@ Import Namespace="System.Data"%>
<%@ Import Namespace="System.Data.SqlClient"%>
<script runat=server>

void Page_Load(Object sender, EventArgs e) {
    if (!IsPostBack) {
        DataSub();
    }
}

void DataSub() {
    SqlCommand OurCommand;
    SqlConnection OurConnection;
    SqlDataAdapter OurDataAdapter;
    DataSet OurDataSet;
    OurDataSet = new DataSet();
    OurConnection = new SqlConnection("Server=server;
    ➥uid=newriders;pwd=password;database=Northwind");
    OurCommand = new SqlCommand("Select ProductName, QuantityPerUnit, UnitPrice,
    ➥UnitsInStock From Products",OurConnection);
    OurDataAdapter = new SqlDataAdapter(OurCommand);
    OurDataAdapter.Fill(OurDataSet, "Products");
    DataView OurDataTable = new DataView(OurDataSet.Tables["Products"]);
    OurDataGrid.DataSource = OurDataTable;
    OurDataGrid.DataBind();
    OurLabel.Text = "Page " + (OurDataGrid.CurrentPageIndex + 1).ToString() +
    ➥" of " + (OurDataGrid.PageCount).ToString();
```

```
}

void OurPager(Object sender, DataGridPageChangedEventArgs e) {
    OurDataGrid.CurrentPageIndex = e.NewPageIndex;
    DataSub();
}

</script>

<html>
<head>
<title>Web Datagrid</title>
</head>
<body bgcolor="#FFFFFF" text="#000000">
<form runat="server">
<h3 style="font-family:Verdana">Our Products</h3>
<asp:DataGrid id="OurDataGrid"
    BorderWidth="1"
    BorderColor="#000000"
    CellPadding="3"
    CellSpacing="0"
    Font-Name="Verdana"
    Font-Size="12px"
    HeaderStyle-BackColor="#AAAAAA"
    ItemStyle-BackColor="#EEEEEE"
    AutoGenerateColumns="false"
    AllowPaging="true"
    OnPageIndexChanged="OurPager"
    PageSize="10"
    PagerStyle-NextPageText="Next"
    PagerStyle-PrevPageText="Prev"
    PagerStyle-HorizontalAlign="Right"
    runat="server">
    <Columns>
        <asp:BoundColumn
            HeaderText="Product Name"
            DataField="ProductName" />
        <asp:BoundColumn
            HeaderText="Quantity Per Unit"
            DataField="QuantityPerUnit" />
        <asp:BoundColumn
            HeaderText="Unit Price"
            DataField="UnitPrice" DataFormatString="{0:c}"
            ItemStyle-HorizontalAlign="right"  />
        <asp:BoundColumn
            HeaderText="Stock"
            DataField="UnitsInStock"
            ItemStyle-HorizontalAlign="center" />
    </Columns>
</asp:DataGrid>
<asp:Label id="OurLabel" runat="server" />
</form>
</body>
</html>
```

Notice in the code how the `CurrentPageIndex` and `PageCount` properties are used to create a display to inform users about what page they're on and what the total pages are. You can, see the results of this code example in Figure 9.12. Notice that the navigation for paging was generated by the `DataGrid`, and all I needed to do was set a few properties.

FIGURE 9.12

The DataGrid *provides a way for you to easily control how many items users will see in their browsers, as well as the navigation to move through the pages of data.*

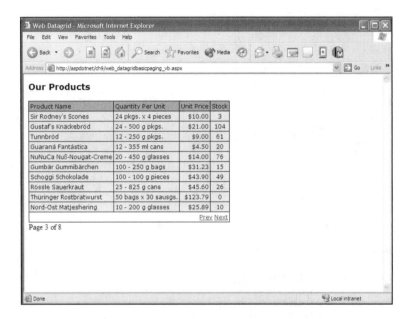

This type of paging is fine for smaller amounts of data, but when you're dealing with larger amounts of data, it might make more sense to deliver to the data source only the data that you need for the current page. Doing so would prevent large amounts of data from being stored in the web server's memory. ASP.NET makes provision for this type of paging, where you take bite-sized portions of the data you want so that the server's memory usage is preserved. This technique of paging with the ASP.NET `DataGrid` is called *chunking*.

Visual Basic .NET—**web_datagridchunkpaging_vb.aspx**

```
<%@ page language="vb" runat="server"%>
<%@ Import Namespace="System.Data"%>
<%@ Import Namespace="System.Data.SQLClient"%>
<script runat=server>
Dim i as integer

Sub Page_Load(sender As Object, e As EventArgs)
```

```
        if Not IsPostBack then
            DataSub
            i = 0
        end if
    end sub

Sub DataSub()
    dim OurCommand as SQLCommand
    dim OurCountCommand as SQLCommand
    dim OurConnection as SQLConnection
    dim OurDataAdapter as SQLDataAdapter
    dim OurDataSet as New DataSet()
    OurConnection = New SQLConnection("Server=server;
    ➥uid=newriders;pwd=password;database=Northwind")
    OurCountCommand = New SQLCommand("Select Count(*) From Products",
    ➥OurConnection)
    OurCountCommand.Connection.Open()
    OurDataGrid.VirtualItemCount = OurCountCommand.ExecuteScalar()
    OurCountCommand.Connection.Close()
    OurCommand = New SQLCommand("Select ProductName, QuantityPerUnit, UnitPrice,
    ➥UnitsInStock From Products Where ProductID Between " & i & " and " & i +
    ➥OurDataGrid.PageSize,OurConnection)
    OurDataAdapter = New SQLDataAdapter(OurCommand)
    OurDataAdapter.Fill(OurDataSet, "Products")
    dim OurDataTable as New DataView(OurDataSet.Tables("Products"))
    OurDataGrid.DataSource = OurDataTable
    OurDataGrid.DataBind()
    OurLabel.Text = "Page " & (OurDataGrid.CurrentPageIndex + 1) & " of " &
    ➥(OurDataGrid.PageCount)
End Sub

Sub OurPager(sender As Object, e As DataGridPageChangedEventArgs)
    i = e.NewPageIndex * OurDataGrid.PageSize
    OurDataGrid.CurrentPageIndex = e.NewPageIndex
    DataSub()
end sub
</script>
<html>
<head>
<title>Web Datagrid</title>
</head>
<body bgcolor="#FFFFFF" text="#000000">
<form runat="server">
<h3 style="font-family:Verdana">Our Products</h3>
<asp:DataGrid id="OurDataGrid"
    BorderWidth="1"
    BorderColor="#000000"
    CellPadding="3"
    CellSpacing="0"
    Font-Name="Verdana"
    Font-Size="12px"
    HeaderStyle-BackColor="#AAAAAA"
```

continues

Visual Basic .NET—(continued)

```
            ItemStyle-BackColor="#EEEEEE"
            AutoGenerateColumns="false"
            AllowPaging="true"
            OnPageIndexChanged="OurPager"
            PageSize="10"
            PagerStyle-NextPageText="Next"
            PagerStyle-PrevPageText="Prev"
            PagerStyle-HorizontalAlign="Right"
            AllowCustomPaging="true"
            runat="server" >
            <Columns>
                <asp:BoundColumn
                    HeaderText="Product Name"
                    DataField="ProductName" />
                <asp:BoundColumn
                    HeaderText="Quantity Per Unit"
                    DataField="QuantityPerUnit" />
                <asp:BoundColumn
                    HeaderText="Unit Price"
                    DataField="UnitPrice" DataFormatString="{0:c}"
                    ItemStyle-HorizontalAlign="right"  />
                <asp:BoundColumn
                    HeaderText="Stock"
                    DataField="UnitsInStock"
                    ItemStyle-HorizontalAlign="center" />
            </Columns>
        </asp:DataGrid>
        <asp:Label id="OurLabel" runat="server" />
    </form>
    </body>
    </html>
```

C#—web_datagridchunkpaging_cs.aspx

```
<%@ page language="c#" runat="server"%>
<%@ Import Namespace="System.Data"%>
<%@ Import Namespace="System.Data.SqlClient"%>
<script runat=server>
int i;

void Page_Load(Object sender, EventArgs e) {
    if (!IsPostBack) {
        DataSub();
        i = 0;
    }
}

void DataSub() {
    SqlCommand OurCommand;
```

```
    SqlCommand OurCountCommand;
    SqlConnection OurConnection;
    SqlDataAdapter OurDataAdapter;
    DataSet OurDataSet = new DataSet();
    OurConnection = new SqlConnection("Server=server;
    ➥uid=newriders;pwd=password;database=Northwind");
    OurCountCommand = new SqlCommand("Select Count(*) From Products",
    ➥OurConnection);
    OurCountCommand.Connection.Open();
    OurDataGrid.VirtualItemCount = (int)OurCountCommand.ExecuteScalar();
    OurCountCommand.Connection.Close();
    OurCommand = new SqlCommand("Select ProductName, QuantityPerUnit, UnitPrice,
    ➥UnitsInStock From Products Where ProductID Between " + i.ToString() + " and "
    ➥+ i.ToString() + OurDataGrid.PageSize,OurConnection);
    OurDataAdapter = new SqlDataAdapter(OurCommand);
    OurDataAdapter.Fill(OurDataSet, "Products");
    DataView OurDataTable = new DataView(OurDataSet.Tables["Products"]);
    OurDataGrid.DataSource = OurDataTable;
    OurDataGrid.DataBind();
    OurLabel.Text = "Page " + (OurDataGrid.CurrentPageIndex + 1).ToString() +
    ➥" of " + (OurDataGrid.PageCount).ToString();
}

void OurPager(Object sender, DataGridPageChangedEventArgs e) {
    i = e.NewPageIndex * OurDataGrid.PageSize;
    OurDataGrid.CurrentPageIndex = e.NewPageIndex;
    DataSub();
}
</script>

<html>
<head>
<title>Web Datagrid</title>
</head>
<body bgcolor="#FFFFFF" text="#000000">
<form runat="server">
<h3 style="font-family:Verdana">Our Products</h3>
<asp:DataGrid id="OurDataGrid"
    BorderWidth="1"
    BorderColor="#000000"
    CellPadding="3"
    CellSpacing="0"
    Font-Name="Verdana"
    Font-Size="12px"
    HeaderStyle-BackColor="#AAAAAA"
    ItemStyle-BackColor="#EEEEEE"
    AutoGenerateColumns="false"
    AllowPaging="true"
    OnPageIndexChanged="OurPager"
    PageSize="10"
    PagerStyle-NextPageText="Next"
    PagerStyle-PrevPageText="Prev"
```

continues

C#—(continued)

```
        PagerStyle-HorizontalAlign="Right"
        AllowCustomPaging="true"
        runat="server" >
        <Columns>
            <asp:BoundColumn
                HeaderText="Product Name"
                DataField="ProductName" />
            <asp:BoundColumn
                HeaderText="Quantity Per Unit"
                DataField="QuantityPerUnit" />
            <asp:BoundColumn
                HeaderText="Unit Price"
                DataField="UnitPrice" DataFormatString="{0:c}"
                ItemStyle-HorizontalAlign="right"  />
            <asp:BoundColumn
                HeaderText="Stock"
                DataField="UnitsInStock"
                ItemStyle-HorizontalAlign="center" />
        </Columns>
    </asp:DataGrid>
    <asp:Label id="OurLabel" runat="server" />
    </form>
    </body>
    </html>
```

When you look at Figure 9.13, you can see that the results don't really look any different to the end user, but the web server is handling only 10 records at a time, rather than the 80 potential records that it would contain for all 8 pages of this data source. Notice the creation of a variable called i in the OurPager function. When this is passed to the data source, this value is used to deliver back only those records for the desired page.

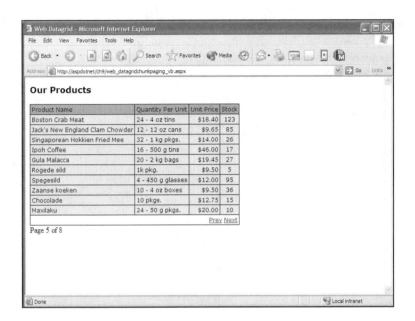

FIGURE 9.13

*To the end user,
page chunking
a* DataGrid
*might not look
any different, but if
you're using large
data sources, your
web server will
thank you.*

Displaying, sorting, and navigating in the DataGrid is pretty cool, but it doesn't
stop there. The DataGrid also provides ways for you to edit your data right within
the DataGrid, as well. Take a look.

Visual Basic .NET—**web_datagridedit_vb.aspx**

```
<%@ page language="vb" runat="server"%>
<%@ Import Namespace="System.Data"%>
<%@ Import Namespace="System.Data.SqlClient"%>
<script runat=server>
Sub Page_Load(sender As Object, e As EventArgs)
    if Not IsPostBack then
        DataSub
    end if
end sub

Sub DataSub()
    dim OurCommand as SqlCommand
    dim OurConnection as SqlConnection
    dim OurDataAdapter as SqlDataAdapter
    dim OurDataSet as New DataSet()
    OurConnection = New SqlConnection("Server=server;
    ➥uid=newriders;pwd=password;database=Northwind")
    OurCommand = New SqlCommand("Select EmployeeID, FirstName, LastName From
    ➥Employees",OurConnection)
    OurDataAdapter = New SqlDataAdapter(OurCommand)
    OurDataAdapter.Fill(OurDataSet, "Employees")
```

continues

Visual Basic .NET—(continued)

```
      dim OurDataTable as New DataView(OurDataSet.Tables("Employees"))
      OurDataGrid.DataSource = OurDataTable
      OurDataGrid.DataBind()
End Sub

Sub Edit(sender As Object, e As DataGridCommandEventArgs)
      OurDataGrid.EditItemIndex = e.Item.ItemIndex
      DataSub
End Sub

Sub Cancel(sender As Object, e As DataGridCommandEventArgs)
      OurDataGrid.EditItemIndex = -1
      DataSub
End Sub

Sub Update(sender As Object, e As DataGridCommandEventArgs)
      dim objFirstName, ObjLastName as TextBox
      dim FirstName, LastName, EmployeeID as String
      objFirstName = e.Item.Cells(1).Controls(0)
      objLastName = e.Item.Cells(2).Controls(0)
      EmployeeID = e.Item.Cells(0).Text
      FirstName = objFirstName.Text
      LastName = objLastName.Text
      dim OurCommand as SqlCommand
      dim OurConnection as SqlConnection
      OurConnection = New SqlConnection("Server=server;
      ➥uid=newriders;pwd=password;database=Northwind")
      OurCommand = New SqlCommand("Update Employees Set FirstName = '" & FirstName &
      ➥"', LastName = '" & LastName & "' Where EmployeeID = " & EmployeeID,
      ➥OurConnection)
      OurCommand.Connection.Open()
      OurCommand.ExecuteNonQuery()
      OurCommand.Connection.Close()
      OurDataGrid.EditItemIndex = -1
      DataSub
End Sub
</script>

<html>
<head>
<title>Web Datagrid</title>
</head>
<body bgcolor="#FFFFFF" text="#000000">
<form runat="server">
<asp:DataGrid id="OurDataGrid"
    BorderWidth="1"
    BorderColor="#000000"
        CellPadding="3"
        CellSpacing="0"
        Font-Name="Verdana"
        Font-Size="12px"
```

```
              HeaderStyle-BackColor="#AAAAAA"
              ItemStyle-BackColor="#EEEEEE"
              AutoGenerateColumns="false"
       OnEditCommand="Edit"
       OnCancelCommand="Cancel"
       OnUpdateCommand="Update"
       runat="server">
       <Columns>
           <asp:BoundColumn
               HeaderText="EmployeeID"
               DataField="EmployeeID"
               readonly="true" />
           <asp:BoundColumn
               HeaderText="First Name"
               DataField="FirstName" />
           <asp:BoundColumn
               HeaderText="Last Name"
               DataField="LastName" />
           <asp:EditCommandColumn
               EditText="Edit"
               CancelText="Cancel"
               UpdateText="Update"/>
       </Columns>
   </asp:DataGrid>
   </form>
   </body>
   </html>
```

C#—web_datagridedit_cs.aspx

```
<%@ page language="c#" runat="server"%>
<%@ Import Namespace="System.Data"%>
<%@ Import Namespace="System.Data.SqlClient"%>
<script runat=server>
void Page_Load(Object sender, EventArgs e) {
    if (!IsPostBack) {
        DataSub();
    }
}

void DataSub() {
    SqlCommand OurCommand;
    SqlConnection OurConnection;
    SqlDataAdapter OurDataAdapter;
    DataSet OurDataSet = new DataSet();
    OurConnection = new SqlConnection("Server=server;
    ➥uid=newriders;pwd=password;database=Northwind");
    OurCommand = new SqlCommand("Select EmployeeID, FirstName, LastName From
    ➥Employees",OurConnection);
    OurDataAdapter = new SqlDataAdapter(OurCommand);
    OurDataAdapter.Fill(OurDataSet, "Employees");
```

continues

C#—(continued)

```
    DataView OurDataTable = new DataView(OurDataSet.Tables["Employees"]);
    OurDataGrid.DataSource = OurDataTable;
    OurDataGrid.DataBind();
}

void Edit(Object sender, DataGridCommandEventArgs e) {
    OurDataGrid.EditItemIndex = e.Item.ItemIndex;
    DataSub();
}

void Cancel(Object sender, DataGridCommandEventArgs e) {
    OurDataGrid.EditItemIndex = -1;
    DataSub();
}

void Update(Object sender, DataGridCommandEventArgs e) {
    TextBox objFirstName, objLastName;
    string FirstName, LastName;
    int EmployeeID;
    objFirstName = (TextBox)e.Item.Cells[1].Controls[0];
    objLastName = (TextBox)e.Item.Cells[2].Controls[0];
    EmployeeID = Int32.Parse(e.Item.Cells[0].Text);
    FirstName = objFirstName.Text;
    LastName = objLastName.Text;
    SqlCommand OurCommand;
    SqlConnection OurConnection;
    OurConnection = new SqlConnection("Server=server;
    ➥uid=newriders;pwd=password;database=Northwind");
    OurCommand = new SqlCommand("Update Employees Set FirstName = '" + FirstName +
    ➥"', LastName = '" + LastName + "' Where EmployeeID = " + EmployeeID,
    ➥OurConnection);
    OurCommand.Connection.Open();
    OurCommand.ExecuteNonQuery();
    OurCommand.Connection.Close();
    OurDataGrid.EditItemIndex = -1;
    DataSub();
}
</script>

<html>
<head>
<title>Web Datagrid</title>
</head>
<body bgcolor="#FFFFFF" text="#000000">
<form runat="server">
<h3 style="font-family:Verdana">Employees</h3>
```

```
<asp:DataGrid id="OurDataGrid"
    BorderWidth="1"
    BorderColor="#000000"
        CellPadding="3"
        CellSpacing="0"
        Font-Name="Verdana"
        Font-Size="12px"
        HeaderStyle-BackColor="#AAAAAA"
        ItemStyle-BackColor="#EEEEEE"
        AutoGenerateColumns="false"
    OnEditCommand="Edit"
    OnCancelCommand="Cancel"
    OnUpdateCommand="Update"
    runat="server">
    <Columns>
        <asp:BoundColumn
            HeaderText="EmployeeID"
            DataField="EmployeeID"
            readonly="true" />
        <asp:BoundColumn
            HeaderText="First Name"
            DataField="FirstName" />
        <asp:BoundColumn
            HeaderText="Last Name"
            DataField="LastName" />
        <asp:EditCommandColumn
            EditText="Edit"
            CancelText="Cancel"
            UpdateText="Update"/>
    </Columns>
</asp:DataGrid>
</form>
</body>
</html>
```

Notice in the preceding code example, in the `DataGrid` opening tag, three events called `OnEditCommand`, `OnUpdateCommand`, and `OnCancelCommand`. The events occur when you click on their corresponding links in the `EditCommandTemplate` column and call the functions to which their values are set. This is how the editing capability of the `DataGrid` is supplied.

You can see the results of this code example in Figure 9.14. Without ever creating a single input text box, the `DataGrid` produces the interface element necessary to perform edit capabilities. You must write what you want to happen within these functions, but all the interface work is done for you. Voilá!!!

FIGURE 9.14

The DataGrid gives you the power to perform edits to your data right within the interface the DataGrid produces.

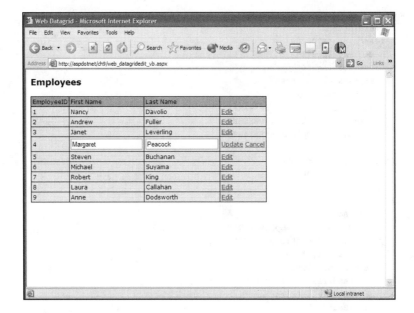

Summary

As I mentioned in the beginning of this chapter, I was faced with a chicken-and-egg type of scenario in deciding whether to deal with data delivery or data display first. I decided to cover the chicken (or the egg, depending on your viewpoint) first. I've given you a lot of material and covered the most commonly used functions of the data-bound controls so you can display your data in whatever methods you want.

Now it's time to move on to the egg (or the chicken, depending on your viewpoint) and discover how to use ADO.NET to query databases and deliver data from those databases to your ASP.NET pages. See you on the next page!

<Part> **III**

ADVANCED FEATURES IN ASP.NET

ADO.NET

Data, data everywhere, and not a drop to drink!

The previous chapter covered displaying data with ASP.NET server controls, and I asked you to overlook how the data was delivered to the page. Now you are going to investigate how you get the data to your pages out of your databases.

What Is ADO.NET?

I live in New York state about an hour north of Manhattan. For this I consider myself lucky. Within a short drive I am able to enjoy all the wonders and experiences that New York City has to offer. Some of the greatest attractions in the world are in NYC, including some of the best restaurants, museums, and Broadway musicals and plays.

More often than not, when I want to enjoy the city, my wife and I will go to Mulberry Street in Little Italy to the world famous La Mela restaurant. They have gnocchi and tortellini to die for there. When I get a hankering for that delicious cuisine, we jump in the car and hit the highway.

We get down to the Hudson River and, thanks to the wonders of modern engineering, simply pay a toll and cross the George Washington Bridge to enter Manhattan and proceed down the island to our destination.

Could you imagine what I'd need to go through to get to La Mela if we had no bridge to Manhattan Island? It would make that trip a nightmare, and I would probably never go and enjoy the La Mela or anything else in NYC. It would take all that dynamic activity out of my life.

ADO.NET is like the George Washington Bridge in these previous paragraphs. It provides a method to achieve all kinds of dynamic productivity at a new level. It is the unsung hero of the .NET Framework, which makes all the rich information and data in our databases accessible to ASP.NET pages.

Just like the George Washington Bridge has different components—the towers, trusses, cables, anchors, and roadway decks that make crossing the gap between New Jersey and New York possible—ADO.NET has components and players.

ADO.NET has the `Connection`, which is like the towers that support the entire bridge, and the `Command`, which is like the giant cables that support the bridge from the towers. The `DataAdapter` connects the cables to the roadway deck sections. The `DataReader`, `DataTable`, and `DataView` are like roadway decking, and the `DataSet` is the collection of `DataTable` roadway deck sections that make up the entire span.

All these different things may seem confusing to you now, but as you go through them, you will see how they all play their little parts to help you cross the gap, river, or chasm between your ASP.NET pages and your database.

The first thing to note about ADO.NET and how it deals with databases is that it splits them into two categories: Microsoft SQL Server and everything else. Pretty clear and easy-to-understand delineation, huh? The reason for this is that this allows ADO.NET to deal with SQL Server through a different mechanism than the OLE DB or ODBC providers that have been used in the past. This provides a highly optimized bridge for Microsoft SQL Server. The other databases, such as Microsoft Access and Oracle, use the OLE DB provider.

Table 10.1 lists namespaces and their necessary objects.

TABLE 10.1 Data Namespaces

Namespace	Description
System.Data.SqlClient	This is the Microsoft SQL Server data provider namespace. You need to import this namespace if you will be communicating with Microsoft SQL Server.
System.Data.OleDb	This is the OLE DB .NET data provider. You need to import this namespace if you will be communicating with an OLE DB database.
System.Data	This namespace contains the classes that build the ADO.NET architecture. These objects allow you to manage data from multiple data sources with the centerpiece being the ADO.NET DataSet.

When using ADO.NET to connect and communicate with a database, you will generally use two out of the three namespaces in Table 10.1 that contain the necessary objects. You will always use the System.Data namespace, but you will use either one or the other of the remaining namespaces, depending on which type of database you are using: SQL Server or the others.

Table 10.2 describes each namespace and the important objects that they contain for connecting and manipulating data in databases.

TABLE 10.2 *System.Data.SQLClient* Namespace

Class	Description
SQLConnection	This represents an open connection to your SQL Server database. This is the equivalent of a network connection to a server.
SQLCommand	This represents a SQL statement or stored procedure that you want to execute against your SQL Server database.
SQLDataReader	Provides a means for reading rows of data from your SQL Server in a "forward-only" situation. This means you can iterate through the rows of the DataReader only forward, and you cannot return to the beginning of the Reader. It is the equivalent of the previous ADO version's Recordset object, with a cursor type of forward-only.
SQLDataAdapter	Represents a set of data commands and a data connection that are used to manipulate DataSets and update your SQL Server database.

The objects provide all the towers, cables, anchors, and trusses for a bridge to your SQL Server database. Parallel objects are also available for OLE DB data sources as well. Table 10.3 gives you a look at them.

TABLE 10.3 *System.Data.OleDb* Namespace

Class	Description
OleDbConnection	This represents an open connection to your OLE DB data source. This is the equivalent of a network connection to a server.
OleDbCommand	This represents a SQL statement or stored procedure that you want to execute against your OLE DB data source.
OleDbDataReader	Provides a means for reading rows of data from your OLE DB data source in a "forward-only" situation. This means you can iterate through the rows of the DataReader only forward, and you cannot return to the beginning of the Reader. It is the equivalent of the previous ADO version's Recordset object, with a cursor type of forward-only.
OleDbDataAdapter	Represents a set of data commands and a data connection that are used to manipulate DataSets and update your OLE DB data source.

As you can see, these hardly differ from the SQL Server version of these objects, but they are necessary for connecting to databases other than Microsoft SQL Server.

Throughout the rest of this chapter I will show you the objects and examples for the SQL Server only. But, never fear. These two groups of objects are exactly the same with one exception: their names. So any place I use the SQL object, you would just use the OLE DB equivalent. I have also included OLE DB versions of all the examples for download on the New Riders Publications web site located at http://www.newriders.com.

One thing I will give you is a few examples of connection strings for the SQLConnection and OleDbConnection objects.

SQLConnection String Example

```
server=servername;user id=userid;password=password;database=databasename
```

OleDbConnection String Example

```
Microsoft Access
Provider=Microsoft.Jet.OLEDB.4.0; Data Source=c:\accessdatabase.mdb;
```

N O T E

There might be times when you don't know the full path to your Access database—for instance, when you are hosting a website on a web server where you don't have administrative access. There is a property of the ASP.NET Page object called Server that has a method called MapPath() that enables you to programmatically map the path to your database.

Imagine that the page you're working on is located in one directory level from the web application's root, and the access database is located in a directory called Database in the application's root. The MapPath() method takes a single string parameter, which is the path to the file or database from that current page's location. To bump out one directory level to the root directory, you use dot, dot, forward slash (../). This puts you in the root directory. Then you append the path to the database from there. So, the connection string would look like the following:

```
Microsoft Access with Server.MapPath
"Provider=Microsoft.Jet.OLEDB.4.0;Data Source=" +
Server.MapPath("../_database/northwind.mdb");


Oracle 8i
Provider=MSDAORA; Data Source=ORACLE8i7; User ID=OLEDB; Password=OLEDB
```

This should provide you with enough basic information to connect to the most common databases. If you need additional information, I recommend referring to the .NET Framework SDK, because there are many ways to create connection strings, and the SDK gives many examples, especially with regard to the `SQLConnection` object.

Now look at the `System.Data` namespace and its pertinent objects in Table 10.4. You need to import this namespace whether you are using a SQL Server database or an OLE DB database.

TABLE 10.4 *System.Data* Namespace

Class	Description
DataTable	This represents one table of in-memory data.
DataRelation	This object represents a parent/child relationship between two DataTable objects.
DataSet	Represents an in-memory cache of data. It consists of a collection of DataTable objects that can be related to each other with the DataRelation object.
DataView	This represents a databindable view of a DataTable that can be sorted, filtered, search, edited, and navigated.

So in plain English, this is how the `System.Data` namespace works:

- `SQLConnnection` or `OleDBConnection` connects to the database.
- `SQLCommand` or `OleDbCommand` tells the database what data you're working with.
- `DataReader` holds the data.
- `DataSet` creates a framework for holding `DataTables` of data.
- `SQLDataAdapter` or `OleDbDataAdapter` passes data in and out of the `DataTables` and databases.
- `DataView` manipulates snapshots of data in our dataset.

As I said, you will use two out of the three namespaces mentioned, depending on what type of data source you are using. The following is the code necessary to make these namespaces available, and it should be placed immediately after the @page directive of your ASP.NET page. This code is identical for both Visual Basic.NET and C#.

SQL Server Databases

```
<%@ Import Namespace="System.Data"%>
<%@ Import Namespace="System.Data.SQLClient"%>
```

Ole Db Databases

```
<%@ Import Namespace="System.Data"%>
<%@ Import Namespace="System.Data.OleDb"%>
```

Now let's investigate the different ways you can use ADO.NET to manipulate and query databases.

Querying Data

You will most often be trying to pull data out of your data source to display it on your ASP.NET pages. To do so, you would use a SQL Select statement. In these examples, the Northwind database is the data source and a DataReader is populated with the results of the SQL command.

DataReader

Remember, a DataReader is a forward-only group of rows of data. You can iterate through the DataReader to display its contents with the DataReader's Read() method, and you can find many examples of that in the SDK. I've also read that many sources are saying that a DataReader cannot be databound to the server controls you saw in the last chapter. I have not found that to be the truth, and I stand as the shining light in the darkness of misinformation. The following is an example of a DataReader being databound to a DataGrid just like the ones you saw in Chapter 9.

Visual Basic .NET—**ado_query_reader_sql_vb/cs.aspx**

```
<%@ page language="vb" runat="server"%>
<%@ Import Namespace="System.Data"%>
<%@ Import Namespace="System.Data.SqlClient"%>
<script runat=server>
Sub Page_Load()
    dim OurConnection as SqlConnection
    dim OurCommand as SqlCommand
    dim OurDataReader as SqlDataReader
```

continues

Visual Basic .NET—(continued)

```
OurConnection = New SqlConnection("Server=server;
➥uid=newriders;pwd=password;database=Northwind")
OurConnection.Open()
OurCommand = New SqlCommand("Select Top 15 ProductName,UnitPrice From
➥Products" ,OurConnection)
OurDataReader = OurCommand.ExecuteReader()
OurDataGrid.DataSource=OurDataReader
DataBind()

OurDataReader.Close()
OurConnection.Close()


End Sub

</script>
<html>
<head>
<title>ADO DataReader</title>
</head>
<body bgcolor="#FFFFFF" text="#000000">
<ASP:DataGrid id="OurDataGrid"
    BorderWidth="1"
    BorderColor="#000000"
    CellPadding="3"
    CellSpacing="0"
    Font-Name="Verdana"
    Font-Size="12px"
    HeaderStyle-BackColor="#AAAAAA"
    ItemStyle-BackColor="#EEEEEE"
    AutoGenerateColumns="false"
    runat="server">
    <Columns>
        <asp:BoundColumn
            HeaderText="Product Name"
            DataField="ProductName" />
        <asp:BoundColumn
            HeaderText="Unit Price"
            DataField="UnitPrice"
            DataFormatString="{0:c}"/>
    </Columns>
</asp:DataGrid>
</body>
</html>
```

C# —**ado_query_reader_sql_vb/cs.aspx**

```
<%@ page language="cs" runat="server"%>
<%@ Import Namespace="System.Data"%>
<%@ Import Namespace="System.Data.SqlClient"%>
<script runat=server>
void Page_Load(){
    SqlConnection OurConnection;
    SqlCommand OurCommand;
    SqlDataReader OurDataReader;

    OurConnection = new
    ➡SqlConnection("Server=server;uid=newriders;pwd=password;database=Northwind");
    OurConnection.Open();
    OurCommand = new SqlCommand("Select Top 20 ProductName,UnitPrice From
    ➡Products" ,OurConnection);
    OurDataReader = OurCommand.ExecuteReader();
    OurDataGrid.DataSource=OurDataReader;
    OurDataGrid.DataBind();
    OurDataReader.Close();
    OurConnection.Close();
}

</script>
<html>
<head>
<title>ADO DataReader</title>
</head>
<body bgcolor="#FFFFFF" text="#000000">
<ASP:DataGrid id="OurDataGrid"
    BorderWidth="1"
    BorderColor="#000000"
    CellPadding="3"
    CellSpacing="0"
    Font-Name="Verdana"
    Font-Size="12px"
    HeaderStyle-BackColor="#AAAAAA"
    ItemStyle-BackColor="#EEEEEE"
    AutoGenerateColumns="false"
    runat="server">
    <Columns>
        <asp:BoundColumn
            HeaderText="Product Name"
            DataField="ProductName" />
        <asp:BoundColumn
            HeaderText="Unit Price"
            DataField="UnitPrice"
            DataFormatString="{0:c}"/>
    </Columns>
</asp:DataGrid>
</body>
</html>
```

As you can see in Figure 10.1, the DataReader bound the data just marvelously to the DataGrid. In this example, I first created variables that represented the object types with which they would be filled. Then I used SQLConnection to connect to the Northwind SQL Server database. I then used the SQLCommand to pass a SQL statement to the database to retrieve the ProductName and UnitPrice columns from the Products table.

FIGURE 10.1

The DataReader returned the results of the Select statement.

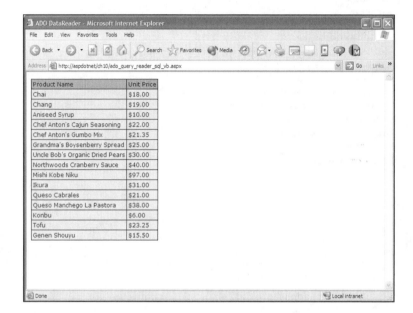

Next, I used the SQLCommand's ExecuteReader() method to populate the DataReader variable with the results from the SQLCommand. Next, as I've said and many would contradict, I bound the DataReader to the DataGrid.

The last thing to do is close the DataReader and then the Connection. When using a DataReader, you must do this explicitly, because the DataReader actively uses the Connection to directly populate the data to its destination and isn't capable of destroying itself or the Connection.

This isn't the case with the DataSet, though. The DataSet is a disconnected, memory-based version of the data that you are operating on from the database. It inherently manages its own cleanup, and you won't need to issue any Close() methods for it. Take a look at the DataSet now.

DataSet

Do you remember that I said that the DataSet is a collection of DataTable road-way decking in the bridge to the database? The DataSet is capable of holding and manipulating the contents of many in-memory tables of data. These tables are called DataTables. Look at an example of delivering many tables of data to an ASP.NET web page with the DataSet.

Visual Basic .NET—ado_query_dataset_vb.aspx

```
<%@ page language="vb" runat="server"%>
<%@ Import Namespace="System.Data"%>
<%@ Import Namespace="System.Data.SqlClient"%>
<script runat=server>
Sub Page_Load()

    dim OurConnection as SQLConnection
    dim OurCommand as SQLCommand
    dim OurCommand2 as SQLCommand
    dim OurDataAdapter as SQLDataAdapter
    dim OurDataAdapter2 as SQLDataAdapter
    dim OurDataSet as New DataSet()

    OurConnection = New SQLConnection("Server=server;
    ➥uid=newriders;pwd=password;database=Northwind")
    OurCommand = New SQLCommand("Select Top 10 ProductName, QuantityPerUnit,
    ➥UnitPrice, UnitsInStock From Products",OurConnection)
    OurCommand2 = New SQLCommand("Select CategoryName,Description From
    ➥Categories",OurConnection)
    OurDataAdapter = New SQLDataAdapter(OurCommand)
    OurDataAdapter2 = New SQLDataAdapter(OurCommand2)
    OurDataAdapter.Fill(OurDataSet, "Products")
    OurDataAdapter2.Fill(OurDataSet, "Categories")
    OurDataGrid.DataSource = OurDataSet.Tables("Products")
    OurDataGrid2.DataSource = OurDataSet.Tables("Categories")
    DataBind()


End Sub

</script>
<html>
<head>
<title>ADO DataSet</title>
</head>
<body bgcolor="#FFFFFF" text="#000000">
<ASP:DataGrid id="OurDataGrid"
    BorderWidth="1"
    BorderColor="#000000"
    CellPadding="3"
```

continues

Visual Basic .NET—(continued)

```
            CellSpacing="0"
            Font-Name="Verdana"
            Font-Size="12px"
            HeaderStyle-BackColor="#AAAAAA"
            ItemStyle-BackColor="#EEEEEE"
            AutoGenerateColumns="false"
            runat="server">
            <Columns>
                <asp:BoundColumn
                    HeaderText="Product Name"
                    DataField="ProductName" />
                <asp:BoundColumn
                    HeaderText="Unit Price"
                    DataField="UnitPrice"
                    DataFormatString="{0:c}"/>
            </Columns>
        </asp:DataGrid>
        <br>
        <ASP:DataGrid id="OurDataGrid2"
            BorderWidth="1"
            BorderColor="#000000"
            CellPadding="3"
            CellSpacing="0"
            Font-Name="Verdana"
            Font-Size="12px"
            HeaderStyle-BackColor="#AAAAAA"
            ItemStyle-BackColor="#EEEEEE"
            AutoGenerateColumns="false"
            runat="server">
            <Columns>
                <asp:BoundColumn
                    HeaderText="Category Name"
                    DataField="CategoryName" />
                <asp:BoundColumn
                    HeaderText="Description"
                    DataField="Description" />
            </Columns>
        </asp:DataGrid>
    </body>
</html>
```

C#—ado_query_dataset_cs.aspx

```
<%@ page language="c#" runat="server"%>
<%@ Import Namespace="System.Data"%>
<%@ Import Namespace="System.Data.SqlClient"%>
<script runat=server>
void Page_Load(){

    SqlConnection OurConnection;
    SqlCommand OurCommand;
    SqlCommand OurCommand2;
    SqlDataAdapter OurDataAdapter;
    SqlDataAdapter OurDataAdapter2;
    DataSet OurDataSet;
    OurDataSet = new DataSet();

    OurConnection = new SqlConnection("Server=server;
    ➥uid=newriders;pwd=password;database=Northwind");
    OurCommand = new SqlCommand("Select Top 10 ProductName, QuantityPerUnit,
    ➥UnitPrice, UnitsInStock From Products",OurConnection);
    OurCommand2 = new SqlCommand("Select CategoryName,Description From
    ➥Categories",OurConnection);
    OurDataAdapter = new SqlDataAdapter(OurCommand);
    OurDataAdapter2 = new SqlDataAdapter(OurCommand2);
    OurDataAdapter.Fill(OurDataSet, "Products");
    OurDataAdapter2.Fill(OurDataSet, "Categories");
    OurDataGrid.DataSource = OurDataSet.Tables["Products"];
    OurDataGrid2.DataSource = OurDataSet.Tables["Categories"];
    DataBind();
}

</script>
<html>
<head>
<title>ADO DataSet</title>
</head>
<body bgcolor="#FFFFFF" text="#000000">
<ASP:DataGrid id="OurDataGrid"
    BorderWidth="1"
    BorderColor="#000000"
    CellPadding="3"
    CellSpacing="0"
    Font-Name="Verdana"
    Font-Size="12px"
```

continues

C#—(continued)

```
            HeaderStyle-BackColor="#AAAAAA"
            ItemStyle-BackColor="#EEEEEE"
            AutoGenerateColumns="false"
            runat="server">
            <Columns>
                <asp:BoundColumn
                    HeaderText="Product Name"
                    DataField="ProductName" />
                <asp:BoundColumn
                    HeaderText="Unit Price"
                    DataField="UnitPrice"
                    DataFormatString="{0:c}"/>
            </Columns>
        </asp:DataGrid>
        <br>
        <ASP:DataGrid id="OurDataGrid2"
            BorderWidth="1"
            BorderColor="#000000"
            CellPadding="3"
            CellSpacing="0"
            Font-Name="Verdana"
            Font-Size="12px"
            HeaderStyle-BackColor="#AAAAAA"
            ItemStyle-BackColor="#EEEEEE"
            AutoGenerateColumns="false"
            runat="server">
            <Columns>
                <asp:BoundColumn
                    HeaderText="Category Name"
                    DataField="CategoryName" />
                <asp:BoundColumn
                    HeaderText="Description"
                    DataField="Description" />
            </Columns>
        </asp:DataGrid>
    </body>
</html>
```

Again, as you can see, the SQLConnection and SQLCommand do exactly the same thing as a DataReader does, but you actually create two commands and use the SQLDataAdapter objects to insert the selected data into two different tables in the dataset. Then you bind the data from these two different DataTables in the DataSet to two different DataGrid objects and DataBind(), then voilá!! Notice that I didn't have to explicitly execute a DataBind() on each table. I basically caused databinding on all objects that had data sources and that could be data-bound by calling the DataBind() method without any specific object ID. You can see the results in Figure 10.2.

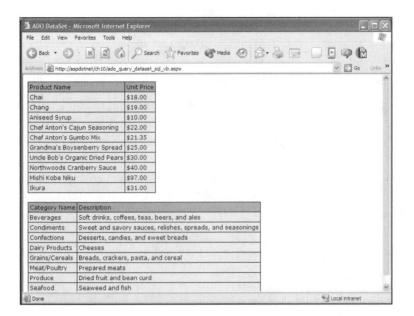

FIGURE 10.2

The DataSet *object can hold multiple tables of data.*

DataRelation

In pre-.NET ADO, there was a function of dealing with related data that was called *data shaping*. It allowed you to iterate through one parent table and iterate through the child data for each record of parent data. For instance, imagine you had a Fruit table and a Fruit Type table. The parent Fruit table would have many related Fruit Types.

- Apples (Fruit)
  - Macintosh (Fruit Type)
  - Red Delicious (Fruit Type)
  - Granny Smith (Fruit Type)
- Berry (Fruit)
  - Raspberry (Fruit Type)
  - Blueberry (Fruit Type)
  - Strawberry (Fruit Type)

Data shaping would allow you to define this type of parent/child relationship between two tables. The `DataRelation` object also allows you to replicate this function, and building multiple level dependencies is as easy as creating additional `DataTables` and `DataRelations`.

To create the dependencies, you have to tell the `DataRelation` object which columns of the `DataTables` are related. This operates much as a primary key/ foreign key relationship does in a database scenario. In the following example I create a few variables of datatypes you haven't seen yet. The `DataColumn` and `DataRow` are objects that make up a `DataTable`. I use these variables as a way to easily reference my columns when setting `DataRelations` and reference my rows when iterating through the data.

Visual Basic .NET—`ado_query_relation_sql_vb.aspx`

```
<%@ page language="vb" runat="server"%>
<%@ Import Namespace="System.Data"%>
<%@ Import Namespace="System.Data.SqlClient"%>
<script runat=server>
Sub Page_Load()

    dim OurConnection as SQLConnection
    dim OurCommand as SQLCommand
    dim OurCommand2 as SQLCommand
    dim OurDataAdapter as SQLDataAdapter
    dim OurDataAdapter2 as SQLDataAdapter
    dim OurDataSet as New DataSet()
    dim OurDataColumn as DataColumn
    dim OurDataColumn2 as DataColumn
    dim OurDataRelation as DataRelation
    dim Category as DataRow
    dim Product as DataRow
    dim ArrRows() as DataRow

    OurConnection = New SQLConnection("Server=server;
    ➡uid=newriders;pwd=password;database=Northwind")
    OurCommand = New SQLCommand("Select Top 10 ProductName, QuantityPerUnit,
    ➡UnitPrice, UnitsInStock, CategoryID From Products",OurConnection)
    OurCommand2 = New SQLCommand("Select CategoryName,Description, CategoryID From
    ➡Categories",OurConnection)
    OurDataAdapter = New SQLDataAdapter(OurCommand)
    OurDataAdapter2 = New SQLDataAdapter(OurCommand2)
    OurDataAdapter.Fill(OurDataSet, "Products")
    OurDataAdapter2.Fill(OurDataSet, "Categories")
    OurDataColumn = OurDataSet.Tables("Products").Columns("CategoryID")
    OurDataColumn2 = OurDataSet.Tables("Categories").Columns("CategoryID")
    OurDataRelation = new DataRelation("ProductCategories", OurDataColumn2,
OurDataColumn)
```

```
OurDataSet.Relations.Add(OurDataRelation)


for each Category in OurDataSet.Tables("Categories").Rows
    ArrRows=Category.GetChildRows(OurDataSet.Relations("ProductCategories"))
    if ArrRows.Length > 0 then
        OurLabel.Text += "<u><b>" + Category("CategoryName") + "</b></u><br>"
        OurLabel.Text += "<ul>"
        for each Product in ArrRows
            OurLabel.Text += "<li>" + Product("ProductName") + "</li><br>"
        next
        OurLabel.Text +="</ul>"
    end if
next


End Sub


</script>
<html>
<head>
<title>ADO DataSet</title>
</head>
<body bgcolor="#FFFFFF" text="#000000">
<asp:Label
    id="OurLabel"
    font-name="verdana"
    font-size="11px"
    runat="server" />
</body>
</html>
```

C#—ado_query_relation_sql_cs.aspx

```
<%@ page language="c#" runat="server"%>
<%@ Import Namespace="System.Data"%>
<%@ Import Namespace="System.Data.SqlClient"%>
<script runat=server>
void Page_Load() {

    SqlConnection OurConnection;
    SqlCommand OurCommand, OurCommand2;
    SqlDataAdapter OurDataAdapter, OurDataAdapter2;
    DataSet OurDataSet = new DataSet();
    DataColumn OurDataColumn, OurDataColumn2;
    DataRelation OurDataRelation;
    DataRow[] ArrRows;

    OurConnection = new SqlConnection("Server=server;
    ➥uid=newriders;pwd=password;database=Northwind");
    OurCommand = new SqlCommand("Select Top 10 ProductName, QuantityPerUnit,
    ➥UnitPrice, UnitsInStock, CategoryID From Products",OurConnection);
```

continues

C#—(continued)

```
OurCommand2 = new SqlCommand("Select CategoryName,Description, CategoryID From
➥Categories",OurConnection);
OurDataAdapter = new SqlDataAdapter(OurCommand);
OurDataAdapter2 = new SqlDataAdapter(OurCommand2);
OurDataAdapter.Fill(OurDataSet, "Products");
OurDataAdapter2.Fill(OurDataSet, "Categories");
OurDataColumn = OurDataSet.Tables["Products"].Columns["CategoryID"];
OurDataColumn2 = OurDataSet.Tables["Categories"].Columns["CategoryID"];
OurDataRelation = new DataRelation("ProductCategories", OurDataColumn2,
➥OurDataColumn);
OurDataSet.Relations.Add(OurDataRelation);

foreach(DataRow Category in OurDataSet.Tables["Categories"].Rows) {
    ArrRows=Category.GetChildRows(OurDataSet.Relations["ProductCategories"]);
    if (ArrRows.Length > 0){
        OurLabel.Text += "<u><b>" + Category["CategoryName"] + "</b></u><br>";
        OurLabel.Text += "<ul>";
        foreach(DataRow Product in ArrRows) {
            OurLabel.Text += "<li>" + Product["ProductName"] + "</li><br>";
        }
        OurLabel.Text +="</ul>";
    }
}
}

</script>
<html>
<head>
<title>ADO DataRelation</title>
</head>
<body bgcolor="#FFFFFF" text="#000000">
<asp:Label
    id="OurLabel"
    font-name="verdana"
    font-size="11px"
    runat="server" />
</body>
</html>
```

What this code does is associate or relate two tables in the DataSet called
Products and Categories. The Categories table has a column called CategoryID
that is its primary key Field, and the Products table has a CategoryID field that
is a foreign key field to CategoryID in the Categories table.

As you can see in Figure 10.3, the DataRelation properly displayed the products that were selected from the Products table under their related categories from the Categories table.

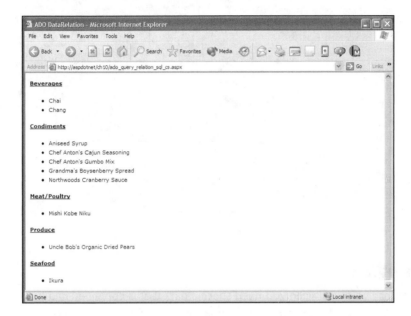

FIGURE 10.3

The
DataRelation
*object allows you
to establish
relationships
between tables in
the* DataSet.

Primary Keys and Foreign Keys, although they may sound intimidating, are pretty simple concepts to understand. They are terms used in databases to help identify or relate rows to each other. A Primary Key is a column or group of columns that represent a unique identifier for each row. Often this is an integer that increments automatically by a set value as new rows are added to a table to ensure that no two primary keys are the same. A *foreign key* is a column or group of columns in a table that represent an identity that can be associated with another table's primary key. Take a look at Figure 10.4 to see a visual of two tables, each with a primary key, and one having a foreign key relationship the other.

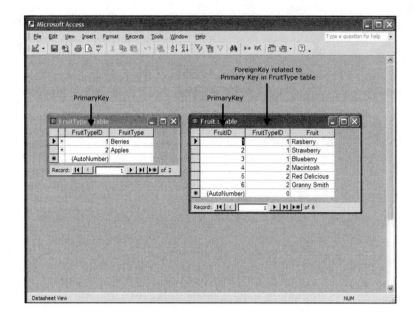

DataView

There may be times when you need specific data that is contained in a DataTable in your DataSet. Maybe you need multiple versions of that data to contain different rows. Enter the DataView. The DataView object in basic form is a copy of the data in a DataTable that you can manipulate independent of the DataTable.

In the following example, I am going to build a DataTable that contains all the products in the Northwind database. Then I will populate two DataViews with that data and filter them differently. One DataView's rows will be filtered by CategoryID = 3, which is all the Confection products, and the other DataView's rows will be filtered by CategoryID = 8, which is all the Seafood products.

Visual Basic .NET—**ado_query_dataview_vb.aspx**

```
<%@ page language="vb" runat="server"%>
<%@ Import Namespace="System.Data"%>
<%@ Import Namespace="System.Data.SqlClient"%>
<script runat=server>
Sub Page_Load()

    dim OurConnection as SQLConnection
    dim OurCommand as SQLCommand
    dim OurDataAdapter as SQLDataAdapter
    dim OurDataSet as New DataSet()
```

```
OurConnection = New SQLConnection("Server=server;
➥uid=newriders;pwd=password;database=Northwind")
OurCommand = New SQLCommand("Select CategoryID, ProductName, UnitPrice From
➥Products",OurConnection)
OurDataAdapter = New SQLDataAdapter(OurCommand)
OurDataAdapter.Fill(OurDataSet, "Products")
dim OurDataView1 as new DataView(OurDataSet.Tables("Products"))
dim OurDataView2 as new DataView(OurDataSet.Tables("Products"))


OurDataView1.RowFilter = "CategoryID = 3"
OurDataView2.RowFilter = "CategoryID = 8"



OurDataGrid.DataSource = OurDataView1
OurDataGrid2.DataSource = OurDataView2
DataBind()


End Sub

</script>
<html>
<head>
<title>ADO DataView</title>
</head>
<body bgcolor="#FFFFFF" text="#000000">
<table border="0" cellpadding="0" cellspacing="20">
<tr><td>
<h4>Confections</h4>
<ASP:DataGrid id="OurDataGrid"
    BorderWidth="1"
    BorderColor="#000000"
    CellPadding="3"
    CellSpacing="0"
    Font-Name="Verdana"
    Font-Size="12px"
    HeaderStyle-BackColor="#AAAAAA"
    ItemStyle-BackColor="#EEEEEE"
    AutoGenerateColumns="false"
    runat="server">
    <Columns>
        <asp:BoundColumn
            HeaderText="Product Name"
            DataField="ProductName" />
        <asp:BoundColumn
            HeaderText="Unit Price"
            DataField="UnitPrice"
            DataFormatString="{0:c}"/>
    </Columns>
</asp:DataGrid>
</td><td valign="top">
<h4>Seafood</h4>
```

continues

Visual Basic .NET—(continued)

```
<ASP:DataGrid id="OurDataGrid2"
    BorderWidth="1"
    BorderColor="#000000"
    CellPadding="3"
    CellSpacing="0"
    Font-Name="Verdana"
    Font-Size="12px"
    HeaderStyle-BackColor="#AAAAAA"
    ItemStyle-BackColor="#EEEEEE"
    AutoGenerateColumns="false"
    runat="server">
    <Columns>
        <asp:BoundColumn
            HeaderText="Product Name"
            DataField="ProductName" />
        <asp:BoundColumn
            HeaderText="Unit Price"
            DataField="UnitPrice"
            DataFormatString="{0:c}"/>
    </Columns>
</asp:DataGrid>
</td></tr>
</table>
</body>
</html>
```

C#—ado_query_dataview_cs.aspx

```
<%@ page language="c#" runat="server"%>
<%@ Import Namespace="System.Data"%>
<%@ Import Namespace="System.Data.SqlClient"%>
<script runat=server>

void Page_Load() {

    SqlConnection OurConnection;
    SqlCommand OurCommand;
    SqlDataAdapter OurDataAdapter;
    DataSet OurDataSet = new DataSet();
    OurConnection = new SqlConnection("Server=server;
    ➥uid=newriders;pwd=password;database=Northwind");
    OurCommand = new SqlCommand("Select CategoryID, ProductName, UnitPrice From
    ➥Products",OurConnection);
    OurDataAdapter = new SqlDataAdapter(OurCommand);
    OurDataAdapter.Fill(OurDataSet, "Products");
    DataView OurDataView1 = new DataView(OurDataSet.Tables["Products"]);
    DataView OurDataView2 = new DataView(OurDataSet.Tables["Products"]);

    OurDataView1.RowFilter = "CategoryID = 3";
```

```
    OurDataView2.RowFilter = "CategoryID = 8";


    OurDataGrid.DataSource = OurDataView1;
    OurDataGrid2.DataSource = OurDataView2;
    DataBind();


}

</script>
<html>
<head>
<title>ADO DataView</title>
</head>
<body bgcolor="#FFFFFF" text="#000000">
<table border="0" cellpadding="0" cellspacing="20">
<tr><td>
<h4>Confections</h4>
<ASP:DataGrid id="OurDataGrid"
    BorderWidth="1"
    BorderColor="#000000"
    CellPadding="3"
    CellSpacing="0"
    Font-Name="Verdana"
    Font-Size="12px"
    HeaderStyle-BackColor="#AAAAAA"
    ItemStyle-BackColor="#EEEEEE"
    AutoGenerateColumns="false"
    runat="server">
    <Columns>
        <asp:BoundColumn
            HeaderText="Product Name"
            DataField="ProductName" />
        <asp:BoundColumn
            HeaderText="Unit Price"
            DataField="UnitPrice"
            DataFormatString="{0:c}"/>
    </Columns>
</asp:DataGrid>
</td><td valign="top">
<h4>Seafood</h4>
<ASP:DataGrid id="OurDataGrid2"
    BorderWidth="1"
    BorderColor="#000000"
    CellPadding="3"
    CellSpacing="0"
    Font-Name="Verdana"
    Font-Size="12px"
    HeaderStyle-BackColor="#AAAAAA"
    ItemStyle-BackColor="#EEEEEE"
    AutoGenerateColumns="false"
```

continues

C#—(continued)

```
runat="server">
<Columns>
    <asp:BoundColumn
        HeaderText="Product Name"
        DataField="ProductName" />
    <asp:BoundColumn
        HeaderText="Unit Price"
        DataField="UnitPrice"
        DataFormatString="{0:c}"/>
</Columns>
</asp:DataGrid>
</td></tr>
</table>
</body>
</html>
```

The results of this can be seen in Figure 10.5. The two `DataViews` have been filtered independently of each other and provide two different views of the data that is contained in the `DataTable`.

FIGURE 10.5

`DataViews` *let you make independent copies of* `DataTables` *that can filter, sort, and edit.*

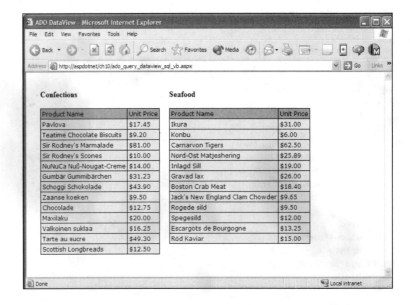

Inserting, Updating, and Deleting Data

Another part of dealing with data in ASP.NET applications is being able to insert new records, update existing records, and delete records from your database tables. With these three types of functions that you can execute against your database, you will be able to manipulate the contents of your database to do just about anything you want.

ADO.NET provides a bunch of ways for you to perform these functions, from simple to automated, to providing you with the tools to be very detailed and specific about how your database and ASP.NET pages interact. Let's move along to the following sections and look at some of the ways you can use ADO.NET to affect your data.

Command

The SQLCommand object has a method called ExecuteNonQuery(), which provides a means by which you can run Insert, Update, and Delete statements against your database by writing the appropriate T-SQL statement as the SQLCommand's CommandText property. Let's have look.

Visual Basic .NET—**ado_sqlcommand_iud_vb.aspx**

```
<%@ page language="vb" runat="server" %>
<%@ Import Namespace="System.Data" %>
<%@ Import Namespace="System.Data.SqlClient" %>
<script runat=server>
Sub Page_Load()
    If (Not IsPostBack) then
        LoadData()
    End If
End Sub

Sub LoadData()
    dim OurConnection as SqlConnection
    dim OurCommand as SqlCommand
    dim OurDataAdapter as SQLDataAdapter
    dim OurDataSet as New DataSet()

    OurConnection = New SqlConnection("Server=server;
    ➥uid=newriders;pwd=password;database=Northwind")
    OurConnection.Open()
    OurCommand = New SqlCommand("Select Top 15 EmployeeID,FirstName,LastName from
    ➥Employees" ,OurConnection)
    OurDataAdapter = New SQLDataAdapter(OurCommand)
    OurDataAdapter.Fill(OurDataSet, "Employees")
```

continues

Visual Basic .NET—(continued)

```
    OurDataGrid.DataSource=OurDataSet.Tables("Employees")
    UpdateEmployeeID.DataSource=OurDataSet.Tables("Employees")
    DeleteEmployeeID.DataSource=OurDataSet.Tables("Employees")
    DataBind()


End Sub

Sub UpdateSetup(sender As Object, e As System.EventArgs)

    UpdateSelect.Visible="False"
    UpdateTextBoxes.Visible="True"
    dim SelectedID as String = UpdateEmployeeID.SelectedItem.Value
    UpdateButton.CommandArgument = SelectedID
    dim OurConnection as SqlConnection
    OurConnection = New SqlConnection("Server=server;
    ➥uid=newriders;pwd=password;database=Northwind")
    OurConnection.Open()
    dim OurCommand as SqlCommand
    dim OurDataReader2 as SqlDataReader
    OurCommand = New SqlCommand("Select FirstName, LastName From Employees Where
    ➥EmployeeID = " + SelectedID ,OurConnection)
    OurDataReader2 = OurCommand.ExecuteReader()
    OurDataReader2.Read()
    UpdateFirstName.Visible="True"
    UpdateLastName.Visible="True"
    UpdateFirstName.Text = OurDataReader2("FirstName")
    UpdateLastName.Text = OurDataReader2("LastName")
    OurConnection.Close()
    OurDataReader2.Close()

    LoadData()
End Sub

Sub UpdateReset(sender As Object, e As System.EventArgs)
    UpdateSelect.Visible="True"
    UpdateTextBoxes.Visible="False"
    LoadData()
End Sub

Sub InsertCommand(sender As Object, e As System.EventArgs)
    dim OurConnection as SqlConnection
    OurConnection = New SqlConnection("Server=server;
    ➥uid=newriders;pwd=password;database=Northwind")
    dim OurCommand as SqlCommand
    OurCommand = New SqlCommand("Insert Into Employees (FirstName, LastName)
    ➥Values (@FirstName, @LastName)" ,OurConnection)
    OurCommand.Parameters.Add("@FirstName", SqlDbType.Varchar, 10).Value =
    ➥InsertFirstName.Text
    OurCommand.Parameters.Add("@LastName", SqlDbType.Varchar, 20).Value =
    ➥InsertLastName.Text
```

```
    OurConnection.Open()
    OurCommand.ExecuteNonQuery()
    OurConnection.Close()

    LoadData()
End Sub

Sub UpdateCommand(sender As Object, e As
➡System.Web.UI.WebControls.CommandEventArgs)
    dim OurConnection as SqlConnection
    dim OurCommand as SqlCommand
    dim EmployeeID as String = e.CommandArgument
    OurConnection = New SqlConnection("Server=server;
    ➡uid=newriders;pwd=password;database=Northwind")
    OurCommand = New SqlCommand("Update Employees Set Firstname = @FirstName,
    ➡LastName = @LastName Where EmployeeID = " + EmployeeID, OurConnection)
    OurCommand.Parameters.Add("@FirstName", SqlDbType.Varchar, 10).Value =
    ➡UpdateFirstName.Text
    OurCommand.Parameters.Add("@LastName", SqlDbType.Varchar, 20).Value =
    ➡UpdateLastName.Text
    OurConnection.Open()
    OurCommand.ExecuteNonQuery()
    OurConnection.Close()

    LoadData()
End Sub

Sub DeleteCommand(sender As Object, e As System.EventArgs)
    dim OurConnection as SqlConnection
    dim SelectedID as String = DeleteEmployeeID.SelectedItem.Value
    dim OurCommand as SqlCommand
    OurConnection = New SqlConnection("Server=server;
    ➡uid=newriders;pwd=password;database=Northwind")
    OurCommand = New SqlCommand("Delete Employees Where EmployeeID = " +
    ➡SelectedID, OurConnection)
    OurConnection.Open()
    OurCommand.ExecuteNonQuery()
    OurConnection.Close()

    LoadData()
End Sub
</script>
<html>
<head>
<title>ADO SQLCommand -Insert,Update,Delete</title>
</head>
<body bgcolor="#FFFFFF" text="#000000">
<form runat="server">
<table border="0" cellpadding="0" cellspacing="20">
<tr><td>
<ASP:DataGrid
    id="OurDataGrid"
```

continues

Visual Basic .NET—(continued)

```
        EnableViewState="false"
        BorderWidth="1"
        BorderColor="#000000"
        CellPadding="3"
        CellSpacing="0"
        Font-Name="Verdana"
        HeaderStyle-BackColor="#AAAAAA"
        ItemStyle-BackColor="#EEEEEE"
        runat="server" />
</td><td>
<h4>Insert</h4>
First Name: <asp:TextBox id="InsertFirstName" runat="server" /><br>
Last Name: <asp:TextBox id="InsertLastName" runat="server" />
<asp:button runat="server" OnClick="InsertCommand" text="Submit" /><br><br>
<hr style="height:1px">
<h4>Update</h4>
<asp:Panel id="UpdateSelect" runat="server" >
EmployeeID:
<asp:DropDownList
    id="UpdateEmployeeID"
    DataTextField="EmployeeID"
    DataValueField="EmployeeID"
    runat="server" />
<asp:button runat="server" text="Select" OnClick="UpdateSetup" />
</asp:Panel>
<asp:Panel id="UpdateTextBoxes" Visible="false" runat="server" >
First Name: <asp:TextBox id="UpdateFirstName" runat="server" />
<asp:button
    id="UpdateButton"
    onCommand="UpdateCommand"
    runat="server"
    text="Update" /><br>
Last Name: <asp:TextBox id="UpdateLastName"  runat="server" />
<asp:button id="CancelUpdateButton" runat="server" onClick="UpdateReset"
➥text="Select Other" />
</asp:Panel><br>
<hr style="height:1px">
<h4>Delete</h4>
EmployeeID:
<asp:DropDownList
    id="DeleteEmployeeID"
    DataTextField="EmployeeID"
    DataValueField="EmployeeID"
    runat="server" />
<asp:button runat="server" text="Delete" onClick="DeleteCommand" />
</td></tr>
</table>
</form>
</body>
</html>
```

C#—ado_sqlcommand_iud_cs.asxp

```csharp
<%@ page language="c#" runat="server" %>
<%@ Import Namespace="System.Data" %>
<%@ Import Namespace="System.Data.SqlClient" %>
<script runat=server>
void Page_Load() {
    if (!IsPostBack) {
        LoadData();
    }
}

void LoadData() {
    SqlConnection OurConnection;
    SqlCommand OurCommand;
    SqlDataAdapter OurDataAdapter;
    DataSet OurDataSet = new DataSet();
    OurConnection = new SqlConnection("Server=server;
    ➥uid=newriders;pwd=password;database=Northwind");
    OurConnection.Open();
    OurCommand = new SqlCommand("Select Top 15 EmployeeID,FirstName,LastName from
    ➥Employees" ,OurConnection);
    OurDataAdapter = new SqlDataAdapter(OurCommand);
    OurDataAdapter.Fill(OurDataSet, "Employees");
    OurDataGrid.DataSource=OurDataSet.Tables["Employees"];
    UpdateEmployeeID.DataSource=OurDataSet.Tables["Employees"];
    DeleteEmployeeID.DataSource=OurDataSet.Tables["Employees"];
    DataBind();
}

void UpdateSetup(Object sender, System.EventArgs e) {
    UpdateSelect.Visible=false;
    UpdateTextBoxes.Visible=true;
    String SelectedID = UpdateEmployeeID.SelectedItem.Value.ToString();
    UpdateButton.CommandArgument = SelectedID;
    SqlConnection OurConnection;
    OurConnection = new SqlConnection("Server=server;
    ➥uid=newriders;pwd=password;database=Northwind");
    OurConnection.Open();
    SqlCommand OurCommand;
    SqlDataReader OurDataReader2;
    OurCommand = new SqlCommand("Select FirstName, LastName From Employees Where
    ➥EmployeeID = " + SelectedID ,OurConnection);
    OurDataReader2 = OurCommand.ExecuteReader();
    OurDataReader2.Read();
    UpdateFirstName.Visible=true;
    UpdateLastName.Visible=true;
    UpdateFirstName.Text = OurDataReader2["FirstName"].ToString();
    UpdateLastName.Text = OurDataReader2["LastName"].ToString();
    OurConnection.Close();
    OurDataReader2.Close();
    LoadData();
```

continues

C#—(continued)

```csharp
}

void UpdateReset(Object sender, System.EventArgs e) {
    UpdateSelect.Visible=true;
    UpdateTextBoxes.Visible=false;
    LoadData();
}

void InsertCommand(Object sender, System.EventArgs e) {
    SqlConnection OurConnection;
    OurConnection = new SqlConnection("Server=server;
    ➥uid=newriders;pwd=password;database=Northwind");
    SqlCommand OurCommand;
    OurCommand = new SqlCommand("Insert Into Employees (FirstName, LastName)
    ➥Values (@FirstName, @LastName)" ,OurConnection);
    OurCommand.Parameters.Add("@FirstName", SqlDbType.VarChar, 10).Value =
    ➥InsertFirstName.Text;
    OurCommand.Parameters.Add("@LastName", SqlDbType.VarChar, 20).Value =
    ➥InsertLastName.Text;
    OurConnection.Open();
    OurCommand.ExecuteNonQuery();
    OurConnection.Close();
    LoadData();
}

void UpdateCommand(Object sender, System.Web.UI.WebControls.CommandEventArgs e) {
    SqlConnection OurConnection;
    SqlCommand OurCommand;
    String EmployeeID = e.CommandArgument.ToString();
    OurConnection = new
SqlConnection("Server=server;uid=newriders;pwd=password;database=Northwind");
    OurCommand = new SqlCommand("Update Employees Set Firstname = @FirstName,
    ➥LastName = @LastName Where EmployeeID = " + EmployeeID, OurConnection);
    OurCommand.Parameters.Add("@FirstName", SqlDbType.VarChar, 10).Value =
    ➥UpdateFirstName.Text;
    OurCommand.Parameters.Add("@LastName", SqlDbType.VarChar, 20).Value =
    ➥UpdateLastName.Text;
    OurConnection.Open();
    OurCommand.ExecuteNonQuery();
    OurConnection.Close();
    LoadData();
}

void DeleteCommand(Object sender, System.EventArgs e) {
    SqlConnection OurConnection;
    String SelectedID = DeleteEmployeeID.SelectedItem.Value;
    SqlCommand OurCommand;
    OurConnection = new
SqlConnection("Server=server;uid=newriders;pwd=password;database=Northwind");
    OurCommand = new SqlCommand("Delete Employees Where EmployeeID = " +
    ➥SelectedID, OurConnection);
```

```
        OurConnection.Open();
        OurCommand.ExecuteNonQuery();
        OurConnection.Close();
        LoadData();
    }
</script>
<html>
<head>
<title>ADO SqlCommand -Insert,Update,Delete</title>
</head>
<body bgcolor="#FFFFFF" text="#000000">
<form runat="server">
<table border="0" cellpadding="0" cellspacing="20">
<tr><td>
<ASP:DataGrid
    id="OurDataGrid"
    EnableViewState="false"
    BorderWidth="1"
    BorderColor="#000000"
    CellPadding="3"
    CellSpacing="0"
    Font-Name="Verdana"
    HeaderStyle-BackColor="#AAAAAA"
    ItemStyle-BackColor="#EEEEEE"
    runat="server" />
</td><td>
<h4>Insert</h4>
First Name: <asp:TextBox id="InsertFirstName" runat="server" /><br>
Last Name: <asp:TextBox id="InsertLastName" runat="server" />
<asp:button runat="server" OnClick="InsertCommand" text="voidmit" /><br><br>
<hr style="height:1px">
<h4>Update</h4>
<asp:Panel id="UpdateSelect" runat="server" >
EmployeeID:
<asp:DropDownList
    id="UpdateEmployeeID"
    DataTextField="EmployeeID"
    DataValueField="EmployeeID"
    runat="server" />
<asp:button runat="server" text="Select" OnClick="UpdateSetup" />
</asp:Panel>
<asp:Panel id="UpdateTextBoxes" Visible="false" runat="server" >
First Name: <asp:TextBox id="UpdateFirstName" runat="server" />
<asp:button
    id="UpdateButton"
    onCommand="UpdateCommand"
    runat="server"
    text="Update" /><br>
Last Name: <asp:TextBox id="UpdateLastName"  runat="server" />
<asp:button id="CancelUpdateButton" runat="server" onClick="UpdateReset"
➡text="Select Other" />
</asp:Panel><br>
<hr style="height:1px">
```

continues

C#—(continued)

```
<h4>Delete</h4>
EmployeeID:
<asp:DropDownList
    id="DeleteEmployeeID"
    DataTextField="EmployeeID"
    DataValueField="EmployeeID"
    runat="server" />
<asp:button runat="server" text="Delete" onClick="DeleteCommand" />
</td></tr>
</table>
</form>
</body>
</html>
```

As you can see in the code examples, there are three different functions that address separately inserting, updating, and deleting. The three functions are pretty similar, with the difference being that I simply set the CommandText property of the SQLCommand to the appropriate T-SQL statement, depending on whether I want to insert, update, or delete data. This is a fairly complex system that allows inserting, updating, and deleting from the same page and also queries the database to populate the DataGrid and the two DropDownLists with the EmployeeID in them.

You can see the result of this page in Figure 10.6, and as you reflect on the code example, realize that each individual function is really a SQLCommand statement unto itself and can be used as an example of how each of these functions can be used individually.

FIGURE 10.6

The SQLCommand's ExecuteNonQuery() method enables you to use the SQLCommand to execute inserts, updates, and deletes.

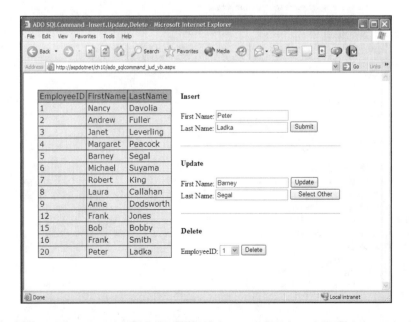

If you look at the `UpdateCommand` function, you will notice the `Command` object's text has `@FirstName` and `@LastName` in the string. These are parameters of the `Command` object that act as placeholders for values that you intend to replace.

```
OurCommand = New SqlCommand("Update Employees Set Firstname = @FirstName, LastName
➥= @LastName Where EmployeeID = " + EmployeeID, OurConnection)
    OurCommand.Parameters.Add("@FirstName", SqlDbType.Varchar, 10).Value =
    ➥UpdateFirstName.Text
    OurCommand.Parameters.Add("@LastName", SqlDbType.Varchar, 20).Value =
    ➥UpdateLastName.Text
```

The `Command.Parameters.Add().Value` method is the way to replace a placeholder or parameter in `Command.Text`. The three parameters that you pass to the `Add()` method are the name of the parameter to replace or receive, the DataType of the Parameter, and the size of the data being contained in the Parameter. The `SqlDBType` namespace contains the DataTypes that are specific to SQL Server and information about these DataTypes can be found in the .NET Framework SDK at the following address:

```
ms-help://MS.NETFrameworkSDK/cpref/html/frlrfsystemdatasqltypes.htm
```

Inserts, updates, and deletes are performed in exactly the same manner as they are when you query the database: First you create a connection, and then you build the command. But rather than fill `DataSets` or `DataReaders` with data from the command, you use the `ExecuteNonQuery()` method, which then performs what the `CommandText` states, without expecting data to be returned from the T-SQL statement.

DataAdapter

The `DataAdapter`, as I've said earlier, is a set of commands and database connections that are used to fill the `DataSet` object and update the database. It provides several ways to communicate between the database and dataset, including an automated method to build and execute T-SQL statements against your database, based from data contained in a `DataSet`.

InsertCommand, UpdateCommand, DeleteCommand

These properties of the `DataAdapter` work almost exactly the same as writing the T-SQL statements into the `Command` object. As a matter of fact, these properties are instances of the `SQLCommand` or `OledbCommand` object, so you deal with them in exactly the same way. The difference is you use the `Update()` method of the `DataAdapter`, rather than the `ExecuteNonQuery()` method of the `Command`, to execute the change. You will use the `Update()` method, whether you are using the `InsertCommand`, `UpdateCommand`, or `DeleteCommand`.

This is what opens the doors for making edits to a `DataTable` in a `DataSet` and then having this affect the values of the database afterwards. In other words, you can insert, update, or delete records in a `DataTable`, then after you conclude editing the `DataTable`, call the `DataAdapter`'s `Update()` method, and this method will insert, update, or delete records according to edits you've made to the `DataTable`.

What I show in the following code example is just the `UpdateCommand` to demonstrate a straightforward example of editing five rows in a `DataTable` and then back to the data source using the `DataAdapter`'s `Update()` method.

Visual Basic .NET—ado_dataadapter_iud_sql_vb.aspx

```
<%@ page language="vb" runat="server"%>
<%@ Import Namespace="System.Data"%>
<%@ Import Namespace="System.Data.SqlClient"%>
<script runat=server>

Sub Page_Load()
    If IsPostBack Then
        Update()
    End If
    DataSub()
End Sub

Sub DataSub()
    dim OurConnection as SqlConnection
    dim OurCommand as SqlCommand
    dim OurDataAdapter as SqlDataAdapter
    dim OurDataSet as new DataSet()
    OurConnection = new SqlConnection("Server=server;
    ➥uid=newriders;pwd=password;database=Northwind")
    OurCommand = new SqlCommand("Select Top 5 ProductID, ProductName, UnitPrice
    ➥From Products",OurConnection)
    OurDataAdapter = new SqlDataAdapter(OurCommand)
    OurDataAdapter.Fill(OurDataSet, "Products")
    OurDataGrid.DataSource = OurDataSet.Tables("Products")
    DataBind()
```

```
    ProductName1.Text = OurDataSet.Tables("Products").Rows(0).Item("ProductName")
    UnitPrice1.Text = OurDataSet.Tables("Products").Rows(0).Item("UnitPrice")
    ProductName2.Text = OurDataSet.Tables("Products").Rows(1).Item("ProductName")
    UnitPrice2.Text = OurDataSet.Tables("Products").Rows(1).Item("UnitPrice")
    ProductName3.Text = OurDataSet.Tables("Products").Rows(2).Item("ProductName")
    UnitPrice3.Text = OurDataSet.Tables("Products").Rows(2).Item("UnitPrice")
    ProductName4.Text = OurDataSet.Tables("Products").Rows(3).Item("ProductName")
    UnitPrice4.Text = OurDataSet.Tables("Products").Rows(3).Item("UnitPrice")
    ProductName5.Text = OurDataSet.Tables("Products").Rows(4).Item("ProductName")
    UnitPrice5.Text = OurDataSet.Tables("Products").Rows(4).Item("UnitPrice")
End Sub

Sub Update()
    dim OurConnection as SqlConnection = new SqlConnection("Server=server;
    ➥uid=newriders;pwd=password;database=Northwind")
    dim OurCommand as SqlCommand = new SqlCommand("Select Top 5 ProductID,
    ➥ProductName, UnitPrice From Products",OurConnection)
    dim OurDataAdapter as SqlDataAdapter = new SqlDataAdapter(OurCommand)
    dim OurDataSet as new DataSet()
    dim OurTable as DataTable
    OurDataAdapter.Fill(OurDataSet, "Products")
    OurDataAdapter.UpdateCommand = new SqlCommand("Update Products Set ProductName
    ➥= @ProductName, UnitPrice = @UnitPrice Where ProductID = @ProductID",
    ➥OurConnection)
    OurDataAdapter.UpdateCommand.Parameters.Add("@ProductName", SqlDbType.VarChar,
    ➥40, "ProductName")
    OurDataAdapter.UpdateCommand.Parameters.Add("@UnitPrice", SqlDbType.Money, 8,
    ➥"UnitPrice")
    OurDataAdapter.UpdateCommand.Parameters.Add("@ProductID", SqlDbType.Int, 4,
    ➥"ProductID")
    OurTable = OurDataSet.Tables("Products")
    OurTable.Rows(0).Item("ProductName") = ProductName1.Text
    OurTable.Rows(0).Item("UnitPrice") = UnitPrice1.Text
    OurTable.Rows(1).Item("ProductName") = ProductName2.Text
    OurTable.Rows(1).Item("UnitPrice") = UnitPrice2.Text
    OurTable.Rows(2).Item("ProductName") = ProductName3.Text
    OurTable.Rows(2).Item("UnitPrice") = UnitPrice3.Text
    OurTable.Rows(3).Item("ProductName") = ProductName4.Text
    OurTable.Rows(3).Item("UnitPrice") = UnitPrice4.Text
    OurTable.Rows(4).Item("ProductName") = ProductName5.Text
    OurTable.Rows(4).Item("UnitPrice") = UnitPrice5.Text
    OurDataAdapter.Update(OurTable)
End Sub
</script>
<html>
<head>
<title>ADO DataSet</title>
</head>
<body bgcolor="#FFFFFF" text="#000000">
<form runat="server">
<ASP:DataGrid id="OurDataGrid"
    BorderWidth="1"
    BorderColor="#000000"
```

continues

Visual Basic .NET—(continued)

```
            CellPadding="3"
            CellSpacing="0"
            Font-Name="Verdana"
            Font-Size="12px"
            HeaderStyle-BackColor="#AAAAAA"
            ItemStyle-BackColor="#EEEEEE"
            AutoGenerateColumns="false"
            runat="server">
            <Columns>
                <asp:BoundColumn
                    HeaderText="Product ID"
                    DataField="ProductID"
                    ReadOnly="True" />
                <asp:BoundColumn
                    HeaderText="Product Name"
                    DataField="ProductName" />
                <asp:BoundColumn
                    HeaderText="Unit Price"
                    DataField="UnitPrice"
                    DataFormatString="{0:c}"/>
            </Columns>
</asp:DataGrid>
<table>
<tr>
<td>Product Name</td>
<td>Unit Price</td>
</tr>
<tr>
<td><asp:TextBox id="ProductName1" runat="server" /></td>
<td><asp:TextBox id="UnitPrice1" runat="server" /></td>
</tr>
<tr>
<td><asp:TextBox id="ProductName2" runat="server" /></td>
<td><asp:TextBox id="UnitPrice2" runat="server" /></td>
</tr>
<tr>
<td><asp:TextBox id="ProductName3" runat="server" /></td>
<td><asp:TextBox id="UnitPrice3" runat="server" /></td>
</tr>
<tr>
<td><asp:TextBox id="ProductName4" runat="server" /></td>
<td><asp:TextBox id="UnitPrice4" runat="server" /></td>
</tr>
<tr>
<td><asp:TextBox id="ProductName5" runat="server" /></td>
<td><asp:TextBox id="UnitPrice5" runat="server" /></td>
</tr>
</table>
<asp:Button id="Submit" text="Submit" runat="server" />
</form>
</body>
</html>
```

C#—ado_dataadapter_iud_sql_cs.aspx

```csharp
<%@ page language="c#" runat="server"%>
<%@ Import Namespace="System.Data"%>
<%@ Import Namespace="System.Data.SqlClient"%>
<script runat=server>

void Page_Load() {
    if (IsPostBack) {
        Update();
    }
    DataSub();
}

void DataSub()      {
    SqlConnection OurConnection;
    SqlCommand OurCommand;
    SqlDataAdapter OurDataAdapter;
    DataSet OurDataSet = new DataSet();
    OurConnection = new SqlConnection("Server=server;
    ➥uid=newriders;pwd=password;database=Northwind");
    OurCommand = new SqlCommand("Select Top 5 ProductID, ProductName, UnitPrice
    ➥From Products",OurConnection);
    OurDataAdapter = new SqlDataAdapter(OurCommand);
    OurDataAdapter.Fill(OurDataSet, "Products");
    OurDataGrid.DataSource = OurDataSet.Tables["Products"];
    DataBind();
    ProductName1.Text = OurDataSet.Tables["Products"]
    ➥.Rows[0]["ProductName"].ToString();
    UnitPrice1.Text = OurDataSet.Tables["Products"]
    ➥.Rows[0]["UnitPrice"].ToString();
    ProductName2.Text = OurDataSet.Tables["Products"]
    ➥.Rows[1]["ProductName"].ToString();
    UnitPrice2.Text = OurDataSet.Tables["Products"]
    ➥.Rows[1]["UnitPrice"].ToString();
    ProductName3.Text = OurDataSet.Tables["Products"]
    ➥.Rows[2]["ProductName"].ToString();
    UnitPrice3.Text = OurDataSet.Tables["Products"]
    ➥.Rows[2]["UnitPrice"].ToString();
    ProductName4.Text = OurDataSet.Tables["Products"]
    ➥.Rows[3]["ProductName"].ToString();
    UnitPrice4.Text = OurDataSet.Tables["Products"]
    ➥.Rows[3]["UnitPrice"].ToString();
    ProductName5.Text = OurDataSet.Tables["Products"]
    ➥.Rows[4]["ProductName"].ToString();
    UnitPrice5.Text = OurDataSet.Tables["Products"]
    ➥.Rows[4]["UnitPrice"].ToString();

}

void Update() {
    SqlConnection OurConnection = new SqlConnection("Server=server;
    ➥uid=newriders;pwd=password;database=Northwind");
```

continues

C#—(continued)

```csharp
    SqlCommand OurCommand = new SqlCommand("Select Top 5 ProductID, ProductName,
    ➡UnitPrice From Products",OurConnection);
    SqlDataAdapter OurDataAdapter = new SqlDataAdapter(OurCommand);
    DataSet OurDataSet = new DataSet();
    DataTable OurTable;
    OurDataAdapter.Fill(OurDataSet, "Products");
    OurDataAdapter.UpdateCommand = new SqlCommand("Update Products Set ProductName
    ➡= @ProductName, UnitPrice = @UnitPrice Where ProductID = @ProductID",
    ➡OurConnection);
    OurDataAdapter.UpdateCommand.Parameters.Add("@ProductName", SqlDbType.VarChar,
    ➡40, "ProductName");
    OurDataAdapter.UpdateCommand.Parameters.Add("@UnitPrice", SqlDbType.Money, 8,
    ➡"UnitPrice");
    OurDataAdapter.UpdateCommand.Parameters.Add("@ProductID", SqlDbType.Int, 4,
    ➡"ProductID");
    OurTable = OurDataSet.Tables["Products"];
    OurTable.Rows[0]["ProductName"] = ProductName1.Text;
    OurTable.Rows[0]["UnitPrice"] = UnitPrice1.Text;
    OurTable.Rows[1]["ProductName"] = ProductName2.Text;
    OurTable.Rows[1]["UnitPrice"] = UnitPrice2.Text;
    OurTable.Rows[2]["ProductName"] = ProductName3.Text;
    OurTable.Rows[2]["UnitPrice"] = UnitPrice3.Text;
    OurTable.Rows[3]["ProductName"] = ProductName4.Text;
    OurTable.Rows[3]["UnitPrice"] = UnitPrice4.Text;
    OurTable.Rows[4]["ProductName"] = ProductName5.Text;
    OurTable.Rows[4]["UnitPrice"] = UnitPrice5.Text;
    OurDataAdapter.Update(OurTable);
}
</script>
<html>
<head>
<title>ADO DataSet</title>
</head>
<body bgcolor="#FFFFFF" text="#000000">
<form runat="server">
<ASP:DataGrid id="OurDataGrid"
    BorderWidth="1"
    BorderColor="#000000"
    CellPadding="3"
    CellSpacing="0"
    Font-Name="Verdana"
    Font-Size="12px"
    HeaderStyle-BackColor="#AAAAAA"
    ItemStyle-BackColor="#EEEEEE"
    AutoGenerateColumns="false"
    runat="server">
    <Columns>
```

```
            <asp:BoundColumn
                HeaderText="Product ID"
                DataField="ProductID"
                ReadOnly="True" />
            <asp:BoundColumn
                HeaderText="Product Name"
                DataField="ProductName" />
            <asp:BoundColumn
                HeaderText="Unit Price"
                DataField="UnitPrice"
                DataFormatString="{0:c}"/>
        </Columns>
</asp:DataGrid>
<table>
<tr>
<td>Product Name</td>
<td>Unit Price</td>
</tr>
<tr>
<td><asp:TextBox id="ProductName1" runat="server" /></td>
<td><asp:TextBox id="UnitPrice1" runat="server" /></td>
</tr>
<tr>
<td><asp:TextBox id="ProductName2" runat="server" /></td>
<td><asp:TextBox id="UnitPrice2" runat="server" /></td>
</tr>
<tr>
<td><asp:TextBox id="ProductName3" runat="server" /></td>
<td><asp:TextBox id="UnitPrice3" runat="server" /></td>
</tr>
<tr>
<td><asp:TextBox id="ProductName4" runat="server" /></td>
<td><asp:TextBox id="UnitPrice4" runat="server" /></td>
</tr>
<tr>
<td><asp:TextBox id="ProductName5" runat="server" /></td>
<td><asp:TextBox id="UnitPrice5" runat="server" /></td>
</tr>
</table>
<asp:Button id="Submit" text="Submit" runat="server" />
</form>
</body>
</html>
```

If you look at the results in Figure 10.7, you can see that I first affected the rows in the DataTable that I wanted to edit, then called the Update() method to mirror those changes back to the database.

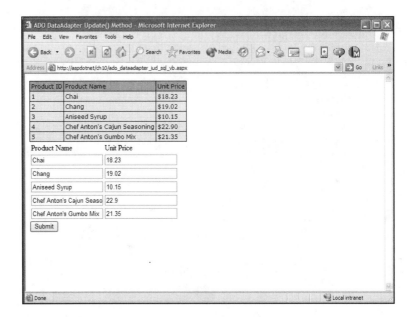

There are many ways to take advantage of these properties of the `DataAdapter` and suspend connection to the database until all changes have been made to the `DataTable`.

CommandBuilder

The `DataAdapter`'s `InsertCommand`, `UpdateCommand`, and `DeleteCommand` provide a great way to pass data back and forth between the `DataSet` object and your database. But wouldn't it be great if the `DataAdapter` could automatically build the `InsertCommand`, `UpdateCommand`, and `DeleteCommand` for you? The `CommandBuilder` object does just that. It provides a way to automatically generate commands to a single table and reconcile changes made to a `DataSet` with your database.

This is pretty cool when you think about inserting, updating, and deleting rows from a `DataSet` and then being able to create an instance of the `CommandBuilder` object and have it dynamically handle reconciling the changes back to the database.

Visual Basic .NET—**ado_dataadapter_iud_cb_sql_vb.aspx**

```
<%@ page language="vb" runat="server"%>
<%@ Import Namespace="System.Data"%>
<%@ Import Namespace="System.Data.SqlClient"%>
```

```
<script runat=server>

Sub Page_Load()
    If Not IsPostBack Then
        DataSub()
    End If
End Sub

Sub DataSub()
    dim OurConnection as SqlConnection
    dim OurCommand as SqlCommand
    dim OurDataAdapter as SqlDataAdapter
    dim OurDataSet as new DataSet()
    OurConnection = new SqlConnection("Server=server;
    ➥uid=newriders;pwd=password;database=Northwind")
    OurCommand = new SqlCommand("Select ProductID, ProductName, UnitPrice From
    ➥Products",OurConnection)
    OurDataAdapter = new SqlDataAdapter(OurCommand)
    OurDataAdapter.Fill(OurDataSet, "Products")
    OurDataGrid.DataSource = OurDataSet.Tables("Products")
    DataBind()
End Sub

Sub Edit(sender As Object, e As DataGridCommandEventArgs)
    OurDataGrid.EditItemIndex = e.Item.ItemIndex
    DataSub
End Sub

Sub Cancel(sender As Object, e As DataGridCommandEventArgs)
    OurDataGrid.EditItemIndex = -1
    DataSub
End Sub

Sub Update(sender As Object, e As DataGridCommandEventArgs)
    dim OurConnection as SqlConnection = new SqlConnection("Server=server;
    ➥uid=newriders;pwd=password;database=Northwind")
    dim OurCommand as SqlCommand = new SqlCommand("Select ProductID, ProductName,
    ➥UnitPrice From Products",OurConnection)
    dim OurDataAdapter as SqlDataAdapter = new SqlDataAdapter(OurCommand)
    dim OurCommandBuilder as SqlCommandBuilder = new
    ➥SqlCommandBuilder(OurDataAdapter)
    dim OurDataSet as new DataSet()
    dim OurDataTable as DataTable
    dim OurDataRow as DataRow
    dim PrimaryKeys(1) as DataColumn
    OurDataAdapter.Fill(OurDataSet, "Products")
    OurDataTable = OurDataSet.Tables("Products")
    PrimaryKeys(0) = OurDataTable.Columns("ProductID")
    OurDataTable.PrimaryKey = PrimaryKeys
    OurDataRow = OurDataTable.Rows.Find(e.Item.Cells(0).Text)
    OurDataRow(1) = CType(e.Item.Cells(1).Controls(0), TextBox).Text
    OurDataRow(2) = CType(CType(e.Item.Cells(2).Controls(0), TextBox).Text,
    ➥Decimal)
```

continues

Visual Basic .NET—(continued)

```
        OurDataGrid.EditItemIndex = -1
        OurDataAdapter.Update(OurDataTable)
        OurDataGrid.DataSource = OurDataTable
        OurDataGrid.DataBind()
End Sub



</script>
<html>
<head>
<title>ADO DataSet</title>
</head>
<body bgcolor="#FFFFFF" text="#000000">
<form runat="server">
<ASP:DataGrid id="OurDataGrid"
    BorderWidth="1"
    BorderColor="#000000"
    CellPadding="3"
    CellSpacing="0"
    Font-Name="Verdana"
    Font-Size="12px"
    OnEditCommand="Edit"
    OnCancelCommand="Cancel"
    OnUpdateCommand="Update"
    HeaderStyle-BackColor="#AAAAAA"
    ItemStyle-BackColor="#EEEEEE"
    AutoGenerateColumns="false"
    runat="server">
    <Columns>
        <asp:BoundColumn
            HeaderText="Product ID"
            DataField="ProductID"
            ReadOnly="True" />
        <asp:BoundColumn
            HeaderText="Product Name"
            DataField="ProductName" />
        <asp:BoundColumn
            HeaderText="Unit Price"
            DataField="UnitPrice"
            DataFormatString="{0:c}"/>
        <asp:EditCommandColumn
            HeaderText="Edit"
            EditText="Edit"
            CancelText="Cancel"
            UpdateText="Update"/>
    </Columns>
</asp:DataGrid>
</form>
</body>
</html>
```

C#—ado_dataadapter_iud_cb_sql_cs.aspx

```
<%@ page language="c#" runat="server"%>
<%@ Import Namespace="System.Data"%>
<%@ Import Namespace="System.Data.SqlClient"%>
<script runat=server>

void Page_Load() {
    if (!IsPostBack) {
        DataSub();
    }
}

void DataSub() {
    SqlConnection OurConnection;
    SqlCommand OurCommand;
    SqlDataAdapter OurDataAdapter;
    DataSet OurDataSet = new DataSet();
    OurConnection = new SqlConnection("Server=server;
    ➡uid=newriders;pwd=password;database=Northwind");
    OurCommand = new SqlCommand("Select ProductID, ProductName, UnitPrice From
    ➡Products",OurConnection);
    OurDataAdapter = new SqlDataAdapter(OurCommand);
    OurDataAdapter.Fill(OurDataSet, "Products");
    OurDataGrid.DataSource = OurDataSet.Tables["Products"];
    DataBind();
}

void Edit(Object sender, DataGridCommandEventArgs e) {
    OurDataGrid.EditItemIndex = e.Item.ItemIndex;
    DataSub();
}

void Cancel(Object sender, DataGridCommandEventArgs e) {
    OurDataGrid.EditItemIndex = -1;
    DataSub();
}

void Update(Object sender, DataGridCommandEventArgs e) {
    SqlConnection OurConnection = new SqlConnection("Server=server;
    ➡uid=newriders;pwd=password;database=Northwind");
    SqlCommand OurCommand = new SqlCommand("Select ProductID, ProductName,
    ➡UnitPrice From Products",OurConnection);
    SqlDataAdapter OurDataAdapter = new SqlDataAdapter(OurCommand);
    DataSet OurDataSet = new DataSet();
    SqlCommandBuilder OurCommandBuilder = new SqlCommandBuilder(OurDataAdapter);
    DataTable OurDataTable;
    DataRow OurDataRow;
    DataColumn[] PrimaryKeys = new DataColumn[1];
    OurDataAdapter.Fill(OurDataSet, "Products");
    OurDataTable = OurDataSet.Tables["Products"];
    PrimaryKeys[0] = OurDataTable.Columns["ProductID"];
    OurDataTable.PrimaryKey = PrimaryKeys;
```

continues

C#—(continued)

```csharp
    OurDataRow = OurDataTable.Rows.Find(e.Item.Cells[0].Text);
    OurDataRow[1] = (e.Item.Cells[1].Controls[0] as TextBox).Text;
    OurDataRow[2] = Decimal.Parse((e.Item.Cells[2].Controls[0] as
    ➥TextBox).Text.Replace("$", ""));
    OurDataGrid.EditItemIndex = -1;
    OurDataAdapter.Update(OurDataTable);
    OurDataGrid.DataSource = OurDataTable;
    OurDataGrid.DataBind();
}


</script>
<html>
<head>
<title>ADO DataSet</title>
</head>
<body bgcolor="#FFFFFF" text="#000000">
<form runat="server">
<ASP:DataGrid id="OurDataGrid"
    BorderWidth="1"
    BorderColor="#000000"
    CellPadding="3"
    CellSpacing="0"
    Font-Name="Verdana"
    Font-Size="12px"
    OnEditCommand="Edit"
    OnCancelCommand="Cancel"
    OnUpdateCommand="Update"
    HeaderStyle-BackColor="#AAAAAA"
    ItemStyle-BackColor="#EEEEEE"
    AutoGenerateColumns="false"
    runat="server">
    <Columns>
        <asp:BoundColumn
            HeaderText="Product ID"
            DataField="ProductID"
            ReadOnly="True" />
        <asp:BoundColumn
            HeaderText="Product Name"
            DataField="ProductName" />
        <asp:BoundColumn
            HeaderText="Unit Price"
            DataField="UnitPrice"
            DataFormatString="{0:c}"/>
        <asp:EditCommandColumn
            HeaderText="Edit"
            EditText="Edit"
            CancelText="Cancel"
            UpdateText="Update"/>
    </Columns>
</asp:DataGrid>
</form>
</body>
</html>
```

As you can see in the code example, the `DataAdapter` was sent as a parameter to the `CommandBuilder` object so it knows which `DataAdapter` to build the commands for. Then the `DataAdapter`'s `Update()` method was called, with the `DataSet` and `DataTable` passed as parameters. The rest is truly magic. The `CommandBuilder` watches the rows of the `DataSet` to determine whether they've changed; if they have, it creates the proper T-SQL statement to properly reconcile the data back to the database.

Stored Procedures

One of the great advantages of Microsoft SQL Server and Oracle databases are stored procedures. Unfortunately, Microsoft Access doesn't support them. The simple explanation is that they are just Transact SQL statements that are stored in the database. This makes compartmentalizing function that is associated with the database, in the database a bit more real. But there is more to it than that.

Stored procedures allow true logical function before data is ever passed across the connection to ASP.NET pages. You can perform logical functions—such as branching—right within SQL Server, so you are really only delivering data through ADO.NET that you need.

Stored procedures also allow multi-part interaction with your database, as well. For instance, imagine if you wanted to insert data into two separate tables and then retrieve the unique identity or primary key of the newly inserted row in one of the tables. Using the standard methods would involve some very complicated code within your ASP.NET pages.

Stored procedures enable you to write all the code encapsulated in a single procedure. You pass in the information you want to insert as parameters to the stored procedure, and it handles it from there. You can also have one of the functions of the procedure be retrieving the primary key of the newly inserted information from the table you want and passing it back to you as an output parameter.

So essentially, you pass parameters in, the stored procedure does the work, and it passes the data back out. 1, 2, 3. But the advantages do not end there.

Stored procedures are also compiled pieces of code that reside in the SQL Server's memory. They don't have to be "processed" every time they are called. They are just sitting there in memory waiting to be called and BANG!!! They do their work. In other words, in most cases there are significant performance advantages to using stored procedures.

Querying with Stored Procedures

The following examples show two simple stored procedures that perform select statements. The first one simply returns the CategoryID and CategoryName of every row in the Categories table into an SqlDataReader. I will use this to populate a DropDownList server control so I can pick what products I want to see on the page.

Stored Procedure—ProductTypes

```
CREATE PROCEDURE ProductTypes

AS

Select CategoryID, CategoryName From Categories

GO
```

The second procedure has two parameters in it: one that supplies a value to the stored procedure, and one that the stored procedure returns. These are called *input parameters* and *output parameters*, respectively. The input parameter passing in is the CategoryID that was selected from the DropDownList server control. The stored procedure uses that CategoryID to filter the Products table by that value against the CategoryID column. The procedure returns the proper products according to the value of the @CategoryID input parameter provided. The @AveragePrice output parameter is set to return the average unit price of the selected category of products. SQL Server's Avg() function performs that calculation.

Stored Procedure—ProductsByType

```
CREATE PROCEDURE ProductsByType

    @CategoryID int,
    @AveragePrice    Money output

AS

Select  ProductName,UnitPrice From Products where CategoryID = @CategoryID
Select @AveragePrice = Avg(UnitPrice) From Products where CategoryID = @CategoryID

GO
```

Now, as you look at the following code, notice that the DropDownList server control is populated with the contents of the SqlDataReader if it's the first time the Page_Load event has fired. If the page is posting back, the selected product category is sent to the stored procedure and a datagrid is populated with the returned contents of the first statement. The average price of the selected products is returned in the @AveragePrice Output parameter.

Visual Basic .NET—**ado_sproc_select_vb.aspx**

```
<%@ page language="vb" runat="server" %>
<%@ Import Namespace="System.Data" %>
<%@ Import Namespace="System.Data.SqlClient" %>
<script runat=server>
Sub Page_Load()
    if (Not IsPostBack) then
        dim OurConnection as SqlConnection
        dim OurCommand as SqlCommand
        dim OurDataReader as SqlDataReader

        OurConnection = New SqlConnection("Server=server;
        ➥uid=newriders;pwd=password;database=Northwind")
        OurCommand = New SqlCommand("ProductTypes" ,OurConnection)
        OurCommand.CommandType = CommandType.StoredProcedure
        OurConnection.Open()
        OurDataReader = OurCommand.ExecuteReader()
        OurDropDown.DataSource = OurDataReader
        OurDropDown.DataTextField="CategoryName"
        OurDropDown.DataValueField="CategoryID"
        OurDropDown.DataBind()

        OurDataReader.Close()
        OurConnection.Close()
    else
        dim OurConnection as SqlConnection
        dim OurCommand as SqlCommand
        dim OurDataAdapter as SqlDataAdapter
        dim OurDataSet as new DataSet

        OurConnection = New SqlConnection("Server=server;
        ➥uid=newriders;pwd=password;database=Northwind")
        OurCommand = New SqlCommand("ProductsByType" ,OurConnection)
        OurCommand.CommandType = CommandType.StoredProcedure
        OurCommand.Parameters.Add("@CategoryID", SqlDbType.Int, 4).Value =
        ➥OurDropDown.SelectedItem.Value
        OurCommand.Parameters.Add("@AveragePrice", sqlDBType.Float).Direction =
        ➥ParameterDirection.Output
        OurDataAdapter = new SqlDataAdapter(OurCommand)
        OurDataAdapter.Fill(OurDataSet, "Products")
        OurDataGrid.DataSource = OurDataSet.Tables("Products")
        DataBind()
```

continues

Visual Basic .NET—(continued)

```
          dim UnitAve as Double = OurCommand.Parameters("@AveragePrice").Value
          OurLabel.Text = "Average Unit Price of All Products: " +
          ➥UnitAve.ToString("C")
          end if
End Sub

</script>
<html>
<head>
<title>ADO Stored Procedures - Select</title>
</head>
<body bgcolor="#FFFFFF" text="#000000">
<form runat="server">
<asp:DropDownList id="OurDropDown" runat="server" />
<asp:Button id="OurButton" Text="Get Products" runat="server" /><br><br>
<ASP:DataGrid
    id="OurDataGrid"
    EnableViewState="false"
    BorderWidth="1"
    BorderColor="#000000"
    CellPadding="3"
    CellSpacing="0"
    Font-Name="Verdana"
    HeaderStyle-BackColor="#AAAAAA"
    ItemStyle-BackColor="#EEEEEE"
    AutoGenerateColumns="False"
    runat="server">
    <Columns>
        <asp:BoundColumn
            HeaderText="Product Name"
            DataField="ProductName" />
        <asp:BoundColumn
            HeaderText="Unit Price"
            DataField="UnitPrice"
            DataFormatString="{0:c}"/>
    </Columns>
</asp:DataGrid>
<asp:Label id="OurLabel"  Font-Name="Verdana" runat="server" />
</form>
</body>
</html>
```

C#—ado_sproc_select_cs.aspx

```
<%@ page language="c#" runat="server" %>
<%@ Import Namespace="System.Data" %>
<%@ Import Namespace="System.Data.SqlClient" %>
<script runat=server>
void Page_Load() {
```

```
    if (!IsPostBack) {
        SqlConnection OurConnection;
        SqlCommand OurCommand;
        SqlDataReader OurDataReader;

        OurConnection = new SqlConnection("Server=server;
        ➥uid=newriders;pwd=password;database=Northwind");
        OurCommand = new SqlCommand("ProductTypes" ,OurConnection);
        OurCommand.CommandType = CommandType.StoredProcedure;
        OurConnection.Open();
        OurDataReader = OurCommand.ExecuteReader();
        OurDropDown.DataSource = OurDataReader;
        OurDropDown.DataTextField="CategoryName";
        OurDropDown.DataValueField="CategoryID";
        OurDropDown.DataBind();
        OurDataReader.Close();
        OurConnection.Close();
    }
    else {
        SqlConnection OurConnection;
        SqlCommand OurCommand;
        SqlDataAdapter OurDataAdapter;
        DataSet OurDataSet = new DataSet();

        OurConnection = new SqlConnection("Server=server;
        ➥uid=newriders;pwd=password;database=Northwind");
        OurCommand = new SqlCommand("ProductsByType" ,OurConnection);
        OurCommand.CommandType = CommandType.StoredProcedure;
        OurCommand.Parameters.Add("@CategoryID", SqlDbType.Int, 4).Value =
        ➥OurDropDown.SelectedItem.Value;
        OurCommand.Parameters.Add("@AveragePrice", SqlDbType.Float).Direction =
        ➥ParameterDirection.Output;
        OurDataAdapter = new SqlDataAdapter(OurCommand);
        OurDataAdapter.Fill(OurDataSet, "Products");
        OurDataGrid.DataSource = OurDataSet.Tables["Products"];
        DataBind();
        Double UnitAve = (Double)OurCommand.Parameters["@AveragePrice"].Value;
        OurLabel.Text = "Average Unit Price: " + UnitAve.ToString("C");
        }
}

</script>
<html>
<head>
<title>ADO Stored Procedure - Select</title>
</head>
<body bgcolor="#FFFFFF" text="#000000">
<form runat="server">
<asp:DropDownList id="OurDropDown" runat="server" />
<asp:Button id="OurButton" Text="Get Products" runat="server" /><br><br>
<ASP:DataGrid
    id="OurDataGrid"
```

continues

C#—(continued)

```
        EnableViewState="false"
        BorderWidth="1"
        BorderColor="#000000"
        CellPadding="3"
        CellSpacing="0"
        Font-Name="Verdana"
        HeaderStyle-BackColor="#AAAAAA"
        ItemStyle-BackColor="#EEEEEE"
        AutoGenerateColumns="False"
        runat="server">
        <Columns>
            <asp:BoundColumn
                HeaderText="Product Name"
                DataField="ProductName" />
            <asp:BoundColumn
                HeaderText="Unit Price"
                DataField="UnitPrice"
                DataFormatString="{0:c}"/>
        </Columns>
    </asp:DataGrid><br>
    <asp:Label id="OurLabel"  Font-Name="Verdana" runat="server" />
    </form>
    </body>
    </html>
```

As you can see in Figure 10.8, the DropDownList was properly populated, the input parameter from the DropDownList has both filtered the Products table and caused the @AveragePrice output parameter to perform only the Avg() function on the selected products. The @AveragePrice is displayed as the Text parameter of OurLabel.

But querying data isn't the only thing that you can do with stored procedures. As I said, you can perform all the functions that you can with T-SQL statements, including inserting, updating, and deleting.

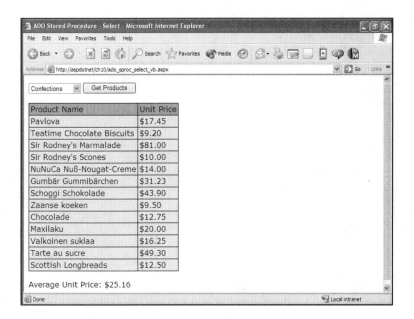

FIGURE 10.8

*Stored procedures
let you perform
multiple functions on
the database server,
as opposed to
performing the logic
on the web server.*

Inserting, Updating, and Deleting with Stored Procedures

Stored procedures add a lot of flexibility to processing data. When using standard T-SQL statements to perform insert, update, and delete functions, you are kind of pigeonholed into doing things in a certain way. Stored procedures not only provide enhanced performance in most cases, but they also give you a much broader way to approach creating functions in your ASP.NET applications.

Here you can look back at the example that I used for the command version of inserting, updating, and deleting, but now all the functions are performed within the confines of a stored procedure. Each function within this ASP.NET page calls the same stored procedure and sends the Action parameter so I can branch within the stored procedure to execute the insert, update, or delete function.

Stored Procedure—`Products_IUD`

```
CREATE PROCEDURE [Products_IUD]

    @Action varchar(10),
    @EmployeeID Int,
    @FirstName varchar(10),
    @LastName varchar(20)

AS
    if @Action = 'Insert'
        Insert Into Employees (FirstName, LastName)
                Values (@FirstName, @LastName)

    if @Action = 'Update'
        Update Employees Set Firstname = @FirstName,
                LastName = @LastName
                Where EmployeeID = @EmployeeID

    if @Action = 'Delete'
        Delete Employees Where EmployeeID = @EmployeeID
GO
```

As you can see, there are three branches in the stored procedure. You can do a whole host of things within a stored procedure—much more than I can cover here—but this shows a simple branch that executes an insert, update, or delete function, depending on which branch shows true.

Stored procedures also make cleaning up the code a bit easier, because the stored procedure expects uniform input parameters no matter what branch is executing. What I've done is utilize the `CommandName` property of the `Button` server control to pass the action that's being performed and to have all three types of action be performed in the same function, instead of having a function each for the insert, update, and delete.

I could have achieved this the same way with the `SqlCommand`, but it would make things a bit messy. I would have needed to build the T-SQL statements through concatenation of strings and the server controls that are delivering the data. I would be restricted from using the `Parameters.Add()` method because all three statements require different parameters.

The following is the more consolidated code that parallels the function of the
`SqlCommand` insert, update, and delete functions covered earlier in this chapter.

Visual Basic .NET—**ado_sproc_iud_vb.aspx**

```
<%@ page language="vb" runat="server" %>
<%@ Import Namespace="System.Data" %>
<%@ Import Namespace="System.Data.SqlClient" %>

<script runat=server>
Sub Page_Load()
    If (Not IsPostBack) then
        LoadData()
    End If
End Sub

Sub LoadData()
    dim OurConnection as SqlConnection
    dim OurCommand as SqlCommand
    dim OurDataAdapter as SQLDataAdapter
    dim OurDataSet as New DataSet()

    OurConnection = New SqlConnection("Server=server;
    ➥uid=newriders;pwd=password;database=Northwind")
    OurConnection.Open()
    OurCommand = New SqlCommand("Select Top 15 EmployeeID,FirstName,LastName from
    ➥Employees" ,OurConnection)
    OurDataAdapter = New SQLDataAdapter(OurCommand)
    OurDataAdapter.Fill(OurDataSet, "Employees")
    OurDataGrid.DataSource=OurDataSet.Tables("Employees")
    UpdateEmployeeID.DataSource=OurDataSet.Tables("Employees")
    DeleteEmployeeID.DataSource=OurDataSet.Tables("Employees")
    DataBind()


End Sub

Sub UpdateSetup(sender As Object, e As System.EventArgs)

    dim SelectedID as String = UpdateEmployeeID.SelectedItem.Value
    dim OurConnection as SqlConnection
    dim OurCommand as SqlCommand
    dim OurDataReader2 as SqlDataReader

    UpdateSelect.Visible="False"
    UpdateTextBoxes.Visible="True"
    UpdateButton.CommandArgument = SelectedID

    OurConnection = New SqlConnection("Server=server;
    ➥uid=newriders;pwd=password;database=Northwind")
    OurConnection.Open()
```

continues

Visual Basic .NET—(continued)

```vbnet
    OurCommand = New SqlCommand("Select FirstName, LastName From Employees Where
    ➥EmployeeID = " + SelectedID ,OurConnection)
    OurDataReader2 = OurCommand.ExecuteReader()
    OurDataReader2.Read()
    UpdateFirstName.Text = OurDataReader2("FirstName")
    UpdateLastName.Text = OurDataReader2("LastName")
    OurConnection.Close()
    OurDataReader2.Close()

    LoadData()
End Sub

Sub UpdateReset(sender As Object, e As System.EventArgs)
    UpdateSelect.Visible="True"
    UpdateTextBoxes.Visible="False"
    LoadData()
End Sub

Sub Products_Function(sender As Object, e As System.Web.UI
➥.WebControls.CommandEventArgs)
    dim Action as String = e.CommandName
    dim FirstName as String
    dim LastName as String
    dim EmployeeID as Integer
    FirstName = ""
    LastName = ""

    Select Case Action
    Case "Insert"
        FirstName = InsertFirstName.Text
        LastName = InsertLastName.Text
    Case "Update"
        FirstName = UpdateFirstName.Text
        LastName = UpdateLastName.Text
        EmployeeID = e.CommandArgument
    Case "Delete"
        EmployeeID = DeleteEmployeeID.SelectedItem.Value
    End Select

    dim OurConnection as SqlConnection
    dim OurCommand as SqlCommand
    OurConnection = New SqlConnection("Server=server;
    ➥uid=newriders;pwd=password;database=Northwind")
    OurCommand = New SqlCommand("Products_IUD",OurConnection)
    OurCommand.CommandType = CommandType.StoredProcedure
    OurCommand.Parameters.Add("@Action", SqlDbType.Varchar, 10).Value = Action
    OurCommand.Parameters.Add("@FirstName", SqlDbType.Varchar, 10).Value =
    ➥FirstName
    OurCommand.Parameters.Add("@LastName", SqlDbType.Varchar, 20).Value = LastName
    OurCommand.Parameters.Add("@EmployeeID", SqlDbType.Int, 4).Value = EmployeeID
    OurConnection.Open()
```

```
        OurCommand.ExecuteNonQuery()
        OurConnection.Close()

        LoadData()
End Sub

</script>
<html>
<head>
<title>ADO SQLCommand -Insert,Update,Delete</title>
</head>
<body bgcolor="#FFFFFF" text="#000000">
<form runat="server">
<table border="0" cellpadding="0" cellspacing="20">
<tr><td>
<ASP:DataGrid
    id="OurDataGrid"
    EnableViewState="false"
    BorderWidth="1"
    BorderColor="#000000"
    CellPadding="3"
    CellSpacing="0"
    Font-Name="Verdana"
    HeaderStyle-BackColor="#AAAAAA"
    ItemStyle-BackColor="#EEEEEE"
    runat="server" />
</td><td>
<h4>Insert</h4>
First Name: <asp:TextBox id="InsertFirstName" runat="server" /><br>
Last Name: <asp:TextBox id="InsertLastName" runat="server" />
<asp:button
    OnCommand="Products_Function"
    CommandName="Insert"
    text="Submit"
    runat="server" /><br><br>
<hr style="height:1px">
<h4>Update</h4>
<asp:Panel id="UpdateSelect" runat="server" >
EmployeeID:
<asp:DropDownList
    id="UpdateEmployeeID"
    DataTextField="EmployeeID"
    DataValueField="EmployeeID"
    runat="server" />
<asp:button runat="server" text="Select" OnClick="UpdateSetup" />
</asp:Panel>
<asp:Panel id="UpdateTextBoxes" Visible="false" runat="server" >
First Name: <asp:TextBox id="UpdateFirstName" runat="server" />
<asp:button
    id="UpdateButton"
    onCommand="Products_Function"
    CommandName="Update"
```

continues

Visual Basic .NET—(continued)

```
        runat="server"
        text="Update" /><br>
Last Name: <asp:TextBox id="UpdateLastName"  runat="server" />
<asp:button id="CancelUpdateButton" runat="server" onClick="UpdateReset"
➥text="Select Other" />
</asp:Panel><br>

<hr style="height:1px">
<h4>Delete</h4>
EmployeeID:
<asp:DropDownList
    id="DeleteEmployeeID"
    DataTextField="EmployeeID"
    DataValueField="EmployeeID"
    runat="server" />
<asp:button
    onCommand="Products_Function"
    CommandName="Delete"
    text="Delete"
    runat="server" />
</td></tr>
</table>
</form>
</body>
</html>
```

C#—ado_sproc_iud_cs.aspx

```
<%@ page language="c#" runat="server" %>
<%@ Import Namespace="System.Data" %>
<%@ Import Namespace="System.Data.SqlClient" %>

<script runat=server>
void Page_Load() {
    if (!IsPostBack) {
        LoadData();
    }
}

void LoadData() {
    SqlConnection OurConnection;
    SqlCommand OurCommand;
    SqlDataAdapter OurDataAdapter;
    DataSet OurDataSet = new DataSet();

    OurConnection = new SqlConnection("Server=server;
    ➥uid=newriders;pwd=password;database=Northwind");
    OurConnection.Open();
    OurCommand = new SqlCommand("Select Top 15 EmployeeID,FirstName,LastName from
    ➥Employees" ,OurConnection);
```

```
        OurDataAdapter = new SqlDataAdapter(OurCommand);
        OurDataAdapter.Fill(OurDataSet, "Employees");
        OurDataGrid.DataSource=OurDataSet.Tables["Employees"];
        UpdateEmployeeID.DataSource=OurDataSet.Tables["Employees"];
        DeleteEmployeeID.DataSource=OurDataSet.Tables["Employees"];
        DataBind();


}

void UpdateSetup(Object sender, EventArgs e) {

        String SelectedID = UpdateEmployeeID.SelectedItem.Value;
        SqlConnection OurConnection;
        SqlCommand OurCommand;
        SqlDataReader OurDataReader2;

        UpdateSelect.Visible=false;
        UpdateTextBoxes.Visible=true;
        UpdateButton.CommandArgument = SelectedID;

        OurConnection = new SqlConnection("Server=server;
        ➥uid=newriders;pwd=password;database=Northwind");
        OurConnection.Open();
        OurCommand = new SqlCommand("Select FirstName, LastName From Employees Where
        ➥EmployeeID = " + SelectedID ,OurConnection);
        OurDataReader2 = OurCommand.ExecuteReader();
        OurDataReader2.Read();
        UpdateFirstName.Text = OurDataReader2["FirstName"].ToString();
        UpdateLastName.Text = OurDataReader2["LastName"].ToString();
        OurConnection.Close();
        OurDataReader2.Close();

        LoadData();
}

void UpdateReset(Object sender, EventArgs e) {
        UpdateSelect.Visible=true;
        UpdateTextBoxes.Visible=false;
        LoadData();
}

void Products_Function(Object sender, System.Web.UI.WebControls.CommandEventArgs e) {
        String Action = e.CommandName;
        String FirstName;
        String LastName;
        int EmployeeID = 0;
        FirstName = "";
        LastName = "";

        switch (Action.ToLower()) {
        case "insert":
```

continues

C#—(continued)

```
        FirstName = InsertFirstName.Text;
        LastName = InsertLastName.Text;
        break;
    case "update":
        FirstName = UpdateFirstName.Text;
        LastName = UpdateLastName.Text;
        EmployeeID = Int32.Parse(e.CommandArgument.ToString());
        break;
    case "delete":
        EmployeeID = Int32.Parse(DeleteEmployeeID.SelectedItem.Value);
        break;
    default:
        break;
    }

    SqlConnection OurConnection;
    SqlCommand OurCommand;
    OurConnection = new SqlConnection("Server=server;
➥uid=newriders;pwd=password;database=Northwind");
    OurCommand = new SqlCommand("Products_IUD",OurConnection);
    OurCommand.CommandType = CommandType.StoredProcedure;
    OurCommand.Parameters.Add("@Action", SqlDbType.VarChar, 10).Value = Action;
    OurCommand.Parameters.Add("@FirstName", SqlDbType.VarChar, 10).Value =
➥FirstName;
    OurCommand.Parameters.Add("@LastName", SqlDbType.VarChar, 20).Value =
➥LastName;
    OurCommand.Parameters.Add("@EmployeeID", SqlDbType.Int, 4).Value = EmployeeID;
    OurConnection.Open();
    OurCommand.ExecuteNonQuery();
    OurConnection.Close();
    LoadData();
}

</script>
<html>
<head>
<title>ADO SqlCommand -Insert,Update,Delete</title>
</head>
<body bgcolor="#FFFFFF" text="#000000">
<form runat="server">
<table border="0" cellpadding="0" cellspacing="20">
<tr><td>
<ASP:DataGrid
    id="OurDataGrid"
    EnableViewState="false"
    BorderWidth="1"
    BorderColor="#000000"
    CellPadding="3"
    CellSpacing="0"
    Font-Name="Verdana"
    HeaderStyle-BackColor="#AAAAAA"
```

```
                    ItemStyle-BackColor="#EEEEEE"
                    runat="server" />
</td><td>
<h4>Insert</h4>
First Name: <asp:TextBox id="InsertFirstName" runat="server" /><br>
Last Name: <asp:TextBox id="InsertLastName" runat="server" />
<asp:button
    OnCommand="Products_Function"
    CommandName="Insert"
    text="voidmit"
    runat="server" /><br><br>
<hr style="height:1px">
<h4>Update</h4>
<asp:Panel id="UpdateSelect" runat="server" >
EmployeeID:
<asp:DropDownList
    id="UpdateEmployeeID"
    DataTextField="EmployeeID"
    DataValueField="EmployeeID"
    runat="server" />
<asp:button runat="server" text="Select" OnClick="UpdateSetup" />
</asp:Panel>
<asp:Panel id="UpdateTextBoxes" Visible="false" runat="server" >
First Name: <asp:TextBox id="UpdateFirstName" runat="server" />
<asp:button
    id="UpdateButton"
    onCommand="Products_Function"
    CommandName="Update"
    runat="server"
    text="Update" /><br>
Last Name: <asp:TextBox id="UpdateLastName"  runat="server" />
<asp:button id="CancelUpdateButton" runat="server" onClick="UpdateReset"
➥text="Select Other" />
</asp:Panel><br>

<hr style="height:1px">
<h4>Delete</h4>
EmployeeID:
<asp:DropDownList
    id="DeleteEmployeeID"
    DataTextField="EmployeeID"
    DataValueField="EmployeeID"
    runat="server" />
<asp:button
    onCommand="Products_Function"
    CommandName="Delete"
    text="Delete"
    runat="server" />
</td></tr>
</table>
</form>
</body>
</html>
```

Notice that the single `Products_Function` provides all the functionality of the `InsertCommand`, `UpdateCommand`, and `DeleteCommand` of the `SqlCommand` example given earlier in this chapter.

Use a `Select` statement to evaluate which action is being performed, which is established via the `CommandName` variable. This is just the tip of the iceberg when it comes to what stored procedures can do for you when manipulating data in your databases and how they can help consolidate code in your ASP.NET pages.

Experiment and be creative. You will be surprised at the power of stored procedures, and after you start using them, you will begin to wonder how many unnecessary lines of code you've written doing things the conventional way.

Summary

ADO.NET is a HUGE, HUGE, HUGE subject, but in the space of this chapter I have given you a good foundation of ways to tackle many of the common tasks needed when interacting with a database in your ASP.NET applications. What you've learned here is also something you can build on as you experiment and move forward to creating more and more complex functions in your applications. ADO.NET is something that you grow into. It has many facets that, as with all the other objects in the .NET Framework, will begin to reveal themselves as you grow in knowledge. Don't be afraid to dig into the .NET Framework SDK in the `System.Data`, `System.Data.SqlClient`, and `System.Data.Oledb` namespaces. You will find other powerful ways to manipulate the objects that are contained within these namespaces.

Now that you have ADO.NET under your belt, it's time to move forward and investigate another bridge that the .NET Framework handsomely addresses, which is the stateless nature of the web and how that affects programming your ASP.NET pages and applications.

State Management in ASP.NET

I'll never forget what's-his-name…

The web is a mysterious and anonymous place. People come and go; ships pass in the night without even knowing it. This unfortunately creates some problems when developing web applications. You need to know who people are, and at the very least you need to be able to identify individual users of the web site.

The problem originates in a web server's bad attitude. If it were up to the web server, all it would do is deliver pages. It doesn't care who wants the page, to whom it sent pages, or whether those users are coming back. This rotten attitude has created quite a quandary for web designers.

What Is State Management?

In the past, you had to jump through some flaming hoops to maintain the identity of a visitor to a web site. You had to use hidden form fields that you passed from page to page, use a unique ID that you passed in the URL, use cookies, or use the ASP Session object. If you've programmed dynamic web applications at all, you know that this was a pain in the posterior!!! I'm not even mentioning simple things like maintaining form field values across page posts, such as you need to do when you perform server-side validation.

To clarify, it would be helpful to identify what state management is and what types you will be faced with when building ASP.NET web applications. State management, or maintaining state, is the process of preserving the condition and information regarding an individual's visit to a single web page, a user's entire visit to your web site, or the condition of your web application as a whole.

According to this definition, state management is used to preserve two things:

- Condition
- Information

Maintaining condition can be preserving which value was selected in a drop-down list when a page is posted back to itself for validation. Maintaining information may be assigning a customer ID to a visitor and having that ID follow them throughout their visit to your website.

The definition also states that condition and information are preserved in three different areas:

- Page state
- User state
- Application state

I am going to go into the three different areas and explore some methods that may be familiar to you, but most are pretty new and exciting parts of the .NET Framework.

Page State

As I said before, the web server doesn't care about user information or condition. If you were creating a form that would post back to itself, it would be your job as a designer to maintain the information a user entered into the form across posts; otherwise, the information the user inserted would be lost when the page was delivered back. The following is a simple example of this in traditional ASP.

Traditional ASP—`trad_page_stat.asp`

```
<%@LANGUAGE="VBSCRIPT"%>
<%dim vFirstName,vLastName,vPhone,vEmail
vFirstName = ""
vLastName = ""
vPhone = ""
vEmail = ""

if Request.Form("submit") <> "" then
    vFirstName = Request.Form("firstname")
    vLastName = Request.Form("lastname")
    vPhone = Request.Form("phone")
    vEmail = Request.Form("email")
end if
%>
<html>
<head>
<title>Traditional ASP - Page State</title>
</head>
<body>
<form name="form1" method="post" action="">
    <input type="text" name="firstname" value="<%=vFirstName%>">
    First Name<br>
    <input type="text" name="lastname" value="<%=vLastName%>">
    Last Name<br>
    <input type="text" name="phone" value="<%=vPhone%>">
    Phone Number<br>
    <input type="text" name="email" value="<%=vEmail%>">
    Email Address<br>
    <input type="submit" name="Submit" value="Submit">
</form>
</body>
</html>
```

Yes, I know there are shorter ways to do this, but I really wanted to demonstrate what is necessary to repopulate form text boxes.

ViewState

Now let's take a look at a similar page in ASP.NET, and observe what you have to do to maintain the state of the TextBox server controls.

ASP.NET—**dotnet_page_state.aspx**

```
<html>
<head>
<title>Traditional ASP - Page State</title>
</head>
<body>
<form runat="server">
<asp:TextBox id="FirstName" runat="server" />
First Name<br>
<asp:TextBox id="LastName" runat="server" />
Last Name<br>
<asp:TextBox id="Phone" runat="server" />
Phone Number<br>
<asp:TextBox id="Email" runat="server" />
Email Address<br>
<asp:Button id="Submit" text="Submit" runat="server" />
</form>
</body>
</html>
```

Do you see how it's done? Look really hard! Still don't see it? No matter how hard you look, you ain't gonna see it because there's nothing there. ASP.NET handles page-level state for you without you lifting a finger. Actually, the only time you need to write any code with reference to maintaining page state in an ASP.NET web form is if you DON'T WANT IT!! That is correct. If you don't want to maintain state, you have to explicitly say so.

For you to see the magic you would have to look at the delivered page's source code. The preceding page's rendered source code looks like this:

ASP.NET—**dotnet_page_state.aspx rendered source**

```
<html>
<head>
<title>Traditional ASP - Page State</title>
</head>
<body>
<form name="_ctl0" method="post" action="dotnet_page_state.aspx" id="_ctl0">
<input type="hidden" name="__VIEWSTATE" value=
➥"dDwtMTE4NzE2NjU2MDs7PkesEtdwWxQyics7BpduSPBkw6L/" />

<input name="FirstName" type="text" id="FirstName" />
```

```
First Name<br>
<input name="LastName" type="text" id="LastName" />
Last Name<br>
<input name="Phone" type="text" id="Phone" />
Phone Number<br>
<input name="Email" type="text" id="Email" />
Email Address<br>
<input type="submit" name="Submit" value="Submit" id="Submit" />
</form>
</body>
</html>
```

The secret lies in the hidden input field called __VIEWSTATE, which is at the core of ASP.NET's capability to maintain the state of an ASP.NET page. Data about the condition and information on a web form is stored in this <input type="hidden"> tag named __VIEWSTATE.

ViewState isn't necessary at all times, and at times it can be pretty costly because it can become quite bloated with conditions and information for a page with many controls or large DataGrids on it. For instance, if you look at Figure 11.1, you will see a DataGrid from an example in Chapter 9. In the original example I didn't have a <form runat="server"> tag on the page, so no ViewState was created, but for demonstration I took that simple DataGrid with the Top 10 products in the Northwind database and wrapped it in a <form runat="server"> tag so a __ViewState would be created. Here is the generated ViewState:

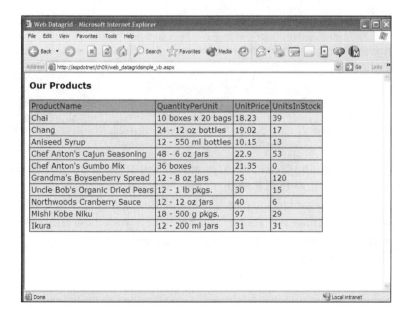

FIGURE 11.1

ViewState *can be expensive on things such as a* DataGrid.

```
<input type="hidden" name="__VIEWSTATE"
value="dDwtNTcyNzE4MDk2O3Q8O2w8aTwxPjs+O2w8dDw7bDxpPDE+Oz47bDx0PEAwPHA8cDxsPFBhZ2V
Db3VudDtfIUl0ZW1Db3VudDtfIURhdGFTb3VyY2VJdGVtQ291bnQ7RGF0YUtleXM7PjtsPGk8MT47aTwxM
D47aTwxMD47bDw+Oz4+Oz0zs7Ozs7OztAMDxAMDxwPGw8SGVhZGVyVGV4dDtEYXRhRmllbGGQ7U29ydEV
4cHJlc3Npb247UmVhZE9ubHk7PjtsPFByb2R1Y3RZROYW1lO1Byb2R1Y3RZROYW1lO1Byb2R1Y3RZROYW1lO288Z
j47Pj47Ozs7PjtAMDxwPGw8SGVhZGVyVGV4dDtEYXRhRmllbGGQ7U29ydEV4cHJlc3Npb247UmVhZE9ubHk
7PjtsPFF1YW50aXR5UGVyVW5pdDtRdWFudGl0eVBlclVuaXQ7UXVhbnRpdHlQZXJVbml0O288Zj47Pj47O
zs7PjtAMDxwPGw8SGVhZGVyVGV4dDtEYXRhRmllbGGQ7U29ydEV4cHJlc3Npb247UmVhZE9ubHk7PjtsPFV
uaXRQcmljZTtVbml0UHJpY2U7VW5pdFByaWNlO288Zj47Pj47Ozs7PjtAMDxwPGw8SGVhZGVyVGV4dDtEY
XRhRmllbGGQ7U29ydEV4cHJlc3Npb247UmVhZE9ubHk7PjtsPFVuaXRzSW5TdG9jaztVbml0c0luU3RvY2s
7VW5pdHNJbk0b2Nr0288Zj47Pj47Pjs+Oz47bDxpPDA+Oz47bDx0PDtsPGk8MT47aTwyPjtpPDM+O
2k8ND47aTw1PjtpPDY+O2k8Nz47aTw4PjtpPDk+O2k8MTA+Oz47bDx0PDtsPGk8MD47aTwxPjtpPDI+O2k
8Mz47PjtsPHQ8cDxwPGw8VGV4dDs+O2w8Q2hhaTs+Pjs+Ozs+O3Q8cDxwPGw8VGV4dDs+O2w8MTAgYm94Z
XMgeCAyMCByYWdzOz4+Oz4+Ozt+O3Q8cDxwPGw8VGV4dDs+O2w8MTguMDAwMDs+Pjs+Ozs+O3Q8cDxwPGw8VGV4d
Ds+O2w8Q2hhbmc7PjtsPGk8MD47aTwxPjtpPDI+Oz47PjtsPHQ8cDxwPGw8VGV4dDs+O2w8MTkuMDAwMDs+P
js+Ozs+O3Q8cDxwPGw8VGV4dDs+O2w8MTkuMDAwMDs+Pjs+Ozs+O3Q8cDxwPGw8VGV4dDs+O2w8MTAwMDs+P
j47Pjs7Pjt0PDtsPGk8MD47aTwxPjtpPDI+Oz47PjtsPHQ8cDxwPGw8VGV4dDs+O2w8QW5pc2VlZCBTeXJ1cDs+P
js7Pjt0PHA8cDxsPFRleHQ7PjtsPDEwIC0gNTUwIG1sIGJvdHRsZXM7Pjs+Ozs+O3Q8cDxwPGw8VGV4dDs+O2w8MTAuMDA7P
j47Pj47O3Q8cDxwPGw8VGV4dDs+O2w8MTMuMDAwMDs+Pjs+O3Q8cDxwPGw8VGV4dDs+O2w8NzA7Pj47Pjs7Pj
j47Pjs7PjtAMDxwPGw8VGV4dDs+O2w8MzYyZXM4ZXM+O3Q8cDxwPGw8VGV4dDs+O2w8MTAwMDs+Pjs+Ozs7
+Pjs+O3Q8cDxwPGw8VGV4dDs+O2w8MzYgYm94ZXM+O3Q8cDxwPGw8VGV4dDs+O2w8MTAwMDs+P
jt0PHA8cDxsPFRleHQ7PjtsPEdyYXZhZC1sYXg7Pjs+Ozs+O3Q8cDxwPGw8VGV4dDs+O2w8bWMkbWEncyBMaWJlcnR5I
EVuY3lCC2Jl3ZW5iZXJyeSBTrcHJlYWQ7Pj47PjsPHA8cDxsPFRleHQ7PjtsPDEyIC0gOCBvei
BqYXJzOz4+Oz47Oz47bDx0PHA8cDxsPFRleHQ7PjtsPDI1Oz4+Oz47Pj47O3Q8cDxwPGw8VGV4dDs+O2w8MTIwMDs+
+Pjs+Ozs+O3Q8cDxwPGw8VGV4dDs+O2w8MTIwOz4+Oz47PjtsPFVuY2xlIEJvYidzIE9yZ2FuaWMgRHJpZWQgUGVhcnM7Pj
s7Pjt0PHA8cDxsPFRleHQ7PjtsPDEyIC0gMSBsYiBwa2dzLjs+Ozs+O3Q8cDxwPGw8VGV4dDs+O2w8O3c7PjtsPHA8cDxsP
FRleHQ7PjtsPDI5Oz4+Oz47Pj47O3Q8cDxwPGw8VGV4dDs+O2w8MTAwMDs+Pjs+O3Q8cDxwPGw8VGV4dDs+O2w8
+Pjs+Ozs+O3Q8cDxwPGw8VGV4dDs+O2w8MTAwMDs+Pjs+O3Q8cDxwPGw8VGV4dDs+O2w8MTIwOz4+Oz47PjtsPE5vcnRod29
vZHMgQ3JhbmJlcnJ5IFNhdWNlOz4+Oz47Oz47bDx0PHA8cDxsPFRleHQ7PjtsPDEyIC0gMTIgb96IGphcnM7Pjt0PHA8cDxsP
FRleHQ7PjtsPDQwOz4+Oz47Oz47bDx0PHA8cDxsPFRleHQ7PjtsPDIwOz4+Oz47PjtsPFNpc3JhIEtvbmdlbTdRs+Pjs+Ozs+O2w
8MTggLSA1MDAgZyBwa2dzLjs+Ozs+O3Q8cDxwPGw8VGV4dDs+O2w8O3c7PjtsPHA8cDxsPFRleHQ7PjtsPDI1Oz4+Oz47Pj47
leHQ7PjtsPElrdXJhXJhOz4+Oz47bDx0PHA8cDxsPFRleHQ7PjtsPDI1IDwMCBtCBtCBqYXJzOz4+Oz47Oz47
z47bDxwPHA8cDxsPFRleHQ7PjtsPDwzMTs+Pjs+O3Q8cDxwPGw8VGV4dDs+O2w8MzE7Pj47Pjs+Pjs+Pjs
+Pjs+Pjs+Pjs+iUF+nF87Ysehxpz4JqGSmZvddnU=" />
```

Hearty, huh? That's a touch over 3Kb for maintaining state on that `DataGrid`. Although this looks large (and it is) there may be times when this is the better route to take with regard to the performance of your application. You will need to weigh the requirements of your application to determine how and when to use `ViewState`. Just for reference, this 3Kb of data will take less than 1 second to download over a 56Kbps modem.

> **N O T E**
>
> __VIEWSTATE *is generated only when a page has a* <form runat="server"> *tag. You can have* DataGrids *on pages without this tag and no* __VIEWSTATE *will be generated.*

You will generally find ViewState very useful on forms where you want to maintain the condition of the user interface across postbacks.

As I said, you don't need to use ViewState. ASP.NET enables you to control whether an ASP.NET web form handles ViewState, or you can set it on a server control level also. The property of the Page and server controls that controls whether that object's state information will be maintained in ViewState is called EnableViewState.

To set a page's ViewState, you set this property in the @Page directive at the top of the page.

```
<%@ page language="vb" EnableViewState="False" runat="server"%>
<%@ page language="c#" EnableViewState="False" runat="server"%>
```

This property of the page is true by default, so if you want ViewState enabled on a page, you can either explicitly set it to true or not include the property declaration.

Setting the ViewState of a server control is no different, really, than setting any other property of a control. The following is a block of code from a code example in Chapter 10 where a DropDownList server control was used to filter a DataTable that populates a DataGrid. Because the DataGrid will be filtered and repopulated on each PostBack, its EnableViewState property can be set to false. The DropDownList is a different story. Here it's important to maintain the data and which value was selected across posts. ViewState repopulates the DropDownList and sets it to the value selected before the post.

Excerpt from ch10/ado_sproc_select_vb.aspx or ch10/ado_sproc_select_cs.aspx

```
<html>
<head>
<title>ADO Store Procedure - Select</title>
</head>
<body bgcolor="#FFFFFF" text="#000000">
<form runat="server">
<asp:DropDownList id="OurDropDown" runat="server" />
<asp:Button id="OurButton" Text="Get Products" runat="server" /><br><br>
```

continues

Excerpt from `ch10/ado_sproc_select_vb.aspx` **or** `ch10/ado_sproc_select_cs.aspx` (continued)

```
<ASP:DataGrid
    id="OurDataGrid"
    EnableViewState="False"
    BorderWidth="1"
    BorderColor="#000000"
    CellPadding="3"
    CellSpacing="0"
    Font-Name="Verdana"
    HeaderStyle-BackColor="#AAAAAA"
    ItemStyle-BackColor="#EEEEEE"
    AutoGenerateColumns="False"
    runat="server">
    <Columns>
        <asp:BoundColumn
            HeaderText="Product Name"
            DataField="ProductName" />
        <asp:BoundColumn
            HeaderText="Unit Price"
            DataField="UnitPrice"
            DataFormatString="{0:c}"/>
    </Columns>
</asp:DataGrid><br>
<asp:Label id="OurLabel"  Font-Name="Verdana" runat="server" />
</form>
</body>
</html>
```

This code example causes the `DropDownList`'s state to be maintained, but the `DataGrid`'s state is not maintained in the `ViewState`.

StateBag

In the past, when you needed to pass a value back to the server that you didn't want the user to see in the browser window, you would use an `<input type="hidden">` tag. ASP.NET provides a object called the `StateBag` (of which `ViewState` is really just an instance) for you to pass data back to the server while it's hidden from the user's view.

The `StateBag` serves this purpose and is treated no differently than any other collection, such as the `Request` collection or `Application` collection. You can get and set values of `StateBag` contents. The following example looks briefly at this.

Visual Basic .NET—**StateBag** Set and Get

```
ViewState("FirstName") = "Peter"
ViewState("Publisher") = "New Riders"


vFirstName = ViewState("FirstName")
vPublisher = ViewState("Publisher")
```

C#—**StateBag** Set and Get

```
ViewState["FirstName"] = "Peter"
ViewState["Publisher"] = "New Riders"


vFirstName = ViewState["FirstName"]
vPublisher = ViewState["Publisher"]
```

As you can see, it's not really that big a deal. You use the word ViewState to address the StateBag collection and place the name of the item you want to set or get in the StateBag you want.

Page state management is a big part of building ASP.NET applications, but you don't usually build one-page applications. Applications can span across many pages, and you need to be able to identify a user from one page to the next. This is where User State and Session State come into play.

Session State

As I mentioned at the beginning of this chapter, there were several ways to handle the state information of a user's visit or session on your web site. All the methods had an inherent problem in one factor or another. Let's look at a few of the problems that some of the solutions used in the past have faced.

Session Object

- Lost data if web services were stopped and restarted

- Not very scalable; server resources required

- Won't work in a web farm

- Won't work with user's cookies disabled

Cookies

- Won't work with user's cookies disabled

- Hidden text boxes

- Information is exposed to anyone that knows how to view source

- Can be tampered with if a malicious visitor wants to

- Work only if a user submits a form

QueryString

- Exposed in the browser's address bar and can be tampered with, making it less than reliable

Now don't get ridiculously excited because ASP.NET doesn't provide any miraculous answers for these problems, but it does supply reasonable remedies and tools to overcome these problems. Are they foolproof? No. Is there any perfect solution? If there were it would be the only one available in ASP.NET, but there are still a bunch of different methods you can use. So you will still be left with some choices, but they are a bit more solid than they used to be, and if you run a SQL Server there is a totally new option available that is quite interesting. Let's address them one by one and see how .NET addresses the individual problems associated with the different methods.

Sessions

By default, sessions in ASP.NET are just like their counterparts in traditional ASP. When a user visits your web site for the first time, ASP.NET generates a 120-bit unique ID for that user, assigns a piece of the server's memory to that ID, and sets a temporary cookie with that ID on the user's machine to maintain the association between the partition of memory and the visitor.

How to Use Sessions

Using session variables isn't much different than using the `StateBag` that was discussed earlier, except you use the word `Session` rather than `ViewState` to address the object.

Visual Basic .NET—session_standard_vb.aspx

```
<%@ page language="vb" runat="server"%>
<script runat=server>
Sub Page_Load()
    Session("OurSession") = "Sessions hold stuff"
    OurLabel.Text = Session("OurSession")
End Sub
</script>

<html>
<head>
<title>Session State - Set Get</title>
</head>
<body bgcolor="#FFFFFF" text="#000000">
<asp:label id="OurLabel" runat="server" />
</body>
</html>
```

C#—session_standard_cs.aspx

```
<%@ page language="c#" runat="server"%>
<script runat=server>
void Page_Load(){
    Session["OurSession"] = "Sessions hold stuff";
    OurLabel.Text = Session["OurSession"].ToString();
}
</script>

<html>
<head>
<title>Session State - Set Get</title>
</head>
<body bgcolor="#FFFFFF" text="#000000">
<asp:label id="OurLabel" runat="server" />
</body>
</html>
```

Pretty simple. One thing to take note of is that C# requires you to use the ToString() method to set the label's text property because C# generally doesn't convert data types on the fly, as Visual Basic .NET will do gracefully.

By default, a session has a lifetime of 20 minutes of inactivity. The server releases the memory set aside for that session and discards the data it contains. The time-out of a session is flexible, though. The Session object is really an instance of the HttpSessionState object, which has a property of Timeout.

This `timeout` property is valued in minutes, so if you want your session to time out after 10 minutes of inactivity, you need to insert the following code on your page in both Visual Basic .NET and C#.

```
Session.Timeout = 10
```

You can also set the session's timeout `property` across the application by placing the `<sessionstate/>` tag inside the `<system.web>` section of the web.config file.

```
<configuration>
    <system.web>
        <sessionState timeout="10" />
    </system.web>
</configuration>
```

Pretty simple either way. Again, the first example of setting the `timeout` is page-specific. In other words, only people that load a page with that code on it will have the `timeout` property set, whereas setting it in the web.config file sets the timeout application-wide.

As I've implied, each session has a beginning and an end as far as your application is concerned, and ASP.NET gives you a way to use those events in your applications. These events are called `Session_Start` and `Session_End`, and they can be referenced in your global.asax file in your application's root folder.

Visual Basic .NET—`global.asax`

```
<script language="vb" runat=server>
Sub Application_OnStart()
    Application("SessionNum") = 0
End Sub

Sub Session_Start()
    dim NumSessions as Integer = Application("SessionNum")
    Application("SessionNum") = NumSessions + 1
End Sub
Sub Session_End()
    dim NumSessions as Integer = Application("SessionNum")
    Application("SessionNum") = NumSessions - 1
End Sub
</script>
```

C#—`global.asax`

```
<script language="c#" runat=server>
void Application_OnStart(){
    Application["SessionNum"] = 0;
}

void Session_Start(){
    int NumSessions = int.Parse(Application["SessionNum"].ToString());
    Application["SessionNum"] = NumSessions + 1;
}
void Session_End(){
    int NumSessions = int.Parse(Application["SessionNum"].ToString());
    Application["SessionNum"] = NumSessions - 1;
}
</script>
```

As you can see, whenever a new session starts, an application variable called
`SessionNum` is incremented by one. Whenever a session ends, this application
variable is decremented by one. There are other applications for using the
`Session_Start` and `Session_End` events in your applications, so keep this
in your pocket for those occasions.

What you've seen so far is a use of the session in a way that parallels a traditional
ASP `Session` object. ASP.NET provides some methods to overcome some of the
session's trouble spots that I mentioned earlier.

In traditional ASP, if the Web Service decides to take a vacation and you need to
restart Web Services, all the data that were stored in memory for the people with
a current session on the web site would lose their state information. That's too
bad if someone is scoping out a $5,000 diamond ring on your jewelry web site
and is ready to buy, but the shopping cart has just gotten dumped because of a
Web Service restart.

This is how sessions run by default and this is called an `InProc` session. `InProc`
sessions are "In the same process" in which ASP.NET is running and is the default
mode of the `SessionState`, but there are three alternatives to running `InProc`.
One doesn't take any explanation at all. It is Off, which means that `SessionState`
is disabled.

```
<configuration>
    <system.web>
        <sessionState mode="Off" />
    </system.web>
</configuration>
```

This information isn't very useful for the discussion here, but for the sake of being thorough I had to mention it. The other two options for `SessionState` are `StateServer` and `SQLServer`. Look first at the `StateServer` mode and see what problems it helps you overcome.

StateServer

With the `StateServer` mode, you can cause sessions to be processed either in a separate process on the same web server where you are running your ASP.NET pages, or you can have these sessions processed on a totally different server.

This addresses to one degree or another three of the four issues that session variables have had in traditional ASP. First, because they run in a totally separate process, either on your web server or a server dedicated to handling session information, if there's a problem with the Web Service and you need to stop and restart this service, a user won't lose session information.

Second, it provides a greater path for scalability because you can utilize a machine that is dedicated to handling session information, thus taking the load and respon-sibility for maintaining this data off your web server. The scalability issues are also coupled with the third issue that `StateServer` addresses.

Finally, sessions can reach across web farms when you have a machine dedicated to state management. All the machines in your web farm can utilize the same `StateServer` for their state information.

These possibilities make storing session state information in memory a more viable option. In traditional ASP this type of system for maintaining state was largely frowned upon because of scalability issues.

There are certain things you must do to use `StateServer` that either runs out of process on your web server or runs on a different server all together.

First, whatever machine you want to run as your `StateServer` must have a service called ASP.NET State Service. To start that service, go to Start Menu, Settings, Control Panel, Administrative Tools, Services. There you can see the service with that title, and it probably has a Startup Type of Manual. Double-click ASP.NET State Service and set the Startup Type to Automatic. This starts this service immediately and assures that it starts every time the server is rebooted.

Second, you must set up the web.config file so that the mode of `SessionState` and another attribute of `SessionState`, called `stateConnectionString`, are set properly.

Web.config

```
<configuration>
    <system.web>
        <sessionState mode="StateServer"
            stateConnectionString="tcpip=server:port" />
    </system.web>
</configuration>
```

The mode attribute needs to be set to StateServer. The stateConnectionString attribute needs to be set to the server name or IP address and port separated by a colon (:). This is required if the mode is set to StateServer.

SQL Server

Another alternative to running session data in the memory of either the web server or a SessionState server is using Microsoft SQL Server to store it in a database.

The reality in using sessions, just like with the StateServer, is that there is absolutely no difference. You set them and get them exactly the same way. The only thing that's different is how the .NET Framework handles the data from there, which depends on the mode that is set in the web.config file.

When you run in SQLServer mode, all your sets and gets of Session variables will cause the information to be written or read from the database rather than from the web server or StateServer's memory. This is another scalable way to handle session information out-of-process, but is not without its drawbacks, either.

First, there is a small performance sacrifice. The benchmarks, articles, and whatever other data I could find all state that using SQLServer for storing session data will result in approximately 75%-80% of the performance of session data being stored in process. The plus side to this is that as the number of users grows, the SQLServer method will scale much better because its limitations for holding and delivering data are much less than those of a web server's memory.

Second, this system was designed with enterprises in mind, and it therefore assumes that you run a dedicated Microsoft SQL Server database server to which you have administrative access. I assume that many readers of this book use Microsoft SQL Server in a shared environment, where this type of access wouldn't be available. Unfortunately, this system wasn't designed for that type of environment.

If you want to enable Microsoft SQL Server as the location where session data is managed, there are a few things that you must do.

You must properly set the mode of `sessionState` in the web.config file, as follows:

```
<configuration>
    <system.web>
        <sessionState
            mode="SQLServer"
            sqlConnectionString="data source=server;user
            ➥id=username;password=password"
            timeout="10" />
    </system.web>
</configuration>
```

Set the `mode` attribute of the `sessionState` tag in the web.config file to `SQLServer`. The other attribute you must provide is `sqlConnectionString`, which is simply a connection string to your database server with the server path, hostname or IP address, user ID, and password. This provides the .NET Framework with the necessary information to use your database as the session storage unit. But wait…there's more! Your database needs to be prepared, also.

Microsoft has written a nifty little SQL script that you can run from Query Analyzer in SQL Server's Enterprise Manager. Enterprise Manager is the utility that Microsoft provides with SQL Server so you can administer the database server.

The necessary SQL script for preparing your SQL Server to handle sessions is called `InstallSQLState.sql` and was placed on the server in the <Drive>:\ WINNT\Microsoft.NET\Framework\<version> directory when you installed the .NET Framework. What this script does is create a new database on the server called ASPState and create a bunch of stored procedures that are necessary for managing session data. It also adds two tables to the system database called tempdb.

Let's proceed by opening Enterprise Manager and then selecting and opening the proper database server from the tree menu on the left. After you've done this, go to the Tools menu and select SQL Query Analyzer. From there you can either copy and paste the contents of the InstallSQLState.sql file or open it using File, Open.

After you have the file open or pasted in the window, you must execute it by either pressing the green arrow in the tool bar, through the Query, Execute Query menu option or Pressing F5. This process will take more than an instant to process, so wait until you see the results appear in a second window, as shown in Figure 11.2.

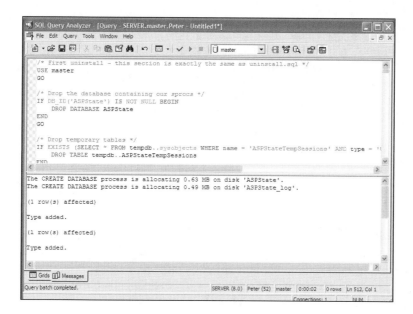

FIGURE 11.2

Executing the InstallSQLState.sql query in Query Analyzer.

Now you are ready to start using SQL Server for your session information. Let's run the files that I created earlier, called either session_standard_vb.aspx or session_standard_cs.aspx, for Visual Basic .NET and C# respectively.

Visual Basic .NET—session_standard_vb.aspx

```
<%@ page language="vb" runat="server"%>
<script runat=server>
Sub Page_Load()
    Session("OurSession") = "Sessions hold stuff"
    OurLabel.Text = Session("OurSession")
End Sub
</script>

<html>
<head>
<title>Session State - Set Get</title>
</head>
<body bgcolor="#FFFFFF" text="#000000">
<asp:label id="OurLabel" runat="server" />
</body>
</html>
```

C#—`session_standard_cs.aspx`

```
<%@ page language="c#" runat="server"%>
<script runat=server>
void Page_Load(){
    Session["OurSession"] = "Sessions hold stuff";
    OurLabel.Text = Session["OurSession"].ToString();
}
</script>

<html>
<head>
<title>Session State - Set Get</title>
</head>
<body bgcolor="#FFFFFF" text="#000000">
<asp:label id="OurLabel" runat="server" />
</body>
</html>
```

The results of this can be seen in Figure 11.3 and they are displayed just as you'd expect. Again, setting and getting session variables when using SQL Server for session storage is not different than using sessions on a web server or a StateServer. You create the session, and then the Text property of the Label server control is set to that session's value. Now take a look at SQL Server and see whether anything happened.

In Figure 11.4 you can see that I've opened up a table called ASPStateTempSessions that resides in the tempdb database and was created when I ran the InstallSQLState.sql in Query Analyzer. This table stores SessionID, created and expired date information, timeout length, and the session info, which is stored in <binary> form in the last two columns. For each variable a row is created and affected by your session gets and sets in your ASP.NET pages.

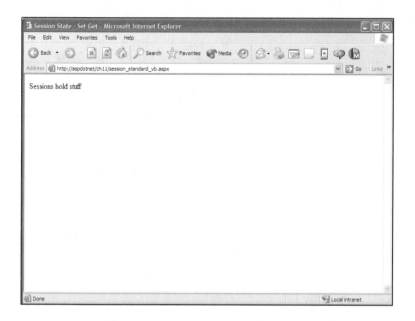

FIGURE 11.3

To store session data with SQL Server, use the same method of getting and setting session variables as you do when you use in-memory sessions.

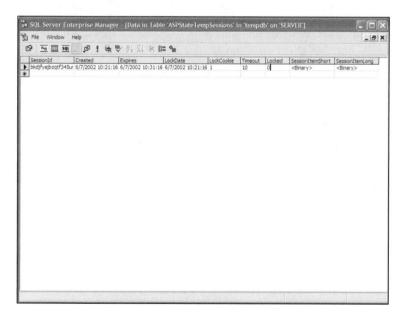

FIGURE 11.4

SQL Server stores session information in a table called ASPStateTempSessions in the tempdb database.

Going Cookieless

Although this may seem like it's a cookie issue and that it should go in the section where I cover cookies, this is really a session issue. All the mentioned methods of in-process and out-of-process session management use a single in-memory (meaning it isn't written to the user's hard drive) cookie to hold the `SessionID` so the server knows who is making the request. This is how it associates session data with that user.

What happens with users who have an older (much older) browser that doesn't support cookies, or those who have opted to turn cookie functionality off in their browsers? That person is alienated from using your web site if you use session variables to store session information.

The .NET Framework provides a way around that using a technique called URL munging. Now I forewarn you that I will not use that word again simply because I hate it. I don't know who coined the phrase but I just want to let them I think it's dumb. To me, that word represents the stuff you step in at the bottom of a lake that squishes between you toes and makes you run back to the shore. Yuck!!! From now on I'll use words like embed and such. Thanks for understanding.

To let the .NET Framework know you want to run your application cookieless, you must set another attribute in the `sessionState` tag in the web.config file named, oddly enough, cookieless.

```
<configuration>
    <system.web>
        <sessionState
            cookieless="true"
            mode="InProc" />
    </system.web>
</configuration>
```

Now let's run the session_standard_vb.aspx or session_standard_cs.aspx for Visual Basic .NET and C# respectively and see what happens to our page.

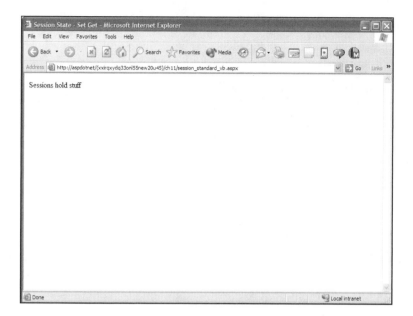

FIGURE 11.5

The .NET Framework embeds the SessionID *information in the URL when running session state with* cookieless *equal to true.*

If you look at the URL in the address bar, you can see that (xxirqxydq33on155new20u45) is embedded in there between the root address and the ch11 directory. This is how the .NET Framework deals with this issue. It embeds the SessionID at the root of the application for uniformity. This provides the necessary information for ASP.NET to identify the user and properly associate session data.

Again, this method isn't without problems. The first problem is a security issue. A malicious person (idiot) could easily capture the URL and subsequently the person's SessionID and masquerade as them and potentially access sensitive data. The second problem is that the user can mung (okay, one small exception, but I mean it in a totally different way) their own URL. This can cause a loss of association with the session data if the user alters the SessionID.

One more problem is losing the SessionID in certain linking situations. ASP.NET handles embedding the SessionID into hyperlinks with relative paths, but it doesn't embed it into fully qualified paths. A solution for that might be to use an HTMLAnchor server control on your page and set the control's href property during Page_Load so you can retrieve the session's SessionID property and construct the link.

Visual Basic .NET—`session_url_vb.aspx`

```
<%@ page language="vb" runat="server"%>
<script runat=server>
Sub Page_Load()
    OurHref.HRef = "http://aspdotnet/(" + Session.SessionID + ")/
    ➥ch11/dotnet_page_state.aspx"
End Sub
</script>

<html>
<head>
<title>Session State - Set Get</title>
</head>
<body bgcolor="#FFFFFF" text="#000000">
<a href="dotnet_page_state.aspx">relative</a><br>
<a id="OurHref" runat="server">full</a>
</body>
</html>
```

C#—`session_url_cs.aspx`

```
<%@ page language="c#" runat="server"%>
<script runat=server>
void Page_Load(){
    OurHref.HRef = "http://aspdotnet/(" + Session.SessionID + ")/
    ➥ch11/dotnet_page_state.aspx";
}
</script>
<html>
<head>
<title>Session State - Set Get</title>
</head>
<body bgcolor="#FFFFFF" text="#000000">
<a href="dotnet_page_state.aspx">relative</a><br>
<a id="OurHref" runat="server">full</a>
</body>
</html>
```

If you plan on using a cookieless session environment, this is something that you need to be mindful of. Make sure that on any link other than those that are relative, you will be responsible for maintaining this ID.

Using Cookies to Maintain Session State

The previous section discussed using session variables to store session state information. Session variables are stored server-side, on the web server, a state server, or Microsoft SQL Server, and they use a single cookie that holds the `SessionID` to maintain an association between the client machine and the session information stored server-side.

Now we are going to talk about storing much of the information that would be stored in session variables in cookies. For clarity, a cookie is a text file that resides on the client's machine that can be used from the server-side to store and retrieve information. It is a domain-specific mechanism that allows a web server to set and get information in a cookie associated with its own domain.

Because of this layer of security, it is a safe way to store data such as a login, password information, or a customer ID. Cookies are really a great alternative to using server-side session variables because they utilize the client's resources as opposed to server-side resources. The only downfall is that visitors to your web site aren't guaranteed to support them or to have them enabled.

Cookies are controlled and manipulated through the `HttpCookie` object located in the `System.Web` namespace. The easiest way to manipulate cookies with .NET is through the `HttpRequest` and `HttpResponse` objects. The `HttpCookieCollection` is a property of each of these objects and is referenced as a property called `Cookies`. And as you saw in Chapter 4, you reference the `Request` and `Response` objects as properties of the page. So to reference the `HttpCookieCollection` from within your ASP.NET pages you would simply use:

- Request.Cookies
- Response.Cookies

From there you address the individual cookies as items of the collection like anything else. Take a look.

Visual Basic .NET—`cookies_simple_vb.aspx`

```
<%@ page language="vb" runat="server"%>
<script runat=server>
Sub Page_Load()

    If Not IsPostBack then
        Response.Cookies("Test").Value = "CookieValue"
    Else
        OurLabel.Text=Request.Cookies("Test").Value
    End If

End Sub
</script>

<html>
<head>
<title>Cookie - Simple</title>
</head>
<body bgcolor="#FFFFFF" text="#000000">
<form runat="server">
<asp:Label id="OurLabel" runat="server" /><br>
<asp:Button Text="test" runat="server" />
</form>
</body>
</html>
```

C#—`cookies_simple_cs.aspx`

```
<%@ page language="c#" runat="server"%>
<script runat=server>
void Page_Load(){

    if (!IsPostBack){
        Response.Cookies["Test"].Value = "CookieValue";
    }else{
        OurLabel.Text=Request.Cookies["Test"].Value;
    }

}
</script>

<html>
<head>
<title>Cookie - Simple</title>
</head>
```

```
<body bgcolor="#FFFFFF" text="#000000">
<form runat="server">
<asp:Label id="OurLabel" runat="server" /><br>
<asp:Button Text="test" runat="server" />
</form>
</body>
</html>
```

In Figure 11.6, you can see that the cookie was set to CookieValue during the
initial load, and it was retrieved during postback and the value of OurLabel's text
property was set to the value of the cookie. Not very difficult. If you come from a
traditional ASP background this doesn't look too different from what you're used
to, with the exception of the .Value at the end of the Response and Request of
the cookies.

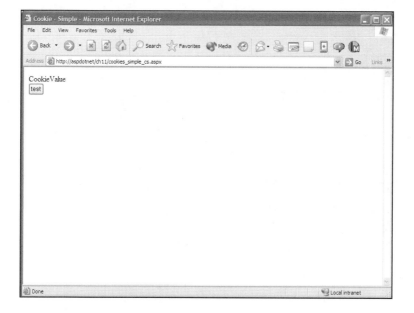

FIGURE 11.6

*Setting the value of
a cookie with the
HttpResponse
object and retrieving
a cookie with the
HttpRequest
object is very simple.*

This cookie type is one that resides in the memory of the client's machine
but doesn't persist after the user closes his browser down and returns. You
can control how long a cookie lasts through the Expires property of the
HttpCookie object.

Visual Basic .NET—`cookies_expires_vb.aspx`

```
<%@ page language="vb" runat="server"%>
<script runat=server>
Sub Page_Load()

    If Not IsPostBack then
        Dim ExpDate as DateTime = Now.AddDays(1)
        Response.Cookies("Test").Value = "CookieValue"
        Response.Cookies("Test").Expires = ExpDate
    Else
        OurLabel.Text=Request.Cookies("Test").Value
    End If

End Sub
</script>

<html>
<head>
<title>Cookie - Expires</title>
</head>
<body bgcolor="#FFFFFF" text="#000000">
<form runat="server">
<asp:Label id="OurLabel" runat="server" /><br>
<asp:Button Text="test" runat="server" />
</form>
</body>
</html>
```

C#—`cookies_expires_cs.aspx`

```
<%@ page language="c#" runat="server"%>
<script runat=server>
void Page_Load(){

    if (!IsPostBack){
        DateTime ExpDate = DateTime.Now.AddDays(1);
        Response.Cookies["Test"].Value = "CookieValue";
        Response.Cookies["Test"].Expires = ExpDate;
    }else{
        OurLabel.Text=Request.Cookies["Test"].Value;
    }

}
</script>

<html>
<head>
<title>Cookie - Expires</title>
</head>
```

```
<body bgcolor="#FFFFFF" text="#000000">
<form runat="server">
<asp:Label id="OurLabel" runat="server" /><br>
<asp:Button Text="test" runat="server" />
</form>
</body>
</html>
```

You can use that function and operate just fine. But ASP.NET also provides a deeper level of cookies in that each cookie can have a collection of name-value pairs in addition to a value itself. ASP.NET hasn't changed the way cookies work any more than it has changed the way HTML works. It simply has given additional functions to cookies that aren't inherent without ASP.NET.

The way you address the collection of name-value pairs within each cookie is to use the .Values("name") property rather than just the .Value property. Notice that the collection has the letter *S* at the end for a plural of Values. Take a look.

Visual Basic .NET—cookies_namevalue_vb.aspx

```
<%@ page language="vb" runat="server"%>
<script runat=server>
Sub Page_Load()

    If Not IsPostBack Then
        Response.Cookies("Customer").Values("CustomerID") = "100"
        Response.Cookies("Customer").Values("OrderID") = "20"
    Else
        If Not (Request.Cookies("Customer") Is Nothing) Then
            OurLabel.Text = Request.Cookies("Customer").Values("CustomerID")
            OurLabel2.Text = Request.Cookies("Customer").Values("OrderID")
        End If
    End If
End Sub 'Page_Load
</script>

<html>
<head>
<title>Cookie - NameValue</title>
</head>
<body bgcolor="#FFFFFF" text="#000000">
<form runat="server">
CustomerID: <asp:Label id="OurLabel" runat="server" /><br>
OrderID: <asp:Label id="OurLabel2" runat="server" /><br>
<asp:Button Text="test" runat="server" />
</form>
</body>
</html>
```

C#—`cookies_namevalue_cs.aspx`

```
<%@ page language="c#" runat="server"%>
<script runat=server>
void Page_Load(){

    if (!IsPostBack){
        Response.Cookies["Customer"].Values["CustomerID"] = "100";
        Response.Cookies["Customer"].Values["OrderID"] = "20";
    }else{
        if(Request.Cookies["Customer"] != null){
            OurLabel.Text = Request.Cookies["Customer"].Values["CustomerID"];
            OurLabel2.Text = Request.Cookies["Customer"].Values["OrderID"];
        }
    }
}
</script>

<html>
<head>
<title>Cookie - NameValue</title>
</head>
<body bgcolor="#FFFFFF" text="#000000">
<form runat="server">
CustomerID: <asp:Label id="OurLabel" runat="server" /><br>
OrderID: <asp:Label id="OurLabel2" runat="server" /><br>
<asp:Button Text="test" runat="server" />
</form>
</body>
</html>
```

You can see that the name-value pair is addressed by the `.Values("name")` property of the `cookie` object. As with just about everything in the .NET Framework, this property is an inherited object called the `NameValueCollection` and is located in the `System.Collections.Specialized` namespace. As you can see, this specialized collection is used to extend the functionality of cookies to perform things like this name–value pair function that cookies don't inherently have.

Also, if you look at the previous code there is something else that is very important to notice. Look at these lines:

Visual Basic .NET

```
If Not (Request.Cookies("Customer") Is Nothing) Then
    OurLabel.Text = Request.Cookies("Customer").Values("CustomerID")
    OurLabel2.Text = Request.Cookies("Customer").Values("OrderID")
End If
```

C#

```
if(Request.Cookies["Customer"] != null){
    OurLabel.Text = Request.Cookies["Customer"].Values["CustomerID"];
    OurLabel2.Text = Request.Cookies["Customer"].Values["OrderID"];
}
```

These two `if` statements are critical to include if you will be checking for cookies that potentially don't exist. For instance, imagine that you have a shopping cart page and you are pulling the `OrderID` out of a cookie on that page, but someone goes there before this cookie has been set. This generates an error because you are trying to address an `HttpCookie` object that doesn't exist. ASP.NET can't do that. It cannot check the value of something that doesn't exist, so you must first check to see whether it exists by using the highlighted `if` statement.

There is also a bit of a shortcut for addressing the `Values` property of the `HttpCookie` object by dropping the `.Values` from your `Response` and `Request`. Take a look.

Visual Basic .NET—`cookies_namevalue_shortcut_vb.aspx`

```
<%@ page language="vb" runat="server"%>
<script runat=server>
Sub Page_Load()

    If Not IsPostBack Then
        Response.Cookies("Customer")("CustomerID") = "100"
        Response.Cookies("Customer")("OrderID") = "20"
    Else
        If Not (Request.Cookies("Customer") Is Nothing) Then
            OurLabel.Text = Request.Cookies("Customer")("CustomerID")
            OurLabel2.Text = Request.Cookies("Customer")("OrderID")
        End If
    End If
End Sub 'Page_Load
</script>

<html>
<head>
<title>Cookie - NameValue Shortcut</title>
</head>
<body bgcolor="#FFFFFF" text="#000000">
<form runat="server">
CustomerID: <asp:Label id="OurLabel" runat="server" /><br>
OrderID: <asp:Label id="OurLabel2" runat="server" /><br>
<asp:Button Text="test" runat="server" />
</form>
</body>
</html>
```

C#—`cookies_namevalue_shortcut_cs.aspx`

```
<%@ page language="c#" runat="server"%>
<script runat=server>
void Page_Load(){

    if (!IsPostBack){
        Response.Cookies["Customer"]["CustomerID"] = "100";
        Response.Cookies["Customer"]["OrderID"] = "20";
    }else{
        if(Request.Cookies["Customer"] != null){
            OurLabel.Text = Request.Cookies["Customer"]["CustomerID"];
            OurLabel2.Text = Request.Cookies["Customer"]["OrderID"];
        }
    }
}
</script>

<html>
<head>
<title>Cookie - Simple</title>
</head>
<body bgcolor="#FFFFFF" text="#000000">
<form runat="server">
CustomerID: <asp:Label id="OurLabel" runat="server" /><br>
OrderID: <asp:Label id="OurLabel2" runat="server" /><br>
<asp:Button Text="test" runat="server" />
</form>
</body>
</html>
```

To use the shortcut, you just eliminate the `.Values` from the reference and voilá…it works the same. Not a big thing, but every little bit helps.

Although cookies provide a great alternative to sessions, the client does have the power to turn them off. It is therefore important that you check to see whether the client has cookies enabled. This is often a difficult subject and many people confuse the issue of a browser's capabilities for handling cookies with the fact that users have the power to disable cookie use if they so desire.

It pays at critical points to run a check to see whether a person has cookies enabled. Now there are a million ways to skin a cat and checking to see whether cookies are enabled is no exception. The following is a simple example of how to check to see whether cookies are enabled. Remember that you must make a round-trip client to truly know whether the user has cookies enabled. Hence the `Response.Redirect` to push us back to the client so we can set the cookie and then return and check to see whether it's set.

Visual Basic .NET—`cookies_test_vb.aspx`

```
<%@ page language="vb" runat="server"%>
<script runat=server>
Sub Page_Load()

    If Not (Request.Cookies("cookiesenabled") Is Nothing) Then
        OurLabel.Text = "Cookies are enabled"
    Else
        If Request.QueryString("ck") <> "true" Then
            Response.Cookies("cookiesenabled").Value = "true"
            Response.Redirect("cookies_test_cs.aspx?ck=true")
        Else
            OurLabel.Text = "Sorry! Cookies are disabled"
        End If
    End If
End Sub 'Page_Load
</script>

<html>
<head>
<title>Cookie - Test</title>
</head>
<body bgcolor="#FFFFFF" text="#000000">
<asp:Label id="OurLabel" runat="server" /><br>
</body>
</html>
```

C#—`cookies_test_cs.aspx`

```
<%@ page language="c#" runat="server"%>
<script runat=server>
void Page_Load(){

    if(Request.Cookies["cookiesenabled"] != null){
        OurLabel.Text = "Cookies are enabled";
    }else{
        if(Request.QueryString["ck"]!="true"){
            Response.Cookies["cookiesenabled"].Value = "true";
            Response.Redirect("cookies_test_cs.aspx?ck=true");
        }else{
            OurLabel.Text = "Sorry! Cookies are disabled";
        }
    }

}
</script>

<html>
<head>
<title>Cookie - Simple</title>
</head>
```

continues

C#—(continued)

```
<body bgcolor="#FFFFFF" text="#000000">
<asp:Label id="OurLabel" runat="server" /><br>
</body>
</html>
```

As I said, this is not the only way to do this, but is only a simple example of how to check to see whether cookies are enabled. Basically, if it's the first time to the page and there is not a cookie called `cookiesenabled`, you should try to set that cookie and then redirect back to the same page with a querystring value to indicate that you've attempted to set the cookie. If you return to the page and the cookie exists, great! Cookies are enabled. But if the cookie doesn't exist and there is a querystring value of `ck=true`, you know that you tried to set a cookie and failed. You can conclude that cookies are disabled and act accordingly, possibly by informing the user that she needs to enable cookies to use the site, or by dealing with state issues in a cookieless way.

Application State

Application state was covered in Chapter 4, which addressed the `Application` property of the ASP.NET `Page` object. I explained that the `Application` property is really an instance of the `HttpApplicationState` object and that you can initialize an `Application` variable in the `Application_OnStart` event that is contained in the Global.asax file located in the root of your application.

First you must remember that `Application` variables are just like `Session` variables, except that they are shared across all users. A `Session` variable holds information that is unique to that user. Application variables hold information that is common to all users.

To reiterate what was covered in Chapter 4, first look at the global.asax file to see how you can initialize `Application` variables.

Visual Basic .NET—`global.asax`

```
<script language="vb" runat=server>
Sub Application_OnStart()
    Application("Publisher") = "New Riders"
    Application("BookTitle") = "ASP.NET for Web Designers"
    Application("Author") = "Peter"
    Application("Rating") = "5 Stars, WHAHOOO!!"
End Sub
</script>
```

C#—`global.asax`

```
<script language="c#" runat=server>
void Application_OnStart(){
    Application["Publisher"] = "New Riders";
    Application["BookTitle"] = "ASP.NET for Web Designers";
    Application["Author"] = "Peter";
    Application["Rating"] = "5 Stars, WHAHOOO!!";
}
</script>
```

This sets the listed `Application` variables when the application first starts, which happens when the first person makes the first request to your web site.

The following are the examples from Chapter 4 that show how to retrieve an `Application` variable. It is no different than retrieving a `Session` variable, except you address the `Application` instead of the `Session`.

Visual Basic .NET—`page_application_vb.aspx`

```
<%@ page language="vb" runat="server"%>
<script  runat=server>

Sub Page_Load()
    Title.Text = "<u>Title:</u> " + Application("BookTitle")
    Publisher.Text = "<u>Publisher:</u> " + Application("Publisher")
    Author.Text = "<u>Author:</u> " + Application("Author")
    BookRating.Text = "<u>Rating:</u> " + Application("Rating")
End Sub

</script>
<html>
<title>Application</title>
<body>
<asp:label id="Title" runat="server"/><br>
<asp:label id="Publisher" runat="server"/><br>
<asp:label id="Author" runat="server"/><br>
<asp:label id="BookRating" runat="server"/>
</body>
</html>
```

C#—`page_application_cs.aspx`

```
<%@ page language="cs" runat="server"%>
<script  runat=server>

void Page_Load(){
    Title.Text = "<u>Title:</u> " + Application["BookTitle"];
    Publisher.Text = "<u>Publisher:</u> " + Application["Publisher"];
    Author.Text = "<u>Author:</u> " + Application["Author"];
    BookRating.Text = "<u>Rating:</u> " + Application["Rating"];
}

</script>
<html>
<title>Application</title>
<body>
<asp:label id="Title" runat="server"/><br>
<asp:label id="Publisher" runat="server"/><br>
<asp:label id="Author" runat="server"/><br>
<asp:label id="BookRating" runat="server"/>
</body>
</html>
```

`Application` variables can be used to hold any type of global information such as database connection. Earlier in this chapter, while describing the `Session_Start` and `Session_End` events, an `Application` variable was actually utilized to keep a running count of active sessions on a web application. There are many uses for `Application` variables for storing global data.

Summary

This chapter covered the subject of `page`, `user`, and `application` states so a conversation between the client and server is possible. By now you can identify a user and persist data throughout a user's visit to your web site. This is the core of making web applications work.

In the next chapter, you are going to go a step further by proceeding not only to identify a user across visits to the website, but also to grant them differentiated access to the site and its pages based on who they are. In other words, it addresses authentication and authorization. See you there.

chapter 12

Form-Based Security in ASP.NET

Can I see some form of
identification, please?

Y ou've come a long way so far. You have a pouch full of tools to build web
applications so that people can visit your site, you can interact with them, and
you can trade information, but up until this point those users have remained
anonymous. You have come to the place where you will learn how to allow
users to identify themselves and then control what information they will be
allowed to see.

This is known as *authentication* and *authorization*. Let me take a minute here to
give some basic definitions of these two words that you'll be studying throughout
this chapter.

- **Authentication**. The process of verifying a user's identity against a known
  and trusted source.

- **Authorization**. To measure or establish the power or permission that has
  been given or granted by an authority.

Although both processes start with the same four letters and are closely integrated, they serve very different purposes in life and hence in your ASP.NET applications. You must first authenticate someone, and only then can you understand what authority or authorization that user might have within your site.

Creating Form-Based Security

As with all things .NET, authentication and authorization have been thoroughly thought out and revisions have been made and objects created to deal with these issues within the .NET Framework. It all starts as most application configuration issues do, in the Web.Config file located in the root of your application.

Now I must start out by explaining that four different modes of authentication are available for use in the .NET Framework for ASP.NET pages.

- **Forms**. Uses ASP.NET form-based authentication.

- **Windows**. Uses the Windows authentication system on the web server.

- **Passport**. Uses Microsoft's Passport Authentication.

- **None**. No authentication, because only anonymous users are expected or because programmers will handle authentication and authorization themselves.

For this chapter, we will be exploring only the Forms mode of authentication. If you are interested in the Windows or Passport method of authentication I would recommend you acquire *Inside ASP.NET*, by Scott Worley, published by New Riders Publishing.

To tell your web application that you will be using the Forms mode of authentication, you need to set the proper entries in the Web.Config file located in the root of your application. If the <authentication> tag is present anywhere but in the root Web.Config file, the .NET Framework generates an error.

Web.Config

```
<configuration>
    <system.web>
        <authentication mode="Forms">
        </authentication>
    </system.web>
</configuration>
```

Of course there's more stuff to add to the Web.Config file, but this is just to demonstrate how to tell your ASP.NET application that you will be using forms-based security.

Understanding Authentication Logic

Now that your application knows that you are using forms-based security, you need to start configuring the application to handle authentication the way you want.

One thing I must mention now is that the techniques discussed in this chapter require that the client's machine be running a cookie-capable and -enabled browser. If this is in question, you need to fabricate an alternate method for authentication. Cookies are required for ASP.NET form-based authentication.

The next thing I want to address is the next tag in the Web.Config file. This is called the `<forms>` tag and is to be located inside the `<authentication>` tag. It has four attributes that I'll cover: `name`, `loginURL`, `protection`, and `timeout`.

Web.Config

```
<configuration>
    <system.web>
            <authentication mode="Forms">
                <forms name="NewRiderAuth"
                loginUrl="ch12/login.aspx"
                protection="All"
                timeout="15">
            </forms>
            </authentication>
    </system.web>
</configuration>
```

The `name` attribute specifies the name of the `HTTPCookie` used for authentication. By default this is `.ASPXAUT`. If you need to run multiple applications under a single domain, and need these applications to run with a unique cookie, this is where you would set it.

The `loginURL` attribute specifies the URL where individuals should be redirected if they haven't been authenticated yet. If none is specified, the default value is `default.aspx`.

The protection attribute has four different possible options: All, None, Encryption, and Validation. The authorization cookie can be encrypted and validated to protect against tampering. You can specify one or the other, both, or none with the different options.

The timeout attribute specifies the time in minutes when the authorization cookie expires, from the time of the last request received. The default is 30 minutes.

Now we have come to a crossroads with regard to what trusted source you are going to use to authenticate a user. In traditional ASP, a database was often used as the source. A user would enter a username and password into a form, and this would be compared against values in a database. The username was compared to a username column, and a password was compared to a password column. If there was a matching record in the database, the user was considered authenticated.

ASP.NET also provides another way to authenticate with form-based authentication, which is to compare a user's input against values in the Web.Config value. I'll explore this method first, then show you how to use a database as the trusted source.

Authenticating Against the Web.Config file.

As I mentioned before, the Web.Config file can hold user data that you can authenticate against, and this is a valid ASP.NET form of validation. The way users are stored is with the addition of two more tags that are placed inside the <forms> tag in the Web.Config file. These tags are the <credentials> tag, and nested within it are <user> tags, one for each user.

Web.Config

```
<configuration>
    <system.web>
            <authentication mode="Forms">
                <forms name="NewRiderAuth"
                loginUrl="ch12/login.aspx"
                protection="All"
                timeout="15">
                <credentials passwordFormat="Clear">
                    <user name="Peter" password="NewRiders"/>
                        <user name="Tom" password="qwerty"/>
                </credentials>
            </forms>
            </authentication>
    </system.web>
</configuration>
```

I will address the passwordFormat attribute of the <credentials> tag in a little bit. In the <user> tag, there are simply a name attribute and a password attribute that are used for the comparison for authentication.

Using the *Authenticate()* Method

Now on to the authentication. I'm not going to get too technical here, but I have to explain a few things. There is a class called FormsAuthentication that handles just about everything we're going to investigate here. Normally, to be able to access an object's methods, you've had to create an instance of that object. If the object was in a namespace that wasn't inherently available in the ASP.NET program, such as System.Web.UI, you've had to import that namespace to create and use that object. We are faced with an exception to this rule here. There are methods of objects that are available for use in ASP.NET pages without importing any namespace and even without creating an instance of an object. These are called *shared/static methods* in Visual Basic .NET and *static methods* in C#.

In a nutshell, all this to say that shared/static methods are always available for use; all you have to do is use a Class.Method() syntax. For the sake of brevity, from now on I will refer to these as "static" methods and drop the "shared" from my explanations. A lot of static methods of the FormsAuthentication object are used throughout this chapter.

In the following example, I am going to introduce you to the first static method, which is a member of the FormsAuthentication object. It is called Authenticate. It takes two parameter: name and password, which are compared against the name and password values in the <user> tag of the Web.Config file. Take a look.

Visual Basic .NET—`authen_simple_vb.aspx`

```
<%@ page language="vb" runat="server"%>
<script runat=server>

Sub Authenticate(Sender as Object, e as EventArgs)
    if FormsAuthentication.Authenticate (Username.Text, Password.Text) then
        OurLabel.Text = "This is a valid login"
    Else
        OurLabel.Text = "This login doesn't exist"
    End If
End Sub

</script>

<html>
<head>
```

continues

Visual Basic .NET—(continued)

```
<title>Login</title>
</head>
<body bgcolor="#FFFFFF" text="#000000">
<form runat="server">
<h3>Login</h3>
<asp:textbox id="Username" runat="server" /> Username<br>
<asp:textbox id="Password" runat="server" />
Password <br><br>
<asp:button text="Login" onClick="Authenticate" runat="server" /><br><br>
<asp:Label id="OurLabel" EnableViewState="False" runat="server" />
</form>
</body>
</html>
```

C#—authen_simple_cs.aspx

```
<%@ page language="cs" runat="server"%>
<script runat=server>

void Authenticate(Object Sender, EventArgs e){
    if (FormsAuthentication.Authenticate (Username.Text, Password.Text)){
        OurLabel.Text = "This is a valid login";
    }else{
        OurLabel.Text = "This login doesn't exist";
    }
}

</script>

<html>
<head>
<title>Login</title>
</head>
<body bgcolor="#FFFFFF" text="#000000">
<form runat="server">
<h3>Login</h3>
<asp:textbox id="Username" runat="server" /> Username<br>
<asp:textbox id="Password" runat="server" />
Password <br><br>
<asp:button text="Login" onClick="Authenticate" runat="server" /><br><br>
<asp:Label id="OurLabel" EnableViewState="False" runat="server" />
</form>
</body>
</html>
```

As you can see, this is very simple. Simply pass the text of the Username and Password text boxes, and the Authenticate static method of FormsAuthentication compares values against all the <user> tags in our Web.Config file. You can see the results in Figure 12.1.

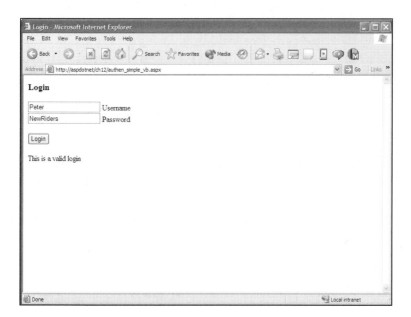

FIGURE 12.1

The Forms Authentication .Authenticate *static method allows you to easily compare usernames and passwords against* <user> *data stored in the Web.Config file.*

> **NOTE**
>
> *When you compare usernames and passwords against the Web.Config* <user> *entries using the* Authenticate *static method, be aware that it is case-sensitive, requiring that the usernames and passwords match precisely.*

Using Hashed Passwords in Web.Config

This is a great method if only trusted people have access to your Web.Config file, because the passwords to your application are exposed. But this doesn't seem very secure if your Web.Config file is located where people other than fully trusted individuals can access it. This means you can't use your favorite password that has been etched on the inside of your forehead.

The .NET Framework has made accommodation for this. Remember, I said that I would touch on the <credentials> tag earlier. In that tag was an attribute called passwordFormat that was set to Clear. The passwordFormat attribute has three possible values: Clear, SHA1, and MD5. The Clear value simply ensures that the password values in the <user> tags are written in plain text.

The SHA1 and MD5 options are cryptographic options called one-way hashes. "What's a hash?" you ask. The long and short of it is that a hash is basically a cryptographic digital fingerprint of a string. A string is converted into a fixed length hash that is a representation of that string in hash form. These two technologies are considered "one-way" hashes, which means that it is "computationally infeasible" to invert and derive the initial string from the hash. In other words, it's simple to take a password and create a hash from it, but it is nearly impossible to take a hash and re-create the password.

These two options for `passwordFormat` allow you to enter hashed passwords, rather than plain text, in the Web.Config file. This way anyone looking at the Web.Config file will see a password that really doesn't make any sense to them.

Now you are faced with creating hashed versions of your passwords. Again, the .NET Framework makes a way. Believe it or not, there is a static method of the `FormsAuthentication` object called `HashPasswordForStoringInConfigFile()`. You simply pass in the password and the hashtype to this method and it returns the hash of that password. The following is an ASP.NET page that I made that uses this static method to hash passwords.

Visual Basic .NET—**password_createhash_vb.aspx**

```
<%@ page language="vb" runat="server"%>
<script runat=server>

Sub CreateHash(sender As Object, e As EventArgs)
    Dim vHash As String
    Dim vHashType As String = HashType.SelectedItem.Text
    Dim vPassword As String = Password.Text
    vHash = FormsAuthentication.HashPasswordForStoringInConfigFile(vPassword,
    ➥vHashType)
    OurLabel.Text = "Your hashed password in " + vHashType + " format"
    OurHash.Text = vHash
End Sub 'CreateHash
</script>

<html>
<head>
<title>Create Password Hash</title>
</head>
<body bgcolor="#FFFFFF" text="#000000">
<form runat="server">
<h3>Hash Password for Web.Config File</h3>
Insert Password <br>
<asp:textbox id="Password" runat="server"/><br>
<asp:RadioButtonList id="HashType" runat="server">
<asp:ListItem text="SHA1"/>
<asp:ListItem text="MD5"/>
</asp:RadiobuttonList>
<asp:Button Text="Create Hash" onClick="CreateHash" runat="server" /><br><br>
```

```
<u><asp:Label id="OurLabel" runat="server" /></u><br>
<asp:Label id="OurHash" runat="server" />
</form>
</body>
</html>
```

C#—password_createhash_cs.aspx

```
<%@ page language="c#" runat="server"%>
<script runat=server>

void CreateHash(object sender, EventArgs e){
    string vHash;
    string vHashType = HashType.SelectedItem.Text;
    string vPassword = Password.Text;
    vHash = FormsAuthentication.HashPasswordForStoringInConfigFile
    ➥(vPassword,vHashType);
    OurLabel.Text = "Your hashed password in " + vHashType + " format";
    OurHash.Text = vHash;
}
</script>

<html>
<head>
<title>Create Password Hash</title>
</head>
<body bgcolor="#FFFFFF" text="#000000">
<form runat="server">
<h3>Hash Password for Web.Config File</h3>
Insert Password <br>
<asp:textbox id="Password" runat="server"/><br>
<asp:RadioButtonList id="HashType" runat="server">
<asp:ListItem text="SHA1"/>
<asp:ListItem text="MD5"/>
</asp:RadiobuttonList>
<asp:Button Text="Create Hash" onClick="CreateHash" runat="server" /><br><br>
<u><asp:Label id="OurLabel" runat="server" /></u><br>
<asp:Label id="OurHash" runat="server" />
</form>
</body>
</html>
```

Creating a hashed password in ASP.NET is simple . If you look at Figure 12.2
you can see I simply entered my desired password into the text box and the static
method called HashPasswordForStoringInConfigFile() generates the appropriate
hash for that password. I enter **NewRiders** into the text box and select MD5 as
the type and it generates my password hash.

FIGURE 12.2

Making hashes of passwords is simple with the static method called `HashPassword-ForStoringIn-ConfigFile()`.

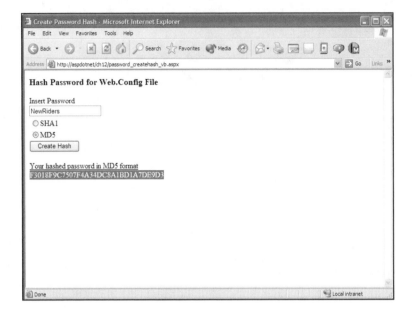

I copy that password hash from the page and paste it into the `password` attribute of my user tag and set the `passwordFormat` to MD5.

Web.Config

```
<credentials passwordFormat="MD5">
    <user name="Peter" password="F3018F9C7507F4A34DC8A1BD1A7DE9D3"/>
</credentials>
```

No changes need to be made to my ASP.NET authentication page. All the changes are made in the Web.Config file. In Figure 12.3, you can see the expected results, when using the MD5 method. Using the SHA1 method is no different, except that you need to make SHA1 versions of hashed passwords and set the `passwordFormat` attribute of the <credentials> tag to SHA1.

Basically what the .NET Framework does is hash the inserted password and compare that to the password entered in the <user> tag.

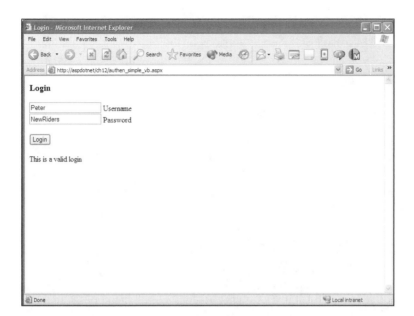

FIGURE 12.3

Using a hash system of passwordFormat *in the* <credentials> *tag in the Web.Config doesn't alter the way people log in to your site.*

This offers another layer of protection with regard to security, but does leave some leeway for people that absolutely want to penetrate the system. This isn't really the best method if you have more than a handful of users, because it can become a bit of a cumbersome way to manage large numbers of users. If you need to manage many user accounts, I recommend using a database. If you need something that is a bit more secure, I recommend managing your users in a secure database environment such as Microsoft's SQL Server. I don't classify Microsoft Access as a secure database environment because there are many readily available utilities that can compromise its less-than-strong security features.

Authenticating Against a Database

As I mentioned, the Web.Config method of managing users is a fine method if security isn't paramount and you aren't dealing with a boatload of users. If either or both of these is the case, though, I recommend a database as your trusted source. I cover using both Microsoft Access and stored procedures in Microsoft SQL Server for authentication in this section. As with the previous section, I will be doing just the "comparison" portion of authentication here. What to do after the comparison process is done is covered in the next section.

For these demonstrations I've added a table called Logins to both the Microsoft Access and Microsoft SQL Server versions of the Northwind database. In Figure 12.4 you can see a screenshot of the database table in Access. It is exactly the same in the SQL Server version.

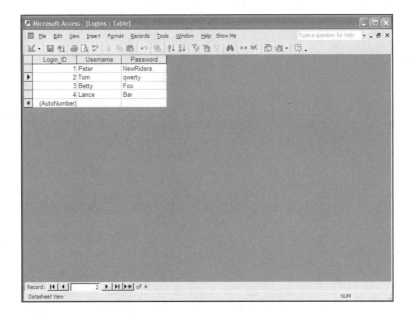

FIGURE 12.4

The database Logins table.

Using Microsoft Access as a Trusted Source

To authenticate against a database demands a slightly different approach than authenticating against the Web.Config file. What I generally do is create another function that calls to the database to compare the username and password. The following is a code example of this.

Visual Basic .NET—**authen_access_vb.aspx**

```
<%@ page language="vb" runat="server"%>
<%@ Import Namespace="System.Data"%>
<%@ Import Namespace="System.Data.OleDb"%>
<script runat=server>


Sub Authenticate(Sender As [Object], e As EventArgs)
    Dim Login_ID As Integer = DBAuthenticate(Username.Text, Password.Text)
    If Login_ID > 0 Then
        OurLabel.Text = "This is a valid login"
    Else
        OurLabel.Text = "This login doesn't exist"
```

```
    End If
End Sub

Function DBAuthenticate(username As String, password As String) As Integer

    Dim OurConnection As OleDbConnection
    Dim OurCommand As OleDbCommand
    Dim OurDataReader As OleDbDataReader
    Dim SQLString As String
    Dim Login_ID As Integer

    SQLString = "Select Login_ID,Password from Logins where Username = '" +
    ➥username + "' and Password = '" + password + "'"
    OurConnection = New OleDbConnection("Provider=Microsoft.Jet.OLEDB.4.0;Data
    ➥Source=" + Server.MapPath("../_database/northwind.mdb"))
    OurConnection.Open()
    OurCommand = New OleDbCommand(SQLString, OurConnection)
    OurDataReader = OurCommand.ExecuteReader()

    If OurDataReader.Read() Then
        If OurDataReader("Password").ToString() = password Then
            Login_ID = Int32.Parse(OurDataReader("Login_ID").ToString())
        Else
            Login_ID = 0
        End If
    Else
        Login_ID = 0
    End If


    OurDataReader.Close()
    OurConnection.Close()

    Return Login_ID
End Function

</script>
<html>
<head>
<title>Login</title>
</head>
<body bgcolor="#FFFFFF" text="#000000">
<form runat="server">
<h3>Login</h3>
<asp:textbox id="Username" runat="server" /> Username<br>
<asp:textbox id="Password" runat="server" />
Password <br><br>
<asp:button text="Login" onClick="Authenticate" runat="server" /><br><br>
<asp:Label id="OurLabel" EnableViewState="False" runat="server" /><br>
</form>
</body>
</html>
```

C#—authen_access_cs.aspx

```
<%@ page language="cs" runat="server"%>
<%@ Import Namespace="System.Data"%>
<%@ Import Namespace="System.Data.OleDb"%>
<script runat=server>

void Authenticate(Object Sender, EventArgs e){
    int Login_ID = DBAuthenticate(Username.Text, Password.Text);
    if (Login_ID > 0){
        OurLabel.Text = "This is a valid login";
    }else{
        OurLabel.Text = "This login doesn't exist";
    }
}

 int DBAuthenticate(string username,string password){

    OleDbConnection OurConnection;
    OleDbCommand OurCommand;
    OleDbDataReader OurDataReader;
    string SQLString;
    int Login_ID;

    SQLString = "Select Login_ID,Password from Logins where Username = '" +
    ➥username + "' and Password = '" + password + "'";
    OurConnection = new OleDbConnection("Provider=Microsoft.Jet.OLEDB.4.0;Data
    ➥Source=" + Server.MapPath("../_database/northwind.mdb"));
    OurConnection.Open();
    OurCommand = new OleDbCommand(SQLString ,OurConnection);
    OurDataReader = OurCommand.ExecuteReader();

    if (OurDataReader.Read()){
        if (OurDataReader["Password"].ToString() == password){
                Login_ID = Int32.Parse(OurDataReader["Login_ID"].ToString());
        }else{
                Login_ID = 0;
        }
    }else{
        Login_ID = 0;
    }


    OurDataReader.Close();
    OurConnection.Close();

    return Login_ID;
}

</script>

<html>
```

```
<head>
<title>Login</title>
</head>
<body bgcolor="#FFFFFF" text="#000000">
<form runat="server">
<h3>Login</h3>
<asp:textbox id="Username" runat="server" /> Username<br>
<asp:textbox id="Password" runat="server" />
Password <br><br>
<asp:button text="Login" onClick="Authenticate" runat="server" /><br><br>
<asp:Label id="OurLabel" EnableViewState="False" runat="server" /><br>
</form>
</body>
</html>
```

Although this may look complicated, it really isn't. The `OnClick` event of the button calls the `Authenticate()` function, which immediately sets an integer variable called `Login_ID` to the returned value of the `DBAuthenticate()` function.

In `DBAuthenticate`, the database is being queried for a record in the Logins table that matches the username and password that is entered in the text boxes. In the `DBAuthenticate` function, if there is a match, the line that reads `if OurDataReader.Read()` will return true. Then you know that you have a match that is not case-sensitive because T-SQL queries like this are not case-sensitive. If this returns false, set `Login_ID` in the `DBAuthenticate` to 0.

To make it a case-sensitive match, do a direct comparison with the line that reads `If OurDataReader("Password").ToString() = password` in Visual Basic .NET and `if (OurDataReader["Password"].ToString() == password)` in C#. This is a case-sensitive check. If the value returned from the database matches this check, then you have a total match and set the `Login_ID` in `DBAuthenticate` to the `Login_ID` from the database table; that is what gets returned to the `Authenticate()` function.

After you're back at the `Authenticate` function, evaluate the Login_ID. If it's 0, you know that the username and password didn't match; otherwise you'll see a value greater than 0 because the `Login_ID`s start at 1. Later I'll show you how to use this value at the `Authentication` cookie, which will make it a snap to pull user-specific data out of the database.

Using Microsoft SQL Server as a Trusted Source

Microsoft SQL Server provides a much more secure environment with which to store your login and password information. It can be protected from unauthorized users, the information is never exposed, and stored procedures allow you to query the database without ever having the username and password information leave the SQL Server database.

The authentication function you are going to explore is very similar to the Access version, except the username and password are sent to a stored procedure. You check for their existence and then return an output parameter called @Login_ID with the Login_ID from the table if they do exist and return @Login_ID with a value of 0 if they don't. Here is the stored procedure.

spLogin

```
CREATE PROCEDURE [spLogin]

    @Username varchar(50),
    @Password varchar(50),
    @Login_ID int output

AS
    if exists (Select * from Logins where username = @username and password =
    ➡@Password)
        Set  @Login_ID = (Select Login_ID from Logins where username = @username
        ➡and password = @Password)
    else
        Set @Login_ID = 0
GO
```

You use the same exact functions as with the Access database, except you run the stored procedure and return the value of @Login_ID to the Authenticate function.

Visual Basic .NET—**authen_sql_vb.aspx**

```
<%@ page language="vb" runat="server"%>
<%@ Import Namespace="System.Data"%>
<%@ Import Namespace="System.Data.SqlClient" %>
<script runat=server>

Sub Authenticate(Sender As [Object], e As EventArgs)
```

```
    Dim Login_ID As Integer = DBAuthenticate(Username.Text, Password.Text)
    If Login_ID > 0 Then
        OurLabel.Text = "This is a valid login"
    Else
        OurLabel.Text = "This login doesn't exist"
    End If
End Sub


Function DBAuthenticate(username As String, password As String) As Integer

    Dim OurConnection As SqlConnection
    Dim OurCommand As SqlCommand
    Dim OurDataReader As SqlDataReader

    OurConnection = New SqlConnection("Server=server;
    ➥uid=newriders;pwd=password;database=Northwind")
    OurCommand = New SqlCommand("spLogin", OurConnection)
    OurCommand.CommandType = CommandType.StoredProcedure
    OurCommand.Parameters.Add("@Username", SqlDbType.VarChar, 50).Value = username
    OurCommand.Parameters.Add("@Password", SqlDbType.VarChar, 50).Value = password
    OurCommand.Parameters.Add("@Login_ID", SqlDbType.Int).Direction =
    ➥ParameterDirection.Output
    OurConnection.Open()
    OurCommand.ExecuteNonQuery()
    Dim Login_ID As Integer = CInt(OurCommand.Parameters("@Login_ID").Value)
    OurConnection.Close()

    Return Login_ID
End Function

</script>

<html>
<head>
<title>Login</title>
</head>
<body bgcolor="#FFFFFF" text="#000000">
<form runat="server">
<h3>Login</h3>
<asp:textbox id="Username" runat="server" /> Username<br>
<asp:textbox id="Password" runat="server" />
Password <br><br>
<asp:button text="Login" onClick="Authenticate" runat="server" /><br><br>
<asp:Label id="OurLabel" EnableViewState="False" runat="server" /><br>
</form>
</body>
</html>
```

C#—authen_sql_cs.aspx

```
<%@ page language="cs" runat="server"%>
<%@ Import Namespace="System.Data"%>
<%@ Import Namespace="System.Data.SqlClient" %>
<script runat=server>

void Authenticate(Object Sender, EventArgs e){
    int Login_ID = DBAuthenticate(Username.Text, Password.Text);
    if (Login_ID > 0){
        OurLabel.Text = "This is a valid login";
    }else{
        OurLabel.Text = "This login doesn't exist";
    }
}


 int DBAuthenticate(string username,string password){

    SqlConnection OurConnection;
    SqlCommand OurCommand;
    SqlDataReader OurDataReader;


    OurConnection = new SqlConnection("Server=server;
    ➥uid=newriders;pwd=password;database=Northwind");
    OurCommand = new SqlCommand("spLogin" ,OurConnection);
    OurCommand.CommandType = CommandType.StoredProcedure;
    OurCommand.Parameters.Add("@Username", SqlDbType.VarChar, 50).Value =
    ➥username;
    OurCommand.Parameters.Add("@Password", SqlDbType.VarChar, 50).Value =
    ➥password;
    OurCommand.Parameters.Add("@Login_ID", SqlDbType.Int).Direction =
    ➥ParameterDirection.Output;
    OurConnection.Open();
    OurCommand.ExecuteNonQuery();
    int Login_ID =  (int)OurCommand.Parameters["@Login_ID"].Value;
    OurConnection.Close();

    return Login_ID;
}

</script>

<html>
<head>
<title>Login</title>
</head>
<body bgcolor="#FFFFFF" text="#000000">
<form runat="server">
<h3>Login</h3>
<asp:textbox id="Username" runat="server" /> Username<br>
<asp:textbox id="Password" runat="server" />
Password <br><br>
```

```
<asp:button text="Login" onClick="Authenticate" runat="server" /><br><br>
<asp:Label id="OurLabel" EnableViewState="False" runat="server" /><br>
</form>
</body>
</html>
```

Although this happens in a different way when you use the stored procedure, the logic isn't very different from the Access version. One thing to note is that although this is a more secure means of storing your sensitive username and password information, you may lose the capacity for case-sensitive authentication, depending on how the database is set up. I have never really found issue with this, but it is something to consider when designing your authentication process.

Completing the Authentication Process

When a user logs in, I highly doubt that all you want to do is set the Text value of a Label as I've done in the past examples. And actually this is only part of the process for ASP.NET to recognize that a user is considered authenticated.

This brings us back to some of the attributes of the <form> tag in the Web.Config file. Let's investigate the name and loginUrl attributes a bit.

```
<authentication mode="Forms">
    <forms name="NewRiderAuth"
        loginUrl="ch12/authen_redirect_vb.aspx"
        protection="All"
        timeout="15">
        <credentials passwordFormat="Clear">
            <user name="Peter" password="NewRiders"/>
                <user name="Tom" password="qwerty"/>
        </credentials>
    </forms>
</authentication>
```

For ASP.NET to consider a user authenticated, that user must have a cookie that matches the name attribute in the <form> tag. Remember that this is the name you are specifying that ASP.NET is to use for the authentication cookie. Also remember that this cookie will be encrypted and validated by ASP.NET when it's created and retrieved, because the protection attribute has been set to All.

The loginUrl attribute tells ASP.NET what page is used to perform the authentication process, or in other words, your login page. The login page basically handles when a user who is not authenticated goes to a page that requires authentication to view. Those users are automatically sent to the URL set in loginUrl if you are using forms security function.

To demonstrate what happens, I have touched on authorization a bit. I have created a directory called "protected" inside my ch12 directory and placed a Web.Config file inside that directory that prevents unauthenticated users from viewing any pages in that directory. The following is the Web.Config file that is in that "protected" directory.

ch12/protected/Web.Config

```
<configuration>
    <system.web>
        <authorization>
            <deny users="?" />
        </authorization>
    </system.web>
</configuration>
```

The question mark (?) in the <deny users="?" /> tag represents anonymous users. I will explain all of this in detail later in this chapter, but basically this authorization says to deny all anonymous users access to this directory and everything contained inside it, including subdirectories that don't have a Web.Config file with explicit authorization settings of its own.

> **T I P**
>
> *Every directory within your application can contain its own Web.Config file to configure the directory that contains it. I recommend that you learn more about configuring your ASP.NET applications by investigating the following URL for the ASP.NET Configuration section in the .NET Framework SDK.*
>
> ms-help://MS.NETFrameworkSDK/cpguidenf/html/cpconaspnetconfiguration.htm

I've create a page inside the protected directory called test_redirect.aspx, which for the purpose of this example is only in Visual Basic .NET.

Test_redirect.aspx

```
<%@ page language="vb" runat="server"%>
<script runat=server>
Sub Page_Load()
    OurLabel.Text = User.Identity.Name
End Sub
</script>

<html>
<head>
<title>Protected Page</title>
```

```
</head>
<body bgcolor="#FFFFFF" text="#000000">
Your user cookie reads: <asp:label id="OurLabel" runat="server" />
</body>
</html>
```

Notice the highlighted text that reads `User.Identity.Name`. To put it simply, it is a shortcut to the `Authentication` cookie in the `name` attribute of the `<forms>` tag in the root Web.Config file. Basically, what this page does is set a `Label`'s `text` property to the value of that cookie.

You can see what happens if I attempt to browse to this file directly in Figure 12.5. Because it resides in a directory that doesn't allow anonymous users (remember the question mark in the `<deny>` tag) I get rejected and redirected to the URL set in the `loginUrl` attribute of the `<forms>` tag in the root Web.Config. In essence, any page that I protect with the ASP.NET `authentication` function will force me to the page at `loginUrl` if I'm not authenticated.

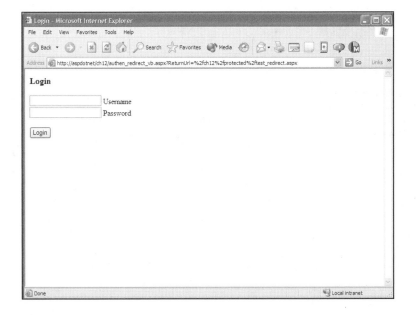

FIGURE 12.5

Going to a page that is protected against unauthenticated users redirects you to the page located in the `loginUrl` *attribute of the* `<forms>` *tag in the application's root Web.Config file.*

If you look at the address bar in Figure 12.4, you can also see that there is a querystring value called `ReturnUrl` with a value of `%2fch12%2fprotected%2ftest_redirect.aspx`. This is a URLEncoded version of the path back to the page I was rejected from, which is the `test_redirect.aspx`. If you carefully look at the gobbledygook value of `ReturnUrl`, you can see that the page's title is there. The `%2f` symbols that litter the value are actually the URLEncoded value for a forward slash (/). If you replace the `%2f` symbols in `ReturnUrl` with forward slashes (/) the result is `/ch12/protected/test_redirect.aspx`. So ASP.NET maintains where you came from when you were rejected. If you are successfully authenticated, ASP.NET has the capability to automatically return you to the URL from which you were originally rejected. Very nice feature.

Using the *RedirectFromLoginPage( )* Method

This leads us to the changes in the authentication process. The following is a modified login page that finishes the authentication process according to ASP.NET.

Visual Basic .NET—**authen_redirect_vb.aspx**

```
<%@ page language="vb" runat="server"%>
<script runat=server>

Sub Authorize(Sender as Object, e as EventArgs)
    if FormsAuthentication.Authenticate (Username.Text, Password.Text) then
        FormsAuthentication.RedirectFromLoginPage (Username.Text, False)
    Else
        OurLabel.Text = "This login doesn't exist"
    End If
End Sub

</script>

<html>
<head>
<title>Login</title>
</head>
<body bgcolor="#FFFFFF" text="#000000">
<form runat="server">
<h3>Login</h3>
<asp:textbox id="Username" runat="server" /> Username<br>
<asp:textbox id="Password" runat="server" />
Password <br><br>
<asp:button text="Login" onClick="Authorize" runat="server" /><br><br>
<asp:Label id="OurLabel" EnableViewState="False" runat="server" />
</form>
</body>
</html>
```

C#—authen_redirect_cs.aspx

```
<%@ page language="cs" runat="server"%>
<script runat=server>

void Authorize(Object Sender, EventArgs e){
    if (FormsAuthentication.Authenticate (Username.Text, Password.Text)){
        FormsAuthentication.RedirectFromLoginPage (Username.Text, false);
    }else{
        OurLabel.Text = "This login doesn't exist";
    }
}

</script>

<html>
<head>
<title>Login</title>
</head>
<body bgcolor="#FFFFFF" text="#000000">
<form runat="server">
<h3>Login</h3>
<asp:textbox id="Username" runat="server" /> Username<br>
<asp:textbox id="Password" runat="server" />
Password <br><br>
<asp:button text="Login" onClick="Authorize" runat="server" /><br><br>
<asp:Label id="OurLabel" EnableViewState="False" runat="server" />
</form>
</body>
</html>
```

Now here's where the magic happens. Notice another static method of FormsAuthentication called RedirectFromLoginPage(). This method does two things when it's called. First, it sets the authentication cookie with the name assigned in the name attribute in the <form> tag of the Web.Config file. You send two parameters with this method to accomplish this. The first one is the value that the authentication cookie should be set to. In the case of the preceding example, this is set to the username that is retrieved from the Username text box's Text property. The second parameter you send is Boolean, true or false, to indicate whether the authentication cookie should persist across browser sessions.

When this parameter is set to true, the cookie's expiration is set to DateTime.Now plus 50 years. No matter how good computers are, I can assure you that your computer and mine will expire long before this cookie does. If you set this parameter to false, the authentication doesn't persist across sessions and is set in memory only.

After the `RedirectFromLoginPage()` method sets the cookies, it redirects you back to the value of `ReturnUrl` in the `QueryString`.

In Figure 12.6 you can see that after I was successfully authenticated I was sent to the page from which I was originally rejected.

FIGURE 12.6

After you are properly authenticated, the `RedirectFromLog inPage()` method automatically returns you to the page from which you were originally rejected.

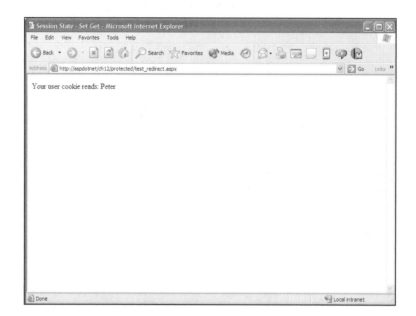

Building Your Own Redirect

Fifty years is a long time for you to wait for a cookie to expire before you force someone to re-authenticate to gain access to restricted areas of your site. But the `RedirectFromLoginPage()` offers only one way to persist the authentication cookie, and I think we all agree that it may be a bit too long for some people.

Thankfully, the .NET Framework provides everything we need. Instead of just calling the `RedirectFromLoginPage()` method with the Username and persisting information, you have to use two different methods to manipulate the cookie and redirect properly.

It is important for you to understand that the `Authentication` cookie actually has two different expirations dates. One is the date to which the `Persist` attribute is tied. This expiration is inside the cookie in an encrypted form. This value can possibly contain two different things. If the `Authentication` cookie is set to persist, this expiration is set to 50 years from the time the cookie was created. If the cookie isn't set to persist, this is set ahead of the time it was created by the number of minutes in the timeout attribute in the `<form>` tag in the root

Web.Config file. The other expiration is the one that the client's browser normally deals with in controlling cookie expiration. The .NET Framework sets this expiration to 1/1/0001 12:00 A.M by default. Apparently around 8000 years from now.

What I'm about to explain is "cheating" by overriding the encrypted expiration of the authentication cookie with the browser's expiration, basically making the cookie inaccessible to the .NET framework because the browser sees it as expired. The encrypted expiration is still set to +50 years from creation. Later you will see how to manipulate the encrypted data in the cookie, but for now we'll cheat.

In this example I'm also going to give users the choice to have their cookies persist or not by providing a check box in which they can indicate their preference.

Visual Basic .NET—authen_cookie_cs.aspx

```
<%@ page language="vb" runat="server"%>
<script runat=server>

Sub Authorize(Sender As [Object], e As EventArgs)
    If FormsAuthentication.Authenticate(Username.Text, Password.Text) Then
        Dim cookie As HttpCookie = FormsAuthentication.GetAuthCookie(Username.Text,
        ➥PersistCookie.Checked)
        cookie.Expires = DateTime.Now.AddDays(14)
        Response.Cookies.Add(cookie)
        Response.Redirect(FormsAuthentication.GetRedirectUrl(Username.Text,
        ➥PersistCookie.Checked))
    Else
        OurLabel.Text = "This login doesn't exist"
    End If
End Sub 'Authorize

</script>

<html>
<head>
<title>Login</title>
</head>
<body bgcolor="#FFFFFF" text="#000000">
<form runat="server">
<h3>Login Page</h3>
<asp:textbox id="Username" runat="server" /> Username<br>
<asp:textbox id="Password" runat="server" />
Password <br>
<asp:checkbox id="PersistCookie" runat="server" />
Save your login status<br><br>
<asp:button text="Login" onClick="Authorize" runat="server" /><br><br>
<asp:Label id="OurLabel" EnableViewState="False" runat="server" />
</form>
</body>
</html>
```

C#—authen_cookie_cs.aspx

```
<%@ page language="cs" runat="server"%>
<%@ Import Namespace="System.Threading"%>
<%@ Import Namespace="System.Security.Principal"%>
<script runat=server>

void Authorize(Object Sender, EventArgs e){
    if (FormsAuthentication.Authenticate (Username.Text, Password.Text)){
        HttpCookie cookie =
        ➥FormsAuthentication.GetAuthCookie(Username.Text,PersistCookie.Checked);
        cookie.Expires = DateTime.Now.AddDays(14);
        Response.Cookies.Add (cookie);
        Response.Redirect (FormsAuthentication.GetRedirectUrl (Username.Text,
        ➥PersistCookie.Checked));
    }else{
        OurLabel.Text = "This login doesn't exist";
    }
}

</script>

<html>
<head>
<title>Login</title>
</head>
<body bgcolor="#FFFFFF" text="#000000">
<form runat="server">
<h3>Login Page</h3>
<asp:textbox id="Username" runat="server" /> Username<br>
<asp:textbox id="Password" runat="server" />
Password <br>
<asp:checkbox id="PersistCookie" runat="server" />
Save your login status<br><br>
<asp:button text="Login" onClick="Authorize" runat="server" /><br><br>
<asp:Label id="OurLabel" EnableViewState="False" runat="server" />
</form>
</body>
</html>
```

To replace the RedirectFromLoginPage() method, I create a variable of the HttpCookie type. Then I use the GetAuthCookie() method, which creates the authentication cookie and sets the cookie variable to the Authentication cookie. Then I set the expiration to DateTime.Now plus 14 days and use the HttpCookie object's Add() method, which adds the cookie to the response back to the client. I then use another method called GetRedirectUrl, which retrieves the value of RedirectUrl from the QueryString and then redirects the user to that page. At that time the cookie is written to the client's machine.

In Figure 12.7 you can see the form with the Checkbox server control that lets the user decide whether the cookie should persist or not. In Figure 12.8 you can see the results of this page when authentication takes place with the check box checked. Look at the two expiration dates. The encrypted expiration is set to 50 years from creation, but it is overridden with the browser's expiration.

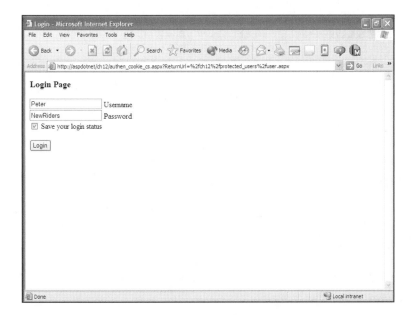

FIGURE 12.7

Form authentication gives you a little play to set cookie expiration for the Authentication *cookie.*

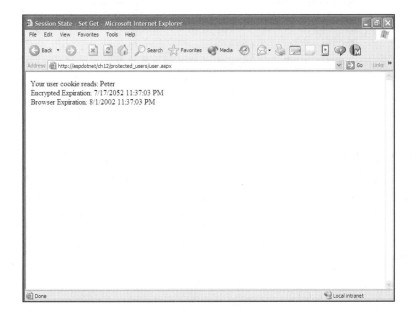

FIGURE 12.8

Notice that the Authentication *cookie has two different expiration dates: one that's contained in the encrypted cookie and one in the browser's normal expiration.*

As I mentioned, you can manipulate the contents of an encrypted cookie, including the expiration. I will explain that later in this chapter. If you prefer to manipulate only the expiration that the .NET Framework deals with, you can use the methods I will explain later to do this.

Understanding Authorization Logic

Now that you've learned about authentication, you are ready to deal with authorization. Again, authorization is to measure or establish the power or permission that has been given or granted by an authority. In ASP.NET applications, the owner of the application or administrator of the application makes determinations about authorization.

Two types of authorization are available:

- **Users**. Authorization that allows or denies access on a user-by-user basis.

- **Roles**. Authorization that allows or denies access based on roles that are used to group users with common permissions or power levels, such as Administrators, Managers, Users, and so on.

These are the two types of authorization schemes that you can deal with. There are also two ways to enforce authorization:

- **Configuratively**. Setting up user and role permissions within Web.Config files in directories on which you want to enforce protection.

- **Programmatically**. Using available methods to check whether a user is authenticated and has the proper permissions to view a page or parts of a page.

The place to start is by addressing user-level authorization.

User Authorization

When I talk about user-level authorization, I am talking about the name attribute placed into the Authentication cookie. This value is used to allow people into a directory or page, and to allow only specific users to view certain data.

For the purpose of all the examples in the user section, I will be using the Web.Config file to authenticate users. I will be using the following users, with their appropriate user names and passwords, to demonstrate this.

```
<credentials passwordFormat="Clear">
    <user name="Peter" password="NewRiders"/>
    <user name="Tom" password="qwerty"/>
</credentials>
```

Configurative

Earlier in the chapter you saw the Web.Config file used to restrict anonymous users from accessing a directory. A Web.Config file was placed in that directory and a tag called <deny> was used to restrict all unauthenticated users. The <deny> tag has a counterpart called the <allow> tag.

```
<configuration>
    <system.web>
        <authorization>
            <allow users="Bob"/>
            <deny users="?"/>
        </authorization>
    </system.web>
</configuration>
```

Two different symbols must be explained: the question mark (?) and the asterisk (*). The question mark is a wild card for all anonymous (unauthenticated) users, and the asterisk is a wild card for all users. Using a combination of these symbols, the users, and the <allow> and <deny> tags, you can enforce simple to very strict rules concerning who is allowed to access the items contained within the directory in which the Web.Config file resides.

N O T E

A Web.Config file controls all the contents of its directory, including other subdirectories, but subdirectories can have their own Web.Config files to either override or add to the security for contents within the directory it controls.

If I set <deny users="?" />, then all unauthenticated users are denied from that directory. If I set a combination, <allow users="Peter" /> and <deny users="*" />, then all users are denied access with the exception of "Peter". (No one can stop me! HAH HAH HAH!!) The following are a few examples of the Web.Config with explanations.

Deny all anonymous users:

```
<configuration>
    <system.web>
        <authorization>
            <deny users="?"/>
        </authorization>
    </system.web>
</configuration>
```

Deny all users, both anonymous and authenticated, with the exception of Peter, Betty, Gene, Frank, and Suzy:

```
<configuration>
    <system.web>
        <authorization>
            <allow users="Peter,Betty,Gene,Frank,Suzy"/>
            <deny users="*"/>
        </authorization>
    </system.web>
</configuration>
```

Deny all anonymous users, as well as Tom, Frank, and Suzy:

```
<configuration>
    <system.web>
        <authorization>
            <deny users="?,Tom,Frank,Suzy"/>
        </authorization>
    </system.web>
</configuration>
```

WARNING!!! The Web.Config file is a mysterious being—if you don't understand it, you will pull your hair out of your head trying to decipher its behavior. In essence, the file reads from the bottom up, and the last rule read takes precedence. The following strange example reinforces the point:

```
<configuration>
    <system.web>
        <authorization>
            <allow users="Peter" />
            <deny users="Peter"/>
        </authorization>
    </system.web>
</configuration>
```

This Web.Config file lets "Peter" access the file in its directory. Why? Because the file is read from bottom to top, the <allow> tag takes precedence over the <deny> tag. Now look at what happens when you swap the <allow> and <deny> tags:

```
<configuration>
    <system.web>
        <authorization>
            <deny users="Peter" />
            <allow users="Peter"/>
        </authorization>
    </system.web>
</configuration>
```

If you place the <allow> tag below the <deny> tag, the <deny> tag takes precedence and "Peter" won't be allowed access to that directory. I mention this so that you understand the flow of rules and you can understand how this affects the way the rules apply.

Later, during the discussion of roles, you'll investigate how to use combinations of users and roles in the Web.Config file to enforce even greater control over the security of your web applications.

Programmatic

You can use programmatic code to enforce permissions on a user. You can also control what a particular user can or cannot see programmatically. If you want to boot anyone who isn't logged in out of a particular page, you can use the User.Identity.IsAuthenticated property to determine whether the user has been authenticated. If they are, this property returns true; otherwise, if the user is still anonymous, this property returns false.

Visual Basic .NET—**author_rejectnonauthenticated_vb.aspx**

```
<%@ page language="vb" runat="server"%>
<script runat=server>

Sub Page_Load()
    If User.Identity.IsAuthenticated = False Then
        Response.Redirect("login.aspx")
    End If
End Sub

</script>

<html>
```

continues

Visual Basic .NET—(continued)

```
<head>
<title>Login</title>
</head>
<body bgcolor="#FFFFFF" text="#000000">
You're Authentic!!
</body>
</html>
```

C#—author_rejectnonauthenticated_cs.aspx

```
<%@ page language="cs" runat="server"%>
<script runat=server>

void Page_Load(){
    if (User.Identity.IsAuthenticated == false){
        Response.Redirect("login.aspx");
    }
}

</script>

<html>
<head>
<title>Login</title>
</head>
<body bgcolor="#FFFFFF" text="#000000">
You're Authentic!!
</body>
</html>
```

You can also control what users see depending on who they are. For instance, the following example show what to do if you want to display one message for unauthenticated users, another message just for the "Peter" user, and a third message for all other authenticated users.

Visual Basic .NET—author_controlusers_vb.aspx

```
<%@ page language="vb" runat="server"%>
<script runat=server>

Sub Page_Load()
    If User.Identity.IsAuthenticated = False Then
        OurLabel.Text = "Welcome anonymous user!"
    ElseIf User.Identity.Name = "Peter" Then
        OurLabel.Text = "Welcome Peter"
```

```
        Else
            OurLabel.Text = "Welcome " + User.Identity.Name
            OurLabel.Text += "<br>Isn't Peter funny looking?"
        End If
End Sub

</script>

<html>
<head>
<title>Authorize</title>
</head>
<body bgcolor="#FFFFFF" text="#000000">
<h3><asp:Label id="OurLabel" runat="server" />
</body>
</html>
```

C#—author_controlusers_cs.aspx

```
<%@ page language="c#" runat="server"%>
<script runat=server>

void Page_Load(){
    if (User.Identity.IsAuthenticated == false){
        OurLabel.Text = "Welcome anonymous user!";
    }else if(User.Identity.Name == "Peter"){
        OurLabel.Text = "Welcome Peter";
    }else{
        OurLabel.Text = "Welcome " + User.Identity.Name;
        OurLabel.Text += "<br>Isn't Peter funny looking?";
    }
}

</script>

<html>
<head>
<title>Login</title>
</head>
<body bgcolor="#FFFFFF" text="#000000">
<h3><asp:Label id="OurLabel" runat="server" />
</body>
</html>
```

In Figure 12.9 you can see the results. The code has checked to see whether a user is authenticated or the User.Identity.Name of the user that is logged in is equal to "Peter".

FIGURE 12.9

*You can program-
matically control
what is delivered to
the browser based
on user information.*

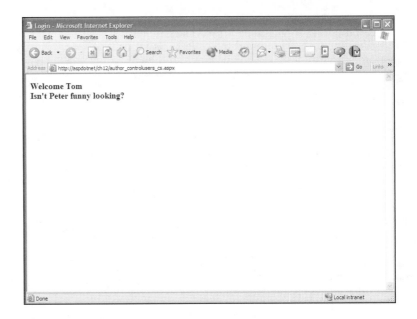

Being able to control information based on users is pretty powerful but can quickly become cumbersome if you are supporting a lot of users. This is where roles authorization comes in.

Roles

Roles authorization is a system of grouping together users with common levels of permission and controlling all the users by affecting authorization and permission control on the role rather than on the individual users.

The .NET Framework has provided a way to handle roles, but from my perspective it is often misunderstood. The object that is used to handle roles security is called the Principal object. There are few or no good references out on the web regarding role-based security or the Principal object, and strangely the .NET Framework SDK is kind of sparse in these areas as well. Never fear, Pierre is here.

There is going to be a bit of information here that may seem like overkill, but it puts all the power of ASP.NET forms-based authentication into your hands. If you want to truly use roles security in your ASP.NET applications, you need to backtrack into the authentication process.

To utilize roles, you need to store those roles somewhere. For security purposes these roles need to be somewhere that an unscrupulous user can't alter them, which is something a persistent cookie usually isn't good for. These are basically text files that someone slick enough can open and edit, and in which he can perhaps assign himself to a role with permissions to areas that he normally isn't allowed to access. You need a secure place to store this information.

As I explained earlier, the authentication cookie is encrypted. You might think that only the name value of the authentication cookie is encrypted, but there is much more in there. There is even a place where you can hide and encrypt roles. It can actually hold anything you want, but this is a great place to hold your roles data because it is encrypted and validated when it is sent to the server.

Let me not get ahead of myself. The first thing I must do is give you a bit of understanding about how the Authentication cookie actually works. I'm not going to get too deep, but if you're going to manipulate this monster manually, you gotta know what's under the hood.

The content of the authentication cookie is actually another object called a FormsAuthenticationTicket. It's a structured group of data that makes up all the important stuff that ASP.NET needs to handle authentication. It contains the following:

- **Version**. Ignore this, you should always set this to 1.

- **Name**. Authentication cookie Name.

- **IssueDate**. Time at which the cookie was issued.

- **Expiration**. Expiration date for the cookie.

- **Expired**. Boolean value to see whether the cookie has expired.

- **isPersistent**. Boolean value to determine whether the cookie persists across sessions.

- **UserData**. User-defined data (this is the magic place).

- **CookiePath**. The path for the cookie.

The only ones you need to concern yourself with are Name, IssueDate, Expiration, IsPersistent, and UserData. As you saw in the previous example, when the `FormsAuthentication.RedirectFromLoginPage()` method is called, ASP.NET does a few things behind the scenes. It creates the `FormsAuthenticationTicket` object, fills it with the listed information, encrypts the ticket, and creates a cookie with the name attribute in the `<forms>` tag in the Web.Config file. Then it places the encrypted ticket into the cookie and adds it to the `HttpResponse` object so that when the server responds back to the client, the client cookie is created. Then it retrieves the value of `ReturnUrl` from the `QueryString` and redirects the user back to that page. WHEW!!!

To access the `UserData` property of the `FormsAuthenticationTicket` object, you need to replicate that process when authentication takes place.

Now you have to get assigned roles from somewhere, and for this example I'm going to modify the Login table from the SQL Server example in the "Authenticating Against a Database" section to contain a column for users' roles. You can see the altered table in Figure 12.10.

FIGURE 12.10

The Login table with a Roles column added.

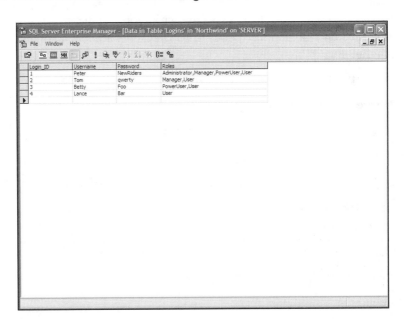

I'm also going to need to alter the stored procedure from that example to return the roles for the authenticated user.

spLogin

```
CREATE PROCEDURE [spLogin]

    @Username varchar(50),
    @Password varchar(50),
    @Login_ID int output,
    @Roles varchar(255) output

AS
    if exists (Select * from Logins where username = @username and password =
    ➥@Password)
        Begin
            Set  @Login_ID = (Select Login_ID from Logins where username =
            ➥@username and password = @Password)
            Set  @Roles = (Select Roles from Logins where username = @username and
            ➥password = @Password)
        End
    else
        Begin
            Set @Login_ID = 0
            Set @Roles = ''
        End
    GO
```

Now you need to authenticate against the SQL Server and retrieve the roles from the database so you can do the magic of building the FormsAuthenticationTicket, placing roles in the UserData property of the ticket, encrypting the ticket and placing it in the Authentication cookie. Then you add the cookie to the Response back to the client, get the RedirectUrl, and redirect the user back to that page.

Visual Basic .NET—author_roles_vb.aspx

```
<%@ page language="vb" runat="server"%>
<%@ Import Namespace="System.Data"%>
<%@ Import Namespace="System.Data.SqlClient" %>
<script runat=server>


Sub Authorize(Sender As [Object], e As EventArgs)
    Dim vUsername As String = Username.Text
    Dim vPassword As String = Password.Text
    Dim OurConnection As SqlConnection
    Dim OurCommand As SqlCommand
    Dim OurDataReader As SqlDataReader
```

continues

Visual Basic .NET—(continued)

```
    OurConnection = New SqlConnection("Server=server;
    ➥uid=newriders;pwd=password;database=Northwind")
    OurCommand = New SqlCommand("spLogin", OurConnection)
    OurCommand.CommandType = CommandType.StoredProcedure
    OurCommand.Parameters.Add("@Username", SqlDbType.VarChar, 50).Value =
    ➥vUsername
    OurCommand.Parameters.Add("@Password", SqlDbType.VarChar, 50).Value =
    ➥vPassword
    OurCommand.Parameters.Add("@Login_ID", SqlDbType.Int).Direction =
    ➥ParameterDirection.Output
    OurCommand.Parameters.Add("@Roles", SqlDbType.VarChar, 255).Direction =
    ➥ParameterDirection.Output
    OurConnection.Open()
    OurCommand.ExecuteNonQuery()
    Dim Login_ID As Integer = CInt(OurCommand.Parameters("@Login_ID").Value)
    Dim Roles As String = CStr(OurCommand.Parameters("@Roles").Value)
    OurConnection.Close()

    If Login_ID > 0 Then
        Dim OurTicket As FormsAuthenticationTicket
        Dim IssueDate As DateTime = DateTime.Now
        Dim ExpireDate As DateTime = DateTime.Now.AddDays(14)
        OurTicket = New FormsAuthenticationTicket(1, vUsername, IssueDate,
        ➥ExpireDate, True, Roles)
        Dim cookie As New HttpCookie(FormsAuthentication.FormsCookieName)
        cookie.Value = FormsAuthentication.Encrypt(OurTicket)
        Response.Cookies.Add(cookie)
        Response.Redirect(FormsAuthentication.GetRedirectUrl(vUsername, True))
    Else
        OurLabel.Text = "This login doesn't exist"
    End If
End Sub 'Authorize

</script>

<html>
<head>
<title>Login</title>
</head>
<body bgcolor="#FFFFFF" text="#000000">
<form runat="server">
<h3>Login Page</h3>
<asp:textbox id="Username" runat="server" /> Username<br>
<asp:textbox id="Password" runat="server" />
Password <br><br>
<asp:button text="Login" onClick="Authorize" runat="server" /><br><br>
<asp:Label id="OurLabel" EnableViewState="False" runat="server" />
</form>
</body>
</html>
```

C#—author_roles_cs.aspx

```
<%@ page language="c#" runat="server"%>
<%@ Import Namespace="System.Data"%>
<%@ Import Namespace="System.Data.SqlClient" %>
<script runat=server>

void Authorize(Object Sender, EventArgs e){
    string vUsername = Username.Text;
    string vPassword = Password.Text;
    SqlConnection OurConnection;
    SqlCommand OurCommand;
    SqlDataReader OurDataReader;

    OurConnection = new SqlConnection("Server=server;
    ➥uid=newriders;pwd=password;database=Northwind");
    OurCommand = new SqlCommand("spLogin" ,OurConnection);
    OurCommand.CommandType = CommandType.StoredProcedure;
    OurCommand.Parameters.Add("@Username", SqlDbType.VarChar, 50).Value =
    ➥vUsername;
    OurCommand.Parameters.Add("@Password", SqlDbType.VarChar, 50).Value =
    ➥vPassword;
    OurCommand.Parameters.Add("@Login_ID", SqlDbType.Int).Direction =
    ➥ParameterDirection.Output;
    OurCommand.Parameters.Add("@Roles", SqlDbType.VarChar, 255).Direction =
    ➥ParameterDirection.Output;
    OurConnection.Open();
    OurCommand.ExecuteNonQuery();
    int Login_ID =  (int)OurCommand.Parameters["@Login_ID"].Value;
    string Roles = (string)OurCommand.Parameters["@Roles"].Value;
    OurConnection.Close();

    if (Login_ID > 0){
        FormsAuthenticationTicket OurTicket;
        DateTime IssueDate = DateTime.Now;
        DateTime ExpireDate = DateTime.Now.AddDays(14);
        OurTicket = new FormsAuthenticationTicket
        ➥(1,vUsername,IssueDate,ExpireDate,true,Roles);
        HttpCookie cookie = new HttpCookie(FormsAuthentication.FormsCookieName);
        cookie.Value = FormsAuthentication.Encrypt(OurTicket);
        Response.Cookies.Add (cookie);
        Response.Redirect(FormsAuthentication.GetRedirectUrl (vUsername, true));
    }else{
        OurLabel.Text = "This login doesn't exist";
    }
}

</script>

<html>
<head>
<title>Login</title>
```

continues

```
</head>
<body bgcolor="#FFFFFF" text="#000000">
<form runat="server">
<h3>Login Page</h3>
<asp:textbox id="Username" runat="server" /> Username<br>
<asp:textbox id="Password" runat="server" />
Password <br><br>
<asp:button text="Login" onClick="Authorize" runat="server" /><br><br>
<asp:Label id="OurLabel" EnableViewState="False" runat="server" />
</form>
</body>
</html>
```

I know reading this block of code may be a bit like trying to swallow an unchewed piece of steak, and right now it's caught in your throat. Stand back; I'm ready to do the ASP.NET Heimlich Maneuver and pop that big bite outta your windpipe.

The large block of code highlighted in bold does the following:

1. Creates a variable of the `FormsAuthenticationTicket` type.

2. Creates a variable of `DateTime` type and sets it to `Now` for the ticket's `IssueDate` property.

3. Creates a variable of `DateTime` type and sets it to `Now + 14` days for the ticket's `Expiration` property. I chose +14 days just for demonstration purposes. You can set the expiration to whatever you want.

4. Populates the `FormsAuthenticationTicket` with a new `FormsAuthenticationTicket` object through one of its overloaded constructors, which takes six input parameters in the following order: `Version`, `Name`, `IssueDate`, `Expiration`, `IsPersitent`, and `UserData`. As you can see, the `UserData` is populated with the roles information that was returned from the database.

5. Creates a variable of `HttpCookie` type and populates it with a new instance of an `HttpCookie` object with the name value pulled from the Web.Config file. It uses the `FormsAuthentication.FormsCookieName` property.

6. Sets the value of the cookie to the encrypted form of the ticket using the `FormsAuthentication.Encrypt()` method.

7. Adds the cookie to the response back to the client browser so the cookie is created on the user's machine.

8. Redirects, the `Response.Redirect`, to the proper page, which is retrieved with the `FormsAuthetication.GetRedirectUrl` property.

Now you've successfully authenticated and stuffed the appropriate data into the `authentication` cookie, including the roles into the `UserData` property of the `FormsAuthenticationTicket` in the authentication cookie. But this doesn't mean it's doing anything. You will still get rejected from directories and pages that require a specific role to be present.

Now for the next trick. Here is where the `Principal` object comes in. In short, the `Principal` object is used to compare role information against the authorization system, either the Web.Config file or programmatically generated list of specific roles. The actual enforcement processes are covered later, but the first thing to do is to get roles into the `Principal` object.

I have read various papers on the `Principal` object on the web and in some other resources and have come to a conclusion. The `Principal` object is misunderstood. Most examples show the `Principal` object as some magician that persists all by itself across page loads. This may be true for Windows applications built on the .NET Framework where a user is operating in a connected environment with full operational state, but I haven't found it to be true with the disconnected request/response stateless environment of ASP.NET applications.

From my experience, the `Principal` object must be created and populated each time a security check must be done. Fortunately, ASP.NET provides a simple way for this to be done. Every time any type of security check is attempting to be enforced, there is an attempt to fire a function that can possibly exist in the application's global.asax file located in the application's root directory. You must create this function, but if named properly it will fire every time any type of authorization process is executed by the .NET Framework. It is called `Application_AuthenticateRequest()`. In this function, you create all the necessary players to create a `Principal` object, decrypt and pull the roles out of your `FormsAuthenticationTicket`, place them inside the `Principal` object, and associate the `Principal` object with the authenticated user. One important note is that you must import the `System.Security.Principal` namespace into your global.asax file to use the `Principal` object and some of the other associated objects that are necessary.

Visual Basic .NET—`global.asax`

```vb
<%@ Import Namespace="System.Security.Principal"%>
<script language="vb" runat=server>

Sub Application_AuthenticateRequest(sender As Object,e As EventArgs)
    If Request.IsAuthenticated = True Then
        Dim OurTicket As FormsAuthenticationTicket
        OurTicket = FormsAuthentication.Decrypt
        ➥(Request.Cookies(FormsAuthentication.FormsCookieName).Value)
        Dim authName As String = User.Identity.Name
        Dim arrRoles() As String = split(OurTicket.UserData,",")
        Dim OurIdentity As GenericIdentity = New GenericIdentity(authName)
        Context.User = New GenericPrincipal(OurIdentity, arrRoles)
End If
End Sub
</script>
```

C#—`global.aspx`

```csharp
<%@ Import Namespace="System.Security.Principal"%>
<script language="c#" runat=server>

void Application_AuthenticateRequest(Object sender,EventArgs e){
    if (Request.IsAuthenticated == true){
        FormsAuthenticationTicket OurTicket;
        OurTicket = FormsAuthentication.Decrypt(Request.Cookies
        [ccc][FormsAuthentication.FormsCookieName].Value);
        String authName  = User.Identity.Name;
        String[] arrRoles = OurTicket.UserData.Split(',');
        GenericIdentity OurIdentity = new GenericIdentity(authName);
        Context.User = new GenericPrincipal(OurIdentity, arrRoles);
    }
}
</script>
```

This code performs the following steps:

1. Checks to see whether the user is authenticated; if so, it proceeds.

2. Creates a variable of the type `FormsAuthenticationTicket`.

3. Populates that variable with the decrypted contents of the `Authentication` cookie. You retrieve this through a standard `Request.Cookies`, but you retrieve the cookie name from the Web.Config file with the `FormsAuthentication.FormsCookieName` property.

4. Creates a variable of the `string` type and populates it with the authenticated user's `Name` property.

5. Places the UserData property of the ticket into a one-dimensional array.

6. Creates a variable of the GenericIdentity type and populates it with a new instance of a GenericIdentity with the authenticated user's Name property.

7. Assigns a new GenericPrincipal object to the Context.User, which is the current user that the .NET Framework is dealing with in this request. Passes the GenericPrincipal constructor the proper parameters, which are the GenericIdentity and the roles. This enables the Principal object to know who it's associated with so that it can then authorize that user against those roles.

This process may seem complicated, but it really is simple. You're creating a Principal object that contains the roles you want and associating it with the proper user. This object can now be used to check against authorization restrictions that exist both configuratively in the Web.Config file and programmatically.

In Figure 12.11, the login is posted to a page that is protected, allowing only administrators based on the Web.Config file in the ch12/protected_roles directory. You can see the user is Peter and that Administrators is one of the roles in the Principal object.

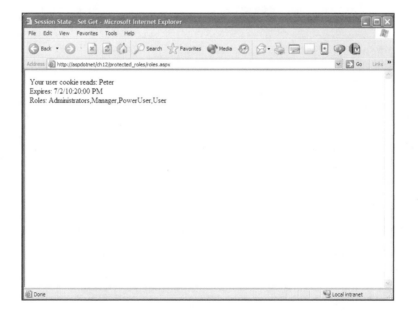

FIGURE 12.11

The Principal *object enables you to control authorization against roles instead of just against users.*

Configurative

Configuring authorization regarding roles in the Web.Config file follows exactly the same rules as users except that you use the word *roles* in its place.

```
<configuration>
    <system.web>
        <authorization>
            <allow roles="Administrators"/>
            <deny roles="*"/>
        </authorization>
    </system.web>
</configuration>
```

This is where the real power in configurative authorization comes in, because you can use combinations of users and roles to control security. For instance, if you wanted to allow all Administrators and also allow just Betty, who is a PowerUser, User, but you want to restrict all other PowerUsers or Users, you can simply add Betty to the <allow> tag as a user.

```
<configuration>
    <system.web>
        <authorization>
            <allow roles="Administrators"
            users="Betty"/>
            <deny roles="*"/>
        </authorization>
    </system.web>
</configuration>
```

Experiment with configurative authorization now that you understand both roles and users. You can have fine control over your applications by using the Web.Config files in different directories, along with the <allow> and <deny> tags, with a combination of users and roles. Just remember that the order of these tags can affect the outcome significantly.

Programmatic

When we were checking users programmatically earlier, we used the `User.Identity.IsAuthenticated` property to check for authorization. To programmatically check role-based authorization, use the `User.IsInRole()` method with the role name being the parameter that you pass in.

Visual Basic .NET—**author_controlroles_vb.aspx**

```
<%@ page language="vb" runat="server"%>
<script runat=server>
```

```
Sub Page_Load()
    If Not User.IsInRole("Administrators") And Not User.IsInRole("Manager") Then
        OurLabel.Text = "You aren't an Administrator or a Manager"
    Else
        If User.IsInRole("Administrators") Then
            OurLabel.Text = "You are an Administrator"
        Else
            OurLabel.Text = "You are a Manager"
        End If
    End If
End Sub

</script>

<html>
<head>
<title>Login</title>
</head>
<body bgcolor="#FFFFFF" text="#000000">
<h3><asp:Label id="OurLabel" runat="server" />
</body>
</html>
```

C#—author_controlroles_cs.aspx

```
<%@ page language="c#" runat="server"%>
<script runat=server>

void Page_Load(){
    if (!User.IsInRole("Administrators") & !User.IsInRole("Manager")){
        OurLabel.Text = "You aren't an Administrator or a Manager";
    }else{
        if (User.IsInRole("Administrators")){
            OurLabel.Text = "You are an Administrator";
        }else{
            OurLabel.Text = "You are a Manager";
        }
    }
}

</script>

<html>
<head>
<title>Login</title>
</head>
<body bgcolor="#FFFFFF" text="#000000">
<h3><asp:Label id="OurLabel" runat="server" />
</body>
</html>
```

In Figure 12.12 you can see the result this page produces when you are logged in as "Peter," who belongs to all the roles, but trips the Administrator branch of this code first.

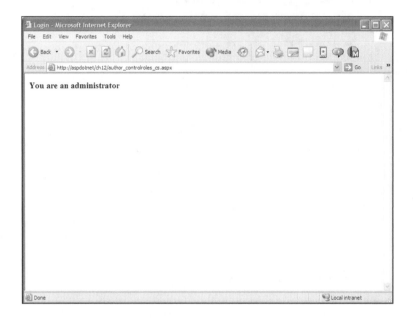

As you can see, role-based security provides a much broader and more powerful way to control who is authorized to see content on your web site, because you can control whole groups of users through a single role.

Summary

The information that I've gone over in this chapter has provided you with powerful systems for security and will enable you to control what content a user—either anonymous or authenticated—can see. These tools can be used in intranet settings where the flow and level of information must be controlled. Or you may use them in an Internet site that is membership-based and in which members can buy different levels of access. The authentication systems and authorization systems present in the .NET Framework will go a long way in helping you protect and secure your applications.

<chapter> **13**

XML in ASP.NET

Say whatever you're gonna say…
I'll figure it out.

I f you've been involved with web design and programming for more that a short
time, you've seen several things come out that have been deemed "THE NEXT
BIG THING" in web design. From little things like the dreaded "blink" tag (I'd like
to kick the guy who created that in the shins) to DHTML being the great interface
savior, to scalable vector graphics changing the way that graphical images will be
delivered to browsers. Not to say that these things don't have their uses or place
(except the blink tag, of course, which has no place in design), but they didn't
reform the web like it was originally reported they would. And funny enough,
scalable vector graphics are really images that are created through XML.

Now the term XML has been floating around for a few years and you've heard
people state that "THIS IS BIG…IT'S REALLY BIG!!!" But you haven't seen any
huge changes at all that are a result of XML. Let me assure you that they are here
now and more changes are coming.

For instance, you may be using or have been hearing about XHTML. This is a strain of XML that is reshaping the direction that browser markup language is going. Go to `http://www.w3c.org` to find out more about this.

Chapter 10 discussed ADO.NET and how it delivers data from databases. XML is used in all the "behind the scenes" activities of ADO.NET. When data is passed back and forth and manipulated with ADO.NET, XML is the vehicle.

The current version of Microsoft SQL Server has an XML layer that enables you to retrieve data from the SQL Server in XML format. As a matter of fact, Microsoft has said that future versions of SQL Server will store all data in XML format.

Having given you these few examples, let me assure you that XML is here and here to stay in a BIG way. Although you've seen XML throughout this book in the Web.Config file, I just want to refresh your memory. XML (Extensible Markup Language) is an open standard language that allows the creation of self-describing, structured information in a standard text document.

XML can be used to describe any type of information you'd like to. The following is a simple example of using XML to describe the people that a fictional person named Bob knows.

bobspeople.xml

```
<?xml version="1.0"?>
<BobsPeople>
    <Family>
        <Wife>
            <Name>Susie</Name>
        </Wife>
        <Children>
            <Child>
                <Name>Betty</Name>
                <Gender>Girl</Gender>
            </Child>
            <Child>
                <Name>Sam</Name>
                <Gender>Boy</Gender>
            </Child>
        </Children>
    </Family>
    <Friends>
        <Friend>
            <Name>Ted</Name>
```

```
        </Friend>
        <Friend>
            <Name>Frank</Name>
        </Friend>
    </Friends>
</BobsPeople>
```

If you look at this file, you can see that Bob's wife's name is Susie. He has two children: a daughter named Betty and a son named Sam. He has two friends, Ted and Frank. This is all pretty self explanatory if you take the time to read the delimiter tags. This is the way XML works. It describes itself.

There is another document type called an XSL document, which is an Extensible Stylesheet Language Transformations stylesheet. This file is used as a template to format XML data. You'll see more on this shortly.

Now, what does this have to do with you or your use of ASP.NET, you ask? Plenty! ASP.NET gives you tools and server controls to do all kinds of stuff with XML data and XML documents.

Let me say that this one little chapter will hardly scratch the surface of XML and barely dent XML's relationship and use in ASP.NET. To master XML's uses within ASP.NET, I recommend a book titled *XML and ASP.NET*, by Kirk Evans, Ashwin Kamanna, and Joel Mueller, from New Riders publishing. That book provides a much more thorough overview of this subject.

The XML Server Control

The first thing to cover is the XML server control. This is located in the `System.Web.UI.WebControls` namespace and looks like the following:

```
<asp:xml runat="server" />
```

As you can see, it is no different from any other server control in the way it is addressed. In inherits the `Control` object (as do all the other Web server controls), which provides it with all the base properties such as `ID`, `EnableViewState`, and `Visible`. If you need a refresher on all the properties it inherits from the `Control` object, refer back to Chapter 7 or the .NET Framework SDK. Table 13.1 looks at the additional properties that we'll be dealing with.

TABLE 13.1 XML Object Properties

Property	Description
Document	Gets or set the `System.Xml.XmlDocument` object to display in the XML control.
DocumentSource	Gets or sets the path to an XML document to display in the XML Control.
Transform	Gets or sets the `System.Xml.Xsl.XslTransform` object that formats the XML document's data for output to the browser.
TransformSource	Gets or sets the path to an XSLT (Extensible Stylesheet Language Transformations) document that formats the XML document before it is sent back to the web browser (usually as HTML or XHTML).

That all may seem like gobbledygook to you now. Let me explain as we progress and it will make a lot more sense. The first thing I'd like to do is give you the XML document that you'll see throughout all of the examples in this chapter.

products.xml

```xml
<?xml version="1.0"?>
<Products>
    <Product>
        <ProductID>1</ProductID>
        <ProductName>Chai</ProductName>
        <Supplier>Exotic Liquids</Supplier>
        <CategoryName>Beverages</CategoryName>
        <UnitPrice>18.23</UnitPrice>
        <UnitsInStock>39</UnitsInStock>
    </Product>
    <Product>
        <ProductID>2</ProductID>
        <ProductName>Chang</ProductName>
        <Supplier>Exotic Liquids</Supplier>
        <CategoryName>Beverages</CategoryName>
        <UnitPrice>19.02</UnitPrice>
        <UnitsInStock>17</UnitsInStock>
    </Product>
    <Product>
        <ProductID>24</ProductID>
        <ProductName>Guarana Fantastica</ProductName>
        <Supplier>Refrescos Americanas LTDA</Supplier>
        <CategoryName>Beverages</CategoryName>
```

```
        <UnitPrice>4.50</UnitPrice>
        <UnitsInStock>20</UnitsInStock>
    </Product>
    <Product>
        <ProductID>34</ProductID>
        <ProductName>Sasquatch Ale</ProductName>
        <Supplier>Bigfoot Breweries</Supplier>
        <CategoryName>Beverages</CategoryName>
        <UnitPrice>14.00</UnitPrice>
        <UnitsInStock>111</UnitsInStock>
    </Product>
</Products>
```

This is an XML document that contains products from the Northwind database. Each product contains a ProductID, ProductName, Supplier, CategoryName, UnitPrice, and UnitsInStock. The XML server control is going to interact with this document in two ways: declaratively and programmatically.

Interacting with XML Declaratively

Internet Explorer 5 and later and Netscape 6 and later have the native capability to display XML documents. You can just request the XML document and the browser will render them. But when you're dealing with XML documents declaratively, you aren't just browsing the XML document; you are browsing to an ASP.NET page with an XML server control on that page. Then you use the DocumentSource and TransformSource properties to assign the XML and XSL documents to the XML server control.

DocumentSource and *TransformSource*

It's possible to just open an XML document in a browser, but here I'll explore the DocumentSource property to demonstrate what a raw XML file looks like in a browser (see Figure 13.1). Because I'm not using an XSL stylesheet, this document's ContentType must be equal to text/xml. Because this content type is XML, it will interpret any HTML tags as XML and actually render them to the browser. For this reason, the entire contents of our page are short and sweet.

Documentsource.xml

```
<%@ Page ContentType="text/xml" %>
<asp:xml id="OurXml" DocumentSource="products.xml" runat="server" />
```

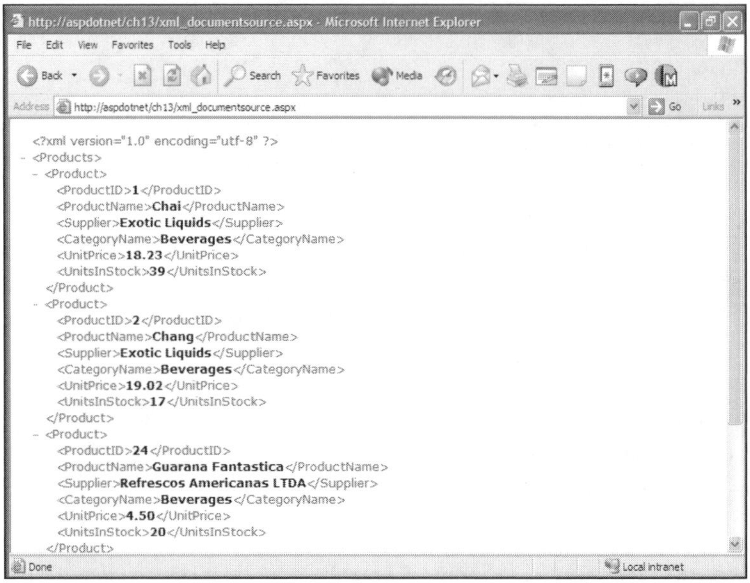

FIGURE 13.1

Raw XML being rendered in the browser window.

When you set the DocumentSource property with a valid XML document, the XML server control renders the document to the browser. This utilization displays the XML document in the browser window. Utilitarian…yes! Pretty…no!!

Enter the XSL stylesheet, which is used to format XML documents. XSL stylesheets contain information and formatting for specific XML documents that describe how the information within the XML document should be rendered to the browser. This is done server-side and produces the desired result. This makes adding XML results to an HTML document possible, as well. The following file is the ASP.NET page that contains the XML server control.

xml_transformsource.aspx

```
<html>
<head>
<title>XML Style Sheet</title>
</head>
<body>
<asp:xml id="OurXml"
    DocumentSource="products.xml"
    TransformSource="products.xsl"
    runat="server" />
</body>
</html>
```

Notice in the XML server control the two properties called DocumentSource and TransformSource. Again, the DocumentSource is the path to the XML file that will supply the data for the XML server control. The TransformSource property is used to set the path of the XSL stylesheet file that will provide formatting for the XML data in the DocumentSource property. Following is the XSL file.

products.xsl

```
<xsl:stylesheet version="1.0" xmlns:xsl='http://www.w3.org/1999/XSL/Transform'>
<xsl:template match="/">
    <style>
    .table-heading {background-color:#CCCCCC;font-family : Verdana,sans-serif;
    ➥font-size:12px;}
    .table-row{font-family : Verdana,sans-serif;font-size:12px;}
    </style>
    <table border="1" cellpadding="3" cellspacing="0">
    <tr class="table-heading">
    <td>ProductID</td>
    <td>Product Name</td>
    <td>Supplier</td>
    <td>Category</td>
    <td>Unit Price</td>
    <td>Units In Stock</td>
    </tr>
        <xsl:for-each select='Products/Product'>
        <tr class="table-row">
            <td><xsl:value-of select='ProductID'/></td>
            <td><xsl:value-of select='ProductName'/></td>
            <td><xsl:value-of select='Supplier'/></td>
            <td><xsl:value-of select='CategoryName'/></td>
            <td><xsl:value-of select='UnitPrice'/></td>
            <td><xsl:value-of select='UnitsInStock'/></td>
            </tr>
        </xsl:for-each>
    </table>
    </xsl:template>
</xsl:stylesheet>
```

If you look at this XSL stylesheet, you will notice that it is made up primarily of familiar <html> tags. An XSL file is really just a formatting template for XML. First I inserted some CSS stylesheets to establish some text formatting for elements in the XSL file. It isn't necessary to include them in this file. They could have just as easily been in the ASP.NET page, but placing them in this file makes the XSL file totally modular.

Then I have created a `<table>` with a `<tr>` containing headings for the data contained in the XML file. Next is where the fun begins. I use the `<xsl:for-each />` block to produce the code delimited by this tag for each `Products/Product` in the XML file. In other words, for each `<Product>` in `<Products>`, do blah, blah, blah.

Basically what this does is create a table row with table cells containing the elements contained inside the `<Products>` tag. Notice that I've assigned the CSS classes to both the table heading row and the product rows.

In Figure 13.2, you can see the results of running the xml_transformsource.aspx file. You can see how different the data appears than it did when I just displayed the raw XML. It is totally formatted by the XSL file that is declared in the `TransformSource` property of the XML server control.

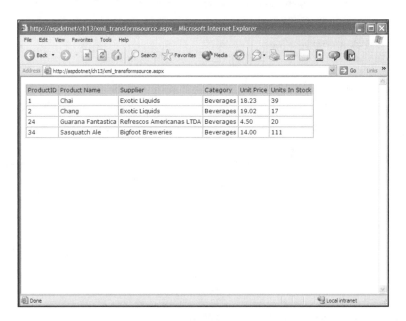

This is how you can declaratively use XML files in your ASP.NET applications, but what if you want to exert more control over XML integration? You can use programming logic in handling XML data as well.

Interacting with XML Programmatically

There are times when you need much more control in handling your XML documents. For instance, what if you want to view the contents of a document and then change its contents, such as by inserting new values?

This requires more control than simple properties can provide. The following is an example of displaying the contents of the products.xml file, but you can also insert items into the XML file. I use a few objects in this example that require that additional namespaces be imported.

System.Data is used because I utilize a DataSet and DataRow. The System.Xml namespace contains the XmlDocument and XmlNodeReader objects. I use these objects to hold and read the products.xml document into the DataSet. System.Xml.Xsl contains the XslTransform object, which holds the XSL file I'm programmatically using.

Visual Basic .NET—**xml_insert_vb.aspx**

```
<%@ page language="vb" runat="server"%>
<%@ Import Namespace="System.Data"%>
<%@ Import Namespace="System.Xml"%>
<%@ Import Namespace="System.Xml.Xsl"%>
<script runat=server>
Private Sub Page_Load()
    Dim OurXmlDocument As XmlDocument = New XmlDocument()
    Dim OurXslTransform As XslTransform = New XslTransform()
    OurXmlDocument.Load(Server.MapPath("products.xml"))
    OurXslTransform.Load(Server.MapPath("products.xsl"))
    OurXml.Transform = OurXslTransform
    If IsPostBack Then
        Dim OurDataSet As DataSet = New DataSet()
        Dim OurXmlReader As XmlNodeReader = New XmlNodeReader(OurXmlDocument)
        OurDataSet.ReadXml(OurXmlReader)
        Dim OurDataRow As DataRow = OurDataSet.Tables("Product").NewRow()
        OurDataRow("ProductID") = ProductID.Text
        OurDataRow("ProductName") = ProductName.Text
        OurDataRow("Supplier") = Supplier.Text
        OurDataRow("CategoryName") = Category.Text
        OurDataRow("UnitPrice") = UnitPrice.Text
        OurDataRow("UnitsInStock") = UnitsInStock.Text
        OurDataSet.Tables("Product").Rows.Add(OurDataRow)
        OurDataSet.AcceptChanges()
        OurDataSet.WriteXml(Server.MapPath("products.xml"))
        Dim OurXmlDataDocument As XmlDataDocument = New
➥XmlDataDocument(OurDataSet)
```

continues

Visual Basic .NET—(continued)

```
        OurXml.Document = OurXmlDataDocument
    Else
        OurXml.Document = OurXmlDocument
    End If
End Sub

</script>

<html>
<body>
<asp:xml id="OurXml" runat="server" EnableViewState="false"/>
<br>
<form runat="server">
<table>
<tr><td>ProductID</td>
<td><asp:TextBox id="ProductID" runat="server"/></td></tr>
<tr><td>Product Name</td>
<td><asp:TextBox id="ProductName" runat="server"/></td></tr>
<tr><td>Supplier</td>
<td><asp:TextBox id="Supplier" runat="server"/></td></tr>
<tr><td>Category</td>
<td><asp:TextBox id="Category" runat="server"/></td></tr>
<tr><td>Unit Price</td>
<td><asp:TextBox id="UnitPrice" runat="server"/></td></tr>
<tr><td>Units In Stock</td>
<td><asp:TextBox id="UnitsInStock" runat="server"/></td></tr>
</table>
<asp:Button id="Submit" text="Submit" runat="server"/>
</form>
</body>
</html>
```

C#—xml_insert_cs.aspx

```
<%@ page language="c#" runat="server"%>
<%@ Import Namespace="System.Data"%>
<%@ Import Namespace="System.Xml"%>
<%@ Import Namespace="System.Xml.Xsl"%>
<script runat=server>
void Page_Load() {
    XmlDocument OurXmlDocument = new XmlDocument();
    XslTransform OurXslTransform = new XslTransform();
    OurXmlDocument.Load(Server.MapPath("products.xml"));
    OurXslTransform.Load(Server.MapPath("products.xsl"));
    OurXml.Transform = OurXslTransform;
    if (IsPostBack) {
        DataSet OurDataSet = new DataSet();
        XmlNodeReader OurXmlReader = new XmlNodeReader(OurXmlDocument);
        OurDataSet.ReadXml(OurXmlReader);
        DataRow OurDataRow = OurDataSet.Tables["Product"].NewRow();
        OurDataRow["ProductID"] = ProductID.Text;
```

```
                OurDataRow["ProductName"] = ProductName.Text;
                OurDataRow["Supplier"] = Supplier.Text;
                OurDataRow["CategoryName"] = Category.Text;
                OurDataRow["UnitPrice"] = UnitPrice.Text;
                OurDataRow["UnitsInStock"] = UnitsInStock.Text;
                OurDataSet.Tables["Product"].Rows.Add(OurDataRow);
                OurDataSet.AcceptChanges();
                OurDataSet.WriteXml(Server.MapPath("products.xml"));
                XmlDataDocument OurXmlDataDocument = new XmlDataDocument(OurDataSet);
                OurXml.Document = OurXmlDataDocument;
        }
        else {
            OurXml.Document = OurXmlDocument;
        }
}

</script>

<html>
<body>
<asp:xml id="OurXml" runat="server" EnableViewState="false"/>
<br>
<form runat="server">
<table>
<tr><td>ProductID</td>
<td><asp:TextBox id="ProductID" runat="server"/></td></tr>
<tr><td>Product Name</td>
<td><asp:TextBox id="ProductName" runat="server"/></td></tr>
<tr><td>Supplier</td>
<td><asp:TextBox id="Supplier" runat="server"/></td></tr>
<tr><td>Category</td>
<td><asp:TextBox id="Category" runat="server"/></td></tr>
<tr><td>Unit Price</td>
<td><asp:TextBox id="UnitPrice" runat="server"/></td></tr>
<tr><td>Units In Stock</td>
<td><asp:TextBox id="UnitsInStock" runat="server"/></td></tr>
</table>
<asp:Button id="Submit" text="Submit" runat="server"/>
</form>
</body>
</html>
```

To give you an idea what happens in the highlighted text, first I create a new XmlDocument object and an XslTransform object. Both these objects have a load method that takes a parameter of the file path to the document that you want to load into them. I used the Server.MapPath() method, which returns the filename in the MapPath parameter and builds the full path to that object, starting from the drive letter forward. This is passed into the XmlDocument and XslTransform objects' Load methods to fill those objects with the XML and XSL files that I want, which is products.xml and products.xsl.

Then I set OurXml's transform property to the value of the XmlTransform object. OurXml is the XML server control in the ASP.NET page.

Then I check to see whether the page is posting back to itself. If it does, then I create a DataSet, create an XmlNodeReader object, and populate it with the XmlDocument object. The XmlNodeReader allows the DataSet's ReadXml method to properly create a DataTable of the contents of the XML document.

After the XmlDocument object is in the DataSet, I create a new DataRow based on the DataTable created by the DataSet's ReadXml method. If fill the DataRow with the values from the TextBox server controls and then use the Add() method to add the DataRow to the Products DataTable in the DataSet and accept the changes with the AcceptChanges() method.

Next, I use the WriteXml() counterpart of the DataSet's ReadXml() method, and write the contents of the DataSet back to the products.xml file.

I then place the contents of the DataSet into an XmlDataDocument, which is an object that allows data to be stored, retrieved, and manipulated through a DataSet, and I set the Document property of the OurXml server control to this object.

If the page hasn't been posted back, it simply uses the XmlDocument object to populate OurXml server control's Document property.

You can see in Figure 13.3 that the values in the edit boxes were added to the table. In theory this means they were added to the XML file.

FIGURE 13.3

When manipulating XML files you can programmatically do just about anything to them that you can do to a database, including inserting data.

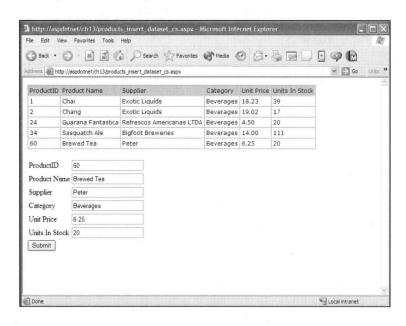

products.xml

```xml
<?xml version="1.0" standalone="yes"?>
<Products>
  <Product>
    <ProductID>1</ProductID>
    <ProductName>Chai</ProductName>
    <Supplier>Exotic Liquids</Supplier>
    <CategoryName>Beverages</CategoryName>
    <UnitPrice>18.23</UnitPrice>
    <UnitsInStock>39</UnitsInStock>
  </Product>
  <Product>
    <ProductID>2</ProductID>
    <ProductName>Chang</ProductName>
    <Supplier>Exotic Liquids</Supplier>
    <CategoryName>Beverages</CategoryName>
    <UnitPrice>19.02</UnitPrice>
    <UnitsInStock>17</UnitsInStock>
  </Product>
  <Product>
    <ProductID>24</ProductID>
    <ProductName>Guarana Fantastica</ProductName>
    <Supplier>Refrescos Americanas LTDA</Supplier>
    <CategoryName>Beverages</CategoryName>
    <UnitPrice>4.50</UnitPrice>
    <UnitsInStock>20</UnitsInStock>
  </Product>
  <Product>
    <ProductID>34</ProductID>
    <ProductName>Sasquatch Ale</ProductName>
    <Supplier>Bigfoot Breweries</Supplier>
    <CategoryName>Beverages</CategoryName>
    <UnitPrice>14.00</UnitPrice>
    <UnitsInStock>111</UnitsInStock>
  </Product>
  <Product>
    <ProductID>60</ProductID>
    <ProductName>Brewed Tea</ProductName>
    <Supplier>Peter</Supplier>
    <CategoryName>Beverages</CategoryName>
    <UnitPrice>6.25</UnitPrice>
    <UnitsInStock>20</UnitsInStock>
  </Product>
</Products>
```

You can see at the bottom of the products.xml file that the information that I inserted into the TextBox server controls has been properly written to the products.xml document.

That is one way of using a `DataSet` and its `ReadXml()` and `WriteXml()` methods to manipulate the product.xml file. There are also objects within the `System.Xml` namespace that enable you to do the same thing that I did with the `DataSet` but do it directly to the XML file.

In the following example, if the page is posted back, I use the `XmlElement` object to build a whole bunch of XML tags. I fill the appropriate `XmlElements` with the contents of the `TextBox` server controls. I then append them as children to the one `XmlElement` object that is named `xmlProduct`. I then place that in the XML document using the `XmlNode` object's `AppendChild()` method and then save the XML document back. It's just another way of doing the same thing, this time with XML and XML objects.

Visual Basic .NET—`xml_insert_purexml_vb.aspx`

```vb
<%@ page language="vb" runat="server"%>
<%@ Import Namespace="System.Data"%>
<%@ Import Namespace="System.Xml"%>
<%@ Import Namespace="System.Xml.Xsl"%>
<script runat=server>
Private Sub Page_Load()
    Dim OurXmlDocument As XmlDocument = New XmlDocument()
    Dim OurXslTransform As XslTransform = New XslTransform()
    OurXmlDocument.Load(Server.MapPath("products.xml"))
    OurXslTransform.Load(Server.MapPath("products.xsl"))
    If IsPostBack Then

        Dim OurXmlNode As XmlNode = OurXmlDocument.DocumentElement
        Dim xmlProduct As XmlElement = OurXmlDocument.CreateElement("Product")
        Dim xmlProductID As XmlElement = OurXmlDocument.CreateElement("ProductID")
        Dim xmlProductName As XmlElement =
➥OurXmlDocument.CreateElement("ProductName")
        Dim xmlSupplier As XmlElement = OurXmlDocument.CreateElement("Supplier")
        Dim xmlCategoryName As XmlElement =
➥OurXmlDocument.CreateElement("CategoryName")
        Dim xmlUnitPrice As XmlElement = OurXmlDocument.CreateElement("UnitPrice")
        Dim xmlUnitsInStock As XmlElement =
➥OurXmlDocument.CreateElement("UnitsInStock")
        xmlProductID.InnerXml = ProductID.Text
        xmlProductName.InnerXml = ProductName.Text
        xmlSupplier.InnerXml = Supplier.Text
        xmlCategoryName.InnerXml = Category.Text
        xmlUnitPrice.InnerXml = UnitPrice.Text
        xmlUnitsInStock.InnerXml = UnitsInStock.Text

        xmlProduct.AppendChild(xmlProductID)
        xmlProduct.AppendChild(xmlProductName)
        xmlProduct.AppendChild(xmlSupplier)
        xmlProduct.AppendChild(xmlCategoryName)
```

```
          xmlProduct.AppendChild(xmlUnitPrice)
          xmlProduct.AppendChild(xmlUnitsInStock)
          OurXmlNode.AppendChild(xmlProduct)
          OurXmlDocument.Save(Server.MapPath("products.xml"))
      End If

      OurXml.Transform = OurXslTransform
      OurXml.Document = OurXmlDocument
  End Sub

</script>

<html>
<body>
<asp:xml id="OurXml" runat="server" EnableViewState="false"/>
<br>
<form runat="server">
<table>
<tr><td>ProductID</td>
<td><asp:TextBox id="ProductID" runat="server"/></td></tr>
<tr><td>Product Name</td>
<td><asp:TextBox id="ProductName" runat="server"/></td></tr>
<tr><td>Supplier</td>
<td><asp:TextBox id="Supplier" runat="server"/></td></tr>
<tr><td>Category</td>
<td><asp:TextBox id="Category" runat="server"/></td></tr>
<tr><td>Unit Price</td>
<td><asp:TextBox id="UnitPrice" runat="server"/></td></tr>
<tr><td>Units In Stock</td>
<td><asp:TextBox id="UnitsInStock" runat="server"/></td></tr>
</table>
<asp:Button id="Submit" text="Submit" runat="server"/>
</form>
</body>
</html>
```

C#—xml_insert_purexml_cs.aspx

```
<%@ page language="c#" runat="server"%>
<%@ Import Namespace="System.Data"%>
<%@ Import Namespace="System.Xml"%>
<%@ Import Namespace="System.Xml.Xsl"%>
<script runat=server>
void Page_Load() {
    XmlDocument OurXmlDocument = new XmlDocument();
    XslTransform OurXslTransform = new XslTransform();
    OurXmlDocument.Load(Server.MapPath("products.xml"));
    OurXslTransform.Load(Server.MapPath("products.xsl"));
    if (IsPostBack) {
```

continues

C#—(continued)

```csharp
            XmlNode OurXmlNode = OurXmlDocument.DocumentElement;
            XmlElement xmlProduct = OurXmlDocument.CreateElement("Product");
            XmlElement xmlProductID = OurXmlDocument.CreateElement("ProductID");
            XmlElement xmlProductName = OurXmlDocument.CreateElement("ProductName");
            XmlElement xmlSupplier = OurXmlDocument.CreateElement("Supplier");
            XmlElement xmlCategoryName = OurXmlDocument.CreateElement("CategoryName");
            XmlElement xmlUnitPrice = OurXmlDocument.CreateElement("UnitPrice");
            XmlElement xmlUnitsInStock = OurXmlDocument.CreateElement("UnitsInStock");
            xmlProductID.InnerXml = ProductID.Text;
            xmlProductName.InnerXml = ProductName.Text;
            xmlSupplier.InnerXml = Supplier.Text;
            xmlCategoryName.InnerXml = Category.Text;
            xmlUnitPrice.InnerXml = UnitPrice.Text;
            xmlUnitsInStock.InnerXml = UnitsInStock.Text;

            xmlProduct.AppendChild(xmlProductID);
            xmlProduct.AppendChild(xmlProductName);
            xmlProduct.AppendChild(xmlSupplier);
            xmlProduct.AppendChild(xmlCategoryName);
            xmlProduct.AppendChild(xmlUnitPrice);
            xmlProduct.AppendChild(xmlUnitsInStock);
            OurXmlNode.AppendChild(xmlProduct);
            OurXmlDocument.Save(Server.MapPath("products.xml"));
        }
    OurXml.Transform = OurXslTransform;
    OurXml.Document = OurXmlDocument;
}

</script>

<html>
<body>
<asp:xml id="OurXml" runat="server" EnableViewState="false"/>
<br>
<form runat="server">
<table>
<tr><td>ProductID</td>
<td><asp:TextBox id="ProductID" runat="server"/></td></tr>
<tr><td>Product Name</td>
<td><asp:TextBox id="ProductName" runat="server"/></td></tr>
<tr><td>Supplier</td>
<td><asp:TextBox id="Supplier" runat="server"/></td></tr>
<tr><td>Category</td>
<td><asp:TextBox id="Category" runat="server"/></td></tr>
<tr><td>Unit Price</td>
<td><asp:TextBox id="UnitPrice" runat="server"/></td></tr>
<tr><td>Units In Stock</td>
<td><asp:TextBox id="UnitsInStock" runat="server"/></td></tr>
</table>
<asp:Button id="Submit" text="Submit" runat="server"/>
</form>
</body>
</html>
```

This just demonstrates the flexibility that the .NET Framework provides for dealing with XML documents. There are many other objects that will help you to play around with XML documents, and I would encourage you to investigate the System.XML namespace and all its objects to further understand how you can use XML in your ASP.NET applications.

One Little Bonus

As a small bonus, I thought it would be fun to show you how to populate a DataSet with two tables and apply an XSL stylesheet that can handle the formatting of both tables in the DataSet.

Visual Basic .NET—**xml_bonus_vb.aspx**

```
<%@ page language="vb" runat="server"%>
<%@ Import Namespace="System.Data"%>
<%@ Import Namespace="System.Data.SqlClient"%>
<%@ Import Namespace="System.Xml"%>
<%@ Import Namespace="System.Xml.Xsl"%>
<script runat=server>
Private Sub Page_Load(ByVal sender As Object, ByVal e As EventArgs)

    Dim OurConnection As SqlConnection = New SqlConnection("Server=server;
    ➥uid=newriders;pwd=password;database=Northwind")
    Dim OurCommand As SqlCommand = New SqlCommand()
    OurCommand.Connection = OurConnection
    Dim OurDataAdapter As SqlDataAdapter = New SqlDataAdapter()
    Dim OurDataSet As DataSet
    OurDataSet = New DataSet("OurDataSet")
    OurCommand.CommandText = "Select Top 10 p.ProductID, p.ProductName,
    ➥s.CompanyName as Supplier, c.CategoryName, UnitPrice, UnitsInStock From
    ➥Products p, Categories c, Suppliers s Where p.CategoryID = c.CategoryID and
    ➥p.SupplierID = s.SupplierID"
    OurDataAdapter.SelectCommand = OurCommand
    OurDataAdapter.Fill(OurDataSet, "Products")
    OurCommand.CommandText = "Select Top 10 Title, TitleOfCourtesy, FirstName,
    ➥LastName, Address, City From Employees"
    OurDataAdapter.Fill(OurDataSet, "Employees")
    Dim OurXmlDocument As XmlDataDocument = New XmlDataDocument(OurDataSet)
    OurXml.Document = OurXmlDocument
End Sub
</script>
<html>
<head>
<title>XML Bonus</title>
</head>
<body bgcolor="#FFFFFF" text="#000000"
<asp:xml id="OurXml" TransformSource="bonus.xsl" runat="server" />
</body>
</html>
```

C#—xml_bonus_cs.aspx

```
<%@ page language="c#" runat="server"%>
<%@ Import Namespace="System.Data"%>
<%@ Import Namespace="System.Data.SqlClient"%>
<%@ Import Namespace="System.Xml"%>
<%@ Import Namespace="System.Xml.Xsl"%>
<script runat=server>
void Page_Load(Object sender, EventArgs e) {

    SqlConnection OurConnection = new SqlConnection("Server=server;
    ➥uid=newriders;pwd=password;database=Northwind");
    SqlCommand OurCommand = new SqlCommand();
    OurCommand.Connection = OurConnection;
    SqlDataAdapter OurDataAdapter = new SqlDataAdapter();
    DataSet OurDataSet;
    OurDataSet = new DataSet("OurDataSet");
    OurCommand.CommandText = "Select Top 5 p.ProductID, p.ProductName,
    ➥s.CompanyName as Supplier, c.CategoryName, UnitPrice, UnitsInStock From
    ➥Products p, Categories c, Suppliers s Where p.CategoryID = c.CategoryID and
    ➥p.SupplierID = s.SupplierID";
    OurDataAdapter.SelectCommand = OurCommand;
    OurDataAdapter.Fill(OurDataSet, "Products");
    OurCommand.CommandText = "Select Top 5 Title, TitleOfCourtesy, FirstName,
    ➥LastName, Address, City From Employees";
    OurDataAdapter.Fill(OurDataSet, "Employees");
    XmlDataDocument OurXmlDocument = new XmlDataDocument(OurDataSet);
    OurXml.Document = OurXmlDocument;
}
</script>
<html>
<head>
<title>XML Bonus</title>
</head>
<body bgcolor="#FFFFFF" text="#000000">
<asp:xml id="OurXml" TransformSource="bonus.xsl" runat="server" />
</body>
</html>
```

This ASP.NET page creates a DataSet, and then pulls data from two different tables in the SQL Server Northwind database and places it into two DataTables: Products and Employees.

Then I take the DataSet and place it in an XmlDataDocument object and set the Document property of the XML server control to the contents of the XmlDataDocument. Basically there are two different tables going into the OurXml server control.

Now you apply two different styles to the two different tables. For this we just create an XSL file. In the above ASP.NET page it was assigned to the TransformSource property of the XML server control and is named bonus.xsl.

bonus.xsl

```
<xsl:stylesheet version="1.0" xmlns:xsl='http://www.w3.org/1999/XSL/Transform'>
<xsl:template match="/">
<style>
.table-heading {background-color:#CCCCCC;font-family : Verdana,sans-serif;
➥font-size:12px;}
.table-row{font-family : Verdana,sans-serif;font-size:12px;}
</style>
<table border="1" cellpadding="3" cellspacing="0">
<tr class="table-heading">
<td>ProductID</td>
<td>Product Name</td>
<td>Supplier</td>
<td>Category</td>
<td>Unit Price</td>
<td>Units In Stock</td>
</tr>
<xsl:for-each select='OurDataSet/Products'>
<tr class="table-row">
<td><xsl:value-of select='ProductID'/></td>
<td><xsl:value-of select='ProductName'/></td>
<td><xsl:value-of select='Supplier'/></td>
<td><xsl:value-of select='CategoryName'/></td>
<td><xsl:value-of select='UnitPrice'/></td>
<td><xsl:value-of select='UnitsInStock'/></td>
</tr>
</xsl:for-each>
</table>
<br /><br />
<table border="1" cellpadding="3" cellspacing="0">
<tr class="table-heading">
<td>Title</td>
<td>Title Of Courtesy</td>
<td>First Name</td>
<td>Last Name</td>
<td>Address</td>
<td>City</td>
</tr>
<xsl:for-each select='OurDataSet/Employees'>
<tr class="table-row">
<td><xsl:value-of select='Title'/></td>
<td><xsl:value-of select='TitleOfCourtesy'/></td>
<td><xsl:value-of select='FirstName'/></td>
<td><xsl:value-of select='LastName'/></td>
<td><xsl:value-of select='Address'/></td>
<td><xsl:value-of select='City'/></td>
</tr>
</xsl:for-each>
</table>
</xsl:template>
</xsl:stylesheet>
```

The real magic happens when I set the `select` attribute of the `<xml:for-each>` tag. You can see the first highlighted group is set to `select='OurDataSet/Products'`. This causes that portion of the XSL file to use the data stored in the Products table of `OurDataSet`.

The second highlighted group is set to `select='OurDataSet/Employees'`, and this subsequently causes that portion of the XSL file to use the data stored in the Employees table of `OurDataSet`.

As you can see in Figure 13.4, the XML server control uses the bonus.xsl stylesheet to format the two different tables from the `DataSet` that were transformed into XML using the `XmlDataDocument` object. These two different tables receive two different formattings based on which data was assigned to the `select` attribute of the `<xml:for-each>` tag.

FIGURE 13.4

XML and XSL provide lots of flexibility for handling data, and the XML server control provides a tool to use these files in your ASP.NET applications.

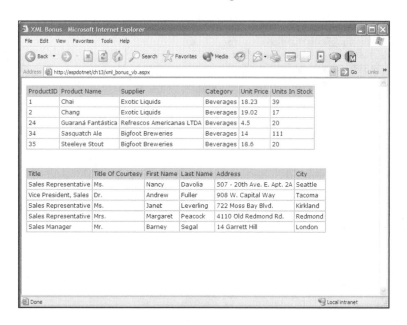

This bonus was intended to show you the flexibility of the XML server control and the versatility of using XSL files to format your XML data. Experiment, have fun, and get used to XML data, because you will be seeing more and more of it as time progresses and XML is adopted to do more things in web development and web applications.

One thing to note is that throughout this chapter I used XML files as the source for the examples, but in real-world situations XML data is more commonly delivered out of a database than an XML file. Considering this, along with the fact that volumes have been written about XML, I will state that I have hardly scratched the surface on this subject. I highly encourage you to explore the web and other books concerning ASP.NET and XML, especially in the area of web services. The following are some additional recommendations of titles covering this area:

- *XML and ASP.NET* by Kirk Evans, Ashwin Kamanna, and Joel Mueller. Published by New Riders Publishing.

- *XML and SQL Server* 2000 by John Griffin. Published by New Riders Publishing.

- *Inside XML* by Steve Holzner. Published by New Riders Publishing.

Summary

I really want to thank you for reading this book. I hope that it was as informative for you in reading as it was rewarding for me to write. I wish you all the success and fun in creating ASP.NET applications, and trust that you will find *ASP.NET for Web Designers* a resource that you can return to often when you need answers, a refresher, or inspiration.

Thank You…It has truly been my pleasure!

God bless you!!!

<Part> IV

APPENDIXES

Installing the .NET Framework

This appendix assumes you already have IIS installed before you install the framework. Although it is possible to install the framework without having IIS installed beforehand, it is not recommended, and that process is not documented here.

Go to `http://www.asp.net/download.aspx`, as shown in Figure A.1.

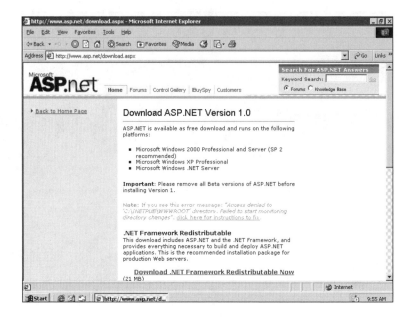

A few paragraphs down the page, there is a link labeled "Download .NET
Framework SDK Now." Clicking on this link takes you to Microsoft's SDK
download page.

The redistributable version contains just the .NET Framework and none of the
documentation. This version is meant for installing on production web servers or
servers that don't need the SDK (Software Developers Kit) samples and tutorials.

For the purposes of this discussion, you should choose the Full SDK Download.

After you agree to the End User License Agreement (EULA), you are prompted
to save the file. The desktop is a good place to download this file to, as shown
in Figure A.2.

After you have obtained the file, double-click the icon on your desktop. You
are asked whether you would like to install the Microsoft .NET Framework
SDK Package as shown in Figure A.3. Answer Yes.

The setup program begins extracting the files necessary to begin installation. This
may take a few minutes. After it has finished, you see the introduction screen, as
in Figure A.4. Click Next.

FIGURE A.2

Save the file to your machine.

FIGURE A.3

Select Yes to installing the .NET Framework SDK to your machine.

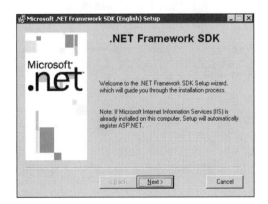

FIGURE A.4

Click Next to proceed with the installation.

You should now be seeing another EULA. Read the agreement, and when you're finished, click the I Accept button and then click Next as shown in Figure A.5.

The following screen allows you to choose what options you'd like to install. The documentation is not optional, and without the SDK, you won't actually be able to run any ASP.NET pages. The samples are optional, but are highly valuable resources, and for the sake of this discussion, it is assumed you will be installing them. Leave all the boxes checked and click Next, as shown in Figure A.6.

Now you have to choose where to install the Framework SDK. Unless you have a compelling reason not to, I suggest using the default location. Leave the Register Environment Variables box checked as you can see in Figure A.7.

FIGURE A.5

Agree to the EULA and click Next to proceed.

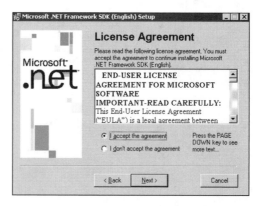

FIGURE A.6

Leave boxes checked to install the SDK and click Next.

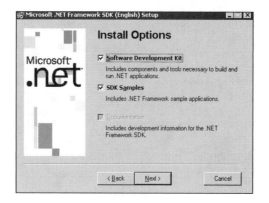

Now the setup program has enough information to go ahead and install the SDK. This takes a few minutes. What you see during this time is represented in Figure A.8

After the installation process runs its course you should see a message informing you that the installation was successful, as shown in Figure A.9. Congratulations! You're finished. You can set up a new web site in IIS and begin run ASP.NET pages.

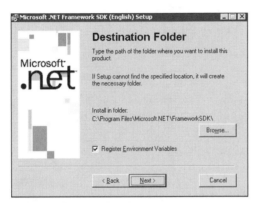

FIGURE A.7

Installing the .NET Framework SDK to the default location.

FIGURE A.8

Waiting for installation to complete.

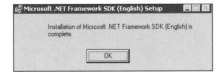

FIGURE A.9

Installation Complete!!

Compiling Custom Objects

W ithin this appendix, you'll see how to compile the ball object created in Chapter 2 into a component that you can place in your application bin directory so you can use it as a fully functional object just like all the ASP.NET server controls.

Just as in the rest of the book, I will demonstrate this in both Visual Basic .NET and C#, but unlike other examples, I won't demonstrate them in parallel. First I will explain the entire process in VB.NET, followed by the entire process in C#.

Visual Basic .NET Example

This section takes the `ball` class from Chapter 2 and compiles it as an object that will be available to the ASP.NET application.

Here is the `ball` class.

ball_vb.vb

```
Namespace Peter.Toybox
    Public Class Ball
        Private _Color as String
        Private _Motion as String

        Public Sub New()
            _Motion = "Still"
        End Sub

        Public Property Color as String
            Get
                Return _Color
            End Get
            Set
                _Color = value
            End Set
        End Property

        Public ReadOnly Property Motion as String
            Get
                Return _Motion
            End Get
        End Property

        Public Sub Roll()
            _Motion="Rolling"
        End Sub
    End Class
End Namespace
```

Enter this source example into your favorite text editor and save this as `ball_vb.vb`.

After you have the file saved, you can try to compile it. On my machine, the files are saved in d:\websites\book\app_b\. If your files are stored in a different location, the exact sequence of commands you need to issue will be slightly different. Substitute your path as appropriate.

1. Click on the Start button.
2. Pick the Run option.
3. Type cmd.
4. Press Enter. You should see a screen similar to Figure B.1.

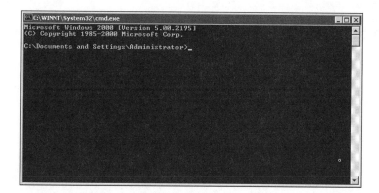

FIGURE B.1

Typing cmd and pressing Enter in the Run dialog box takes you to a command prompt.

The section "C:\Documents and Settings\Administrator>" reflects the current directory. It is separated into two parts: the "C:" and the "\Documents and Settings\Administrator" portion. The "C:" is the drive letter, and the "\Documents and Settings\Administrator" is the path. My files are stored on a different drive. I can go to that by typing **D:**. This places me in the root of the D drive. To change where the files are stored, I type **cd\websites\book\app_b** (see Figure B.2).

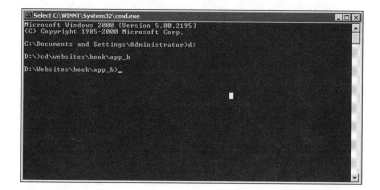

FIGURE B.2

Change to the directory where your class file is located.

Your drive and path will vary depending on where you saved the `ball_vb.vb` file. Now that I am in the same directory as the file, I can try to compile it. Type **vbc /t:library ball_vb.vb**.

- **vbc** is the command to invoke the Visual Basic compiler.
- **/t:library** tells it that I want a compiled library file, not an executable.
- **ball_vb.vb** is the name of the source file.

If all goes well, your screen should now look something like Figure B.3.

However, if you made any mistakes, you may receive an error message, like that in Figure B.4.

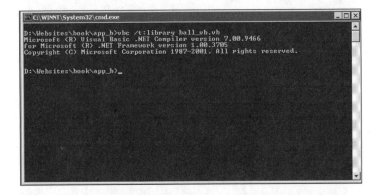

FIGURE B.3

If all goes well, you will return back to the command prompt without any errors.

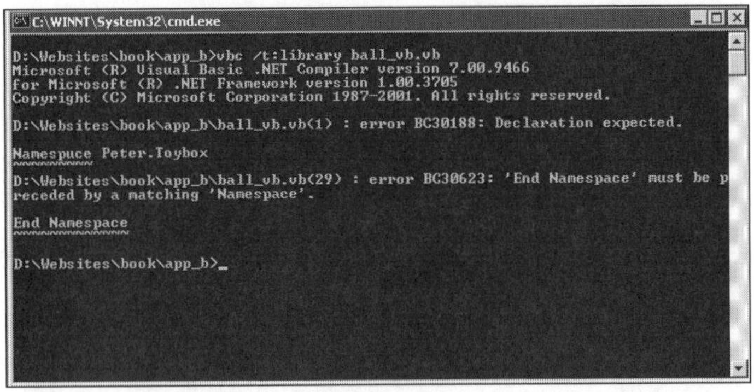

FIGURE B.4

If your file generates errors during compilation, you will receive a detail of the error.

In Figure B.4, I misspelled Namespace. The program doesn't know what to make of it and reports that in the first block. Then, because the namespace wasn't declared properly, it notifies you that there is a closing namespace without an opening one. Both these problems are remedied by simply fixing the typo and issuing the command again.

When you do succeed in compiling your file, the result is a ball_vb.dll file (see Figure B.5). You can check this by using the dir command.

FIGURE B.5

When your compilation is successful, the result is a file with a .dll extension with an identical name as your .vb file. This is your component.

Unfortunately, this file doesn't do much good out here. If you want to use this class in a web application, you need to copy the file into a special directory on the web server called bin. Chances are, this directory doesn't exist yet if this is the first time you've compiled a component.

Using Explorer, navigate to the root of your web site. If you do not see a directory named bin, right-click in the window and select the New option. A submenu should appear asking what you would like to create. Choose Folder. The menu goes away, a new folder is created, and you should be able to type in the name of the folder (see Figure B.6). Type **bin** and press Enter (see Figure B.7).

Now, again using Explorer, go back to where you saved the source file and copy the dll there to the new bin directory you have just created.

FIGURE B.6

Create a new folder.

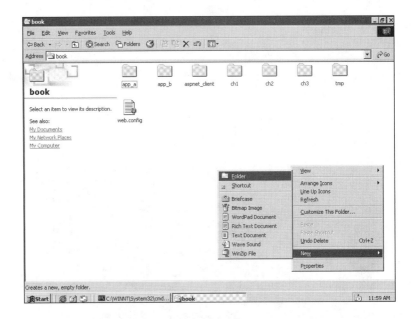

FIGURE B.7

Call the new folder bin.

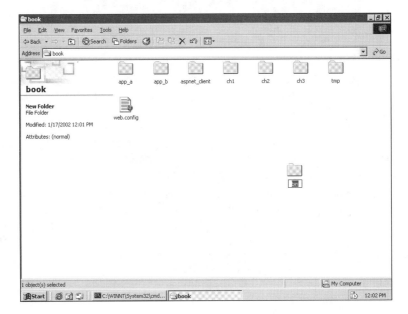

> **NOTE**
>
> Windows considers .dll files to be system files. Depending on your settings, you might not see a dll file where you compiled it. If this is the case, go to the Tools menu of the folder and choose Folder Options (see Figure B.8). Under the View tab, select Show Hidden Files and Folders and uncheck Hide Protected Operating System Files (see Figure B.9). You may also find it helpful to uncheck the option above the Hide Protected Files option, called Hide File Extensions for Known File Types, as well. With this option checked, the files' extensions appear in Explorer so that it will be easier to identify the different file types you are using.

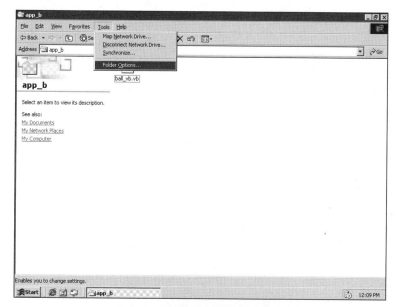

FIGURE B.8

Open the Folder Options dialog box.

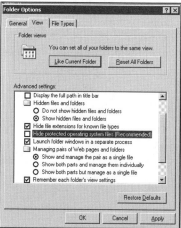

FIGURE B.9

Uncheck the Hide Protected Operating System Files and click OK.

You should now be able to see ball_vb.dll in the directory. Copy this file to the bin directory you created. Now you need a web page to test the component out. Create a page, and enter in the following code:

ball_class_vb.aspx

```
<%@ page language="vb" runat="server"%>
<%@ import namespace="Peter.Toybox"%>
<html>
<title>Run Ball Method</title>
<body>
<%
dim objMyBall as New Ball()

Response.Write("<u>Before Roll Method</u><br>")
Response.Write("MyBall: " & objMyBall.Motion & "<br><br>")

objMyBall.Roll()

Response.Write("<u>After Roll Method</u><br>")
Response.Write("MyBall: " & objMyBall.Motion)

%>
</body>
</html>
```

Save the page as ball_class_vb.aspx, and then browse to it at the location of your application. The example application happens to reside at a local IP of 192.168.1.53. Your file will most likely reside somewhere within the http:// localhost application. See the results in Figure B.10.

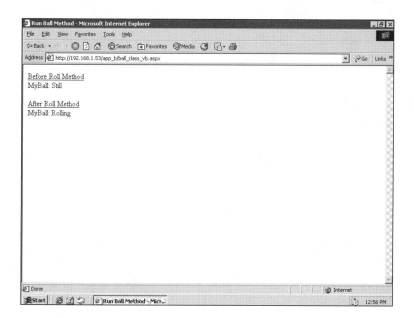

FIGURE B.10

Success!! The ball class is working as expected.

C# Example

This section takes the `ball` class from Chapter 2 and compiles it as an object that will be available to the ASP.NET application.

Here is the `ball` class.

ball_cs.cs

```
namespace Peter.Toybox {

    public class Ball    {
        private string _Color;
        private string _Motion;

         public Ball(){
            _Motion = "Still";
        }

        public string Color{
            get {
                return _Color;
            }
            set {
                _Color = value;
            }
```

continues

___

ball_cs.cs (continued)

```
        }

        public string  Motion {
            get {
                return _Motion;
            }
        }

        public void Roll() {
            _Motion="Rolling";
        }
    }
}
```

Enter this source example into your favorite text editor and save this as ball_cs.cs.

After you have the file saved, you can try to compile it. On my machine, the files are saved in d:\websites\book\app_b\. If your files are stored in a different location, the exact sequence of commands you need to issue will be slightly different. Substitute your path as appropriate.

1. Click the Start button.
2. Pick the Run option.
3. Type cmd.
4. Press Enter.

You should see a screen similar to Figure B.11.

The section "C:\Documents and Settings\Administrator>" reflects the current directory. It is separated into two parts: the "C:" and the "\Documents and Settings\Administrator" portion. The "C:" is the drive letter, and the "\Documents and Settings\Administrator" is the path. My files are stored on a different drive. I can go to that by typing **D:**. This places me in the root of the D drive. To change to where the files are stored, I type **cd\websites\book\app_b**.

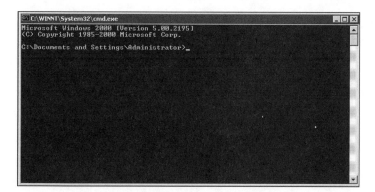

FIGURE B.11

Typing cmd and pressing Enter in the Run dialog box takes you to a command prompt.

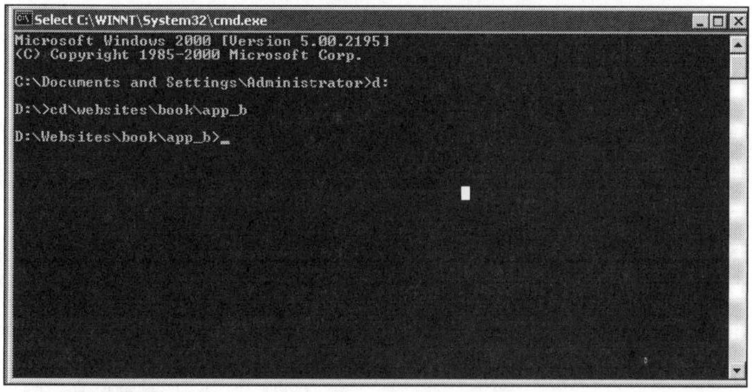

FIGURE B.12

Change to the directory where your class file is located.

Your drive and path will vary depending on where you saved the ball_class_cs.cs file. Now that I am in the same directory as the file, I can try to compile it. Type **csc /t:library ball_cs.cs**.

- **csc** is the command to invoke the C# compiler.

- **/t:library** tells it that I want a compiled library file, not an executable.

- **ball_cs.cs** is the name of the source file.

If all goes well, your screen should now look something like Figure B.13.

If all goes well, you return back to the command prompt without any errors.

However, if you made any mistakes, you may receive an error message, like that in Figure B.14.

If your file generates errors during compilation, you will receive a detail of the error.

In Figure B.14, I misspelled Namespace. The program doesn't know what to make of it, and reports that in the first block. Then because the namespace wasn't declared properly, it notifies you that there is a closing namespace without an opening one. Both these problems are remedied by simply fixing the typo, and issuing the command again.

When you do succeed in compiling your file, the result is a ball_cs.dll file. You can check this by using the dir command. See the results in Figure B.15.

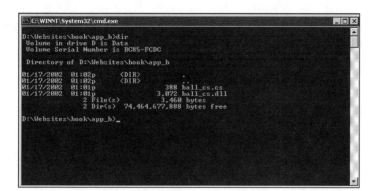

FIGURE B.15

When your compilation is successful, the result is a file with a .dll extension with an identical name as your .vb file. This is your component.

Unfortunately, this file doesn't do much good out here. If you want to use this class in a web application, you need to copy the file into a special directory on the web server called bin. Chances are, this directory doesn't exist yet if this is the first time you've compiled a component.

Using Explorer, navigate to the root of your website. If you do not see a directory named bin, right-click in the window and select the New option. A submenu should appear asking what you would like to create. Choose Folder. The menu goes away, a new folder is created, and you should be able to type in the name of the folder. Type **bin** and press Enter, as shown in Figures B.16 and B.17.

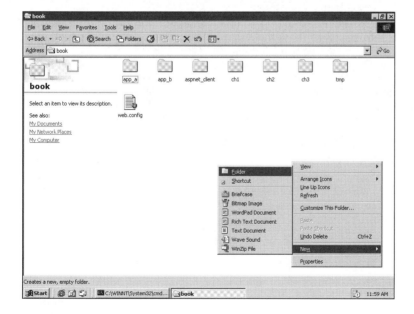

FIGURE B.16

Create a new folder.

FIGURE B.17

Name the folder bin.

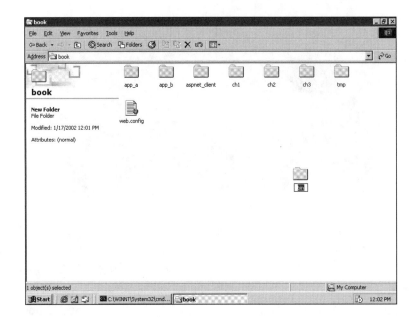

Now, again using Explorer, go back to where you saved the source file and copy the dll there to the new bin directory you have just created.

N O T E

Windows considers .dll files to be system files. Depending on your settings, you might not see a dll file where you compiled it. If this is the case, go to the Tools menu of the folder and choose Folder Options. Under the View tab, select Show Hidden Files and Folders and uncheck Hide Protected Operating System Files. You may also find it helpful to uncheck the option above the Hide Protected Files option, called Hide File Extensions for Known File Types, as well. With this option checked, the files' extensions appear in Explorer so that it will be easier to identify the different file types you are using. You can see this in Figures B.18 and B.19

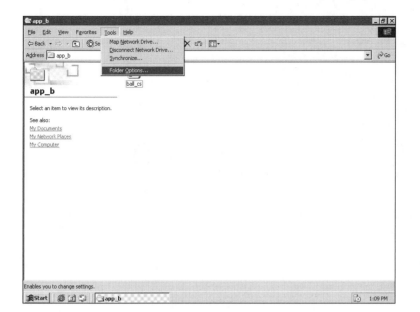

FIGURE B.18

*Open the Folder
Options dialog box.*

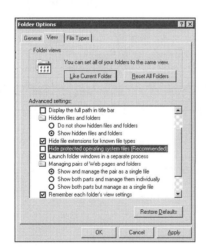

FIGURE B.19

*Uncheck Hide
Protected Operating
System Files option.*

You should now be able to see ball_cs.dll in the directory. Copy this file to the
bin directory you created. Now you need a web page to test the component out.
Create a page, and enter in the following code:

ball_class_cs.aspx

```
<%@ page language="c#" runat="server"%>
<%@ import namespace="Peter.Toybox"%>
<html>
<title>Run Ball Method</title>
<body>
<%
Ball objMyBall = new Ball();

Response.Write("<u>Before Roll Method</u><br>");
Response.Write("MyBall: " + objMyBall.Motion + "<br><br>");

objMyBall.Roll();

Response.Write("<u>After Roll Method</u><br>");
Response.Write("MyBall: " + objMyBall.Motion);

%>
</body>
</html>
```

Save this as `ball_class_cs.aspx`, and then browse to it at the location of your application. The example application happens to reside at a local IP of 192.168.1.53. Your file will most likely reside somewhere within the http://localhost application. See the results in Figure B.20.

FIGURE B.20

Success!! The ball class is working as expected.

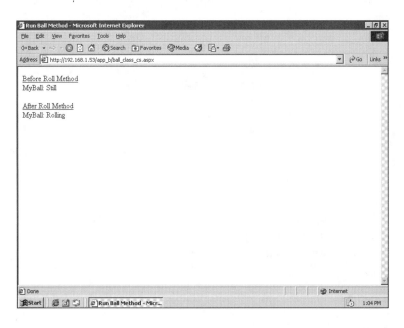

Can you see how easy it is to expand the function and classes that you can use in the .NET Framework? Being able to build and compile your own classes opens up a whole new world of expandability and addresses code reuse that has been a very difficult issue to deal with in the past.

And because the .NET Framework allows you to just drop newly compiled classes into the bin directory without stopping and starting web service in IIS, you can make additions and modifications to your objects without fear of how this might cause interruptions. You can change and recompile an object, drop it into the bin directory, and the next time a new call to the object is made, it will load that class into memory and use it. After all existing uses of the old object are dropped, that object will be completely removed from the server's memory and the new DLL will be used exclusively.

Index

Symbols

A

I-K

void keyword (functions), 122

W

Solutions from experts you know and trust.

www.informit.com

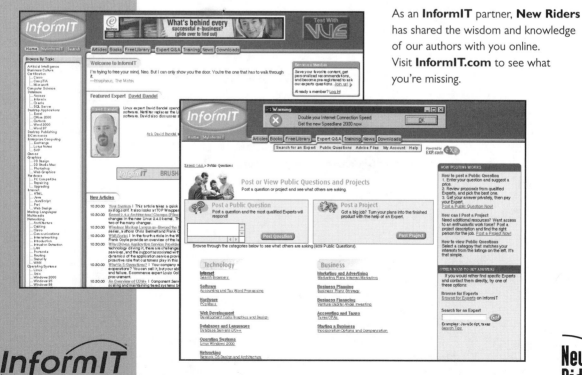

VOICES THAT MATTER

HOW TO CONTACT US

VISIT OUR WEB SITE

WWW.NEWRIDERS.COM

On our Web site you'll find information about our other books, authors, tables of contents, indexes, and book errata. You will also find information about book registration and how to purchase our books.

EMAIL US

Contact us at this address: **nrfeedback@newriders.com**

- If you have comments or questions about this book
- To report errors that you have found in this book
- If you have a book proposal to submit or are interested in writing for New Riders
- If you would like to have an author kit sent to you
- If you are an expert in a computer topic or technology and are interested in being a technical editor who reviews manuscripts for technical accuracy
- To find a distributor in your area, please contact our international department at this address. **nrmedia@newriders.com**
- For instructors from educational institutions who want to preview New Riders books for classroom use. Email should include your name, title, school, department, address, phone number, office days/hours, text in use, and enrollment, along with your request for desk/examination copies and/or additional information.
- For members of the media who are interested in reviewing copies of New Riders books. Send your name, mailing address, and email address, along with the name of the publication or Web site you work for.

BULK PURCHASES/CORPORATE SALES

The publisher offers discounts on this book when ordered in quantity for bulk purchases and special sales. For sales within the U.S., please contact: Corporate and Government Sales (800) 382-3419 or **corpsales@pearsontechgroup.com**. Outside of the U.S., please contact: International Sales (317) 581-3793 or **international@pearsontechgroup.com**.

WRITE TO US

New Riders Publishing
201 W. 103rd St.
Indianapolis, IN 46290-1097

CALL US

Toll-free (800) 571-5840 + 9 + 7477
If outside U.S. (317) 581-3500. Ask for New Riders.

FAX US

(317) 581-4663

WWW.NEWRIDERS.COM

VIEW CART

search ⊙

▸ Registration already a member? Log in. ▸ Book Registration

Publishing
the Voices
that Matter

OUR AUTHORS

PRESS ROOM

| web development | design | photoshop | new media | 3-D | server technologies |

EDUCATORS

ABOUT US

CONTACT US

You already know that New Riders brings you the **Voices That Matter**.

But what does that mean? It means that New Riders brings you the

Voices that challenge your assumptions, take your talents to the next

level, or simply help you better understand the complex technical world

we're all navigating.

Visit **www.newriders.com** to find:

▸ **10% discount** and **free shipping** on all book purchases

▸ Never before published chapters

▸ Sample chapters and excerpts

▸ Author bios and interviews

▸ Contests and enter-to-wins

▸ Up-to-date industry event information

▸ Book reviews

▸ Special offers from our friends and partners

▸ Info on how to join our User Group program

▸ Ways to have your Voice heard

WWW.NEWRIDERS.COM

Colophon

This book was written and edited in Microsoft Word, and laid out in QuarkXPress. The font used for the body text is Bembo and Mono. It was printed on 50# Husky Offset Smooth paper at VonHoffmann Inc. in Owensville, Missouri. Prepress consisted of PostScript computer-to-plate technology (filmless process). The cover was printed at Moore Langen Printing in Terre Haute, Indiana, on 12pt., coated on one side.